Securing Command of the Sea

Securing Command of the Sea

NATO Naval Planning, 1948–1954

Sean M. Maloney

Naval Institute Press
Annapolis, Maryland

© 1995 by Sean M. Maloney

All rights reserved. No part of this book may be reproduced without written permission from the publisher.

Library of Congress Cataloging-in-Publication Data
Maloney, Sean M., 1967–
   Securing command of the sea : NATO naval planning, 1948–1954 / Sean M. Maloney.
     p.   cm.
   Includes bibliographical references (p.   ) and index.
   ISBN 1-55750-562-4 (alk. paper)
   1. North Atlantic Treaty Organization—Armed Forces. 2. Sea-power—Europe. 3. Sea-power—United States. 4. Command and control systems—Europe. 5. Command and control systems—United States. 6. United States—Armed Forces—Europe. I. Title.
UA646.3.M244 1995
359'.03'094—dc20   94-21513

Printed in the United States of America on acid-free paper ∞

02 01 00 99 98 97 96 95   9 8 7 6 5 4 3 2

First printing

Contents

	List of Illustrations	vii
	Foreword Julian Oswald, Admiral of the Fleet, R.N. Adm. Frank B. Kelso II, USN (Ret.)	xi
	Acknowledgments	xiii
	Introduction	1
1	Second World War Command Organization	5
2	An Attack Against One Is an Attack Against All: The Founding of NATO Command Organization, 1947–1949	47
3	Crusade in Europe Revisited and the Third Battle of the Atlantic: SACEUR and SACLANT, 1949–1951	86
4	From the Ditch to the Pillars of Hercules: Command Organization in the Channel, STRIKEFLEETLANT and IBERLANT, 1951–1953	138
5	The Struggle for the Mediterranean: The Development of CinCAFMED, 1951–1954	170
	Conclusion	197
	Appendix 1: Assessing the Soviet Submarine Threat, 1945–1956	205
	Appendix 2: Fleet Structure and Technological Change, 1945–1956	208
	Notes	215
	Glossary	247
	Bibliography	253
	Index	269

Illustrations

1.1.	Second World War command organization types	7
1.2.	Allied coalition command organization, 1942–45	9
1.3.	Arcadia strategic zones	11
1.4.	Allied coalition command organization and supreme allied commands, 1942–45	12
1.5.	Command organization for Torch, 8 November 1942	15
1.6.	Royal Navy organization in the Mediterranean, 1943–45	18
1.7.	RAF command organization in the Mediterranean, 1943	19
1.8.	Command organization for Husky, 10 July 1943	20
1.9.	Mediterranean Allied Air Forces, 1 January 1944	22
1.10.	Mediterranean naval command organization, 1 June 1944	23
1.11.	Mediterranean command organization, 1944–45	24
1.12.	SHAEF organization for Overlord, 1944	25
1.13.	British Area Combined Headquarters, 1940	27
1.14.	Royal Navy commands in the Atlantic, 1939	28
1.15.	Canadian defense organization in the Atlantic area	30
1.16.	Command organization for the Atlantic, 1941–42	33
1.17.	Semiformal arrangements for air-naval cooperation in Newfoundland, October 1941	34
1.18.	U.S. Navy sea frontiers, 1942–45	36
1.19.	U.S. Navy organization for the Atlantic, May 1942–May 1943	37
1.20.	CHOP line, 1 July 1942	39
1.21.	Canadian Northwest Atlantic Command, April 1943	41
1.22.	Canadian defense organization in the Atlantic area, 1943–45	43
1.23.	U.S. Navy Tenth Fleet organization, 1 May 1943	44
2.1.	U.S. postwar naval commands	53

2.2.	U.S.–Canadian organization for defense	55
2.3.	Broiler's estimate of air forces available	58
2.4.	Broiler's estimate of ground forces available	58
2.5.	Broiler's estimate of naval forces available	59
2.6.	Plan Broiler: Ocean areas vulnerable to Soviet air and submarine attack	60
2.7.	Plan Broiler: Allied courses of action—first alternative	61
2.8.	Plan Broiler: Allied courses of action—second alternative	63
2.9.	Proposed organization for British Plan Doublequick	65
2.10.	Broiler/Doublequick division of the Atlantic	66
2.11.	Western Union Defense Organization, June 1948	68
2.12.	WUDO withdrawal organization, July 1948	70
2.13.	Proposed organization for the higher direction of war in Europe, 1948	71
2.14.	Allied higher direction for Doublestar/Speedway/Bullmoose, October 1948	72
2.15.	Atlantic commands for Doublestar/Speedway/Bullmoose	74
2.16.	British view of the North Atlantic Pact organization, 19 February 1949	76
2.17.	The Foulkes proposal, March 1949	78
2.18.	U.S. plan for a peacetime organization for planning under NATO	80
2.19.	NATO regional planning groups, December 1949	81
2.20.	U.S.–British agreement on NATO organization, 18 August 1949	82
2.21.	North Atlantic Treaty Organization, December 1949	84
3.1.	Concept of NATO operations for Crosspiece/Galloper, 1950	90
3.2.	Plan Crosspiece: Vital SLOCs	92
3.3.	U.S. proposal for command in the Atlantic, October 1949	94
3.4.	Proposed U.S. command organization for the Atlantic, October 1949	94
3.5.	Tentative NATO command organization for war, October 1950	101
3.6.	Proposed global coalition command organization, July 1950	102
3.7.	Proposal no. 5, July 1950	104
3.8.	Temporary consensus, August 1950	105
3.9.	Working concept for SACEUR, January 1951	106
3.10.	British SACEUR proposal, January 1951	107

Illustrations ix

3.11.	Alternate British SACEUR proposal, January 1951	108
3.12.	Eisenhower's view of command organization in Europe, January 1951	109
3.13.	Allied command in Europe, November 1951	110
3.14.	SACEUR command boundaries, April 1951	111
3.15.	NAORPG's functional command proposal, July 1950	113
3.16.	NAOR command organization—U.S. proposal, August 1950	114
3.17.	U.S. proposal to NAORPG, August 1950	115
3.18.	British proposal, August 1950	117
3.19.	British view of SACLANT organization, October 1950	119
3.20.	NAORPG recommendation to the NADC, October 1950	120
3.21.	British proposal to eliminate IBERLANT, March 1951	126
3.22.	The McGrigor proposal, April 1951	128
3.23.	SACLANT's provisional organization, February 1952	136
4.1.	Masthead/Binnacle command organization for the higher direction of war	141
4.2.	British concept for command in the Channel area, November 1950	143
4.3.	British concept for command in the Channel and southern North Sea	144
4.4.	Standing Group's interim arrangement for command in the Channel, February 1951	145
4.5.	Channel Command, February 1952	148
4.6.	NATO CHANCOM and coastal commands, February 1952	149
4.7.	Command organization for the Canadian Atlantic Sub-area and its relationship to SACLANT, March 1952	152
4.8.	SACLANT organization, August 1952	155
4.9.	SACLANT command boundaries, August 1952	156
4.10.	U.S. Navy organization, 1951	160
4.11.	SACEUR's Special Air Staff, July 1952	163
4.12.	French IBERLANT proposal, October 1952	165
4.13.	Finalized SACLANT organization, 1952–53	168
5.1.	NATO CinCAFSOUTH organization, January 1951	172
5.2.	NATO CinCAFSOUTH, 1951	173
5.3.	SACEUR and the proposed relationship to SACME—U.S. view, April 1951	177
5.4.	CinCAFME proposal, April 1951	178
5.5.	Incorporation of French area into Mediterranean command plan	179

5.6.	Incorporation of French area into Mediterranean command plan (map)	180
5.7.	British compromise on Mediterranean naval area, May 1951	181
5.8.	British proposal for an eastern Mediterranean command, November 1951	183
5.9.	British proposal for an eastern Mediterranean command, November 1951 (map)	184
5.10.	U.S. proposal for command organization in the Mediterranean and Middle East, December 1951	185
5.11.	British proposal for command organization in the Mediterranean, January 1952	187
5.12.	U.S. proposal for command organization in the Mediterranean, January 1952	188
5.13.	U.S. proposal to the Standing Group at the Lisbon meeting, January 1952	189
5.14.	British proposal for naval command organization in the Mediterranean, November 1952	193
5.15.	Final NATO CinCAFMED organization	195
5.16.	SACEUR's Allied Forces Mediterranean (AFMED), 1954	196
6.1.	Naval command organization for the Korean War, February 1951	200
6.2.	NATO commands, 1990	202

➤ Foreword

It might be thought that in discussions to determine the command structure, the actual mechanism through which the strength of NATO members' forces is exerted, military voices would predominate. That this is far from the case is demonstrated by Sean Maloney in his detailed and thorough analysis of the genesis of NATO's maritime command arrangements. It was international politics, at the highest levels, that spoke the loudest. The author suggests that at times we were at great risk, because the temptation for the Soviets to intervene when alliance partners were clearly in disarray must have been very strong. But as the old English proverb goes, the proof of the pudding is in the eating. The Soviets did not attack, the chilly peace held, and now, forty years on, the threat is rapidly disappearing. Thus it can be argued that the command structures agreed upon by the fractious allies did meet the test—including perhaps the most dangerous incident of all, the Cuban missile crisis—albeit perhaps by a narrow margin.

An understanding of how we arrived where we are is not only interesting but of great value in relation to future changes—not simply possible changes, but inevitable changes. Command philosophy and organization can never stand still, as the demise of CINCHAN and the radical new arrangements recently introduced reveal. Nor will these be the last alterations, not least because the pressure to downsize and economize is now very strong in all NATO countries.

While many aspects of NATO's military organization have, understandably, remained classified until superseded (or even longer), the broad sweep of its grand strategy has always been common knowledge. No matter whether it was massive retaliation or flexible response, it was important in the logic of deterrence for any potential aggressor to know that the alliance would respond and to judge that the response was plausible. Therefore, it is possible to assess the links between successive strategies and developments in command organization. To say the least, they were not always well aligned, as this book shows.

As one who has served in the NATO command structure in many ranks and who has held appointments as Principal Subordinate Commander in Striking Fleet Atlantic, Major Subordinate Commander to SACLANT, and Major NATO Commander (CINCHAN), I learned a great deal from this thorough, painstakingly researched investigative analysis.

JULIAN OSWALD, Admiral of the Fleet, Royal Navy

Sean Maloney has captured the politics and maritime arguments that made formulation of NATO's naval commands so difficult. This book is a very fine reference for historians and practitioners of naval command. The reader will be amazed at the interest shown in NATO's command structure by the military and political "giants" of the World War II era. This structure evolved and continues to evolve as changes take place in the NATO nations and in the world. With every reorganization or realignment the command structure is evaluated and often altered, but each change is carefully examined by the nations and leaders of the alliance. Mr. Maloney has produced a fascinating document that should be studied by officers of the naval profession. I learned much from its well-written pages.

ADM. FRANK B. KELSO II, Chief of Naval Operations, USN (Ret.)

➢ Acknowledgments

With a project of this magnitude, there are inevitably a great many people to thank. I would like to start with thanks to Capt. Peter Swartz, USN (Ret.), and Dr. Michael A. Palmer for their support and encouragement. Albert "Durf" McJoyt did an excellent job on the maps, while Andy Maloney handled the organizational diagrams in a superlative fashion.

The staff and historians of the U.S. Naval Historical Center, both in the Contemporary History Division and the Operational Archives, were a great help, particularly Gina Akers, Dr. Jeff Barlow, Bernard Calvacante, Dr. Mark Jacobsen, Kathy Lloyd, Dr. Ed Marolda, Rick Russell, and Dr. Gary Weir.

I would also like to thank the staff and historians of the Canadian Department of National Defence Director General, History, particularly Isabell Campbell, Dr. Carl Christie, Owen Cooke, Don Graves, Dr. Steve Harris, Anne Martin, Edwich Munn, Donna Porter, Dr. Roger Sarty, and Mike Whitby. I would also like to thank Michael Way from the National Archives of Canada, Government Archives Division. All are indispensable, and it is sad that the cuts made by DND to DG HIST do not recognize this.

On the other side of the Atlantic, I would also like to thank Dr. Eric Grove for his valuable assistance. The Public Record Office, Kew, functions efficiently with its computers and document handlers, so it is difficult to thank any one individual. The security people were helpful and understanding when the wrong material was delivered to me by accident. Richard Ponman of the Cabinet Historical Section in London and his staff were extremely hospitable, and I thank them for allowing me access to documents that they had on hand from the PRO.

I would also like to recognize the staff at the Naval Institute Press. My colleagues Dr. Michael Henessey and Dr. Joel Sokolsky suffered through endless phone calls and brainstorming sessions over the course of two years, and Adm. Charles Duncan and Adm. J. T. Hayward also endured a flood of correspondence. Thanks also to Lt. Cdr. Patricia O'Neill at SACLANT and Lt. Cdr. Horemfins at HQ Allied Forces, Northwestern Europe. Capt. (N) Tony Goode was most hospitable at SEA LINK '92.

I would also like to thank my good friends Glen Barny, Matt Larson, Dave McDermott, Rob Silliman, and Scott Staten for providing forward base areas on my many trips to Washington, D.C., and Mrs. Loretta Scott for providing the same in Ottawa. My good friend Fritz Heinzen, tome acquisitor extraordinaire, also merits recognition. Finally, saving the best for last, I would like to thank my parents, Al and Judy Maloney, for their support and encouragement throughout this project. I would also like to acknowledge the financial assistance of the DND Military and Strategic Studies Programme.

➢ Introduction

The object of naval warfare must always be directly or indirectly either to secure the command of the sea or to prevent the enemy from securing it.
    —Julian S. Corbett, *Some Principles of Maritime Strategy*

Deterrence is the art of producing, in the mind of the enemy, the fear to attack.
    —Dr. Strangelove

Securing the command of the sea has been the primary duty of any major naval power throughout history. From Athens to Lepanto, from the Seven Years War to the campaign of Trafalgar, and from Jutland to Midway and the Battle of the Atlantic, the effects of seapower on the course of any conflict were ignored at great peril. Throughout the twentieth century, actual command of the sea was exercised not only through numbers of ships but through command organization. Since command and control has been essential to any military operation, whether during peace, war, or cold war, this has been reflected in the development of command organizations. In fundamental terms, command organizations are groupings of people that plan and execute operations at the operational and strategic levels of warfare. As such, the need for command organizations to deter aggression during the early stages of the Cold War by providing the NATO alliance with the ability to defend itself was of paramount concern to its members. The purpose of this study is to provide a history of NATO naval command organization with reference to alliance strategy and to the precedents established by the Western coalition during the Second World War.

Several themes are apparent in this study. The importance of command organizations resides in the fact that they are necessary for the attainment of the objective, be it operational or strategic in nature. For the purposes of this study, the objective in both war and cold war is command of the sea; as a result, command organizations provide insights into how NATO and national strategies were formulated, coordinated, and executed; postwar planning was a catalyst for the creation and development of command organizations (both national and coalition), and the two are interlinked.

The Second World War highlighted many problems in the development of strategy, its execution, and command and control over both national military forces and those forces operating within a wartime coalition. In an alliance system problems of national pride, disproportionate national capabilities to make war, and geography place as many strains on allied relationships as do enemy actions. The problems of coordinating one nation's naval, air, and land forces with those of other nations had never been addressed satisfactorily before World War II, primarily because forces of such magnitude and technical sophistication had never been assembled before. The physical problems of signals communication in the rapidly maturing electronic age were also considerable.

Compared to the postwar world, such problems were relatively easy to deal with; the threat of direct, sudden action from an already declared enemy was evident. After 1945, the enemy was more covert and sometimes less concrete, and the conflict was not formally declared; as a result, the problems in determining enemy capabilities and intentions, as well as the dissemination of this information among alliance partners, were difficult. Differing views on the nature of the threat posed more and different problems than they had in the Second World War. Essentially, the Western alliance was engaged in a war without battles; this environment was a new one that policymakers and strategic planners scrambled to assess and deal with.

The immediate postwar period from 1945 to 1948 was a time of confusion. The intoxication of victory was only starting to wear off, and nations were attempting either to rebuild or to restructure for peace. Military alliances did not cease to exist but did languish in a sort of benign neglect. Only after Western political leaders realized that a threat did exist (and had actually existed all along) were the military connections reestablished. However, there were two problems. The first was the rapid demobilization of Western military forces after 1945; second, the only nations capable of conducting any form of military action against the Soviet Union in 1946 were the United States, Great Britain, and members of the Commonwealth. Only as a group could these partners stand up to the Soviet Union, and only the United States had the atomic bomb. It soon became clear that other nations would acquire it, depriving the West of its monopoly.

Relations between the Soviet Union and the West were antagonistic, and this required concerted action from the West to counter Stalin's expansionist tendencies. American allies, particularly Britain, were in a position to challenge the absoluteness of U.S. leadership of the West, and the problems of command and control over coalition forces evident in the Second World War returned to haunt strategic planners. The creation of the North Atlantic Treaty Organization (NATO) in 1949 solved some of the old problems of coalition control but in turn presented new ones. As a result, NATO naval command organizations in the 1950s were an expression of how national strategies and their naval components interacted with other countries' strategies and forces to resolve conflicts over interests and strategic problems.

There is a gap in the historiography of command relationships and their interaction with national strategies in both the Second World War and the Cold War. So far, no historian or political scientist has attempted to link the development of NATO command organizations with the historical experience of World War II, nor has the link between postwar strategy and command organization been made. What was the nature of these links? How did NATO command organization descend from Second World War command organization?

Since NATO command organization can be considered a "descendant" of its World War II "parent," an overview of Second World War commands in the Atlantic and in Europe is crucial. The problem of an allied command in war reached a somewhat mature state by 1945, so this study will commence with an examination of the naval command and control organizations in the Atlantic and Mediterranean theaters in the Second World War, their strategic and operational problems, and the effect that actual command and control problems had on the conduct of the naval war in both theaters. We will then examine the transitional years of 1945 to 1948 and the search for a new coalition command structure; this will be linked to the development of NATO, the Supreme Allied Commander Atlantic (SACLANT), and the naval components of the Supreme Allied Commander, Europe (SACEUR) from 1949 to 1954. Because command and control organizations cannot be separated from the development of strategy and policy, the pertinent national strategies and their differences will be linked to the developing command organizations by examining national and coalition naval strategy for the 1948 to 1954 period. Finally, the evolution of SACLANT from 1951 to 1954 in light of command reorganization will receive scrutiny, as will the creation of the Channel Command (CHANCOM) and Commander in Chief, Allied Forces

Mediterranean (CinCAFMED). Since the focus of this study is on the military aspects of NATO command organization, the political angles of these problems, which are related to higher forms of national foreign policy, will be examined only briefly and only when they are instrumental in the resolution of disputes.

Another theme that runs throughout this study is the nature of the Anglo-American "special relationship" in the early 1950s. The endless transatlantic debate had, in the words of Dwight D. Eisenhower, "sometimes resulted in the creation of schism and division rather than unity and confidence. The difficulties thus created plague us to some extent in trying to put together a command organization that seems to resemble a picture puzzle. The pieces are made up of individual ambitions and rigid conceptions of service function, prestige and tactical doctrine and of nationalistic jealousies, suspicions and economic interests...." The almost Freudian melodrama between the mature but declining British empire and the adolescent American superpower was also played out in the command organization debate.

1 ➤ Second World War Command Organization

I would rather fight an alliance than be part of one.
    —attributed to Napoleon Bonaparte

It has never been our practice to place combined expeditions under either a naval or a military commander in chief and allow him to decide between naval and military exigencies. The danger of possible friction between two commanders in chief came to be regarded as small compared with the danger of a single one making mistakes through unfamiliarity with the limitations of the service to which he does not belong....
    —Corbett, *Some Principles of Maritime Strategy*

The Second World War provides an essential starting point for examining postwar command organization. The sheer size, variety, and technological complexity of the forces involved necessitated a large and complex system of command and control. Until World War II, the need for such a complex system did not exist. Afterward, the nature and magnitude of the operating forces did not regress, and in fact postwar command organization was the logical outgrowth of the Second World War experience. The purpose of this chapter is to discuss the types of command organizations established during the Second World War in both general and specific terms as they relate to the conduct of naval warfare in the Atlantic and the Mediterranean. This will provide a basis for later comparison with postwar command organization. In addition, some examples of friction between Second World War command organizations are provided to highlight postwar changes and to stress some continuing command problems after the establishment of NATO in 1949. Note that the nature of combined operations and interservice cooperation dictates that the naval component cannot be studied in isolation from land and air forces. Because of the complexity of the World War II command situation and given the fact that this study is focused primarily on the postwar period, this chapter is meant as an overview for later comparison and contrast; it should not be considered the definitive word on Second World War command organization.

To conduct complex multiservice operations successfully, all service elements have to interact and coordinate. Interservice and political–service problems that already exist within a single nation are multiplied when groups of nations form coalitions in order to fight an enemy. The Allied coalition of World War II was no exception. By 1942 it was clear to the Allied leadership that the dominant members of the coalition were the United States and Great Britain. The economic and military strengths of the partners were disparate. Great Britain was a world power on the decline, and the United States was assuming the mantle of a great power. While Great Britain had significant experience in conducting coalition war and a proprietary interest in the Second World War up to 1941, it was weak economically; the United States was a relatively inexperienced but undamaged industrial giant that had access to vast reserves of manpower and material. Some means had to be found to coordinate the military activities of these partners.

Thus, in the Second World War the first multinational, multiservice coalition commands, which formed the basis for NATO command organizations, were created. The direct predecessor to NATO's Supreme Allied Commander Europe was the Supreme Headquarters Allied Expeditionary Force, which in turn developed out of the coalition command organizations created to execute the Torch and Husky operations. These transitional commands in the Mediterranean had to interact with the British national command already in place to handle operations in the Mediterranean and the Middle East, which itself was the predecessor of NATO's Commander in Chief, Allied Forces Mediterranean. There was a political imperative to balance the number and prestige of the coalition and national commands among the two senior partners of the coalition, the United States and Britain. This would eventually pose problems in the postwar period when the British became a less than equal partner in the Western coalition. Notwithstanding this, U.S. and British staffs eventually learned to cooperate to overcome many personal, international, and interservice problems by 1944. This experience would form the basis for later NATO cooperation when the arrangements for the Supreme Allied Commander, Europe and Supreme Allied Commander, Atlantic were debated and finalized.

The Higher Direction of War, 1939–1945

Both the United States and Great Britain had national political and national military command organizations; each military was organized into regional command organizations that had operating forces assigned to them. In order to link the two national military commands, an overall coalition command organization and some regional coalition commands were established to eliminate overlap. In very general terms, the coalition command situation in 1942 was similar to figure 1.1.

The British and American political and military command organizations differed in some ways. Great Britain's political organization for war was embodied in the War Cabinet, which consisted of the prime minister (Winston Churchill), the minister of defence (MoD; also Churchill), the secretary of state for foreign affairs (Anthony Eden), the chancellor of the exchequer, the minister of labour, and other governmental posts necessary

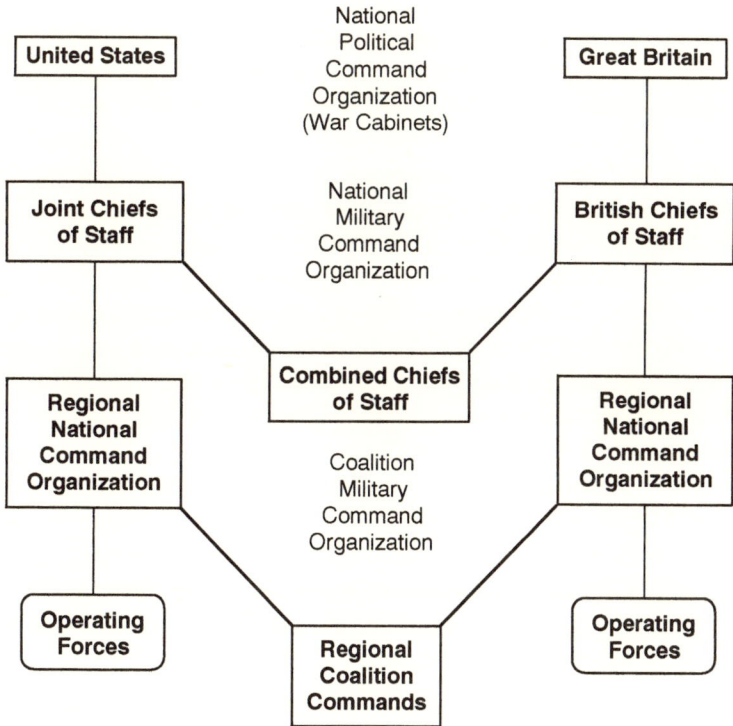

Fig. 1.1. Second World War command organization types

for the conduct of the war from a political standpoint. The military organization was called the British Chiefs of Staff (for the purposes of this paper, the BCS), and it gave strategic direction to the operational joint commands. Its membership consisted of the Chief of the Imperial General Staff (CIGS), Gen. Sir Alan Brooke; the First Sea Lord and Chief of the Naval Staff, Admiral of the Fleet Sir Dudley Pound (later Adm. Sir Andrew Cunningham); the Chief of the Air Staff, Air Chief Marshal Sir Charles Portal; the Chief of Combined Operations, Vice Adm. Louis Mountbatten (later Maj. Gen. R. E. Laycock); and the Chief of Staff, Ministry of Defence, Lt. Gen. Sir Hastings Ismay. The BCS was subordinate to the War Cabinet through the Chief of Staff to the minister of defence, which was almost irrelevant because Churchill himself was the MoD.[1]

The American political and military organization was slightly different from the British system. There was no formalized "war cabinet" in name, but there was a special group that directed the war. The president, Franklin D. Roosevelt, had input from several sources in addition to his usual civilian cabinet members. Adm. William D. Leahy, who was the unofficial Chairman of the Joint Chiefs of Staff (JCS; established in February 1942), was the primary military adviser to the president. Others included the Secretary of the Army, Henry Stimson; the Secretary of the Navy, Frank Knox (later James Forrestal); the Chief of Staff of the Army, Gen. George C. Marshall; Commander in Chief, U.S. Fleet, and the Chief of Naval Operations, Adm. Ernest King; and the Commanding General of the Army Air Forces, Gen. H. H. Arnold. At first glance, it may appear as though the JCS had a more prominent position politically than the BCS even though it commanded only U.S. operational unified and single-service commands; however, formal lines of communication were frequently circumvented by Churchill and Roosevelt in an almost random manner.[2]

How were these national military command organizations linked? The American-British staff conversations (ABC-1) were convened at the Washington conference of 29 January 1941 and included members of the JCS and BCS. The purpose of the conference was to develop a system of coalition warfare, to determine the best methods of defeating Germany if the United States entered the war (with an eye to coordinating U.S. and British planning and agreeing on broad areas of strategic responsibility), and to develop command arrangements. The results of ABC-1 included the establishment of the Combined Chiefs of Staff (CCS) in January 1942, recognition of the need to exchange intelligence, and agreement on an offensive policy ("Germany First") and a defensive policy (the protection

Second World War Command Organization   ➤ 9

of sea lines of communication in the North Atlantic). General principles of command were discussed, including the need for each country to have strategic direction in specific areas of responsibility; these would be established in detail at a later conference, code-named Arcadia. ABC-1 was concluded on 27 March 1941.³

The Arcadia conference (22 December 1941–14 January 1942) in Washington focused on "the need to control forces of differing nations operating within a single theater," and the result was the fine-tuning of a coalition command organization, the CCS (see fig. 1.2).⁴ This body consisted of the top BCS and JCS members, and its task was to "formulate and execute, under the direction of the heads of the countries concerned,

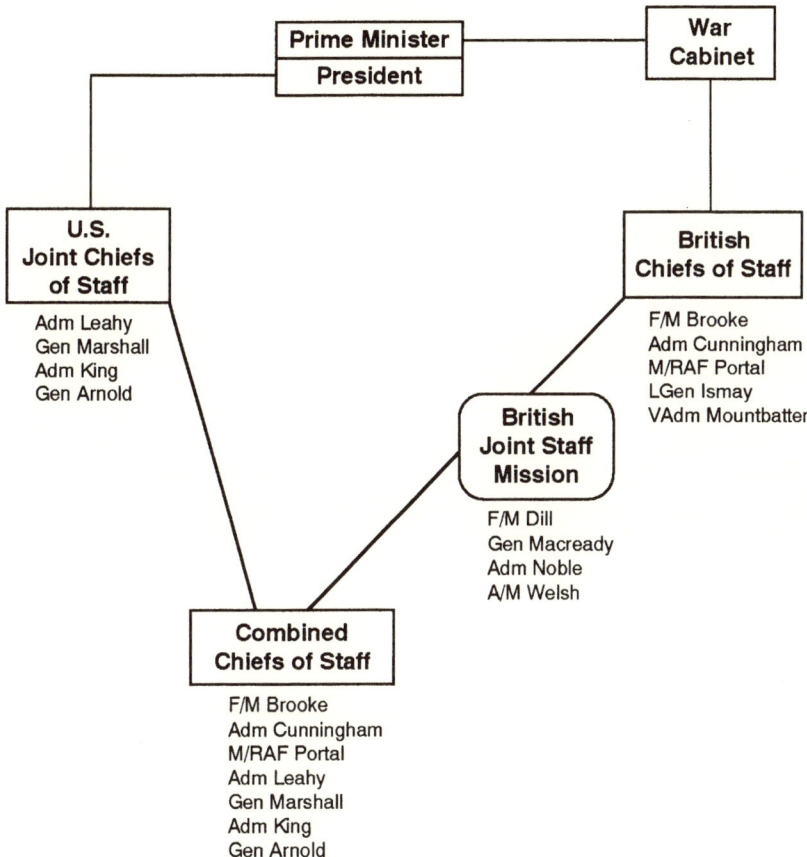

Fig. 1.2. Allied coalition command organization, 1942–45

policies and plans relating to the strategic conduct of the war, allocation of munitions, broad war requirements and transport requirements."[5] In this way, the CCS was the joint responsibility of the BCS and JCS; the link between the two was provided by the British Joint Staff Mission (BJSM) led by Field Marshal Sir John Dill of the British army. The BJSM was located in Washington and acted as a liaison from the BCS to the JCS. The mandate of the CCS was to provide "general jurisdiction over grand strategic policy," while the BCS/JCS mandate was to supply "jurisdiction pertaining to all matters of operational strategy" within theaters of war.[6]

No other Allied nations were represented in the CCS. Canada, for example, did not participate in the dealings of the CCS because it was essentially a middle power; however, Churchill gave assurances to the Canadian political leadership, headed by Mackenzie King, that Canada and other commonwealth nations "would be consulted where her interests were concerned."[7] In addition to other unilateral measures taken to coordinate defense with the United States (these will be discussed later), a Canadian Joint Staff Mission was established in Washington.[8]

Other consequences of Arcadia included the division of the world into British and American strategic theaters of war. These had far-reaching effects into the postwar period as the British and the Americans set the division of labor to reflect national interests and capabilities (see fig. 1.3). Both Roosevelt and Churchill corresponded throughout the first months of 1942 with the express purpose of delineating the coalition war effort in operational terms. Essentially, the United States handled China and the Pacific, while Britain was responsible for the rest of Asia, the Mediterranean, and the Middle East. Europe and the Atlantic were subject to shared control.[9]

Some special fields, however, required special command measures. Combined U.S.–British commands included the Atlantic, the strategic air campaign, and the preparation for land operations in the Mediterranean and Northwest Europe. The Atlantic area was divided into British and U.S. areas of strategic responsibility, and the conduct of the naval war was invested in the naval authorities concerned without consulting the CCS directly. The strategic air offensive in Europe was coordinated through the CCS, the national strategic bombing commands remaining under national operational control (see fig. 1.4).[10]

Another important consequence of the Arcadia conference was the debate over the establishment of supreme allied commands in geographic areas. The differing nature of U.S. and British regional strategic decision-making caused friction. The British system, which will be called here the

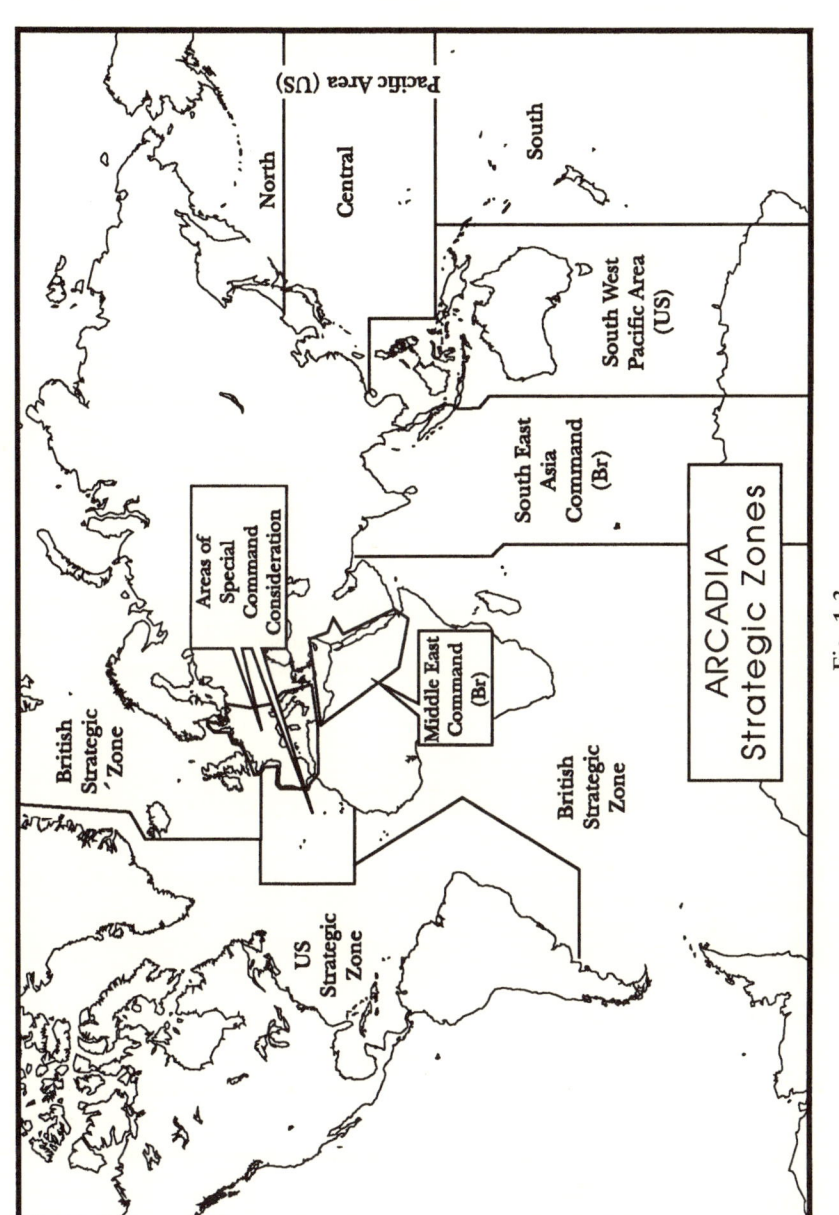

Fig. 1.3.

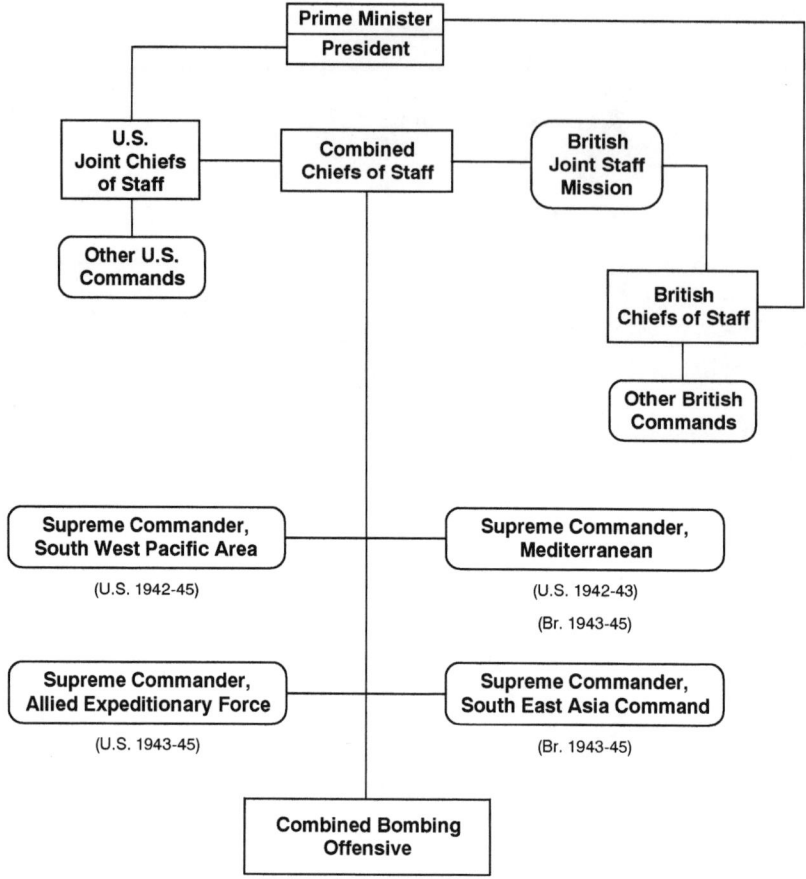

Fig. 1.4. Allied coalition command organization and supreme allied commands, 1942–45

joint committee system, consisted of three commanders in chief, one from each service, all jointly responsible for a geographic command. The land forces commander coordinated the committee and represented it before the CIGS. This system worked well in the Middle East but led to problems in coordination with other countries' forces operating in British geographic areas of command.[11]

The Americans, on the other hand, thought that the joint committee system was inefficient and disrupted a cardinal principle of war, unity of command. The American system, called here the *unified command system,* consisted of three service commanders (for the purposes of this study, the USAAF will be referred to as a separate service) within a geographic command. The service providing the bulk of the resources to that command also provided the supreme commander for that area—usually one of the three service commanders (a practice known as "double hatting"), although sometimes another officer from the same service as the supreme commander would handle those forces operationally. The other service heads in the area were subordinate to the supreme commander. In this way, the Americans believed that a single man had responsibility for the conduct of operations within the area and that confusion and interservice rivalry could be eliminated.[12]

As with the British system, geographic and operational delineation was confusing at times. For example, in March 1942 Marshall and the JCS subdivided the Pacific theater into two areas: the Southwest Pacific Area (SWPA) and the Pacific Ocean Area (POA). The SWPA (a U.S. geographic command and a coalition command established by the CCS after Arcadia) was the realm of the Supreme Commander, Southwest Pacific Area; this was Gen. Douglas MacArthur, who was responsible for the conduct of the war in all land areas in the Pacific from the Philippines to Samoa. However, the national geographic commander for the POA, Adm. Chester W. Nimitz, was double-hatted as the Commander in Chief, U.S. Pacific Fleet, and thus had under his control all U.S. naval operating forces in both the SWPA and the POA.[13]

The result of the Anglo-American debate over joint or unified control was a compromise. In 1942, the United States and Britain agreed to establish one supreme commander to lead all three services in each of the four major theaters of operations: the Pacific, the Middle East, the Mediterranean, and Europe. Initially, Britain had supreme command over the Middle East and the Mediterranean, and the United States over the Pacific; the planned return to the continent of Europe was designated a U.S. supreme commander's responsibility. Once operations in the Mediterranean were under way, however, the Americans provided the supreme commander for this area; to compensate for this politically, the Southeast Asia Command (SEAC) was established under Mountbatten in August 1943 to control all Allied forces in India and Burma. All supreme commands maintained coalition staffs drawn from all services.[14]

Within the Anglo-American geographic commands, national operating forces were commanded by national regional commands. These commands could be administrative or operational in nature and sometimes changed status depending on the degree of military activity within the region. Consequently, specific theaters of operation provide examples of command organization within a particular area. Since this study focuses on the Mediterranean, Atlantic, and European theaters, closer examination of the overall command organizations and their naval components within these areas is necessary. Keeping in mind that the purpose of operations in the Atlantic was to support the land and air efforts in the Mediterranean and Europe, it should be noted here that the focus and specific roles of the naval components in the three theaters were quite different. Naval operations in the Mediterranean and Europe were characteristically offensive in nature, involving antiship activity and support of landing operations with less emphasis on securing safe passage of civilian and military shipping. The effort in the Atlantic, however, was primarily defensive in nature and was geared toward defense of shipping. As a result, the need for diverse elements such as land, naval, tactical, strategic, and coastal air forces to coordinate and interact in the Mediterranean and European theaters was greater than it was in the Atlantic, where the primary services involved in operations were the naval and coastal air forces. This explains to some degree the comparative immaturity of coalition command organization in the Atlantic theater by 1945.

COMMAND ORGANIZATION IN THE MEDITERRANEAN

The first extensive use of Allied coalition command organizations was in the Mediterranean. Until 1942, Britain prosecuted the war in the Mediterranean through its national command organizations. The Royal Navy in the Mediterranean was divided into Commander in Chief, Levant for the eastern Mediterranean and Commander in Chief, Mediterranean for the western Mediterranean. The dividing line ran from Sicily to Tunisia. There was also a Vice Admiral in Charge, Malta to handle the defense of that island. The land forces came under the British Commander in Chief, Middle East (CinCME), headquartered in Egypt; the various air elements (tactical, strategic, and coastal) in Egypt, Iran, and the Persian Gulf were commanded by Headquarters, RAF Middle East.[15]

This all changed with the decision to commit an Allied expeditionary force to the Mediterranean (Operation Torch). While the Middle East remained an inactive theater of war (with the exception of the war in Egypt and some operations in Syria), some British forces in the Mediterranean basin under CinCME were assigned to the new coalition command. The designated leader of this coalition command was an American, Gen. Dwight D. Eisenhower. His position was called Commander in Chief, Allied Expeditionary Force (CinCAF), later changed

Second World War Command Organization   ➢ 15

to Commander in Chief, Allied Forces for security purposes, and he headed Allied Force Headquarters (AFHQ). This organization was a transitional one and would eventually develop into a supreme command under the CCS (see fig. 1.5). CinCAF had direct command over British and American land forces assigned to AFHQ and their associated land-based air support; the air support for Torch was not integrated into one coalition organization, and each air element's commander was directly responsible to AFHQ. Indirect command was exercised by CinCAF over the British naval component, which was under the coalition command of the Allied Naval Commander, Expeditionary Force (NCXF), Adm. Sir Andrew Cunningham (RN). One lesson from the Dieppe operation in August 1942 was the need to create special naval assault forces with their own senior naval officers; tripartite organizations were necessary for the joint planning of the operation, but the command of the entire enterprise to the water's edge had to be handled by the naval leadership. In essential terms, the

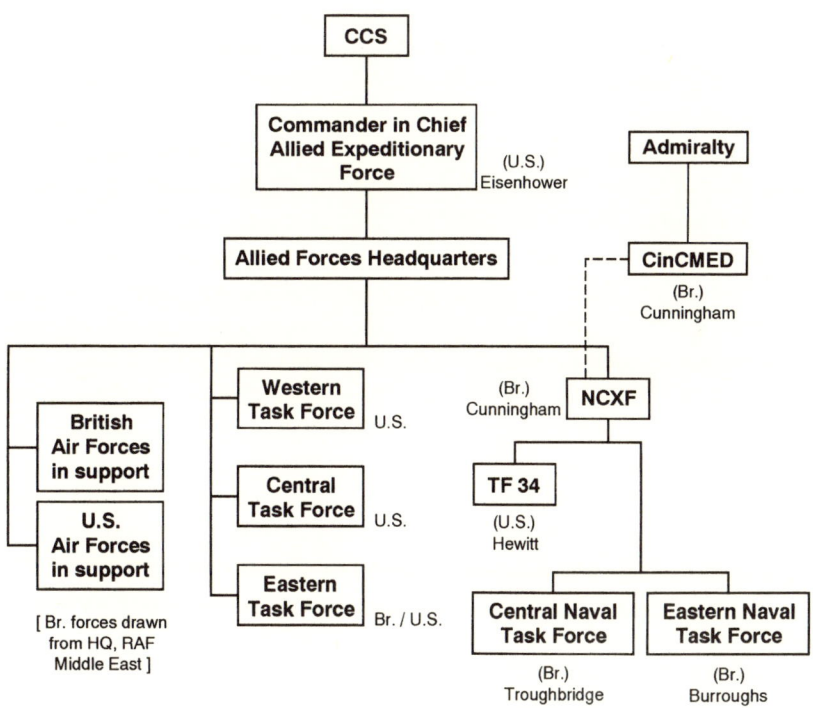

Fig. 1.5. Command organization for Torch, 8 November 1942

British naval operating forces committed to Torch remained under national command, not under coalition command.[16] This was probably done because of the preponderance of Royal Navy operating forces committed to the operation, and it became a precedent that continued into the postwar period.

The American naval force assigned to Torch was called Amphibious Force Atlantic Fleet (Task Force 34) and was under the operational command of Adm. H. K. Hewitt. This national command organization was equipped mostly with assault transports. Its national administrative command was the Commander in Chief, Atlantic Fleet (CinCLANTFLEET), Adm. Ralph Ingersoll. But for the purposes of Torch, Task Force 34 was ultimately under the auspices of NCXF for the purpose of coordination with the other naval forces involved.[17]

There were significant problems involving the interaction between British and American national commands in the Atlantic and the coalition command in the Mediterranean established for Torch. One of these was the issue of COMNAVNAW, a case in which British and U.S. strategic interests and national commands conflicted. In January 1943, CinCAF took control of all coalition operations in the western Mediterranean from Gibraltar to a line running between Tunisia, Tripolitania, and Corfu; the eastern Mediterranean remained under the British national command of the Commander in Chief, Middle East. To maintain congruence with progressing operations, the U.S. Navy in March 1943 established United States Naval Forces, North African Waters (U.S. COMNAVNAW), a geographic command led by Admiral Hewitt, the former Task Force 34 commander. It was subordinate to a renamed NCXF, the Allied Naval Commander in Chief, Mediterranean, Admiral Cunningham (RN). The U.S. naval operating forces assigned to the Mediterranean theater of operations—and, by default, COMNAVNAW—appeared to be part and parcel of the newly established U.S. Eighth Fleet, which was a double-hatted position held by Hewitt. Eighth Fleet also was subordinate to Cunningham's coalition command.[18]

COMNAVNAW, however, was directly under the command of Adm. Ernest King, the U.S. Navy Commander in Chief (COMINCH) based in Washington, D.C., not the Allied Combined Chiefs of Staff. COMNAVNAW had the responsibility of protecting American troop convoys in and around North Africa in support of U.S. operations there and also across the Atlantic in an area already under British operational control. To the British, this was politically unacceptable vis-à-vis the earlier agreements dividing the world into British and American zones of responsibility.[19]

The control of RAF Coastal Command long-range patrol and antisubmarine warfare (ASW) aircraft at Gibraltar initially belonged to the local British combined headquarters there; for Operation Torch, the planes were allocated to Eisenhower in his role as Torch commander. The British were under the impression that this was a temporary state of affairs. The practice continued after Torch was complete, however. This resulted in a disruption of air coverage both for British convoys headed to and from England and for American convoys headed to and from the United States. To the British, it was illogical (not to mention impolite) for RAF Coastal Command to be "hijacked" by the naval commander of an American "incursion" into the British strategic zone to provide protection to American troop convoys; such protection would come at the expense of air protection to British trade convoys transiting to the British Isles through the area.[20] The problem of the Gibraltar approaches was never solved satisfactorily during World War II and would later cause severe problems in the establishment of the NATO command structure in the Atlantic during the 1950s.

Once Torch was completed and operations in Tunisia were under way, complications arising from the establishment of a coalition expeditionary force in the western Mediterranean forced a reorganization of command relationships in the entire Mediterranean theater. The Casablanca conference in January 1943 resulted in the establishment of two distinct theaters of war: the European Theater of Operations (ETO) and the North Africa Theater of Operations (NTO). ETO's geographic area included Iceland, Britain, Scandinavia, France, Germany, and eastern Europe. NTO's included the Iberian Peninsula, Italy, Sicily, Sardinia, Corsica, northwestern Africa, and Tunisia. For the purposes of the strategic bombing campaign, these boundaries were ignored.[21] The coalition commander, CinCAF (Eisenhower), changed titles to become Allied Commander in Chief, Allied Forces North Africa, reflecting the Allied advance and changing strategy. At this point, Allied CinCAFNA did not exercise control over all Allied efforts in the Mediterranean; he coordinated naval, air, and land operations within the western Mediterranean only and was responsible for planning Operation Husky, the invasion of Sicily.

The predominant national command organizations in the Mediterranean in mid-1943 were still the British naval and air commands. The Royal Navy shuffled its resources and finalized the organization portrayed in figure 1.6.[22] The Levant command was abolished, and all Royal Navy forces in the Mediterranean were incorporated under the Commander in Chief, Mediterranean (CinCMED). The flag officers in the various areas

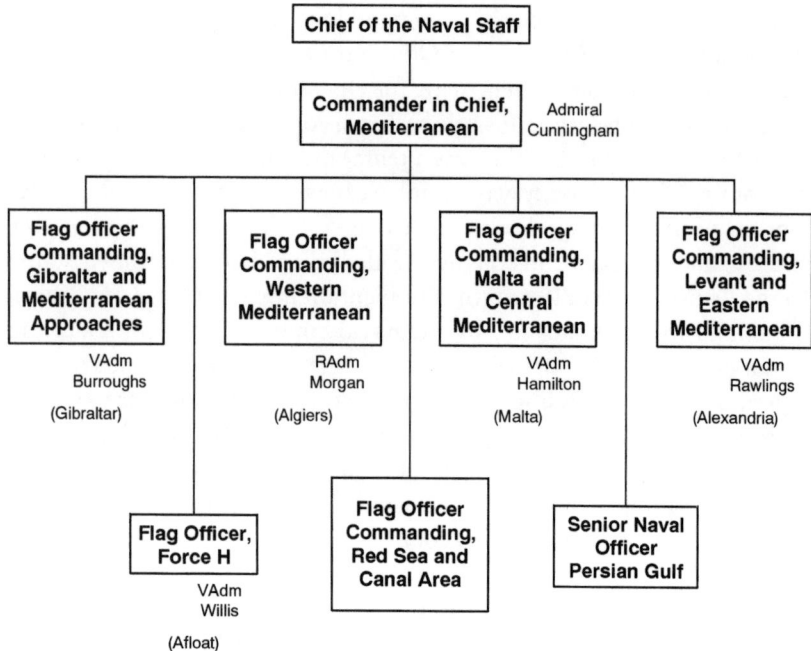

Fig. 1.6. Royal Navy organization in the Mediterranean, 1943–45

had administrative control over facilities in their areas; operating forces were assigned as necessary by CinCMED with the exception of Force H, a collection of battleships, cruisers, and aircraft carriers structured specifically for offensive operations that at times was directly controlled by the Home Fleet or the Flag Officer, Atlantic. Notably, Force H appears to be the ancestor of NATO's Striking Fleet Atlantic.

The Royal Air Force, on the other hand, had command over all RAF activity through its Headquarters, RAF Middle East (HQ RAFME). Previously called the Middle East Air Command, HQ RAFME exercised control over six geographic commands that included areas outside the Mediterranean (see fig. 1.7). In addition, until October 1943 HQ RAFME commanded the Ninth Air Force, a U.S. national command. A potential complication in the development of any coalition command in the Mediterranean was the friction that could have resulted from the placement of a British national command, HQ RAFME, which had widespread responsibilities outside the Mediterranean theater of operations, under an American supreme commander.[23]

Second World War Command Organization   ➢ 19

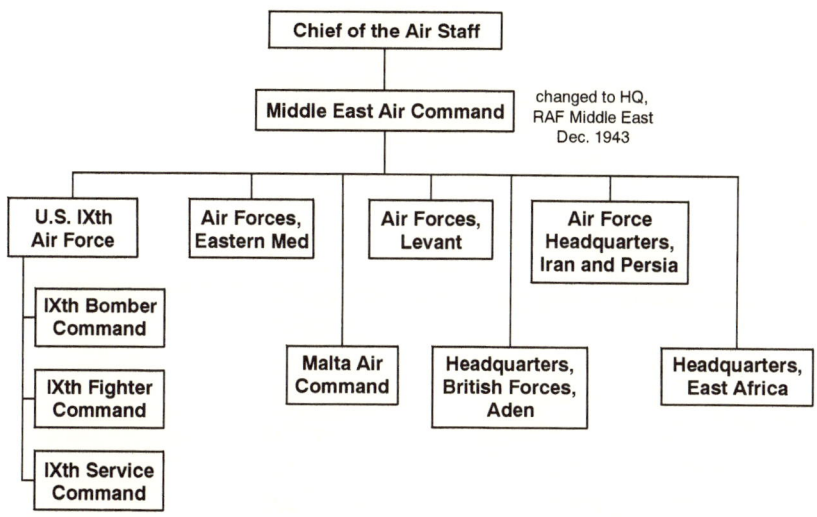

Fig. 1.7. RAF command organization in the Mediterranean, 1943

The command organization established for Operation Husky clearly grew out of the Torch organization (see fig. 1.8; cf. fig. 1.5). The air elements were similar to and appear to have been facilitated by the last British reorganization. Allied CinCAFNA reported to the CCS and maintained the Allied Force Headquarters as he had as CinCAF. His geographic area of command remained the western Mediterranean, and British national commands still were responsible for the eastern Mediterranean to the BCS. Sealift and naval support for Husky was again commanded by the Naval Commander in Chief, a British admiral, and was divided into Eastern and Western naval task forces. The Western Naval Task Force was commanded by Admiral Hewitt (USN) and his Eighth Fleet. The Eastern Naval Task Force was under the command of Admiral Ramsay (RN), and his forces were allocated from Admiral Cunningham in his role as the British national naval commander in the Mediterranean. All ground forces for Husky were placed under the command of Field Marshal Alexander and the 15th Army Group, which included the British Eighth Army and the U.S. Seventh Army.[24]

The air forces were placed under a coalition command called the Mediterranean Air Command (Air Chief Marshal Tedder, RAF), which consisted of the British Middle East Air Command (MEAC) and its subordinates, the Malta Air Command, and the U.S. Ninth Air Force. Allied

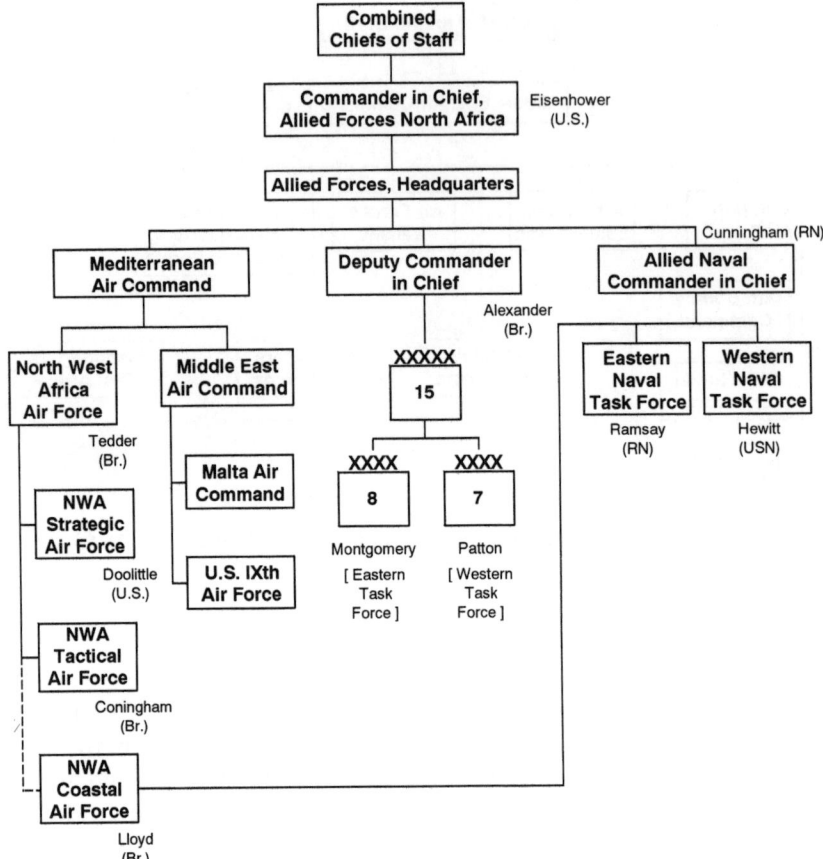

Fig. 1.8. Command organization for Husky, 10 July 1943

air assets in North Africa were placed under a coalition command, the Northwest Africa Air Force (NWAAF; Major General Spaatz, USAAF) and subordinated to the Mediterranean Air Command. NWAAF supported the Western Naval Task Force, and MEAC supported the Eastern Naval Task Force.[25]

Compared to Torch, the Husky organization appears to be less ad hoc. The organization of the air forces was undergoing a shakeout process, while the Allied naval forces grew accustomed to working together under Cunningham. After Sicily was secured in August 1943, the temporary and transitional command organization that existed became a permanent one.

This structure underwent another and final reorganization in late 1943 and early 1944, and the development of coalition command in the Mediterranean reached its maturity.

One problem with the placement of Eisenhower as CinCAFNA was that it tipped the numerical balance of supreme Allied commanders in favor of the Americans, unleashing the predictable political backlash from the British. During the Arcadia conference the Mediterranean was an area of British strategic responsibility. By 1943, General Marshall and the JCS were proposing a single Allied commander in chief for both the Mediterranean theater of operations and the European theater of operations when the Allies returned to the continent in force, instead of two separate supreme commanders. At the same time, the Commander in Chief, U.S. Pacific Fleet indicated that all Allied operations in the Pacific and Indian Oceans should fall under one unified commander. Apparently, Marshall was very concerned about damaging Anglo-American relations by having "too many Yanks in charge." Fortunately, the British simultaneously proposed the establishment of a British coalition commander in the Mediterranean and the creation of SEAC as compensation for American command of the European theater of operations. As a compromise, the Mediterranean theater of operations was not subordinated to the European command.[26]

As a result of this compromise, Allied CinCAFNA became Allied Commander in Chief, Mediterranean Theater in December 1943. At this point, Eisenhower left to become the head of the coalition command, Supreme Headquarters, Allied Expeditionary Force (SHAEF), of which more will be said later. Gen. Sir Henry Maitland of the British army assumed the position of CinC Mediterranean Theater, which was renamed Supreme Allied Commander, Mediterranean Theater. SACMED commanded all Allied forces within the Mediterranean area, including the British national commands in the eastern Mediterranean and the Middle East.

The existing command organization in the Mediterranean was streamlined for the continued prosecution of the war. The convoluted air organization, Mediterranean Air Command, was restructured into the Mediterranean Allied Air Forces (MAAF) (see fig. 1.9). MAAF grouped all strategic bombing aircraft from both the RAF and USAAF into the Mediterranean Allied Strategic Air Force, which was commanded by Lieutenant General Doolittle (USAAF). Tactical air support was centralized under the Mediterranean Allied Tactical Air Force led by a British CinC, Air Marshal Conningham; its operating forces were the RAF Desert Air Force (DAF) and the U.S. Twelfth Air Force. DAF supported British

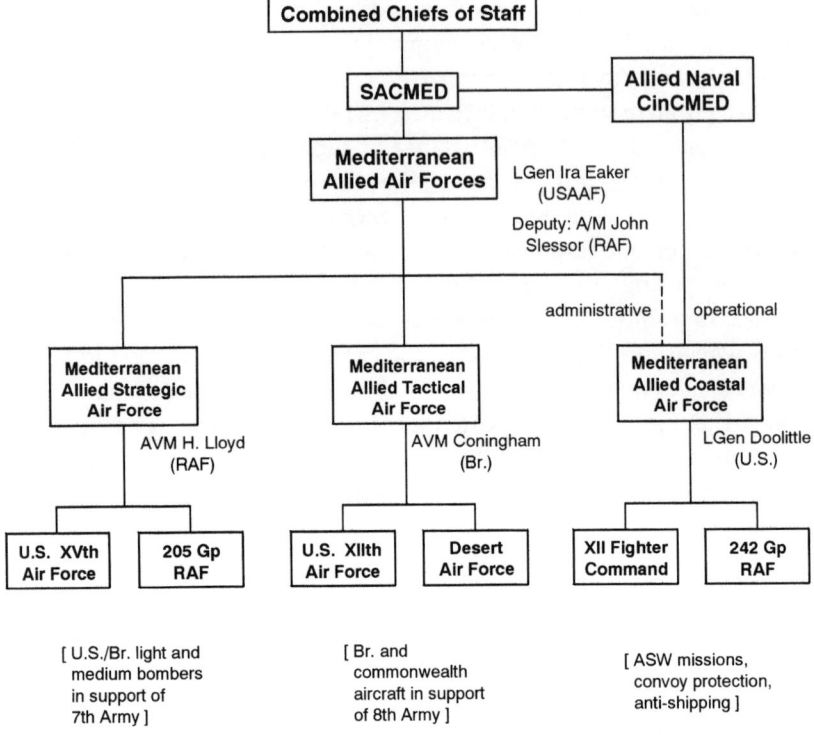

Fig. 1.9. Mediterranean Allied Air Forces, 1 January 1944

and commonwealth forces in the Mediterranean, while the Twelfth Air Force supported American and French ground forces. The role of the Mediterranean Allied Coastal Air Force was to conduct antiship efforts, convoy protection, and antisubmarine warfare. Significantly, MAAF had only administrative control over the Mediterranean Allied Coastal Air Force; it was operationally controlled by the Allied Naval CinCMED, Admiral Cunningham (RN).[27] This was in keeping with British practice whereby the RAF was administratively responsible for maritime air operations while the Royal Navy had operational control.

In his national capacity of commander of Royal Navy forces in the Mediterranean and Middle East, the Allied Naval CinCMED reorganized his national forces into five flag commands within the Mediterranean and two special commands, Persian Gulf and Red Sea/Canal Zone (see fig. 1.10). These national commands also were coalition commands; due to the pre-

Second World War Command Organization

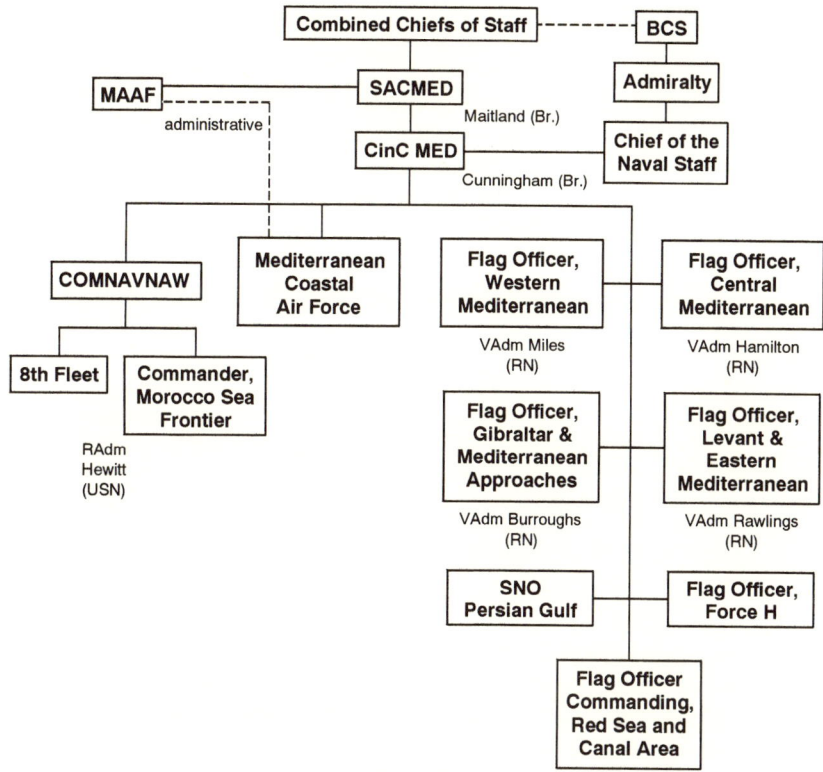

Fig. 1.10. Mediterranean naval command organization, 1 June 1944

ponderance of Royal Navy assets involved, the difference was purely theoretical. As coalition commander, CinCMED retained command of the U.S. national command, the Eighth Fleet, still under Admiral Hewitt.[28]

Thus, by mid-1944 the coalition command in the Mediterranean theater of operations reached its ultimate form (see fig. 1.11). The development of this organization would provide the basis for the transitional command, SHAEF, as a permanent coalition command under the CCS for the European theater of operations.

COMMAND ORGANIZATION FOR WESTERN EUROPE: SHAEF

As a transitional command, SHAEF was quite similar in organization to the command organizations established in the Mediterranean (see fig. 1.12). The control of Allied naval forces for Overlord was delegated to

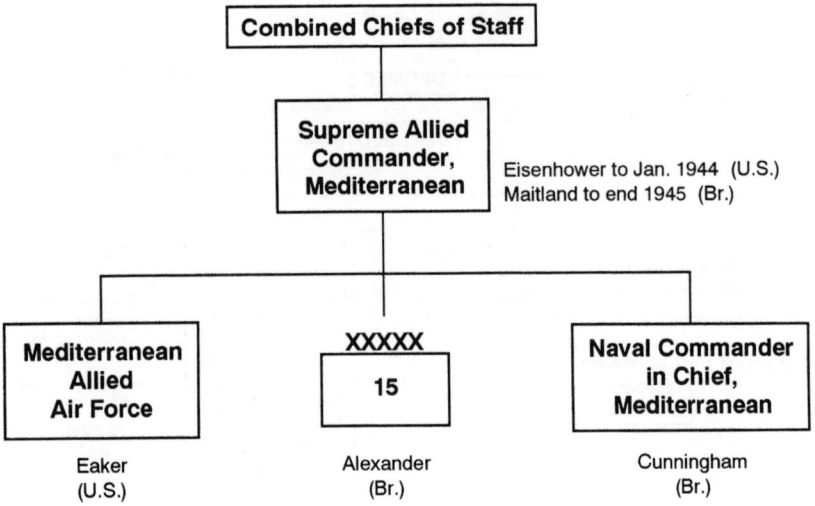

Fig. 1.11. Mediterranean command organization, 1944–45

Admiral Ramsay of the Royal Navy; the naval component for Overlord was called Neptune. As with previous coalition landing operations, there was a western and an eastern task force, under the command of Vice Admiral Kirk (USN) and Vice Admiral Vian (RN), respectively. Vice Admiral Kirk had national operational command over all American naval forces in Europe with the exception of Hewitt's Eighth Fleet and U.S. NAVNAW. The bulk of U.S. naval forces allocated to Neptune consisted of assault amphibious transports and their escorts; some cruisers and second-line battleships were also present. The administrative support for Kirk's command was supplied by the U.S. Navy's headquarters in London, Commander, Naval Forces Europe (COMNAVEUR) under Admiral Stark (USN).[29]

Vice Admiral Vian was allocated naval forces from the Royal Navy's Home Fleet and the various home commands for the purposes of Overlord. The antisubmarine protection for Neptune was an adjunct to Royal Navy and RAF Coastal Command efforts already established for convoy protection since 1942; planning and allocation of these forces was merely extended to the coast of France for the operation.[30] However, once SHAEF was established as a permanent command ashore in France, the emphasis shifted away from a tri-service orientation to dominance by the air and ground forces.

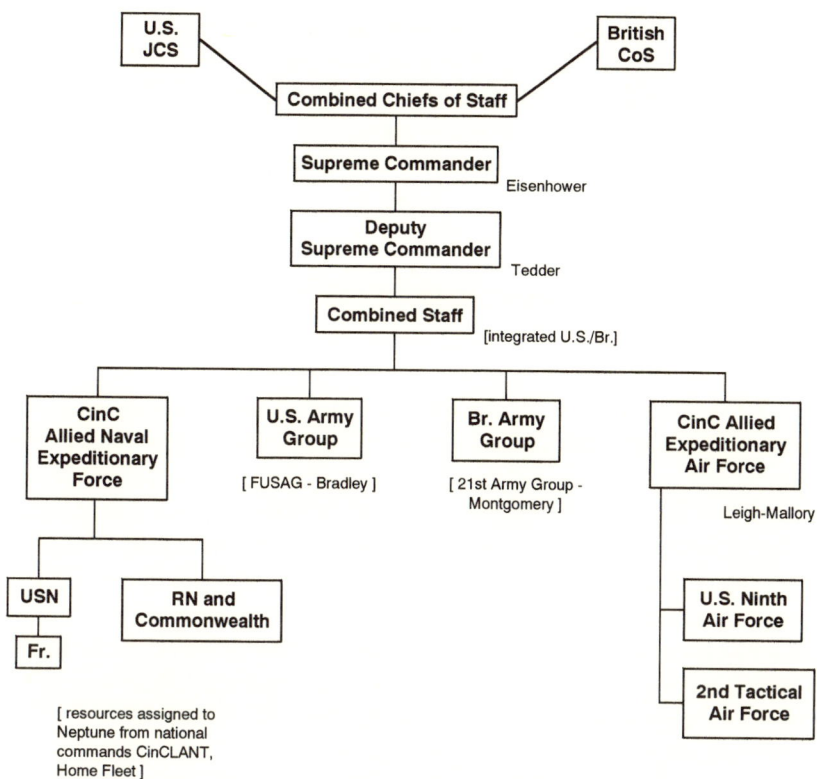

Fig. 1.12. SHAEF organization for Overlord, 1944

Ultimately, the legacy of the Mediterranean and European command organizations would affect the creation of NATO's Supreme Allied Commander, Europe in the 1950s and its interaction with NATO's Supreme Allied Commander, Atlantic, as we will see in later chapters.

Command Organization in the North Atlantic

The debates over command organization for the North Atlantic caused more interallied problems that those over the Mediterranean or Northwest Europe. This was due to the difficulties of coordinating three naval and three air forces engaged in the campaign that would decide fundamentally whether or not the coalition could continue to fight. Additional complicating factors were the lack of official U.S. participation prior to 1941 and the nature of the U.S. unified style of command as opposed to the British joint system. However, from the outset of the war to 1941 the brunt of the Battle of the Atlantic was borne by Great Britain and Canada, and it is their command organizations that will be examined first.

British operational command in coastal areas bordering the Atlantic from 1939 to 1941 was exercised through local joint commands known as Area Combined Headquarters (ACHQs), one overseas ACHQ, and two overseas naval commands. Each ACHQ was a geographic command and had a Royal Navy flag officer, an army general officer, and a Royal Air Force air vice marshal who jointly handled defensive measures for that particular area, including convoy operations as well as air and seaward defenses. These officers and their staffs were co-located at the ACHQ site. Operating forces were allocated to the ACHQ service heads from the British Chiefs of Staff; these could vary, depending on the tasks of the operating forces or the weight of movement through the assigned area. The War Office and Air Ministry dealt with administrative and material support for the Army and RAF respectively, while the Admiralty held sway over material and administrative matters for the Royal Navy as well as operational control at sea. In 1939, the ACHQs for the British Isles included Plymouth, which was the location of the Commander in Chief, Western Approaches (CinCWA); Rosyth; and Chatham, which supported the naval commands Nore and Portsmouth (see fig. 1.13).[31]

Initially the ACHQs were established specifically to coordinate air-sea cooperation in the event of an invasion of Britain. Each ACHQ had operational control over an RAF Coastal Command Group and, occasionally, elements from Fighter Command; however, air cover from this resource could be directed elsewhere at the whim of the Air Staff. As a result, threat information gathered by patrol aircraft could be processed by the ACHQ and fed directly into the Royal Navy's intelligence machinery. A combined air/naval response could thus occur in a timely fashion with a minimum of interservice interference.[32]

The operational naval forces allocated to the ACHQs and naval commands varied greatly, both in type and in numbers. The threat to the sea lines of communication (SLOCs) in the Atlantic, which were vital to the Allies' ability to conduct offensive operations and to prop up Britain's economy, consisted initially of surface raiders and individual U-boats (later operating in wolf packs) augmented by long-range land-based air support. This threat was countered by a three-tiered system that included the evasive routing of convoys with the help of signals intelligence, close escort of convoys, and main battle units to deal with surface raiders. Essentially, escort groups tasked to the ACHQs for the protection of SLOCs provided

Second World War Command Organization 27

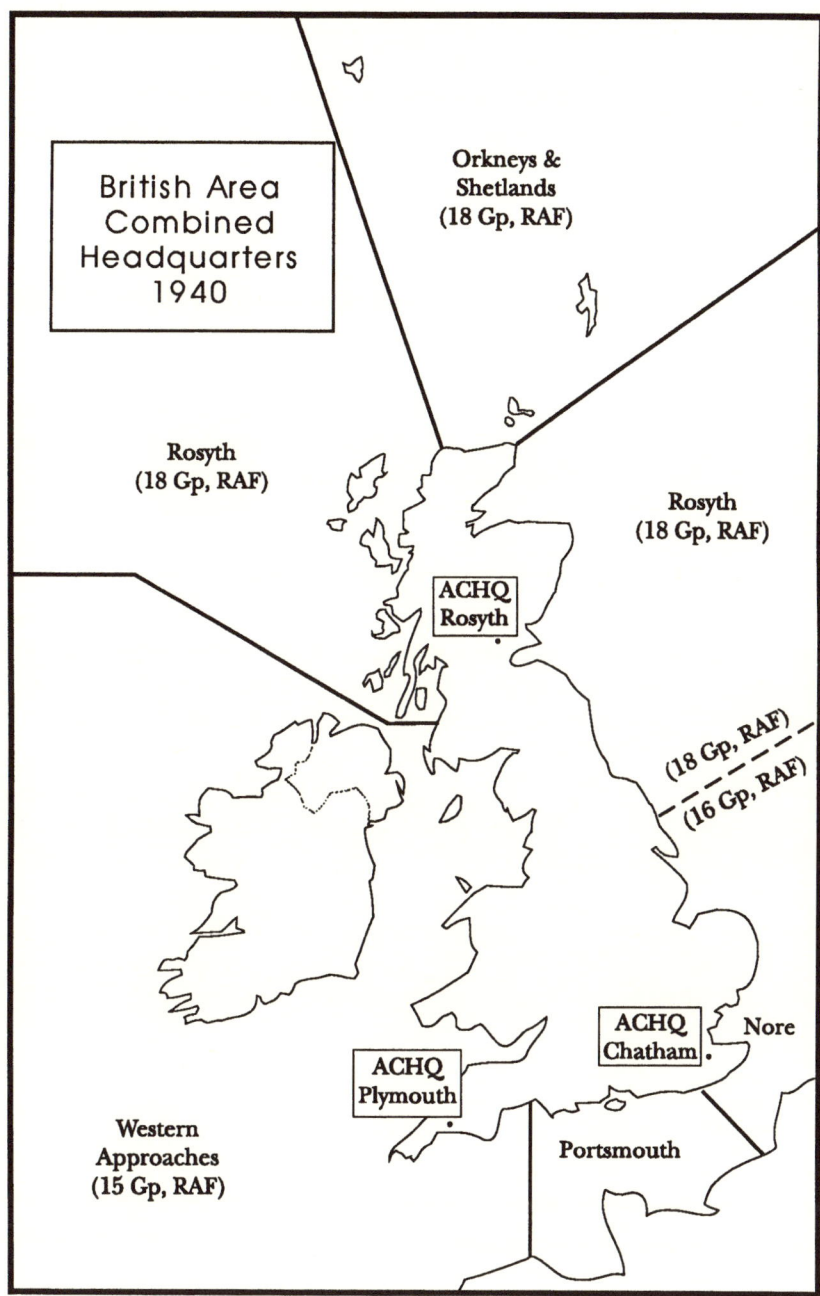

Fig. 1.13.

protection to a particular convoy from start to finish and returned to their areas on the next outward-bound convoy. Offensive forces such as aircraft carriers and battleships remained under the higher direction of Force H at Gibraltar or the Home Fleet at Scapa Flow, which reported directly to the Admiralty.

For overseas operations, the British national commands in the Atlantic that concern us were the North Atlantic naval area and associated Coastal Command Group, commanded by the ACHQ at Gibraltar whose naval commander was Flag Officer North Atlantic; the America and West Indies naval area, commanded by a Commander in Chief, America and West Indies Station (CinCAW&I), located at Bermuda; and the South Atlantic naval area, which had its headquarters at Freetown (see fig. 1.14). These headquarters were also part of a British worldwide control-of-shipping network that was linked to a centralized intelligence organization in the Admiralty.[33]

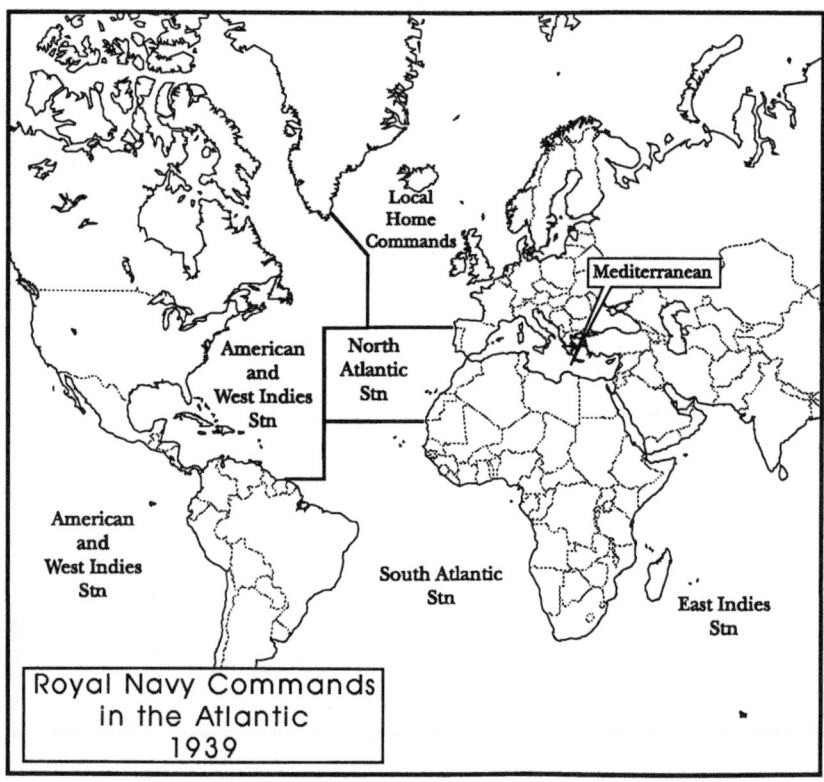

Fig. 1.14.

Great Britain relied on forces allocated to CinCAW&I for naval operations in the western Atlantic from 1939 to 1940. Although the relatively small Royal Canadian Navy (RCN) in the Atlantic logically should have been under the strategic direction of the British CinCAW&I from the outset of the war, this was not promulgated for political reasons. The RCN remained a local force until June 1940 when its destroyers were sent to operate in British waters under British command in the Western Approaches—not to be confused with the functional antisubmarine warfare command of Commander in Chief, Western Approaches (CinCWA), which was established later.[34]

Canadian air-sea cooperation in the Atlantic from 1939 to 1940 was based on the British ACHQ model (see fig. 1.15). The Joint Service Committee, Halifax was established on 28 August 1940; its title later became Joint Service Committee, Atlantic Coast (JSCAC). This group consisted of members from the Canadian Army's Atlantic Command, the fledgling RCAF Eastern Air Command (consisting mostly of elements from RCAF bomber/reconnaissance squadrons), and the RCN's Commanding Officer, Atlantic Coast (COAC). The responsibility for Newfoundland rested with the Joint Services Subcommittee, Newfoundland (JSSC), which was subordinated to the JSCAC; this was not established until June 1941. In 1940, however, a joint operations center in either Halifax or Newfoundland had yet to be established; the number of operating forces was small, and the quality of their equipment was poor.[35]

Notwithstanding the dilapidated state of Canadian defense preparedness, bilateral Canadian–U.S. defense planning shifted into a higher gear in 1940. The Ogdensburg summit of 7 August 1940 between Roosevelt and Canadian Prime Minister King precipitated the organization of the Permanent Joint Board on Defense (PJBD) on 27 August 1940. The PJBD consisted of representatives from the naval, air, and land forces of both countries, as well as political deputies from the Department of External Affairs and the State Department. The responsibilities of the PJBD were directed toward joint defense planning and the reconciliation of strategic direction in North America should it become a theater of war.[36]

The first product of the PJBD was an emergency war plan. Keeping in mind that the United States was not yet a belligerent and that Newfoundland was not yet part of Canada, a Joint Canadian–United States Basic Defense Plan—the Black Plan—was formulated for the defense of the whole of North America in October 1940 in the event that Great Britain was lost to the Axis powers. It was essentially a strategic study that surveyed broad courses of action rather than a blow-by-blow defense plan.[37]

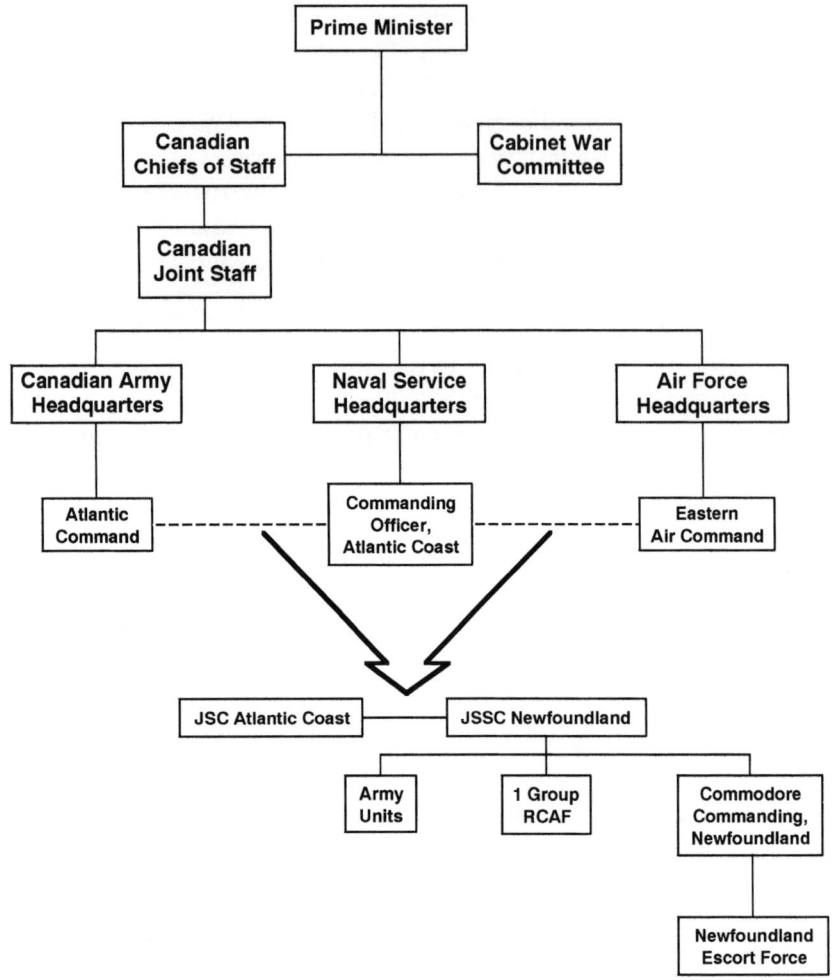

Fig. 1.15. Canadian defense organization in the Atlantic area

A modification of the Black Plan formed the foundations of the worst-case scenario, Joint Operational Plan No. 1, in which the Chief of Staff of the U.S. Army was allowed the "exercise of strategic direction" over Canadian forces with the consent of the Canadian Chiefs of Staff. This would later cause problems in the establishment of a coalition command in the North Atlantic. Under Joint Operational Plan No. 2, which was postulated on the survival of Britain, the U.S. entrance into the war became the basis for bilateral U.S.–Canadian defense talks called ABC-22, which were ancillary to the ABC-1 discussions.[38]

As we have seen, ABC-1 resulted in the broad and ill-defined division of the Atlantic Ocean into eastern and western zones of strategic responsibility if the United States entered the war against Germany. Once this occurred, the United States would control the western Atlantic and would have operational control over its own, British, and Canadian forces operating there; the exception to U.S. control was the territory covered by bilateral Canadian–U.S. agreements. The Canadians did not participate in ABC-1 and were, needless to say, irritated over such cavalier treatment of their strategic needs.[39]

ABC-22 initially was designed as a strategic concept for the defense of North America if Britain was not knocked out of the war. It called for Canada to assume shared command in the Atlantic and a joint command over Newfoundland. Unfortunately, due to misunderstandings on the PJBD the U.S. Navy Hemisphere Defense Plan No. 4, also known as WPL 51, was adopted for ABC-22 by the United States in June 1941. Under the terms of WPL 51, the RCN was operationally subordinated to the U.S. Navy—a decision that the RCN did not like at all. The relationship between WPL 51 and the provision of air support was ambiguous; due to the problem of reconciling two different types of command organization, the U.S. Navy believed that it also controlled the RCAF Eastern Air Command (RCAF EAC). The RCAF liked this state of affairs even less. It was clear that U.S. planners did not understand the joint command relationship that Canadian and British organizations enjoyed; instead, they were still laboring under their own unified command system. WPL 51 remained on the shelf until its implementation in August.[40]

The American view of ABC-22 was that Canadian commands in the Atlantic would be established and subordinated to the U.S. Northeast Defense Command, which was under U.S. commanders using the American unified command system. As a result, the U.S. unified command for the area encompassing Canadian waters was a naval officer and WPL 51 was his staff's product, with its operational naval forces coming from the newly established U.S. Commander in Chief, Atlantic Fleet (U.S. CinCLANT), Adm. Ernest J. King. The only degree of operational control that Canadians exercised over RCN and RCAF forces under WPL 51 involved coastal and inshore operations out to three miles.[41]

Command organization in the Atlantic in late 1941 was a muddled affair. Even though WPL 51 appeared to grant the United States sweeping powers, and even though CinCLANT could exercise strategic direction over RCN and RCAF units outside of Canadian coastal waters, the definition of what actually constituted coastal waters was left somewhat vague. Such a zone, which could be defined as large or as small as Canada chose, could influence the degree of control that the U.S. Navy had over the RCN. Consequently, actual operational participation by the Americans was substantial, the command organization was not rigidly enforced, and of course WPL 51 was still only a planning document.[42]

The Atlantic Conference at Argentia on 10–15 August 1941 formalized the national control authorities for the Battle of the Atlantic, at least until 1943. A meeting between Admiral King (USN) and Admiral Noble (RN) established naval control of shipping arrangements and the terminal authorities in the eastern and western Atlantic; these were the U.S. Eastern Sea Frontier, led by COMEASTSEAFRON, and Britain's Western Approaches Command, led by CinCWA. In addition, the U.S. Navy took responsibility for U.S.–to–Iceland convoys, and the British handled the traffic in the eastern Atlantic.[43]

Since Newfoundland was not part of Canada yet and remained a British territory, the "destroyers for bases" agreement between the United States and Great Britain provided the Americans with the opportunity to establish a task force for antisubmarine warfare in the Atlantic in Newfoundland. To carry this out, WPL 51—which still formed the basis of U.S. thinking—called for the formation of a U.S. Navy ASW task force headquarters, called Task Force 24 (TF 24), which was set up in September 1941. Three months earlier at the suggestion of the British, the RCN had activated Commodore Commanding, Newfoundland (CCNF) to handle its operating forces. CCNF had administrative control over RCN ships operating out of Newfoundland as part of the Newfoundland Escort Force (NEF), which was the keystone of local defenses and was administratively responsible to Commanding Officer, Atlantic Coast (COAC) in Halifax and operationally responsible to CinCWA prior to the establishment of TF-24. COAC's forces were still responsible for coastal operations along the Canadian coast. This resulted in a neutral American admiral having operational control over RCN, U.S. Navy, and Royal Navy forces in the Northwest Atlantic (see fig. 1.16).[44]

A very important command issue from the outset was the integration of land-based airpower into the Atlantic command organizations. For a variety of reasons, the use of aircraft progressed from seaward reconnaissance patrols and antiraider operations to long-range offensive ASW operations.[45] The British-Canadian system of joint command overcame most

Second World War Command Organization

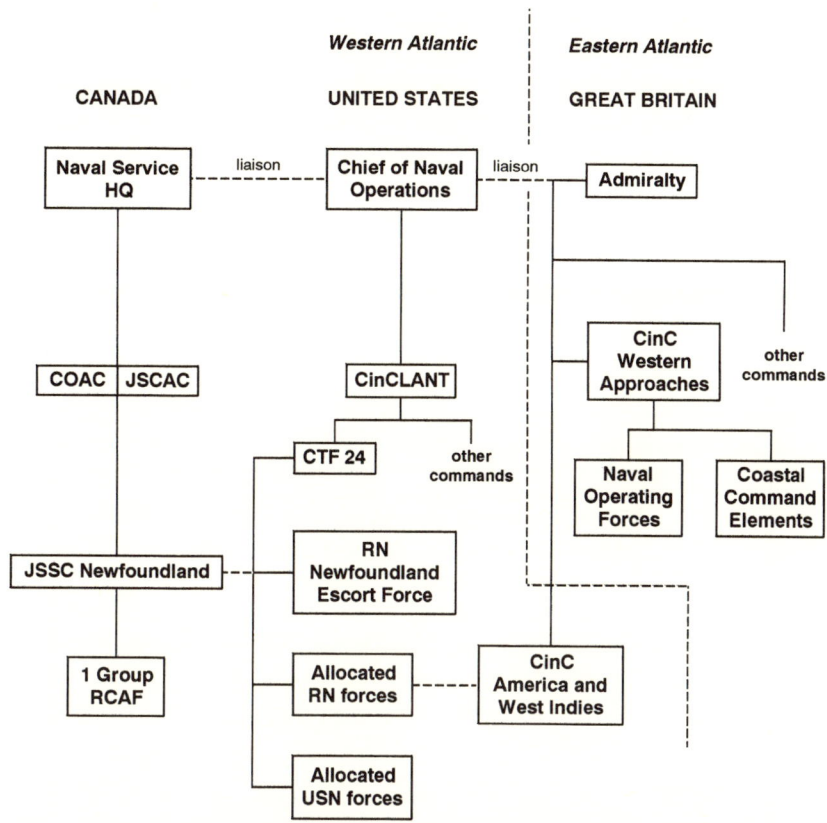

Fig. 1.16. Command organization for the Atlantic, 1941–42

problems of air-sea coordination by granting operational control of air force units engaged in ASW to the navy. Under the U.S. system, long-range patrol assets were split between the Army Air Force and the U.S. Navy, each with different procedures, tactics, and roles. However, coordination between the British-Canadian system and the Americans' unified command system caused problems.

As we have seen, the confusion over WPL 51 led the U.S. Navy to believe that the TF-24 commander had operational control over RCAF Coastal Command units assigned to the Canadian JSCAC. At one point, CTF-24 was told by his staff that RCAF units operating out of Newfoundland were there not to escort convoys in the North Atlantic but to protect convoys within the Canadian coastal zone. The local Canadian

CCNF interpreted this to mean that CTF-24 would use American resources available to him in his role as a U.S. unified commander—that is, aircraft belonging to the U.S. Army Air Force—for long-range aerial support in the North Atlantic. Due to interservice American bickering over the types and missions of aircraft assigned to navy or air force units, CTF-24 could not always secure or coordinate USAAF resources. As incredible as it sounds, there were times when no air support was available to convoys in the western North Atlantic in late 1941.[46]

A meeting between Canadian and American commanders in Newfoundland was called to sort out this very dangerous situation in October 1941. This meeting divided the labor along geographic lines (see fig. 1.17). U.S.

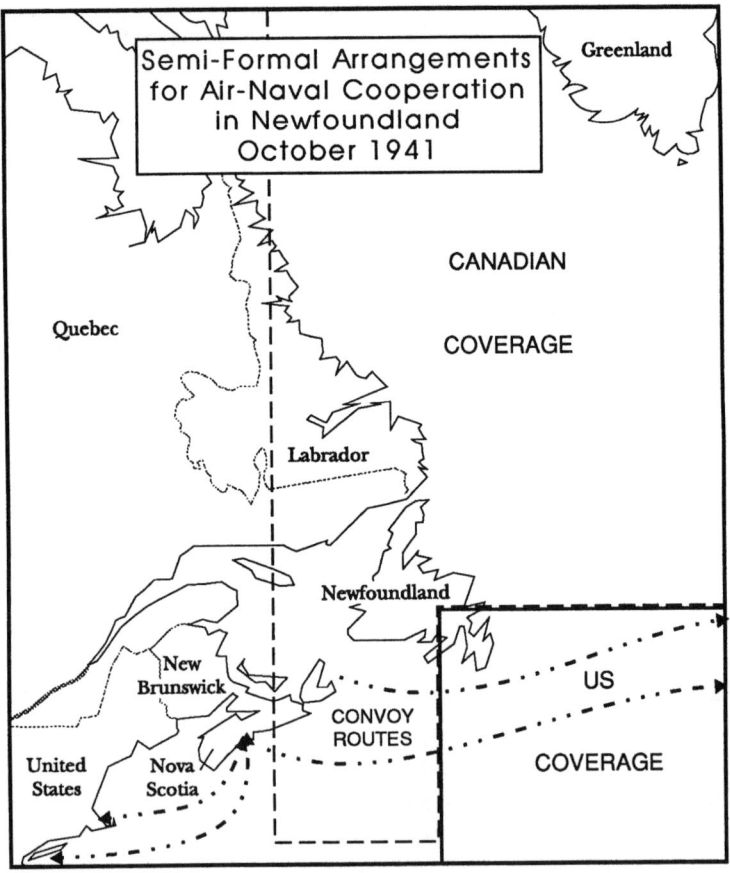

Fig. 1.17.

Navy aircraft under CTF-24 would escort convoys east of 55° west longitude and south of 48° north latitude, while the RCAF would escort convoys in a "coastal air zone" west of 55° west and to the maximum range of their aircraft off Newfoundland north of 48° north. Arrangements with USAAF units would be sorted out later; operational needs from TF-24 became "orders" for U.S. Navy squadrons, "proposals" for 1 Group, RCAF, and "requests" for USAAF units. This arrangement made it more difficult for the United States to influence RCAF operations and preserved the RCAF's relationships to the JSSC Newfoundland.[47]

On the British side of the Atlantic there were no coalition command arrangements to worry about. The ACHQ system performed well, and at least operational friction between RAF Coastal Command and the Royal Navy was minimal. In April 1941, the British established a functional ASW command, Commander in Chief, Western Approaches (CinCWA) under Adm. Sir Percy Noble (later Adm. Sir Max Horton), who was responsible for the conduct of the Battle of the Atlantic within the British strategic zone. A more pressing problem was a lack of long-range aircraft to support convoy operations, and the constant battle with RAF Bomber Command over the allocation of such aircraft.[48]

The importance of the Arcadia conference of December 1941–January 1942 on command organization in the Atlantic manifested itself in two ways: the division of the world into three British and American strategic zones and the formal integration of the United States into the war. Thus, a description of the U.S. Navy's organization on the East Coast is necessary since the United States became a formal partner in the Battle of the Atlantic after 7 December 1941.

On 30 December 1941, Admiral King became the Commander in Chief of the U.S. Fleet (COMINCH) and Adm. Ralph Ingersoll became CinCLANT. Previously, the COMINCH position was called CinCUS ("sink us"), but because of the adverse publicity caused by Pearl Harbor it was renamed. COMINCH was the supreme commander of U.S. Navy operational forces and sea frontiers, and he was responsible for the creation of current war plans. COMINCH appears to have been subordinate to both the Chief of Naval Operations (CNO), who was the chief naval adviser to the president of the United States and a member of the JCS, and the secretary of the navy. The CNO was responsible for the creation of long-range war plans, the strategic direction of the navy, and administrative and logistical requirements. The division of labor was not always clear early in the war; both the CNO and COMINCH attended all important conferences. Adm. Harold Stark was CNO until 14 March 1942, when Admiral King was appointed to fill both posts.[49]

Initially, the U.S. Navy's Sea Frontiers commands (SEAFRONs) had the responsibility for coastal defense. This system of geographic commands was established in July 1941 by Stark and was based on areas extending seaward from the U.S. coast of North America for 200 miles. The ones that concern us here are the Eastern SEAFRON, the Gulf SEAFRON, the Caribbean SEAFRON, and the Panama SEAFRON (see fig. 1.18). These SEAFRONs had complete operational control over all forces allocated to them, including coastal convoys traveling through their areas. Theoretically, air protection was to be furnished to the convoys by USAAF assets. However, interservice problems over the establishment of a U.S. unified command prohibited any close cooperation in early 1942.[50]

A major flaw in the protection of convoys within the American SEAFRONs in early 1942 was the lack of a centralized routing organization similar to the British system. This lack of control within the EAST-

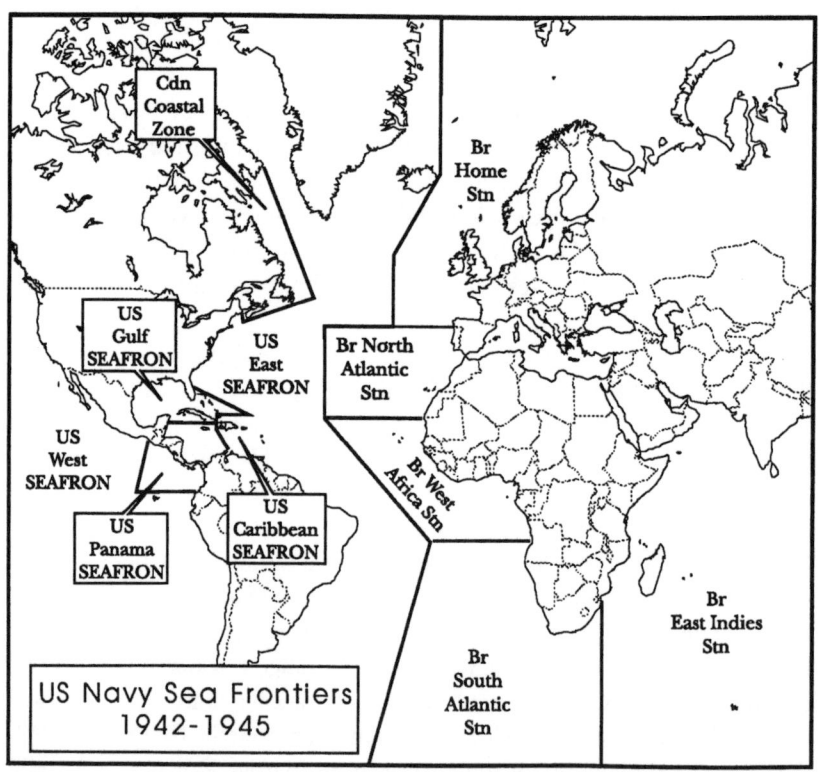

Fig. 1.18.

Second World War Command Organization ➢ 37

SEAFRON in early 1942 resulted in what has been described as "Pearl Harbor East": the massacre of unprotected merchant shipping within sight of the U.S. coast by Doenitz's Operation Paukenschlag.[51]

It appears as though Paukenschlag resulted in an overhaul of American organization in the Atlantic from March to August 1942. Admiral King became both CNO and COMINCH at this time (see fig. 1.19). By May, a centralized convoy and routing (C&R) section for the East coast of the United States (based on the British model) was created and subordinated to COMINCH HQ. The C&R section "assumed full responsibility for routing and reporting of all merchant shipping in the U.S. Strategic Area and for troop convoys to Europe...." Thus, the requirements people told C&R how many, when, and where; CinCLANT provided escorts and

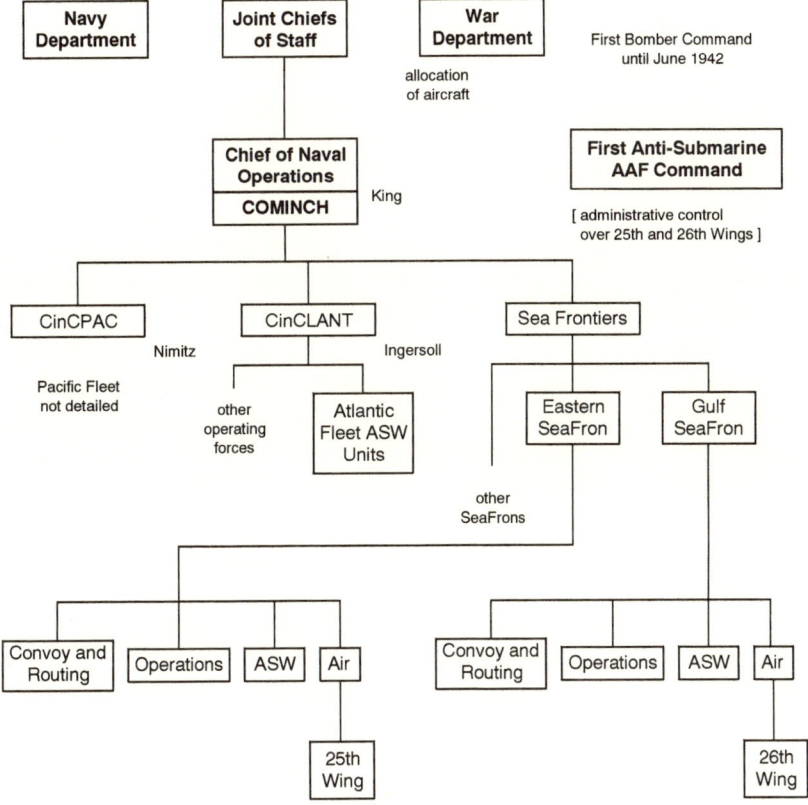

Fig. 1.19. U.S. Navy organization for the Atlantic, May 1942–May 1943

transports; and C&R coordinated routes with the British shipping control organization.[52] In addition, coordination between the SEAFRONs was improved, and an interlocking convoy system between then was organized for coastal traffic.[53]

U.S. air support for the protection of shipping also required reorganization. It was very clear to the Americans that the major limiting factors on the conduct of this very important mission were the ability of the USAAF and the U.S. Navy to cooperate, the lack of training of USAAF crews for the task, and the paucity of navy aircraft capable of doing the job. Prewar agreements limited the navy to owning seaplanes and carrier-based aircraft. The types of planes needed for long-range ASW operations were all in the hands of the USAAF, which adamantly refused to give operational control of them to the navy's SEAFRONs before 1942.[54]

Another Paukenschlag legacy was the hasty organization of the USAAF 1st Bomber Command, which was established for ASW operations in EASTSEAFRON and GULFSEAFRON. Squadrons of the 1st Bomber Command were placed under the operational control of the SEAFRONs, with the USAAF retaining control over administration and training. Unfortunately, the SEAFRONs jealously guarded these new assets and would not cooperate with each other to concentrate aircraft at critical points. Other problems included the lack of common communications equipment. Doctrine was another issue: the USAAF favored concentrating aircraft in "killer groups" to hunt for previously sighted U-boats instead of using single aircraft patrols covering a wide area. Marshall and King reorganized these units into the 1st Antisubmarine Army Air Command and assigned operational control of the 25th and 26th Wings, 1st ASAA Command, to the EASTSEAFRON and the GULFSEAFRON, respectively; even still, problems continued between the 1st ASAA Command and the SEAFRON commanders.[55]

The most important results of the post-Paukenschlag reorganization were the establishment of the change of operational control (CHOP) line at 26° west longitude and the integration of the British and American convoy and routing systems (see fig. 1.20). Prior to June 1942, the convoy routing authority was either British or Canadian; this changed in July 1942 when U.S. Naval Operations (OPNAV) in Washington took control of convoy routing west of the CHOP line. U.S. Navy or RCN ships would escort a convoy from Halifax to Liverpool, for example; after the convoy crossed the CHOP line (which was not actually fixed in one place—it could change slightly depending on the time of day) at 26° west, operational control of the convoy would switch from the Canadians (later the

Second World War Command Organization ➢ 39

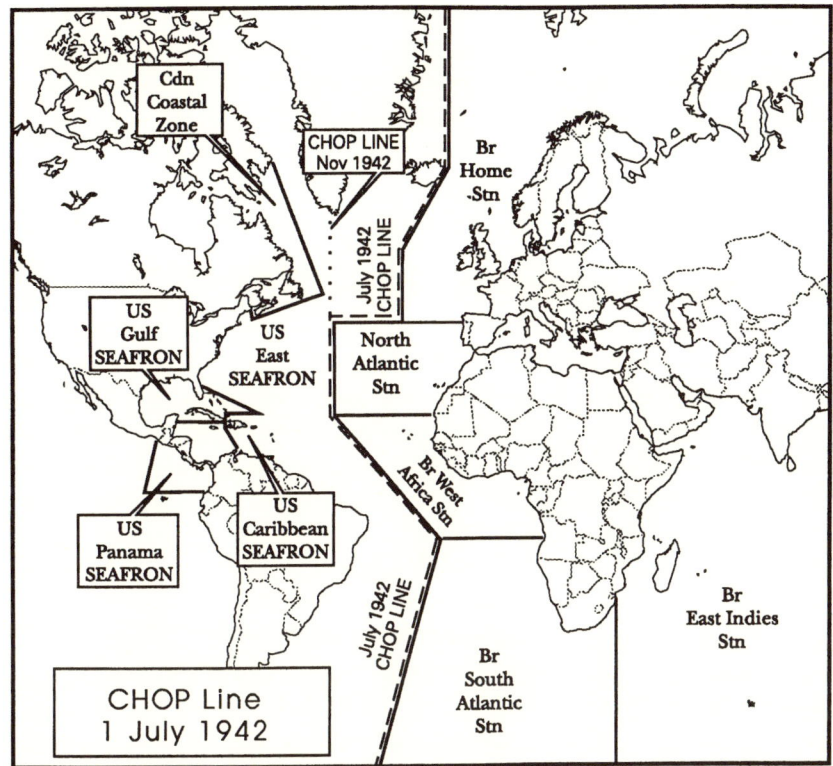

Fig. 1.20.

Americans) to the British, who could alter the convoy's route if enemy action necessitated it. Air coverage as far as possible toward the CHOP line was handled by RCAF or U.S. aircraft out of Newfoundland; RAF, RAAF, or RNZAF units based in England and Iceland took over the rest of the run.[56] Establishment of a clearer system of operational control allowed the Allies to improve their reaction time to developing enemy threats.

Although the convoy control situation had improved, it was far from perfect. In July 1942 convoy ON 113, headed from England to North America, was engaged by U-boats at the CHOP line. The convoy commander chose to head north and evade other U-boats nearby. However, because the convoy was over the CHOP line the American convoy routing authority ordered a course change due south. The convoy commander realized that this would take ON 113 back to the enemy he had just engaged, so he turned east and then south—right into another "rake" of U-boats, where two ships were lost. As a result, the convoy turned a complete 360° circle right in the middle of U-boat-infested waters and needlessly exposed itself. The odyssey of ON 113 highlighted another command and control problem: on the U.S. side of the CHOP line, U.S. naval authorities ashore assumed that they had direct control over all convoys, while on the British side the shore personnel were advisers, leaving the local convoy commander to make the final decision.[57]

The ON 113 problem was noticed by personnel within the Canadian command organizations. In the U.S. strategic zone there were nine command authorities involved in the Battle of the Atlantic (U.S. Navy and USAAF commands ashore in the continental United States, CTF-24, NEF/FONF, RCAF HWE, RCAF 1 Group in Newfoundland, the Canadian JSSC in Newfoundland, COAC/JSCAC in Halifax, and the army commands), each with different ideas on how operations were to be handled. Canadian military and political authorities were concerned about the lack of control the RCN and the RCAF had over their forces. RCN operating forces were essentially controlled by everyone except the RCN. The Canadian solution was to push for a restructuring of commands and the establishment of a Canadian theater. The reasons for this were quite logical. The Canadian contribution to CTF-24 was 48 percent, while the U.S. Navy's contribution was 2 percent. CTF-24 was poorly placed and interfered with Royal Navy–RCN ASW cooperation, as both used the same operational procedures. There was no joint control of all aerial ASW operations in Newfoundland. Finally, the RCN's system of disseminating HF/DF intelligence information was more efficient than the American system, which was overly bureaucratic. The options were either to remove CTF-24 and replace him with a Canadian or Flag Officer Newfoundland (as CCNF had been renamed) or to pull Canadian forces from CTF-24's command.[58]

This meeting bore fruit at the Anglo-American-Canadian Atlantic Convoy Conference of 1 March 1943, which was convened to sort out the Atlantic command organization's Gordian knot. Initially, the United States did not want to confront this issue but finally conceded under duress from the other parties. The British position was that the Canadian organizations should be under the command of CinCWA, which was unacceptable to the United States because this would essentially extend British control as far as Maine, deep in the American strategic zone. The issue of a completely separate Canadian strategic zone was ruled out because both the United States and Great Britain believed that the RCN lacked both a

Second World War Command Organization ➤ 41

balanced fleet that included battleships, cruisers, and aircraft carriers and the experience to handle those forces if they were provided by the Royal Navy and the U.S. Navy.[59]

The results of the conference included the proposal that a North Atlantic area be established with the responsibility for trade convoys and ASW under British and Canadian authorities north of 40° north latitude, while strategic command of the mid-Atlantic remained a U.S. task. COAC would also be responsible for the general direction of all surface and air forces employed in ASW in this new area, which would be called the Canadian Northwest Atlantic Command (see fig. 1.21). A new CHOP line

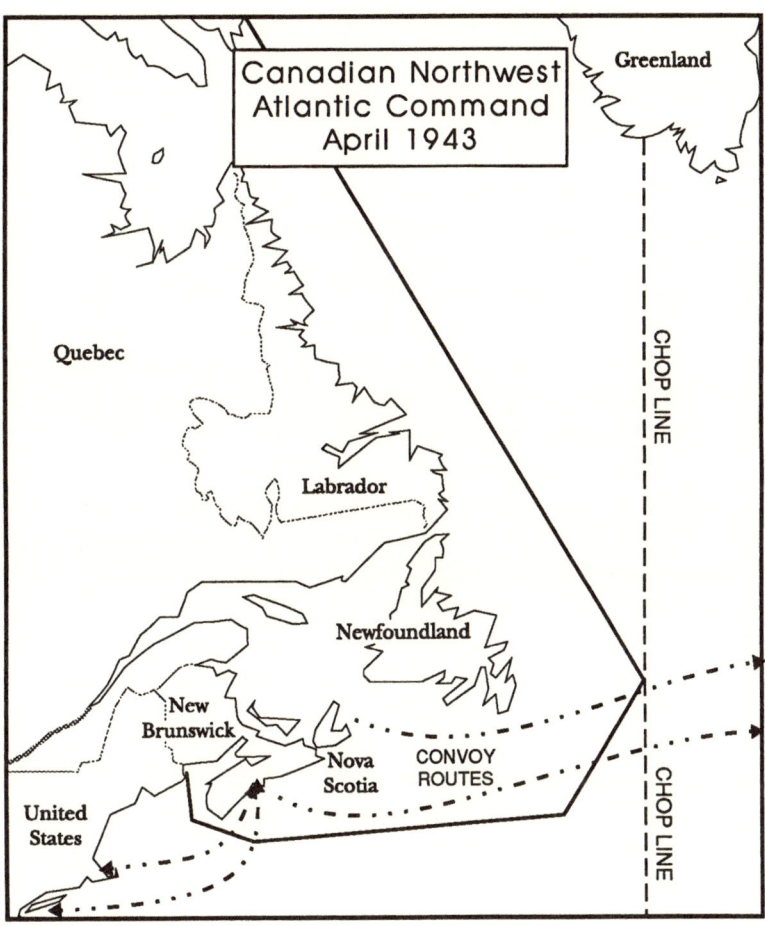

Fig. 1.21.

would be established at 47° west longitude. The routing of convoys west of the CHOP would be controlled by Canada if they were outside the U.S. EASTSEAFRON. The SEAFRONs would remain under U.S. control and could concentrate on southerly convoys servicing U.S. forces in the Mediterranean; as compensation, the United States took control over tanker convoys making the Caribbean-to-Britain run. Air support from long-range patrol aircraft from all Allied countries were to disregard the CHOP line, and all escort carrier support groups (hunter-killer groups based around a CVE) would remain under the strategic control of their commanders. This precedent would have far-reaching effects on the efforts to develop NATO naval command organization in the Atlantic in 1952. In the end, CTF-24 was disbanded, and the United States retained strategic direction in the western Atlantic. The new Canadian command was established by the end of April 1943 with Rear Adm. L. W. Murray (RCN) in command. COAC was renamed Commander in Chief, Canadian Northwest Atlantic; JSCAC was replaced by Commander in Chief, East Coast Defenses, who was put in charge of the former JSSC, Newfoundland (now Commander in Chief, Newfoundland Defenses) (see fig. 1.22). Like their predecessors, CinC East Coast Defenses and CinC Newfoundland Defenses remained joint commands.[60]

The United States also cleaned house and proposed a proper unified command organization for the Atlantic. In April 1943 Admiral King's assistant chief of staff for ASW, Rear Adm. F. S. Low, suggested that a unified command be established under Admiral Ingersoll, the U.S. Navy's CinCLANT. King vetoed the idea; he believed that ASW coordination with the Royal Navy required a higher-ranking officer with the ability to resist political interference. Additionally, the organization had to be able to handle ASW in the Pacific as well as the Atlantic and thus could not be subordinated to EASTSEAFRON. Finally, the new unit required fleet status so it could have equal access to the U.S. Navy communications network.[61]

This new organization, called the Tenth Fleet, was a functional ASW command not unlike the British Western Approaches command. King himself was the Tenth Fleet commander, and Low became his chief of staff. The express purpose of Tenth Fleet was to provide unity of command over U.S. ASW operations within the area under U.S. strategic control. Its specific functions included the destruction of enemy submarines, the protection of coastal merchant shipping, the centralization of control and routing of convoys, and the coordination and supervision of all U.S. Navy ASW training and development (see fig. 1.23). The Tenth Fleet used CinCLANT's ships operationally; CinCLANT issued operational orders

Second World War Command Organization ➢ 43

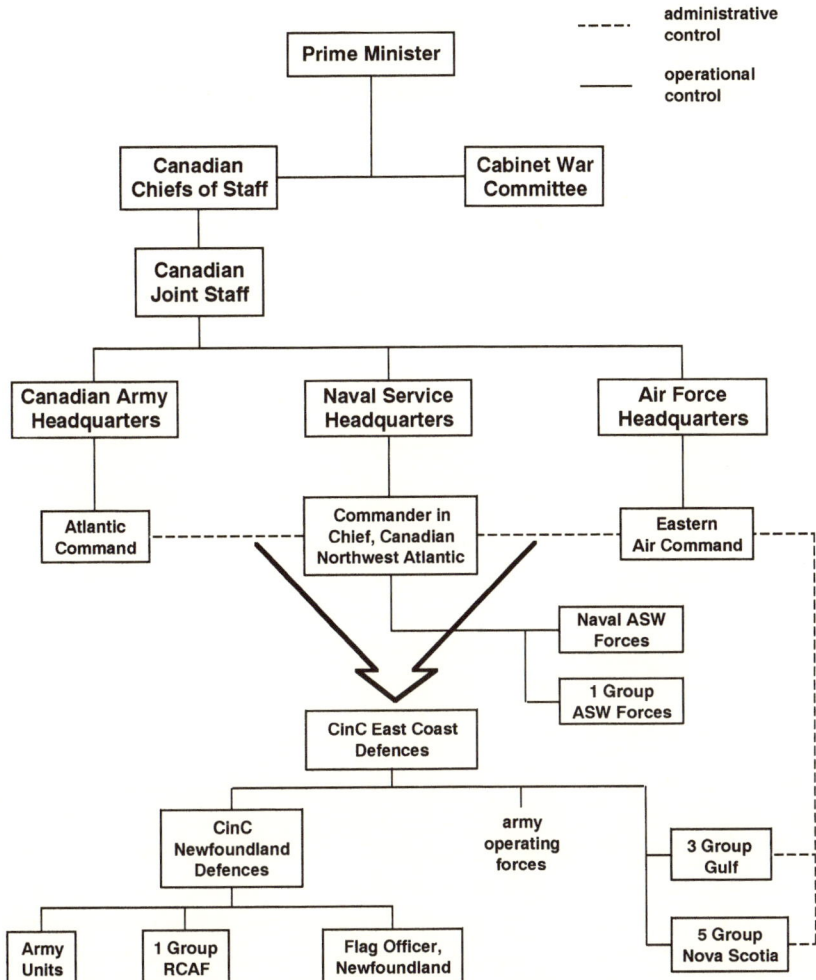

Fig. 1.22. Canadian defense organization in the Atlantic area, 1943–45

to escort groups originating in the United States. The Tenth Fleet was also responsible for the organization and operational control of hunter-killer groups. This concept of a specially tasked fleet would reappear in the postwar organization of the U.S. Navy.[62]

There was no room for USAAF units in the Tenth Fleet organization. Attempts to reproduce the RAF Coastal Command–Royal Navy relationship were doomed: the U.S. Navy and the USAAF could not agree on principles of command or ASW tactics. The USAAF was used to forming

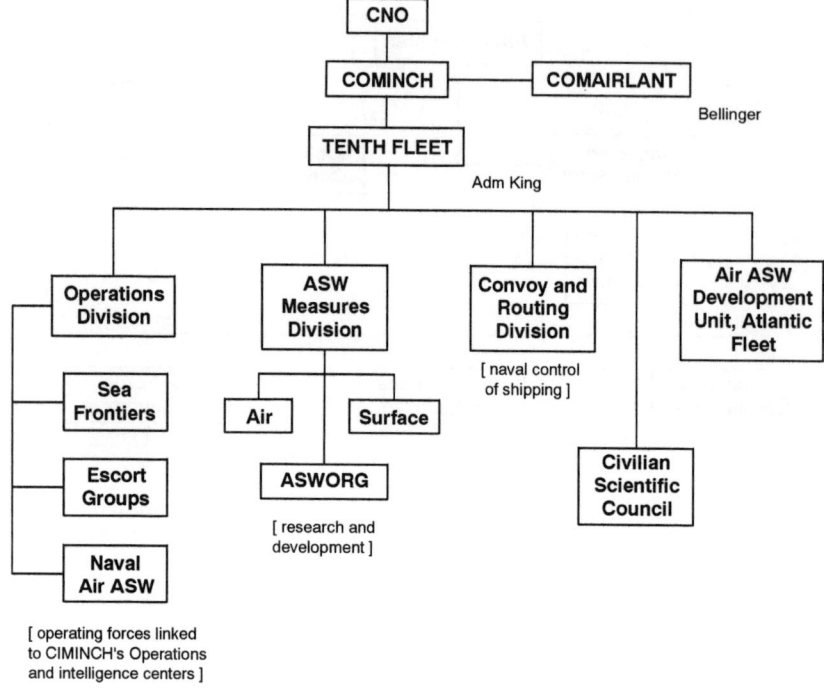

Fig. 1.23. U.S. Navy Tenth Fleet organization, 1 May 1943

units on the basis of types of weapon systems (e.g., all B-17s were in the same organization, all tasked with bombing), while the navy tended toward functional groupings of different types of aircraft and ships tailored for a particular mission. By September 1943, the USAAF agreed to transfer specialized long-range patrol aircraft to the U.S. Navy in exchange for unmodified naval long-range aircraft that were still in the factory. Commander Air Force, Atlantic Fleet (COMAIRLANT) was formed in March 1943 and subordinated to the Tenth Fleet.[63]

Thus, by the middle of March 1943 the transition from fragmented national commands dealing with other fragmented national commands to unified or joint national commands dealing with other unified or joint national commands was under way. One wonders, though, why no coalition command was created to be responsible for the Atlantic in the same way that the Mediterranean was organized.

In fact, there were several proposals for a supreme commander in the Atlantic during the Second World War. The first was put forward by Air

Chief Marshal Phillip Joubert of RAF Coastal Command in September 1942. Joubert proposed a single Allied commander for the Atlantic antisubmarine conflict, with a central and integrated planning staff to "coordinate the separate and often conflicting policies of the British, Canadian, and American naval and air authorities, together with those of the various service authorities in such areas as the Mediterranean, West Africa and Australia...."[64] The official RAF history curtly states: "The scheme was attractive in theory, if liable to give rise to difficulties in practice; and it was pursued for several months before finally being abandoned."[65]

According to the official Royal Navy history, the concept of an Atlantic supreme commander originated with Field Marshal Jan Smuts, who recommended a "Super CinC" and a "Super Air CinC" with the responsibility of handling all (not just ASW) forces involved in the Atlantic battle. The First Sea Lord's staff advised that although such a structure appeared desirable at first, British, Canadian, and American operational practices were too complex and the situation would degenerate into total chaos. Also, there was concern that the Americans would inevitably wish to control this position. The Admiralty could never justify such a scenario politically, since this was considered to be a life-or-death struggle by Britain's leadership and people.[66]

Within the same time frame, however, the U.S. Navy control officer at Londonderry, Capt. L. Hewlett Thebaud, suggested a combined British–U.S. staff under one admiral with total operational control over all British and U.S. escorts, convoys, and ASW warfare. The U.S. Commander, Naval Forces Europe agreed with such a scheme and strove to sell it to the British.[67] Known as the SCAT proposal (Supreme Commander, Atlantic Theater), it also went nowhere.

The main reasons why a supreme allied commander was not set up in the Atlantic during World War II were summed up during the Atlantic Convoy Conference of March 1943. Britain had demonstrated the ability to coordinate Royal Navy–RAF operations in its strategic zone to deal with the U-boat threat; the United States was unable to do so. The U.S. command organization in the Pacific worked only because the vast majority of the operating forces there were American, which facilitated control. U.S. commands in the Atlantic were too divided internally to handle the SCAT concept. Operationally, the United States had lots of different forces in the Atlantic, the British and the Canadians had more experience in ASW, and no British government could have survived politically with an American SCAT. The problems of integrating the Admiralty, British intelligence organizations, and the Department of War Transport with their

American counterparts in the pursuit of a common trade and logistical policy were just too great.[68]

Though no coalition command was established in the Atlantic during the Second World War, an interallied organization was set up to coordinate certain matters. The Allied Antisubmarine Survey Board (AASSB) was established after the Casablanca conference of January 1943. Its objective was to "survey all matters relating to ASW in the Atlantic Ocean" and to make recommendations to the U.S. CNO and Britain's First Sea Lord.[69] Additionally, the Combined Procedure Board was formed to standardize signal and ASW routines for the Royal Navy, the RCN, and the U.S. Navy. This problem was considered too complicated to solve during wartime, and the temporary solution was to eliminate mixed-escort convoy routes, a move long favored by Admiral King.[70] Thus, instead of a coalition command situation under the control of the CCS, the Atlantic was divided into units responsible to their own national naval commanders; these communicated via two trilateral boards that provided coordination in operational procedure and delineations of control.

The Second World War provides a focal point from which to start an examination of NATO command organization in the late 1940s and early 1950s. The command organizations that were established to fight the war in the Mediterranean and the Atlantic developed in response to several factors, the most important being the status of the geographic area in overall strategic policy and the type of operations conducted there. The Mediterranean theater could be regarded as an offensive theater in nature, designed to support directly the land and air efforts in northwestern Europe. The Atlantic theater was defensive in nature, designed to support logistically the offensive operations in northwestern Europe as well as the Mediterranean. The problems in command organization encountered during the conflict—the COMNAVNAW controversy, the attempts at coordinating airpower with land- and seapower in the Atlantic and Mediterranean, the difficulties in combining Canadian, U.S., and British efforts in the Atlantic, the missteps involving convoy ON 113—all were indicators of the weaknesses encountered on the journey toward coalition command, a journey that would not cease with the surrender of Germany in 1945.

2 ➤ An Attack Against One Is an Attack Against All
The Founding of NATO Command Organization, 1947–1949

You may call it coalition, you may call it the accidental and fortuitous concurrence of atoms....
—Lord Palmerston, 1857

Whenever our neighbour's house is on fire, it cannot be amiss for the engines to play a little on our own.
—Edmund Burke, 1790

By 1947, it was clear to the leadership of the free nations that the Soviet Union was exceeding the bounds of its sovereign authority and attempting to live up to its ideal of world domination by any means necessary. Since the Terminal conference in July 1945, the world had lurched from crisis to crisis—in 1946, the situation in Iran, the Corfu Channel incident, Turkey's tension with the Soviet Union, and the Greek civil war; in 1947, the Communist coup in Hungary and the Trieste crisis. Slick diplomacy and economic steps taken to revive a battered Europe (the European Recovery Program, or Marshall Plan) could not prevent the February 1948 coup in Czechoslovakia or the Berlin blockade in March of that year. Something else was needed if Western Europe was not to fall under the hammer and sickle.

Initially, the West's formal military response to Soviet-inspired aggression was limited to a bilateral agreement between Canada and the United States that was a continuation of Second World War practices. This was soon followed by trilateral U.S., Canadian, and British defense arrangements (the ABC relationship). Later, the Western Union Defense Organization (WUDO) was formed, made up of European nations that had signed the Brussels Treaty in 1948. These organizations and arrangements merged to become the North Atlantic Treaty Organization (NATO) in 1949. The purpose of this chapter is to examine these interim arrangements, including their differing concepts for war with the Soviet Union and their proposed command organizations. Additionally, the establishment of NATO and its formally implemented structure will receive attention. All of these areas will be discussed in light of the World War II experience in coalition warfare.

It was obvious to British and American military planners (but not always their political leadership) that in 1946 any military threat in the postwar period would be from the Soviet Union. The discovery of a Soviet intelligence and subversion organization in Canada, the harassment of Allied personnel in Berlin and Vienna, as well as the continued mobilization of a military far larger than actually needed to deter aggression were further indicators of the nature of the postwar relations with the Soviet Union. Consequently, analysis of possible enemy action and responses to such aggression were undertaken close to the formal end of the Second World War.[1]

An example of such an analysis was the U.S. Joint Chiefs of Staff's Pincher study, which undoubtedly had independent British counterparts. The main catalysts for the commissioning of the Pincher study included the continuing confrontation at Venezia Giulia between Allied troops and communist forces, the increasing tensions between the Soviet Union and Turkey over access through the Bosporus, and the Iran crisis of 1946. It was this last event that appears to have directly stimulated Pincher's creation.[2] Pincher's concept of operations assumed that the Soviet Union, "although desiring to avoid a major conflict for the next several years, will commit an act or series of aggressions vitally affecting the security of the British Empire or the United States or both, leading to war between the United States/Britain and the USSR. . . ."[3]

For the Soviet concept of operations, Pincher envisioned a possible two-pronged Soviet attack: one aimed at the Persian Gulf and Suez, the other with the goal of overrunning Western Europe. The motivation for such an attack was as economic as it was ideological. Pincher reasoned that the Soviet Union was developing its economy to compete with that of the developed West in order to be able to spread the communist ideology. The development of this economy would come at the expense of both the Russian people and the occupied neighboring states (Poland, Hungary, Czechoslovakia, Bulgaria, Rumania, and Yugoslavia). In order to accomplish their aims, the Soviets would make use of incremental, politically subversive moves backed by the threat of overwhelming military force.[4]

In broad terms, the Pincher study believed that the Soviets' objective was to "establish a protective barrier of dominated countries along those portions of her border where penetration would imperil the security of vital areas. . . . The USSR will vigorously pursue a policy of ideological penetration in all countries where Soviet influence might be enhanced of U.S. or British interests undermined. . . ."[5] After this barrier was in place, the Soviet Union could go about subverting Western Europe to feed its developing economy and continue the revolution that had begun long before the Second World War. Pincher also considered the relative military capabilities of the Western allies vis-à-vis the Soviet Union's. The Western allies, Britain, the Commonwealth, and the United States had, in the view of one JCS observer, liquidated most of their military strength. Land forces that had beaten the best-trained and best-led army in the world were demobilized; aircraft that had turned Germany's and Japan's cities into rubble were cut up and turned into aluminum siding for houses; great fleets that had triumphed over the U-boat and kamikaze were mothballed. In contrast, the armed forces of the Soviet Union remained mobilized at a war footing long into the postwar period.[6]

Pincher's estimate of Soviet military capabilities in early 1946 was disturbing. Arrayed against token allied occupation forces in Germany consisting of eight American divisions at half strength (i.e., four divisions), four British divisions, and a division-sized French formation were no less than 208 Soviet divisions (156 infantry, 25 armored, 5 airborne, 5 mountain, 12 artillery, and 5 cavalry). Of these, 66 were forward-deployed in Germany and Czechoslovakia, 10 were in the Far East, 12 were an immediate strategic reserve for Europe, and 120 were either involved in training the vast reserve army in the Soviet Union proper or allocated to occupation duty in the new satellites.[7]

Importantly, Pincher assumed that the United States was allied to Britain and the Commonwealth. The country had a strategic reserve of four divisions in the continental United States (most of them at reduced strength), and six more on occupation duty in Japan; Britain had a two-division strategic reserve at home, with two in the Mediterranean and two in the Middle East. Canada could provide one division with little notice, making a total of seventeen allied divisions in reserve.[8]

On the air side, the Soviets had overwhelming numbers in tactical airpower, including 23,500 fighters and close air support aircraft immediately available, with 8,400 in tactical reserve and 18,000 in stored reserve;

11,000 transport aircraft provided airborne formations with a significant lift capability. Fortunately, there was no Soviet strategic air force yet. To stave off this armada, the Western allies could provide 1,500 very heavy bombers, 965 light bombers, and 2,000 fighters. But not all of these allied aircraft were deployed to Europe, while a significant amount of Soviet airpower was tasked to support its ground forces there.[9]

The naval comparisons appeared promising at least initially, since the U.S. Navy and the Royal Navy had access to a vast reserve fleet that included hundreds of each conceivable type of vessel. Much of the Soviet navy was obsolescent, and the Soviet naval experience during World War II had not been a positive one. Even though Soviet strategy did not require a battle fleet, it could provide 9 cruisers, 59 destroyers, 80 escorts, 150 patrol craft, and 150 submarines, 90 of which were classified as oceangoing.[10] However, the study noted that "the acquisition by the Soviets of extensive information about German developments in war material, of large numbers of German naval and technical personnel, scientists and of extensive German production and developmental facilities [provides] a substantial increase in the effectiveness . . . of the Soviet Navy. . . . Very large technical improvements, based on late German developments, may well be incorporated in the design of new Soviet submarines. . . ."[11] With this threat came the potential for a renewal of a Battle of the Atlantic if war came.[12]

Finally, Pincher predicted that the Soviets would acquire the atomic bomb between 1948 and 1956 and noted that they were already experimenting with chemical and biological agents. It should be noted that at this time the entire American stockpile of atomic bombs numbered nine weapons in the 10–15 kiloton range, and the United States possessed only twenty-seven aircraft capable of carrying them. The production of atomic bombs was still the realm of the craftsman, not the mass producer, since each weapon was practically custom-built. This was hardly a credible deterrent in 1946, even if Soviet leaders understood the effects of such weapons, because in all probability they also knew the rough size of the arsenal through their espionage networks.[13]

By assessing Soviet intentions and capabilities vis-à-vis the Western allies, Pincher provided an early basis for American action against the Soviet Union. Though in terms of numbers the situation appeared bleak, it is clear from the document that the creators of Pincher did not consider war with the Soviet Union a likely event during 1946–47 and looked toward 1948–49 as possible start years.[14]

Although Pincher was approved as the conceptual basis for U.S. war planning on 18 June 1946, a number of problems still had to be dealt with. To do so, a meeting of the U.S. Joint Strategic Planning Committee (JSPC) of the Joint Chiefs of Staff was convened on 18 June.[15] The most striking shortcoming of Pincher involved its potential use as a basis of action in the event of war: there was no discussion of the higher direction of war or coalition warfare in the actual document. Adm. Forrest Sherman, the naval member of the JSPC, pointed out that "in view of the assumption of the alliance of the U.S. and Britain, plans should be prepared in a form that might at the proper time be presented to the British for their concurrence on a combined basis...."[16]

It should be kept in mind, however, that political relations between the United States and Britain were rather strained from 1945 to early 1947. These problems stemmed from the termination of lend-lease, the reconciliation of Britain's wartime debt to the United States, the leftist nature of the Labour government in Britain, and the nonresolution of the Palestine problem. Militarily, American politicians wanted the abolition of the Combined Chiefs of Staff and had already obstructed Britain from acquiring its share of atomic bomb technology by enacting the McMahon Act.[17]

To solve the strategic zoning problem (without British input), Sherman recommended that a rough division of labor similar to the Arcadia division of the Second World War be outlined in Pincher, with the United States handling the Pacific and the British handling the Indian Ocean/Persian Gulf region. The Atlantic would be divided at the same CHOP line as it had been in 1943, with the Mediterranean controlled by a British and later a U.S. commander. The U.S. Army member of the JSPC, General Hull, added that the Alaska and North Atlantic areas should be commanded jointly with Canada.[18] There was no mention of a Combined Chiefs of Staff organization, but it was assumed to exist by the JSPC. It is unclear if this information was transmitted to the British or the Canadians, since Pincher was intended for planning purposes only. But clearly, consideration of coalition command organization in the postwar period was based on the World War II experience.

Before Pincher had been approved in June 1946, the JCS set in motion a series of talks aimed at reorganizing the U.S. military into new commands for the immediate postwar period. The division of labor in the Pacific between the CinCPOA and SACSWPA commands broke down in 1945 when the JCS was planning the invasion of Japan and had attempted to merge the positions. Although the personalities of Douglas MacArthur and Chester Nimitz had much to do with the friction, the more serious contrast of command philosophy was quite evident. The navy believed that unified command organizations should be geographic in nature and that the unified commander essentially ruled over his area; the army (and by default the USAAF at the time) believed that commands were functional in nature and should be organized around forces instead of areas.[19]

A series of talks among JCS members occurred between February and December 1946, and the end result was the Unified Command Plan (UCP), eventually approved by President Truman. The UCP established the major U.S. joint national commands for the period under review here. They included the Pacific Command, led by CinCPAC; the Far East Command, led by CinCFE, which replaced CinCPOA and SACSWPA; the Alaskan Command, established in January 1947; the European Command, established in March 1947; the Atlantic Command, formed in November 1947; the Caribbean Command, also formed in November 1947; and the Northeast Command, established in October 1950. Each of these commands utilized the unified command system—that is, one service head as the commander in chief and two others as subordinates. Each CinC was responsible directly to the JCS for command of the geographic area, as well as to the head of his service for the operations of his service forces in the area (see fig. 2.1). More important, a nonjoint command, Strategic Air Command, the future guardian of America's nuclear deterrent, was born on 26 March 1946. All of these commands were directly responsible to the JCS.[20]

In addition, the U.S. Navy reorganized, adding two new commands to those created during the war. The Atlantic and Pacific Fleets were still subordinated to CinCLANT and CinCPAC, as they had been during the war. The naval operating forces for these commands included the Second Task Fleet and the Seventh Task Fleet, respectively. COMNAVNAW became COMNAVMED in 1946; Commander in Chief, U.S. Naval Forces East Atlantic and Mediterranean (CinCNELM) replaced the wartime COMNAVEUR and absorbed COMNAVMED by November 1947. CinCNELM became responsible for naval operations in and around Europe and the Mediterranean, and its primary operating force eventually became the Sixth Task Fleet in 1948.[21]

With stroke of a pen, geographic rather than functional considerations initially appeared to have won out. However, areas of friction outside the Pacific were not solved for some time, notably the delineation between the Atlantic Fleet and the Northeast Command. In 1946 the United States possessed a worldwide command system much like Britain's prior to World War II. U.S. planners had identified a problem in their prewar command and control philosophy and had taken steps to deal with it.

The British naval command situation was not much different from the one established before the Second World War. Command over Royal Navy

An Attack Against One Is an Attack Against All

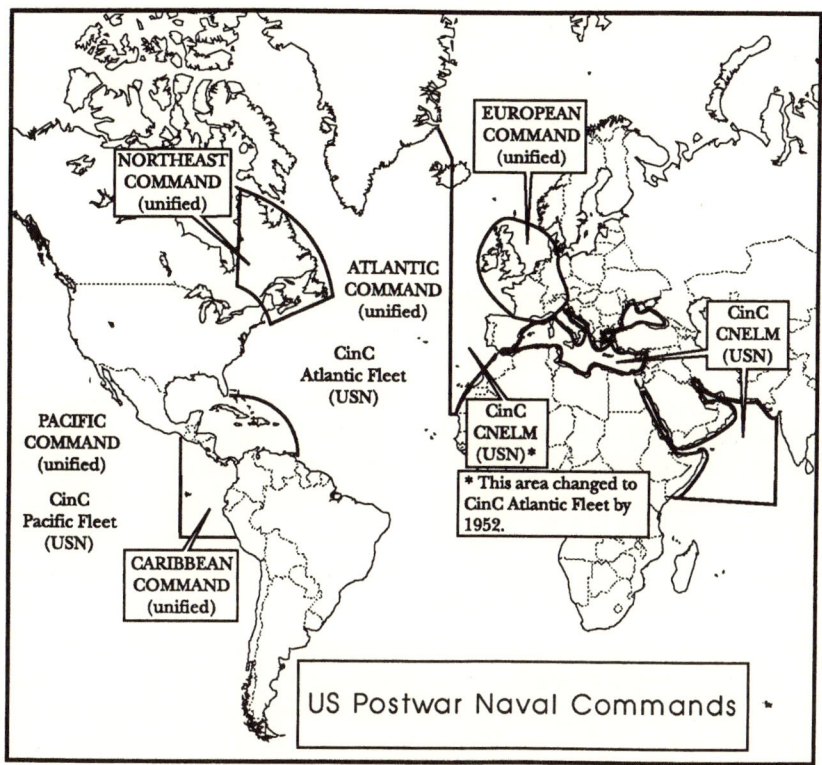

Fig. 2.1.

forces was exercised through geographic commands under a commander in chief, with flag officers handling sub-areas (see chapter 1 for geographic delineations). For interservice purposes, the British still relied on the joint committee system for certain geographic areas such as the Middle East. In their pragmatic way, the Royal Navy noted that "the precise organization that is adopted in any particular war will always depend on the personalities who are in charge of the machine when the crisis arises and particularly on the personality and wishes of the Prime Minister of the day. First World War and Second World War experience shows this. . . ."[22] This British penchant toward the ad hoc allowed for much flexibility when developing coalition command organizations.

If military relations between the United States and Britain became informal in nature from 1946 to 1947, the level of formalization between the United States and Canada remained high. The Canada–U.S. Permanent Joint Board on Defense, created during World War II, was not disestablished at the end of the conflict; on the contrary, the United States wished to use the PJBD to handle postwar Canadian–U.S. defense coordination. However, the primary weakness of the PJBD was that the U.S. military representatives did not necessarily reflect the military climate in Washington.[23]

To solve this, the PJBD initially recommended a combined Canadian–U.S. Chiefs of Staff (modeled on the CCS) that would establish and execute joint planning for operations in and around North America. This idea, known as the CANUSA proposal, was rejected by the JCS because the Americans believed that one bilateral agreement would set a precedent for other current and future allies, and that an entire series of such bilateral agreements would "bog down" defense planning.[24]

In the place of CANUSA, the PJBD recommended that its military members form the Joint Canadian–U.S. Military Cooperation Committee (MCC) and that representatives of the Canadian Chiefs of Staff and the U.S. JCS participate in it (see fig. 2.2). The MCC would be responsible for the creation of a Canada–U.S. security plan based on its own estimate of defense needs, while the PJBD would handle the foreign policy and production aspects of defense. The MCC was formally established in May 1946 and set out to produce its estimate.[25]

The resulting document was the Joint Canadian–U.S. Basic Security Plan 5. This plan was essentially a revision of ABC-22 with added emphasis on the protection of North America against air attack and the protection of sea lines of communication (SLOCs). Though the plan was a broad statement of how war would be fought jointly by the United States and Canada, the general discussions of command arrangements reflected the need to reconcile Canadian joint- and U.S. unified-command organization in order to avoid the convoluted Second World War situation.[26] The key phrase in these arrangements was that "coordination of the military efforts . . . shall be effected by mutual cooperation except where unified command is determined to be appropriate," and then only after consultation with the Canadian Chiefs of Staff.[27] In other words, informal arrangements would be tolerated "on the ground" for a time by the operating forces involved in a particular situation but had to be referred upward for approval.

Stronger links between the American, British, and Canadian planning staffs developed over the course of 1947. Starting out as standardization discussions examining such arcane things as screw threads, the ABC relationship was able to shift rapidly into more critical tasks. These tasks included the harmonization of national strategic concepts and intelligence estimates, and moves toward the development of an ABC logistical system.[28]

An Attack Against One Is an Attack Against All ➢ 55

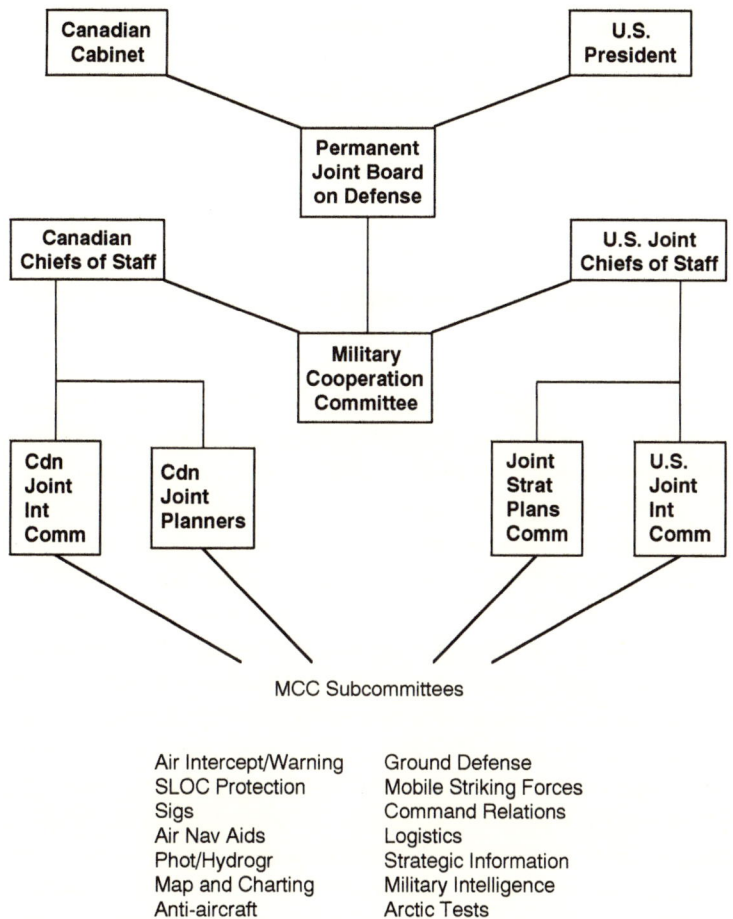

Fig. 2.2. U.S.–Canadian organization for defense

Events in early 1947 gave some urgency to Western defense preparation. Political pressure was brought to bear by the Soviet Union on Norway and Turkey in an effort to acquire bases there, an effort that was firmly renounced by both governments. A Soviet-backed coup occurred in Hungary, and Greece continued to be wracked with violence as it struggled to fend off Soviet-supported indigenous forces. In an effort to economically support noncommunist governments against Soviet interference, the altruistic Marshall Plan was implemented. To protect this effort, and realizing that it was the only nation self-sufficient enough to undertake it, the United States promulgated the Truman Doctrine of economic support to Western Europe and containment of the Soviet Union. This move finally swept away almost all vestiges of the traditional isolationism that had held sway over past U.S. foreign policy. As a further measure, the civilian side of the U.S. defense establishment was reorganized to include an intelligence organization (the Central Intelligence Agency) and an improved system of defense and foreign policy coordination (the National Security Council). The British had undergone a similar reorganization in 1946, but the American reorganization was an indicator of how seriously the U.S. leadership regarded the security situation.[29]

By mid- to late 1947, some agreement was reached between the U.S. and British Chiefs of Staff regarding joint planning. This agreement was established at a secret meeting known as the Dunkirk talks (not to be confused with the Dunkirk Treaty of March 1947). The topics discussed at this meeting included a possible strategic concept in case the Soviet Union invaded Western Europe. This concept, which had already been discussed internally by the Americans in the Pincher study, involved the prompt evacuation of British and American occupation forces from Germany, Austria, and Trieste in the event of a Soviet onslaught.[30] Admiral Connolly (USN) and the Royal Navy's First Sea Lord were responsible for the detailed planning of this evacuation. Previous talks on this subject involving the British had been discontinued on orders from Clement Attlee, the prime minister. Members of the British JPS involved in the talks had problems with the concept: "We feel bound to bring to the notice of the British Chiefs of Staff the extreme danger of embarking on talks of this kind [plans for a withdrawal from Europe] just at the moment when we are doing everything possible to bolster up the determination of the Western European powers to oppose and eradicate communist influence in their countries. . . ."[31] It is quite clear that only U.S. and British military personnel were privy to the Dunkirk talks. The British JPS noted that "it is inappropriate [to] bring the Foreign Office into the secret"—and, by inference, the State Department as well.[32]

The concept of operations discussed at the Dunkirk talks appears to have been taken from the U.S. Plan Broiler. In August 1947, the JSPC was ordered to prepare a plan for war assuming that the United States had to fight in 1948; it was to be derived from the Pincher study and its offshoots. The resulting plan, Broiler, was completed for review on 8 November 1947 and underwent constant revision until 10 March 1948, when it was finally approved by the JCS.[33]

A series of authorized meetings in March and April 1948 (probably stimulated by the Berlin blockade, which started in March) resulted in the creation of formal U.S.–British joint planning machinery. By May 1948, the British version of Broiler was completed. This was Plan Doublequick.[34] Broiler/Doublequick's estimates and concept of operations are worth examining in detail, because they provide the basis for later joint ABC war plans and command organization until the formal inauguration of the North Atlantic Treaty in 1949 and the creation of a new strategic concept to accompany it.

Broiler was a JCS Emergency War Plan (EWP) developed using forces available in 1947 and scheduled for use within a specific time frame—in this case, during 1948 or 1949 if the world situation deteriorated suddenly. It was not the basis for long-term military or budgetary planning as some later plans were. Broiler planners assumed that Britain and the Commonwealth would be U.S. allies; that Scandinavia would be overrun; that Turkey and Spain would be allies of Britain and the United States; and most important, that the United States would use its atomic weapons.[35] The broad objective of Broiler was "to create conditions within the USSR which will insure abandonment of Soviet political and military aggression."[36]

Broiler's rationale for Soviet aggression was essentially unchanged from Pincher—that is, the goal of controlling the Eurasian landmass and later dominating the periphery. Initially, Broiler anticipated that the Soviets would attempt to subjugate Western Europe and the Middle East by all means short of open warfare. In doing so, the Soviets would provoke either severe criticism or a show of force from the West, which would be used as a pretext to invade.[37]

Probable Soviet military objectives included the elimination of Britain as an allied base area; the takeover of the Middle East, with its vital oil resources; the staging of limited operations in the Far East to divert allied forces; and the use of limited attacks to deny the allies base areas that could be used to retake Europe.[38] Broiler's estimate of Soviet and allied forces appears in figures 2.3, 2.4, and 2.5; this was based on Pincher's estimate, with some "fine tuning."

The probable employment of Soviet air and land forces in the Broiler concept would remain in use into the early 1950s. The Soviet attack on Western Europe would presumably follow four axes of advance toward the Channel, the Pyrenees, Denmark, and Italy, to be followed by a fifth push into Norway. Greece and the Bosporus Straits would be taken with two more advances, which would be followed by an airborne attack on the Persian oil fields. Mechanized forces from Azerbaijan would link up with these units and push on to the Suez Canal, while other airborne forces seized bases in the Mediterranean from which airpower would interdict Britain's SLOC there.[39]

USSR Satellite	USSR	Type	Br.	U.S.	Fr.
757	5200	Fighter	516		72
	2250	Ground Attack	48	325 USAF	
	1700	Light/Medium Bomber	168	180 USN	
	1300	Long-Range Bomber	168		
	5000	Transport	240		24

Fig. 2.3. Broiler's estimate of air forces available

USSR Satellite	USSR	Location	U.S.	Br.	Fr.	Cda.
	113	USSR				
	24	Germany	1.3	3		
24	8	Poland				
	3	Austria	0.3	0.3		
17		Czech.				
2	2	Hungary				
10	5	Rumania				
7	9	Bulgaria				
34		Yugoslavia				
		France			3	
		Britain		5		
		U.S.	3.3			
		Canada				0.3
	8	Far East	7			
		Mid East		2.3		
94	172		12.5	10.6	3	0.3
USSR Satellite	USSR		U.S.	Br.	Fr.	Cda.

Fig. 2.4. Broiler's estimate of ground forces available

An Attack Against One Is an Attack Against All ➤ 59

USSR	Type	Br.	U.S.	Cda.	Total
3	BB	2	2		4
	CV	1	11		12
	CVL	3		1	4
	CVE		7		7
8	Ca	3	9		12
3	CI	9	21		30
44	DD	42	131	6	179
31	FF	37			45
			76		
233	SS	25	8		101

Fig. 2.5. Broiler's estimate of naval forces available

Probable Soviet naval operations centered on the need to protect the USSR from amphibious operations and aircraft carrier–based strikes as well as the desire to interdict SLOCs to Britain, thus denying its use as a base. Broiler estimated that the Soviets were capable of operating thirty captured German Type IXCs and would have access to between seven and twenty Type XXIs, with the possibility of assembling thirty-nine more in eighteen months.[40] This was in addition to the 150 Soviet types already in existence. Projected Soviet operations included aerial mining, long-range air attacks, and submarine operations as portrayed in figure 2.6.

The allied strategic plan was based on several very broad objectives. Initially, North and South America would be secured to protect its economic and military potential. Second, base areas outside the Western Hemisphere would be secured; these included Britain, Japan, and Cairo-Suez, with Karachi as an alternate. Simultaneously, the air and sea LOCs to the base areas would be secured, and unconventional warfare would be implemented in the occupied areas. After these conditions were established, a strategic air campaign using both conventional and atomic bombs would sortie from the base areas to destroy the Soviet Union's industrial capability to wage war. There is no follow-up for these actions in Broiler beyond the vague statement, "prepare for later operations."[41] Broiler was to be implemented in three phases: first, the Soviet offensive would be halted while Western mobilization occurred; second, the Middle East and its resources would be liber-

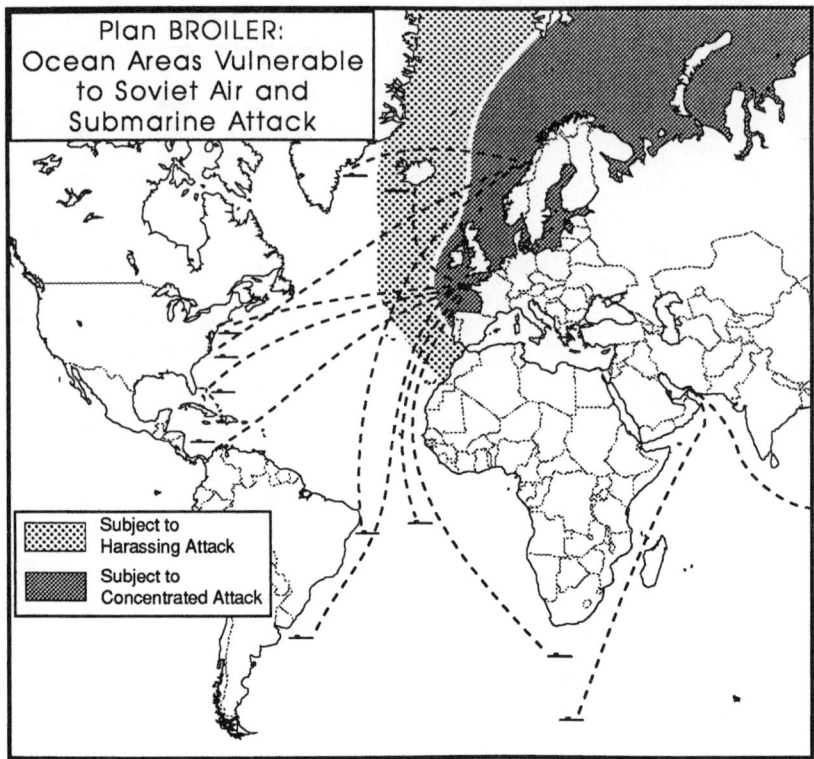

Fig. 2.6.

ated. The final phase was outlined in another vague phrase: "additional measures to permit realization of our national war objectives."[42]

The JSPC planners diverged in their views on how the phases would be executed. All were in agreement over the withdrawal of occupation forces from Germany and the need to defend the Western Hemisphere and Britain, maintain LOCs, and conduct a strategic air offensive. However, the choice of a base area in addition to Britain caused problems. In 1947, the primary delivery system for nuclear weapons was the B-29, which had a combat radius of 1,717 miles with a maximum bomb load. Even conventional bombers like the British Lincoln had a radius of only 1,875 miles.[43] Because in-flight refueling was still undergoing development, secure forward bases were needed from which aircraft could operate in a protracted manner.

One option was to secure the Mediterranean and Cairo-Suez area (see fig. 2.7). There were not enough allied ground forces to do this, however.

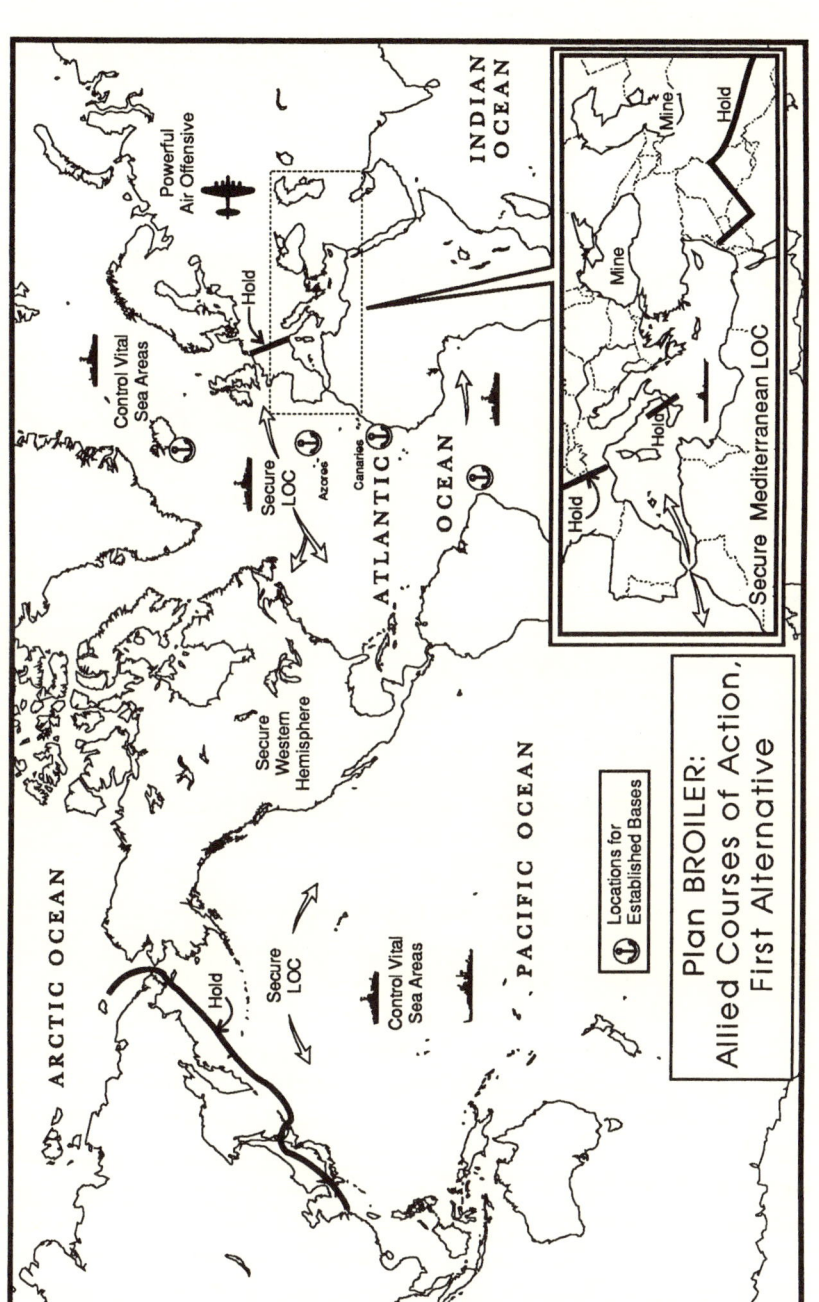

Fig. 2.7.

Instead, the JSPC reasoned that carrier-based aircraft equipped with atomic weapons used in a tactical role could support allied ground forces in Turkey and "thin out" Soviet ground forces heading toward Cairo-Suez and the Persian Gulf. Long-range aircraft with conventional weapons would be used to interdict Soviet land LOCs to the theater. This option was replete with risks. The use of carrier task forces in the Mediterranean assumed that the Soviets had not yet overrun Spain and Malta and that the Cairo-Suez area was secure in the first place; it also assumed that a large share of ASW resources would be made available from other theaters and sent to the Mediterranean.[44]

The second alternative, and the one favored by the JSPC, involved securing Karachi as a base area (see fig. 2.8). This would theoretically entail less risk of scarce resources; to squander them in an attempt to secure a possibly unsecurable base just did not make military sense. However, the political problems with not securing the Mediterranean were a serious disadvantage to this option. A major segment of Britain's economic lifeline ran through the Mediterranean and Suez. If it were not secured, Britain could not be maintained as a base area for future air and land operations since its ability to fight would be impaired. But those operations could not be conducted from Karachi alone. More important, the problems created by British decolonization in the region demonstrated that Karachi would not be a secure area from which to launch offensive operations.[45]

Be that as it may, the JSPC recommended that the best bet was the Karachi option. There were not enough atomic bombs to allow their use on "tactical" targets, and the diversion of long-range airpower from the strategic bombing campaign was unacceptable to the strategic air planners, some of whom undoubtedly had chafed under orders to use strategic air units to interdict LOCs to Normandy during the last war.[46]

The Broiler/Doublequick strategic concept fell under criticism immediately after its acceptance as an emergency war plan. This criticism fell into two broad areas: the lack of a command organization and a conflicting concept of the role of naval operations. Although Broiler was presented to the U.S. secretary of defense to demonstrate to him that an EWP existed and could be implemented "should the situation require such action," the Chief of Naval Operations, Adm. Louis Denfield, had serious reservations about it.[47] Even though Broiler was acceptable as an EWP, it was not a legitimate long-term planning tool because, Denfield believed, "the strategic plan and concept of operations are completely at variance with U.S. foreign policy."[48] Denfield particularly did not agree with leaving conti-

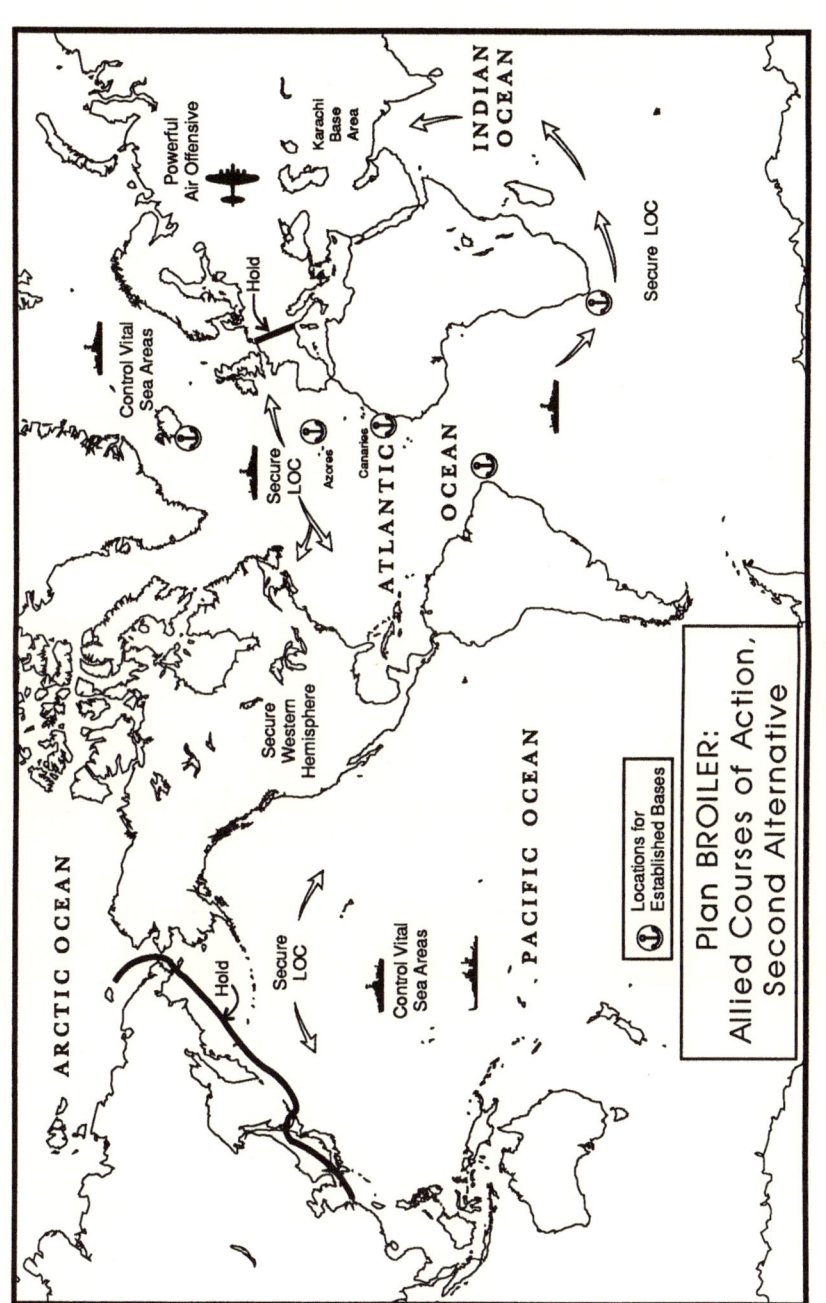

Fig. 2.8.

nental Europe without a fight, because this would neutralize the will of the European people to resist. He also felt that Broiler accepted the loss of the Mediterranean too readily if the Karachi option was selected; political problems would result with the British over this SLOC. Finally, if the Mediterranean were given up, the left flank of the Persian Gulf area would be open and even harder to defend.[49]

As a navy man, Denfield felt that too much emphasis was being placed on strategic bombing as a decisive tool and that Broiler "does not exploit the inherent possibilities of our naval and air power."[50] This reflected an ongoing U.S. interservice debate over the role of airpower to deliver atomic weapons in support of a national strategy.[51]

The Pincher study from 1946 included a strategic concept for naval operations in the event of war based on the need to eliminate the Soviet submarine threat, which was assumed to be composed of Type XXI clones (see appendix 1). This concept revolved around the need to eliminate the submarine base areas and destroy as many submarines as possible there in order to reduce the threat to SLOCs, thereby achieving command of the sea. This was known as "attack at source," and it formed the basis for U.S. Navy planning throughout this period. By 1948, SAC's concept of operations had been formed around the seeming decisiveness of strategic bombing. SAC's leadership argued that land-based bombers equipped with atomic bombs could handle this attack-at-source mission and that the navy should be limited to defensive SLOC protection.[52]

In sum, Denfield thought Broiler was too "worst case" and too narrow in outlook. The attack-at-source concept was virtually ignored—Broiler relegated it to a very low priority after the strategic air campaign had begun.[53] It would, however, reappear phoenixlike in future plans.

The British, on the other hand, were particularly concerned about the lack of command relationships in Broiler and set up a meeting to correct this flaw before proceeding with their version, Doublequick. The British JPS produced an elaborate study that was unveiled at the Washington talks in April 1948.[54] This report was noteworthy because it provided a bridge between Second World War command organization and NATO command organization. In the British scheme, the overall direction of war was placed in the hands of the familiar CCS organization (see fig. 2.9). The defense of the "main support areas" (North America, South Africa, and Australasia) was the responsibility of their respective national command organizations; Britain would handle the defense of its home islands. The strategic air offensive was to be under the direct command of the CCS. Naturally, this commander would be an American since the division of labor between

Britain and the United States with respect to strategic air targeting was to send the SAC to the Soviet Union and to use RAF Bomber Command for missions in support of the base areas.[55]

Coalition command in the active theaters would be delegated to supreme commanders, with each SC having a coalition staff and three commanders in chief to handle the operating forces of the land, sea, and air elements in that command. This was similar to the organization for Normandy in 1944. In Western Europe, the supreme commander would be American, and his deputy would be the RAF officer in charge of the defense of British airspace. Both would be responsible to the Western Union Chiefs of Staff (WUCoS), a coalition command organization to be discussed in detail later. The land forces commander would be French, and he would deal with the withdrawal from Germany.[56]

The Mediterranean and the Middle East, once they became active theaters, would compose a single theater of war. Initially, the supreme com-

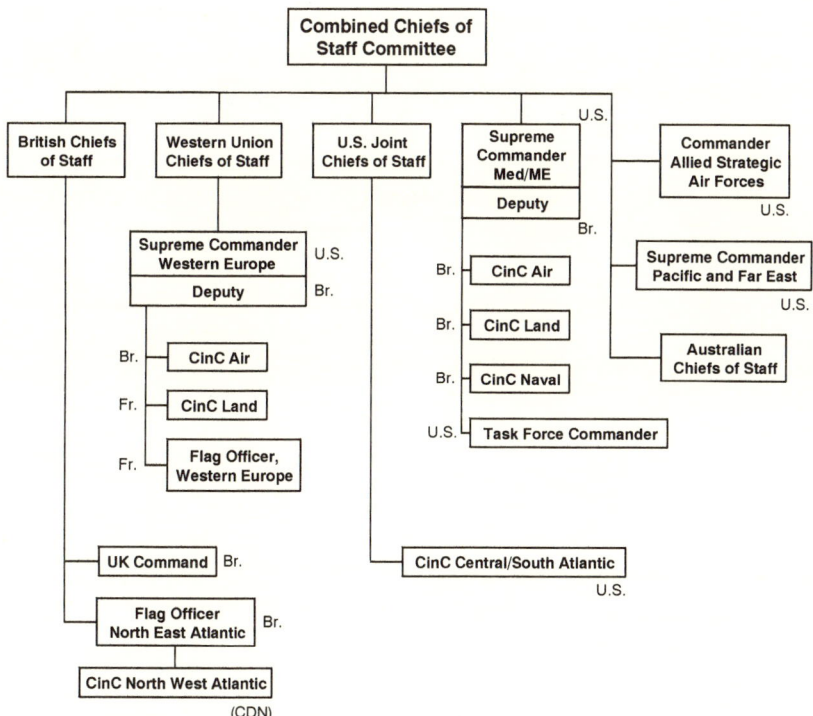

Fig. 2.9. Proposed organization for British Plan Doublequick

mander was to be British, with a British land forces CinC, a U.S. air CinC, and a British naval CinC—again, a structure quite similar to the final version of command organization in the Mediterranean during World War II. Once the preponderance of forces was American, a U.S. supreme commander would take over. The Atlantic was to be divided into a North Atlantic Area under a British commander and a Central/South Atlantic Area under an American, both responsible to their national commands as in the Second World War (see fig. 2.10). The North Atlantic would be subdivided further at the CHOP line into a Canadian CinC, Northwest Area and a British Flag Officer, Northeast Area. Air support for naval operations would be left up to national commands in their areas. The British JPS had noted the World War II COMNAVNAW problem and sought to reconcile it before the actual conflict started. It is uncertain what the American reaction to this proposal was. It appears, however, that discussions over the

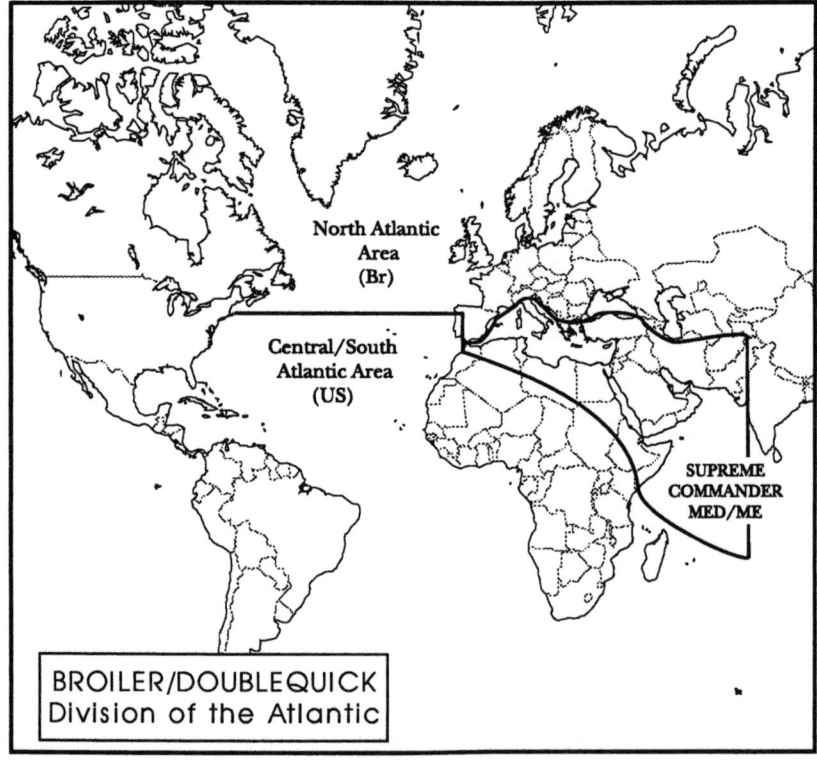

Fig. 2.10.

development of the WUCoS overshadowed this proposal for the time being.⁵⁷

Even though Broiler was the focal point for U.S., British, and Canadian planners during April 1948, Britain's concern over its strategic needs in the Mediterranean and the lack of an agreed-upon command organization combined with the U.S. Navy's dissatisfaction with its role in Broiler led to the revision of Broiler/Doublequick. This revision was initially called Halfmoon (the code name later changed twice, from Fleetwood to Doublestar) by the Americans, Speedway by the British, and Bullmoose by the Canadians. Doublestar's strategic concept was similar to Broiler's but was modified to include the developing Western Union Defense Organization (WUDO).⁵⁸

WUDO played a direct role in the establishment of NATO command organization. At the time of the U.S.–British discussions on joint war planning in late 1947 and early 1948, Britain was also involved in talks to establish a European defense organization involving itself, France, Belgium, Luxembourg, and Holland. Initiated by Ernest Bevin, who at the time was ignorant of the Dunkirk talks, the Western European Union was an economic and military organization that came into being with the signing of the Brussels Treaty on 17 March 1948. Known variously as the Brussels Treaty Organization or the Brussels Pact, its defense component had a Western Union Defense Committee composed of representatives from the member governments plus a Western Union Chiefs of Staff Committee, consisting of representatives from the member nations and American observers (see fig. 2.11).⁵⁹ The WUDO had primarily a land and air orientation due to the nature of the Soviet land threat to Western Europe and was essentially a SHAEF-style command that would be in place prior to the outbreak of a conflict. Naval considerations were not covered in detail except for the English Channel and North Sea areas, which fell under British command.⁶⁰

American participation in a European defense organization was at the time a surprising bonus to the Europeans. It was assumed that after World War II the United States would retreat to an isolationist position. However, it had signed a mutual defense treaty (the Rio Pact) with certain Latin American nations in 1947. This precedent paved the way for closer U.S.–European defense relations. Initially, the State Department was wary. After a series of secret talks over a proposed "Atlantic Approaches Pact of Mutual Assistance" that occurred prior to the Anglo-American-Canadian war plan meetings in Washington during April 1948, the question shifted from whether the United States should participate to the degree to which

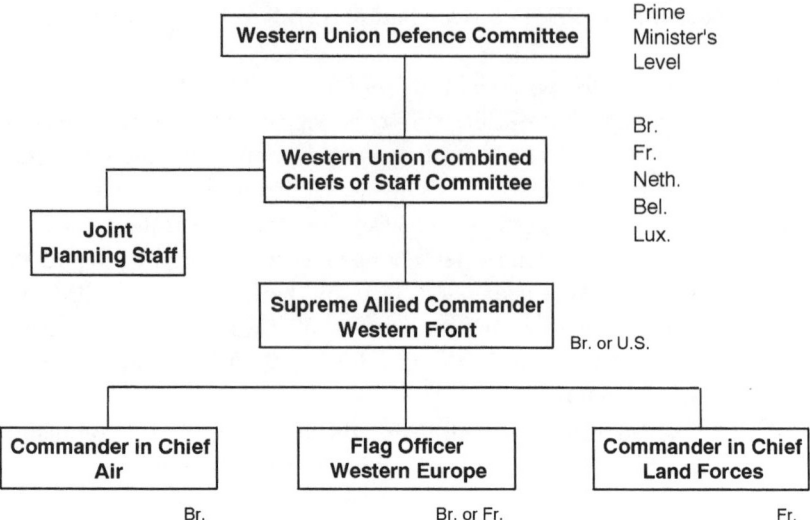

Fig. 2.11. Western Union Defense Organization, June 1948

it should participate. The results of these talks included a U.S. pledge to take part in negotiations for a more comprehensive collective defense agreement and a firm commitment to assist in the defense of Europe if the Soviets attacked.[61]

In light of the concurrent development of the Western Union Defense Organization, Doublestar/Speedway/Bullmoose as a strategic concept differed from Broiler/Doublequick in two important respects: Western Europe would not be abandoned outright if the Soviets invaded, and the role of seapower was considered by the planners in more detail.

The overall assumptions for Doublestar were similar to those in Broiler, as was the projected Soviet concept of operations. A notable addition to the list of expected Soviet actions was the "disruption of vital Allied lines of communications by aggressive submarine warfare, mining and air operations."[62]

The allied strategic concept differed from Broiler in a number of ways. The air offensive was still was a priority item, its purpose being to "exploit the destructive and psychological power of atomic weapons" against the Soviet war-making capability.[63] Other tasks included the securing of the Western Hemisphere and Britain; however, Doublestar diverged from Broiler by placing emphasis on the Cairo-Suez base area instead of the Karachi option. Other added tasks that were given priority in Doublestar included the provision of substantial aid to allies and the creation of underground and psychological warfare groups.[64]

Specific allied operations to be taken under Doublestar's strategic concept were divided into two periods. The emphasis in the first period was the protection of the Western Hemisphere. Doublestar included more detailed planning for this than previous strategic concepts had. It also contained a major revision of Broiler's concept of operations in Western Europe. The intention in Doublestar was for allied occupation forces in Germany to be airlifted to the Rhine immediately; then they were to conduct a fighting withdrawal in concert with the French army either to French ports or to Spain, where they would be evacuated by sea. A simultaneous evacuation would occur in the Mediterranean.[65]

To maintain the security of the Cairo-Suez base area, Doublestar made provisions for the use of British and American carrier airpower to interdict enemy movement with conventional ordnance and to protect allied shipping from Soviet long-range aircraft. In a complete turnaround from Broiler, Doublestar ordered that "carrier task groups will supplement and support the air offensive to the extent practical consistent with their primary task."[66] But like Broiler, Doublestar did little to enlighten its end users as to operations past those described. The second period included only limited operations to maintain the Mediterranean SLOC and the retaking of the Persian Gulf oil fields.[67]

In one respect, then, Doublestar attempted to correct some of the problems revealed in Broiler's concept. The command organization for Doublestar/Speedway/Bullmoose became the subject of much tripartite correspondence. In July 1948, members of WUDO met in Washington and formed the Working Group, which was tasked with the development of the diplomatic basis for a North Atlantic pact. At the same time, the British and American militaries attempted to sort out command arrangements between the United States and WUDO in the event of Soviet hostilities. It is useful to remember that this activity all took place under the Damoclean sword of the Berlin crisis. As participants realized, the shooting down of one allied plane on its way to Berlin would have plunged Europe into a Third World War: "The USSR under Kremlin dictatorship, utilizing the technique of indirect aggression and the threat of indirect aggression, is an implacable enemy to Western Civilization and the present situation in Europe must be regarded as extremely insecure. . . ."[68]

In addition, the JCS had noted that "the United States must pledge real and effective aid in screening Western Europe from Soviet conquest and occupation."[69] To do so, European nations would need a military aid program and some method of coordinating the higher direction of war. The British believed that a combined chiefs of staff based on the World War II model but now involving all the principal participants would be too large to be effective. The U.S.–British relationship was tried and proven, and it would serve for the time being.[70] Politically, the French would be a problem if they felt left out: "The short range emergency plan approved by the JCS for planning purposes, prepared in concert with British and Canadian planners, recognizes the necessity for coordination of the military actions of the United States, the United Kingdom's and French occupation forces prior to and during the initial stages of [war] but does not provide for over all command or recognize the necessity for . . . inclusion in Western Union Forces. . . ."[71]

To get around this, the JCS recommended to the British Chiefs of Staff that the WUCoS organization referred to earlier would constitute a temporary measure until the war "got into gear"; after this point, a U.S.–British CCS would take over. The problem with France could be solved by allowing the French to control land operations during the withdrawal to the Rhine, while the American Allied Commander in Chief would have an integrated liaison staff from the British, U.S., and French fleets in the post of Flag Officer, Western Europe (see fig. 2.12). FOWE was to be responsible for naval activ-

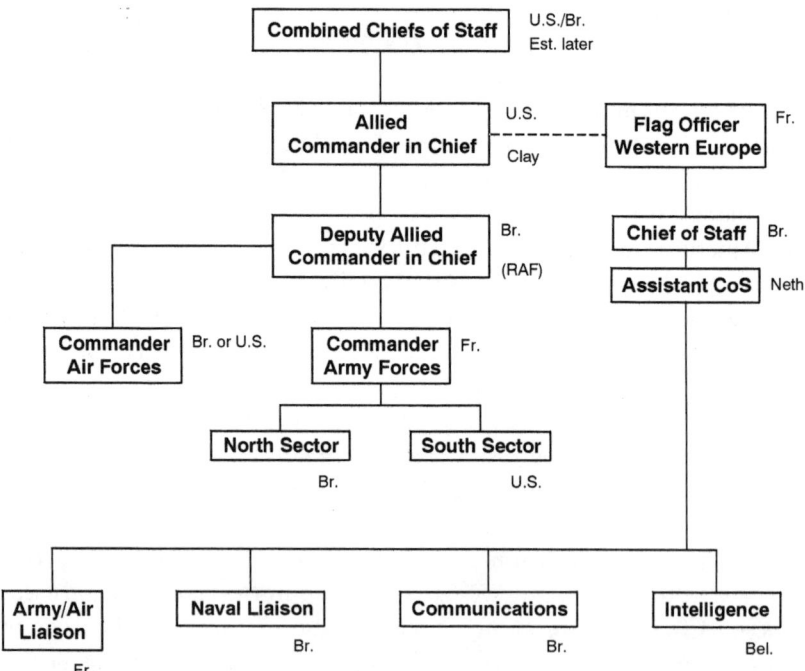

Fig. 2.12. WUDO withdrawal organization, July 1948

ities on the major European rivers in support of the withdrawal and for coordination with seagoing elements of the larger navies during the evacuation from ports.[72]

Under the CCS, the United States proposed that a single supreme allied commander be designated to command all allied forces in Western Europe, the Mediterranean, and the Middle East. The supreme commands for the sort of conflict foreseen by the Doublestar concept included Allied Commander in Chief, Western Europe; Allied CinC, Strategic Air Forces; and Allied CinC, Mediterranean/Middle East. The WUCoS would then become an "advisory body" to the CCS for operations in Europe—a polite way of saying that the French would be frozen out of the higher military decision-making process (see fig. 2.13).[73]

Unbeknownst to the British, internal American deliberations over command arrangements in Europe had taken on a Machiavellian tone as U.S. planners discussed means of keeping a Supreme Allied Commander, Western Europe–Mediterranean and Middle East out of London "so that he would not be unduly influenced by the British Chiefs of Staff," thus avoiding the apparent "danger of having a strong man in there [in command of Western Europe] and drawing everything in to make the operation a tactical success."[74] By inserting a U.S. commander who was in tune

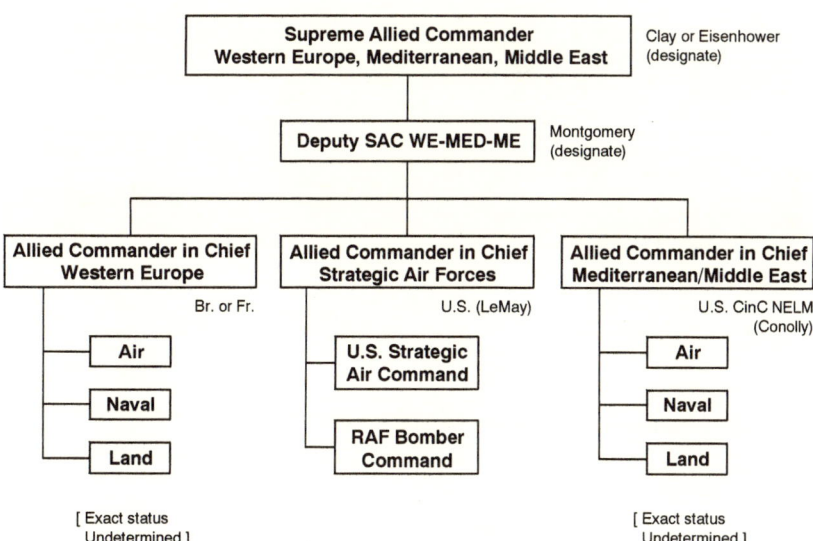

Fig. 2.13. Proposed organization for the higher direction of war in Europe, 1948

with the concept of Doublestar, the planners believed that they could exert control over the entire process. The cracks of diverging U.S. JCS and British CoS views on coalition command organization in the postwar period were starting to appear.

Note that there appears to have been little consideration given to other strategic areas of responsibility, particularly the Atlantic. The British were violently opposed to some aspects of the proposal from Washington—particularly the placement of the U.S. CinCNELM in control of the campaign in the Mediterranean, which was British "turf" in the last war. These factors prompted a special meeting between the U.S. JSPC, the Canadian Joint Planning Committee, and the British JPS in October 1948. An agreement was reached on the Mediterranean/Middle East command problem: there would be a U.S. supreme commander, but with a British deputy. The land and naval commanders would both be British, the air commander American (see fig. 2.14). The U.S. Sixth Task Fleet was placed directly

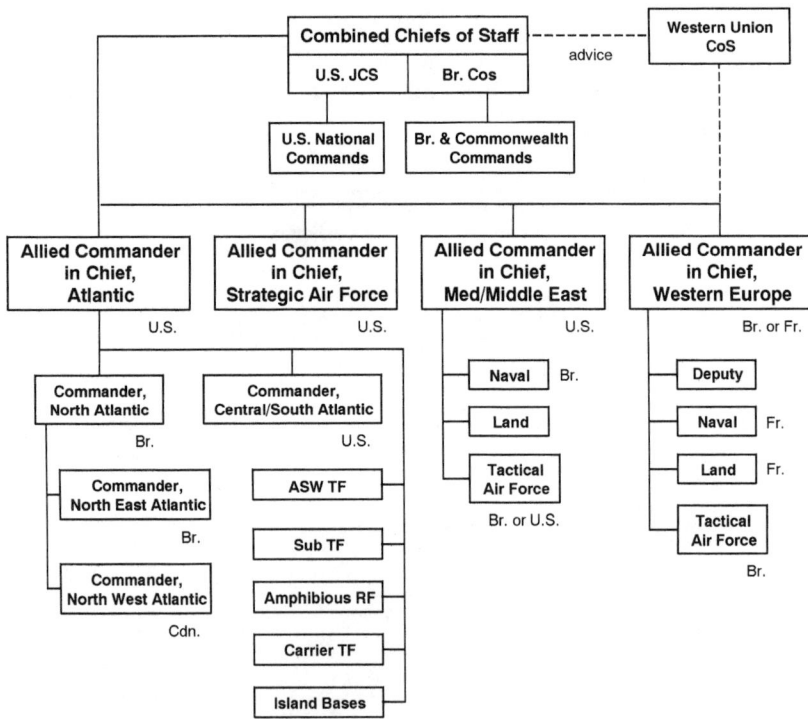

Fig. 2.14. Allied higher direction for Doublestar/Speedway/Bullmoose, October 1948

under the supreme commander's control, presumably to observe the McMahon Act provisions that prohibited U.S. forces armed with nuclear weapons from being under the control of a foreign commander.[75]

The British JPS had no problem with the designation of the U.S. Strategic Air Command commander to handle the strategic air offensive; however, there was still no agreement over command in the Atlantic. Essentially, the United States had changed its mind about the Broiler concept of splitting the Atlantic into British and U.S. zones and wanted strategic command over the entire Atlantic, while the British fell back on the established system of two command zones.[76]

The division of the North Atlantic at 42° north latitude was no longer acceptable to American planners, who thought that the U.S. CinCLANT should "run the whole show" with two subordinates: a Commander, North Atlantic and a Commander, South/Central Atlantic, both with their own national staffs. Commanders of task fleets, ASW task forces, submarine task forces, and island commanders were to be directly under CinCLANT. The arguments for this hierarchy revolved around the need for flexibility and concentration of effort; the Americans believed that U.S. island base commands that contained unified commanders would be easier to integrate under a U.S. supreme commander.[77] Unlike the Supreme Commander, Atlantic Theater proposal of the Second World War, such a supreme commander would have control over all aspects of naval warfare in the Atlantic, not just antisubmarine warfare and the protection of convoys.

British arguments against such a scheme suggested that the area from the North Pole to the Cape of Good Hope was too large for efficient control by one person for political, geographic, and communications reasons. Second, ASW task forces and submarines must come under the orders of a local area commander so that all forces could be coordinated in one place. In addition, putting all forces of one type together in functional groupings was too inflexible. Another important consideration was that the placement of such a commander in Norfolk, Virginia, deprived him of naval control of shipping (NCS) and intelligence information because the communication facilities required for NCS were located in Ottawa, Washington, and London. Finally, the seaward defenses of Britain and the North Atlantic routes to it would be entirely under American control, and "this would be unacceptable to the United Kingdom."[78]

The British countered with a proposal that relegated overall strategic direction (not control) over the entire Atlantic to a U.S. supreme commander located in Washington. This position would go to the CNO, who would be "double-hatted." This commander would also have an integrated U.S., Canadian, and British staff. The British proposal recommended that the Atlantic be divided into two areas along a line south of and parallel to the North Atlantic convoy lanes at 42° north latitude (see fig. 2.15). The Northern Area would be commanded by a British CinCNA with an integrated staff. The Central/South Atlantic Area would be under the command of the U.S. CinCLANT commander, who would also have an integrated staff. However, the Admiralty wanted to reserve the right to issue directions to the CinCNA to divert British naval forces to the defense of Britain as necessary, on top of his responsibilities for defensive ASW and trade protection in his area.[79]

Other important aspects of the British proposal included relegating to the U.S. CNO the operational control of submarines via SUBNA and SUBLANT commands, both to be established with integrated staffs and coor-

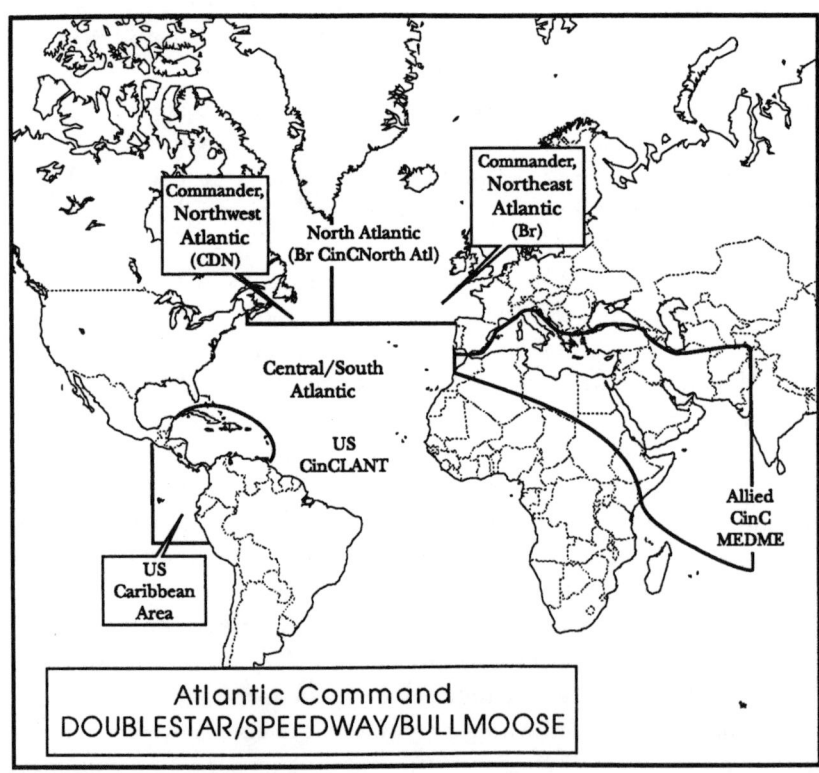

Fig. 2.15.

dination with CinCNA and CinCCSA.⁸⁰ This foreshadowed the creation of the coalition submarine command organization Commander, Submarines Eastern Atlantic under SACLANT in 1952.

At this point, the British proposal came to naught. The debate over the structure and form of the forthcoming North Atlantic pact overshadowed these conversations, as participants focused on a higher direction of war for the new coalition. (The continuing evolution of command organization in the North Atlantic and the development of a strategic concept for its defense are the subjects of chapter 3.) The underpinnings for NATO existed in 1948. These included a strategic concept, a political commitment to collective defense, and a proposed command organization. The next step was to bring them all together. As Lord Ismay wrote in 1954, "On 28 April 1948, the idea of a single mutual defense system, including and superceding the Brussels Treaty system, was publicly put forward by Mr. St. Laurent in the Canadian House of Commons. It was welcomed a week later in Westminster by Mr. Bevin. At about the same time, Senator Vandenberg proposed, in consultation with the State Department, a resolution that recommended in part [that the United States] contribute to the maintenance of peace by making clear its determination to exercise the right of individual or collective self-defense. . . ."⁸¹

On 6 November 1948, President Truman instructed the National Security Council to begin negotiations for a North Atlantic Treaty; the Canadian and European governments had given their consent in October. Ambassadors of the original member nations (Canada, the United States, Great Britain, France, the Netherlands, Belgium, Luxembourg, Portugal, Italy, Denmark, Norway, and Iceland) met in December and gave the go-ahead to the Working Group to draft the actual treaty. From January 1949, the Working Group continued to fine-tune the proposal until the final version was signed on 4 April 1949. Bringing NATO into being as an organization was, at this stage, a comparatively straightforward political and diplomatic act. Creating the structures within it to make NATO work took much longer to accomplish. As Don Cook notes in *Forging the Alliance,* "It would be two years before the superstructure of the North Atlantic Treaty Organization was finally in place on top of the North Atlantic Treaty. . . ."⁸² The military command organization for NATO could be described as rudimentary, and debate continued throughout 1949.

As we have seen, the imperfect Doublestar command organization was the last pre-NATO scheme for the coalition's higher direction of war. By February 1949, the main theme in the command organization debate was how to reconcile the existing WUDO and the developing NATO military commands.

The British Chiefs of Staff served as the link between Europe and North America during these discussions. It was clear that the WUCoS was already too large to be effective, and that expanding it to handle planning outside of Western Europe proper would make it even more unwieldy. But using organizations that were already up and running might streamline the "marrying up" plan. To set the parameters of NATO organization for the higher direction of war, a decision had to be reached over the boundaries of the NATO area. Any command organization had to be able to plan for a war that encompassed Western Europe, the Atlantic Ocean, and the defense of North America and Scandinavia.[83]

The British JPS, however, recognized that different areas had different geographic considerations and that this dictated different command arrangements for each area (see fig. 2.16). The defense of Western Europe required detailed planning and an integrated staff; this was already func-

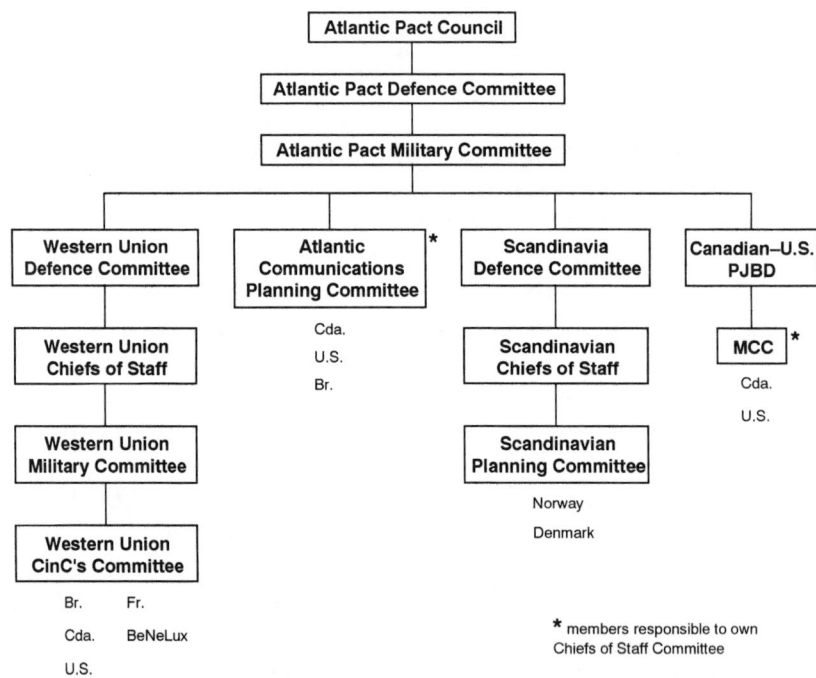

Fig. 2.16. British view of the North Atlantic Pact organization, 19 February 1949

tioning well under the WUDO system. The battle of the Atlantic, reasoned the British chiefs, should be the responsibility of a tripartite Anglo-American-Canadian committee, whose suggested title was the Atlantic Communications Planning Committee. The defense of North America and Scandinavia could be the responsibility of local arrangements. In the U.S.–Canadian case, the PJBD was acceptable. All of these organizations would have some form of connection with a CCS-type organization (an Atlantic Pact Military Council) with the United States and Britain participating. To connect it with political direction, an Atlantic Pact Defense Committee consisting of the defense ministers of the member nations would be responsible to the Atlantic Pact Council, which in turn would consist of representatives from the various heads of state.[84] This would replace the informal connections between heads of state that existed during World War II, since the nations involved in the North Atlantic Treaty were complete sovereign entities as opposed to governments in exile with little or no resources at their disposal.

The Canadians added an improved system that could incorporate the WUDO into this British concept for higher direction. On 7 March 1949, Canadian Gen. Charles Foulkes disseminated a new concept for NATO's military command organization among the members' separate chiefs of staff. At this point the Canadian leadership believed that having a U.S.–British CCS handle the higher direction of war would prove divisive in the event of a conflict. Foulkes's concept recognized that, because of the large number of nations participating in NATO, logistical problems, sovereignty issues, and nationalism could not be discounted as factors. In previous conflicts, the solution had been either to centralize or to decentralize command according to the British or U.S. methods of joint or unified command. Foulkes sought to use both centralization and decentralization in developing the NATO command.[85]

Under the Foulkes concept, candidates for centralized coalition command included Western Europe (with a U.S. supreme commander responsible to a Council of Defense Ministers instead of a CCS clone) and an organization Foulkes called the Strategic Reserve Group. The SRG would have as its members the United States, Britain, and Canada and would have control over all uncommitted military resources and the resource base in North America. The decentralized organizations in the Foulkes concept were called regional groups (RGs) and "should be composed of countries possessing a common interest which, if threatened, would call for immediate action by all countries in that group."[86] Initially, Foulkes believed that there should be three regional groups, covering North

America, Scandinavia, and Western Europe (see fig. 2.17). Each RG would have a defense council with a chiefs of staff committee responsible for planning the defenses of that region. A representative of each RG would report to and advise the supreme commander. Planning at the RG level was to be highly detailed in nature, something that could not be done at a higher level of command. In addition, the concept was compartmentalized and reduced the risk of a security problem.[87]

The Foulkes concept was discussed at Anglo-American-Canadian planning sessions in March 1949. Reaction from both the United States and Britain was positive—in fact, the British JPS revised its February proposal to include Foulkes's regional grouping idea. However, Britain still favored overall U.S.–British control in the event of war. Internal British discussions indicated that exploratory British proposals for military organization within NATO were not to create difficulties in the special relationship or to "interfere with the close working consultation with the U.S. and British Chiefs of Staff."[88]

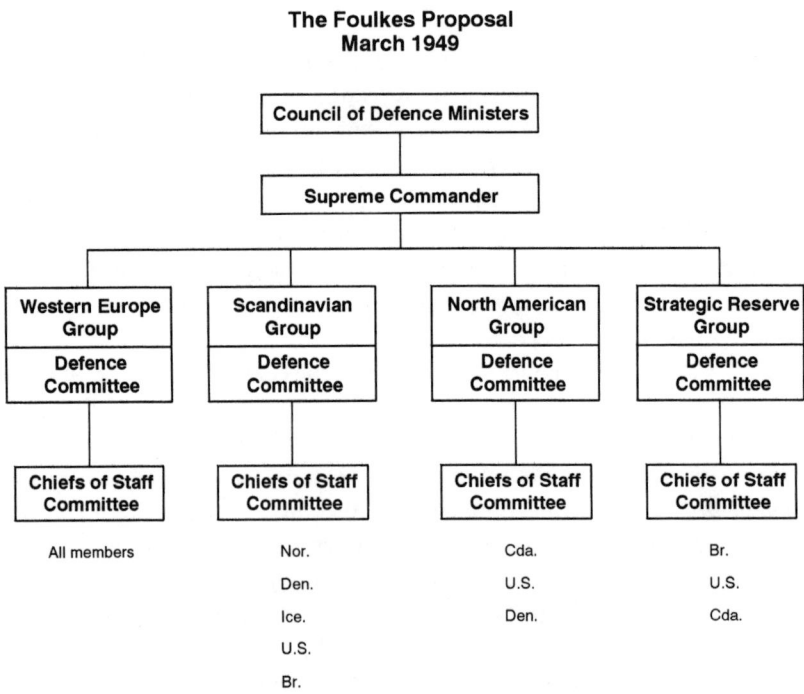

Fig. 2.17. The Foulkes proposal, March 1949

The main obstacle between U.S. and British planners in the development of command organization for Western Europe, the Mediterranean, and the Middle East was the degree of control that any supreme commander would have over the forces assigned to him. The British position was that the WUCoS should have command over the land, sea, and air forces in and around Western Europe while at the same time being responsible to the U.S. supreme commander. Operating forces in the Mediterranean and Middle East would be placed under various commanders in chief responsible to the supreme commander. The U.S. view suggested that the WUCoS was merely an advisory body to the supreme commander and that some arrangements had to be made over the division of labor in other areas. The Doublestar organization would have to be updated.[89]

As we have seen, both U.S. and British concepts of wartime command in Europe, the Mediterranean, and the Middle East focused on the provision of one supreme allied commander for the whole region with several subordinate commanders in chief for the Mediterranean and Middle East. With the development of the North Atlantic Treaty and the end of the Berlin blockade in May 1949, the emphasis in command organization shifted from a concept needed for immediate war-fighting (such as command arrangements for Broiler or Doublestar) to one focused on planning for a war in the near future. The problem of finding a compromise between the two poles was expressed by the U.S. Joint Strategic Planning Committee in April 1949: "It would be highly desirable for the closest collaboration to continue between the U.S. Chiefs of Staff and the British Chiefs of Staff on matters concerning worldwide strategy and the higher direction of war. The U.S. Joint Chiefs of Staff concur with the opinions expressed by the British Chiefs of Staff that discussions of the wartime organization by the North Atlantic Pact countries ought to be avoided for the present...."[90]

By May 1949, even this relationship between the JCS and the British Chiefs of Staff was under careful consideration by the Americans. At some point, the JCS recognized that a Second World War–style CCS was incapable of handling the higher direction of war and that it should be replaced with another body, primarily because of the need to include the French. There was still no agreement with the British over certain command relationships for Doublestar. The primary points of contention were still the role of the WUCoS, command in the Atlantic, and the authority of commanders in chief under the supreme commander. Even Doublestar as a strategic concept was now outdated. Regarding the CCS, U.S. planners noted: "It is by no means beyond the realm of possibility that continuation of the present Combined Chiefs of Staff concept (whether on a sub rosa or 'above the board' basis) would so weaken the mutually cooperative effort of the nations [of NATO].... Adherence to a concept which would appear to other nations as the formation of a U.S.–UK power block might destroy any hope of achieving the maximum effort of the remaining countries of Western Europe...."[91] As far as the bilateral special relationship went: "It is important to emphasize that the United Kingdom Chiefs of Staff no longer represents the British Commonwealth. As such, the resources controlled by them would be limited to those in the UK, which, in the long range view, may be even less than those controlled by France...."[92]

However, the JCS enthusiastically embraced the Canadian regional group concept and incorporated it into its proposals as well. In line with the British tenet that existing organizations should be used when available, the U.S. view on peacetime planning for NATO placed five regional planning groups under the overall direction of a North Atlantic Military Advisory Council (see figs. 2.18 and 2.19). The regional groupings included a Canadian–U.S. Regional Planning Group (CUSRPG), with the existing MCC as an executive body; a North Atlantic Ocean Regional Planning Group (NAORPG), with the U.S. CinCLANT and its British equivalent as executive bodies; the Western Union Chiefs of Staff; a Norway-Denmark Regional Planning Group (later called the Northern Europe Regional Planning Group); and a Mediterranean Regional Planning Group. (The regional planning groups will be discussed in more detail in chapter 3.) The British Chiefs of Staff concurred with this scheme

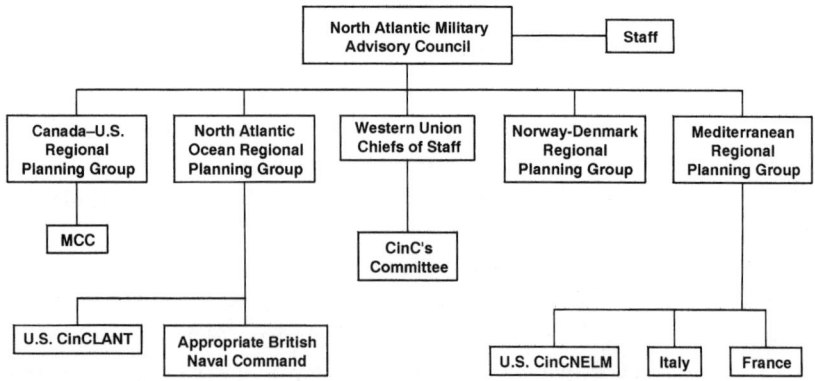

Fig. 2.18. U.S. plan for a peacetime organization for planning under NATO

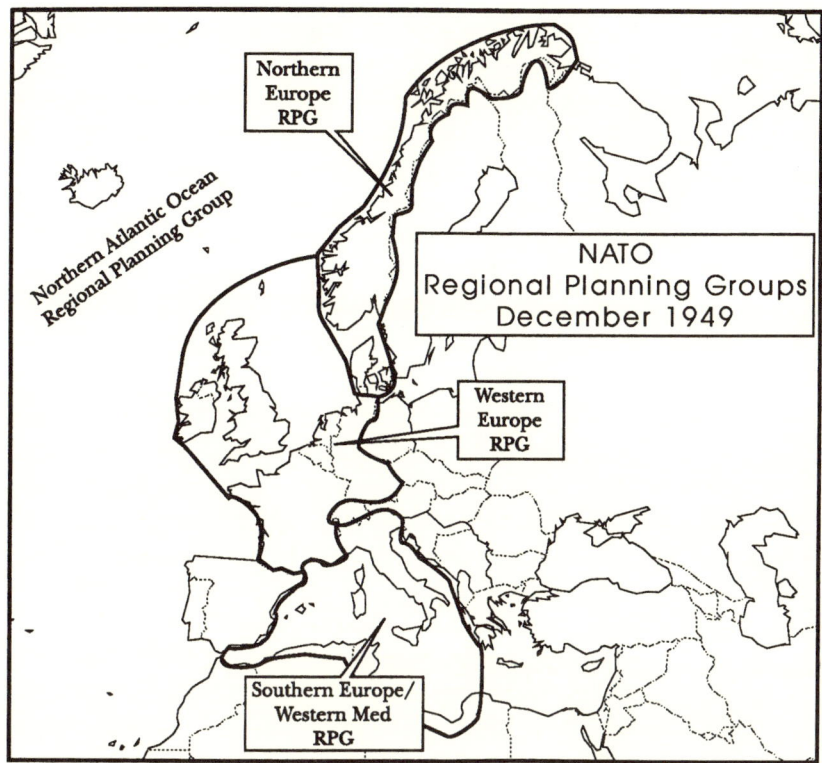

Fig. 2.19.

but still fought a rearguard action to retain bilateral U.S.–British control at some point.[93]

It was quite evident to the JSPC and the British JPS that the implementation of NATO's political organization would alter how a war would be run by its members. Doublestar/Speedway/Bullmoose was geared toward an immediate conflict, and its higher direction was firmly in the hands of a U.S.–British CCS. With the decreased tension after the end of the Berlin blockade, the joint planners noted that "it is highly probable that the [military] command arrangements will require considerable modification as a result of a new change in concept in emergency plans . . . ," and that a study of new command arrangements in time of war should wait until NATO was finalized and a new strategic concept agreed upon.[94] Although NATO's organization was not finalized until December 1949, the JSPC and JPS settled on a virtually identical organization at the end of August 1949 (see fig. 2.20). Both the British and the Americans agreed that discussions of military command organization below the level of the regional planning groups would be deferred to a later date.[95]

One particular impasse that existed between U.S. and British planners was the place of the NATO organization and regional planning in the gestalt of global conflict. After the concept of NATO organization had been agreed to by Britain and the United States, the CCS concept was put to rest. Going back on a previous decision, the JCS indicated to the British that some form of military relationship should continue and that the British Joint Staff Mission (Washington) should continue to be the contact point: "[The] North Atlantic Treaty is a pact arrived at for defensive purposes and, under its terms will not concern itself with a war projected beyond its immediate locale. Planning for a global war which may be

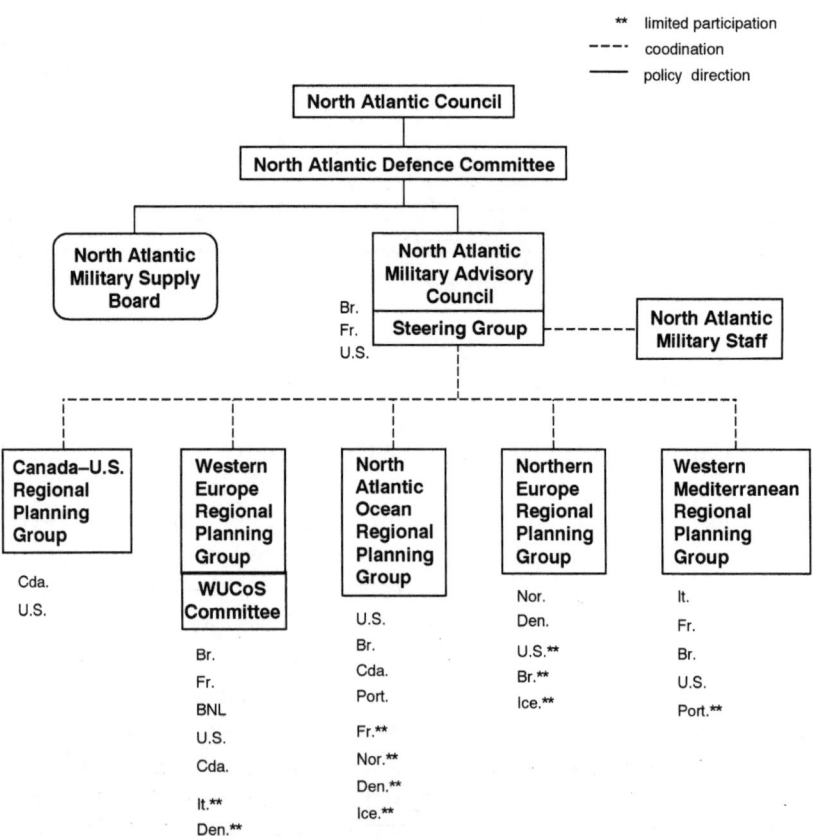

Fig. 2.20. U.S.–British agreement on NATO organization, 18 August 1949

thrust upon the Western powers has been undertaken by ourselves and the British and must be pursued."[96]

The British suggested that some mechanism was still necessary to make joint U.S.–British worldviews known to NATO. This mechanism was initially called the steering group by the Americans who envisioned it to be a device to propel policy; the British view was that such an organization should coordinate policy instead. Eventually, an accord was reached. The body would be known as the Standing Group (SG), it would include representatives from Great Britain, the United States, and France. Its role would be to coordinate planning between the regional planning groups, set the strategic priorities among the members, and prepare an overall strategic concept for approval by the NATO Defence Committee.[97]

NATO's formal organization was established during the first session of the North Atlantic Council (NAC) on 17 September 1949 when the Working Group submitted its final recommendations (see fig. 2.21). The highest political level of responsibility within NATO was originally the North Atlantic Council, which consisted of the foreign ministers (or their representatives) from the member nations. There were two committees under the NAC, the Defence Financial and Economic Committee and the Defence Committee; only the latter concerns us here. The Defence Committee consisted of the defense ministers (or their representatives) from the member nations and was responsible for recommending overall military policy to the NAC for debate and adoption. Under this was the Military Committee, which included representatives from the chiefs of staff of member nations; its job was to advise the Defence Committee on military matters and to give overall policy direction to the Standing Group. The Standing Group, made up of French, U.S., and British representatives, in turn provided guidance and coordination to the regional planning groups.[98]

The recommendations for the regional planning groups were based on the Foulkes proposal and its U.S. and British variants. The provisions adopted gave members who were not part of particular RPGs the ability to participate in them as necessary. The groups were organized geographically and consisted of the Western European RPG, the North Atlantic Ocean RPG, the Canadian–U.S. RPG, the Northern Europe RPG, and the Southern Europe/Western Mediterranean RPG. Each was responsible for developing joint defense plans for its area as well as providing advice to the SG in order to resolve differences between the RPGs.[99]

In summary, the development of post–Second World War command orga-

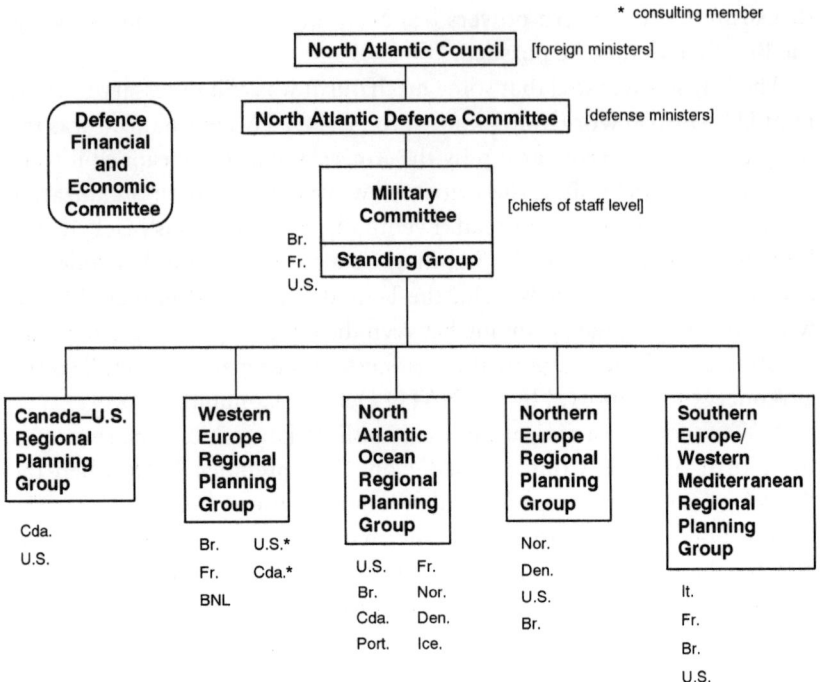

Fig. 2.21. North Atlantic Treaty Organization, December 1949

nization was the consequence of several factors. The need to create a detailed joint U.S.–British strategic concept (Broiler/Doublequick) to defend against the Soviet Union in response to a comprehensive threat estimate (Pincher) produced a formal command organization for implementation in the event of such an immediate war. This organization was based on World War II experiences and arrangements. Simultaneously, a European command organization for the defense of Western Europe, the Western Union Chiefs of Staff, was created independent of U.S.–British arrangements. Its structure was similar to that of SHAEF in the Second World War. With the shift in U.S. political orientation toward Europe during the Berlin blockade, a new joint U.S., British, and Canadian strategic concept, Doublestar/Speedway/Bullmoose, was developed from Broiler/Doublequick; this concept was more comprehensive and attempted to include the Western Union Defense Organization in its command arrangements.

With the end of the Berlin blockade and the establishment of NATO in 1949, the planners' emphasis shifted from an immediate war to a conflict that was projected to occur some years in the future. This was reflected in

NATO's decision in 1949 to create regional planning groups and to formalize an organization for the higher direction of war rather then developing full-fledged NATO military commands for detailed planning purposes. Events, however, would conspire against this outlook in 1950.

While the NATO organization was being finalized, a modified U.S. Air Force B-29 belonging to the 375th Very Long Range Air Weather Reconnaissance Squadron left Eielson Air Force Base in Alaska to carry out an air sampling mission over the Pacific on 3 September 1949. Near the Kamchatka Peninsula, its crew obtained the first indications that the Soviet Union had tested an atomic device on 29 August 1949; U.S. Navy and RAF units produced confirmatory data. The U.S. monopoly on the atomic bomb had been broken.[100] A new strategic concept would be needed—and with it, a new command organization.

3 ➤ Crusade in Europe Revisited and the Third Battle of the Atlantic

SACEUR and SACLANT, 1949–1951

The policy of Lacedaemon was not to exact tribute from her allies, but merely to secure their subservience to her interests by establishing oligarchies among them; Athens, on the contrary, had by degrees deprived hers of their ships, and imposed instead contributions in money on all . . . both found their resources for this war separately to exceed the sum of their strength when the alliance flourished intact. . . .
   —Thucydides, *The Peloponnesian War*

Vigilia Pretium Libertatis (Vigilance is the price of liberty).
   —motto of SACEUR

The brevity of the respite in tension between the end of the Berlin blockade and the explosion of the first Soviet atomic bomb was not lost on the West in early 1950. The Americans were particularly incensed by the loss of China to Maoist forces in late 1949, but there was little that could be done; continued revelations of Soviet spying and subversion in North America added another discordant note. The British were preoccupied with a burgeoning insurgency in Malaya, while French Indochina plunged into open warfare. Attention was, therefore, focused elsewhere as the level of tension in Europe plateaued; the pressure on Greece and Turkey had lessened by 1950, and only sporadic harassment occurred in the Berlin sector.

The fact that tension had plateaued did not alter the viewpoint from which the West watched possible Soviet actions in Western Europe. Soviet military forces still remained mobilized at near wartime levels five years after the Second World

War. Still, NATO planning in early 1950 revolved around the idea that a war would not occur before 1954.

This chapter examines not only the interim NATO peacetime planning organizations established in 1949 but also the Anglo-American strategic concept for war from 1950 to 1952 and the resulting bilateral discussions on possible wartime command organizations in the Atlantic up until the Chinese intervention in Korea in November 1950. In addition, the decision to overhaul NATO's machinery for the higher direction of war in the face of the Korean conflict receives attention. Finally, the creation of the first NATO commands, SACEUR for Europe and SACLANT for the Atlantic Ocean, serves as the focus of the last half of this chapter. The establishment of other NATO commands that provided naval support to SACEUR and SACLANT will be the subject of the next chapter.

Strategic Concepts

Although NATO's organization in late 1949 was geared toward long-term defense, there was still a need to plan for a war that might occur within the 1950–51 time frame. Such planning was already quite advanced between Britain and the United States, and it needed modification to accommodate the new NATO dimension. Both long- and short-term planning concepts provided input for the creation of NATO command organizations from 1950 to 1952.

The debate over a new Anglo-American strategic concept that would include the NATO area commenced at a September–October 1949 meeting of the U.S. and British Chiefs of Staff. Doublestar/Speedway/Bullmoose, the Anglo-American-Canadian concept for war in 1948, had served its purpose and would soon be overtaken by both technological and political events. The United States already had an Emergency War Plan on hand. This was Plan Offtackle, which relied heavily on Doublestar and another U.S. EWP, Trojan; Offtackle appears to have been the basis for these talks. When the Offtackle concept was laid out in September 1949, the British had scathing criticism. The Joint Planning Staff constantly referred to Offtackle as "not militarily sound" because it "does not deploy forces to the best advantage to achieve the political object of preventing Western Europe from being overrun."[1] The JPS also decried the inordinate percentage of U.S. strategic bombers used to pummel the USSR and recommended changes to allow for their use in slowing down the Soviet advance on the Middle East and retaining the SLOC through the Mediterranean. The British were rather self-congratulatory for having "shook the faith of the U.S. planners in their concept," and they demanded some changes to it. These changes were debated and implemented by the JSPC and the JPS.[2] The agreed-upon version of the Emergency War Plan was called Crosspiece by the Americans and Galloper by the British.[3]

The Crosspiece/Galloper concept of Soviet operations was an extrapolation of Pincher, Broiler/Doublequick, and Doublestar/Speedway/Bullmoose and remained the dominant strategic concept from 1950 to 1952. This concept in its NATO incarnation was called MC 14. It anticipated that the Soviets' land campaign against Western Europe was to be followed by an air campaign against Britain. Simultaneous thrusts into Turkey, Greece, and Iran were projected. Limited land operations supported by internal subversion were to be aimed at Japan, Korea, Alaska, and the North American continent. As in previous strategic concepts, a heavy Soviet sea and air offensive against SLOCs to and from North America was predicted. Crosspiece/Galloper also assumed that Scandinavia would be quickly overrun.[4] Crosspiece/Galloper did not contain a detailed breakdown of Soviet forces but assumed that the Soviets possessed the capacity to conduct all of these operations.[5] However, actual Soviet capabilities during the period covered by Crosspiece/Galloper were somewhat different from those discussed in Doublestar/Speedway/Bullmoose in that they were in some ways more lethal.

The most important change was the development of a Soviet strategic air force. The Soviets had copied B-29 aircraft that had been impounded and their crews interrogated during World War II. The reverse-engineered version was called the TU-4. The prototype first flew in 1947, and by 1953 between 1,000 and 1,500 had been produced. With a range of 3,450 nautical miles, the TU-4 could not reach North America from the Soviet Union unless the mission was one way. However, the TU-4 could target any place in Eurasia, including Japan and Britain, with conventional or atomic explosives. Galloper planners estimated that 150 to 300 TU-4s could be directed against Britain, augmented by conventionally armed surface-to-surface missiles, within D+60 days. At the time, Crosspiece/Galloper planners credited the Soviets with having between ten and thirty Nagasaki-size atomic bombs. If the TU-4 was forward-based in Iceland, Greenland, or the Aleutians, significant strikes would be possible against North America. In addition, approximately 20 percent of the TU-4 force was tasked to Soviet naval aviation; if based in Norway, these planes posed a threat to SLOCs in the North Atlantic.[6]

Combined with a long-range air threat, allied estimates of the Soviet submarine threat confirmed previous assertions that the Soviets had the ability to seriously interfere with SLOCs to Europe. According to the Combined Canadian–British–U.S. Working Group on Antisubmarine Doctrine in 1950, "Considerable and effective forces can be brought to bear against Allied shipping within 1000 miles of the west coast of Europe and North Africa, assuming Soviet submarines operate from west European and North Sea bases. . . ."[7] The maximum number of Soviet submarines available for operations totaled 281, of which 25 were German Type XXI equivalents (see appendix 1)—a threat that was considered "imposing but not formidable."[8]

Allied estimates of Soviet land, airborne/airmobile, and naval surface forces in 1950–51 were not significantly different from Broiler/Doublequick's and need not be reviewed here. However, it should be noted that the Soviet capability to conduct ground support and air superiority operations was enhanced by the deployment of jet aircraft in 1950. Aircraft such as the MiG-15, MiG-17, and IL-28 came as a surprise to the West and would have been a definite force multiplier in the early stages of a European conflict in 1950–52.[9]

Notwithstanding technological developments, Crosspiece/Galloper differed significantly from Doublestar/Speedway/Bullmoose in its concept of allied operations (see fig. 3.1). Although its objectives and basic undertakings were the same as those of previous plans, Crosspiece/Galloper planned for the defense of the Rhine River–Italian Alps line in Europe and made active provisions to impede the Soviet advance. The planners realized, however, that this was a best-case situation because allied ground force levels in Europe had not really changed since 1948. Thus, they provided two alternatives, neither of which embraced an immediate evacuation. A fighting withdrawal was to be staged and a substantial bridgehead area in Western Europe held to facilitate later offensive action. If these conditions could not be met, a base area in North Africa would be developed from which an offensive could be mounted.[10]

British and U.S. planners diverged on one important issue: the role and importance of the Middle East and the Cairo-Suez base area. The British considered this area to be a priority on par with the defense of Britain itself because of that nation's historical commitments to the region and dependence on Middle East petroleum resources. The United States, on the other hand, gave it a lower priority, after the Western Hemisphere and Britain. Several factors appear to explain the U.S. divergence. First, to conduct the strategic bombing campaign the Strategic Air Command had acquired the intercontinental B-36 bomber and was in the process of developing in-flight refueling for its shorter-range B-29s and B-50s. This

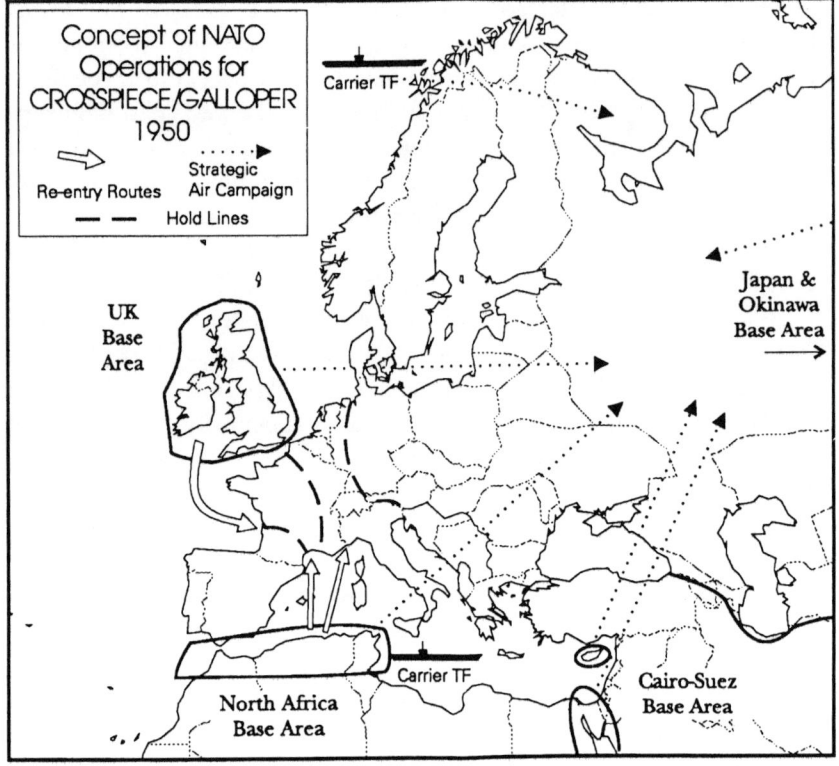

Fig. 3.1.

was in contrast to the conventionally equipped British Lincoln strategic bombers, which did not have long range or an in-flight refueling capability and required forward basing in Cyprus or the Cairo-Suez area. The United States preferred North Africa as a base area for the strategic air campaign because of its proximity to Western Europe, since for political reasons the land counteroffensive against the Soviet Union had to be directed through Western Europe instead of the Middle East. It was also a more defensible area.[11]

In addition, the projected Soviet rate of advance through Turkey and northern Iran was slower than in earlier plans, possibly after more careful consideration of terrain factors; U.S. planners felt that the Middle East would have to be a "British show" because U.S. ground forces would not be available for deployment there for some time. In effect, the Middle East was not as critical as it had been in previous strategic concepts, and the

Soviet capability to conduct operations there was less than originally believed.[12]

The need to retain Britain as an ally and as a base area for a return to the continent led U.S. planners to consider in more detail the role of the Mediterranean, and attention was refocused here instead of the Middle East. The SLOC running through the Mediterranean was one of several considered to be vital. Crosspiece/Galloper advocated limited offensive action in the early stages to prevent Sicily, Sardinia, and Crete from falling to Soviet airborne forces and being used as air bases by long-range aircraft.[13]

The role of naval forces was given more prominent treatment in Crosspiece/Galloper. Naval forces were expected to contribute to all aspects of the strategic concept, including the strategic air campaign: "Carrier forces will supplement and support the strategic air offensive to the extent of their capabilities and as available. . . ."[14] This was a definite departure from earlier plans and seems to have reflected the projected ability of the U.S. Navy to conduct sustained atomic operations from aircraft carriers with the P2VC Neptune interim carrier-based bomber and the AJ-1 and AJ-2 Savage aircraft.[15]

As could be expected, traditional SLOC protection operations predominated Crosspiece/Galloper naval planning (see fig. 3.2). Several vital SLOCs were established in the plan: North America to Britain, Gibraltar, South America, South Africa, and Japan; Britain to Gibraltar and Scandinavia; and Gibraltar to Suez. France was to be responsible for SLOCs between France and North Africa, while Britain would handle east-west SLOCs in the Mediterranean with the support of U.S. carrier task forces from the Sixth Task Fleet. In the European theater, the assumption was that the Soviets would attempt to cut the SLOC to Britain using a combination of long-range airpower, submarine operations in the Western Approaches, and a prodigious quantity of submarine and aerial mines. Some small-scale surface raiding and fast attack craft operations were also expected.[16]

It is interesting to note that the Crosspiece/Galloper planners thought that mines were as much of a threat as submarines to SLOCs leading to Britain. Apparently they believed that the Royal Navy could handle any naval threat but lacked mine countermeasures vessels.[17] Inexplicably, the Galloper estimate of Soviet submarine capabilities diverged from joint Anglo-American-Canadian discussions on antisubmarine warfare by suggesting that "available information tends to show that the Soviets have not so far developed a large number of modern high speed submarines nor

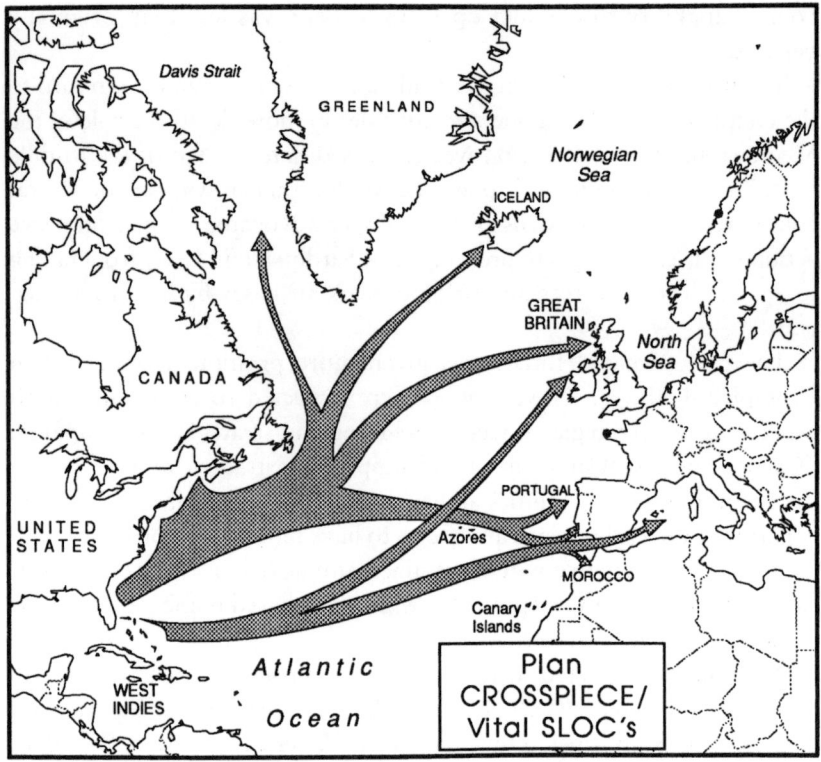

Fig. 3.2.

is their operational efficiency likely to be of a high standard comparable with that of the Germans in the last war. . . ."[18] This difference can probably be credited to conflicting national intelligence estimates.

As with previous U.S.–British intercourse on strategic thinking, command organization for Crosspiece/Galloper became a major point of contention. As the British JPS noted: "No emergency plan can be completed unless it includes intended command arrangements; it is particularly desirable to decide these in slow time in peace since they would be very difficult to resolve quickly in war. . . ."[19]

Since Crosspiece/Galloper contained an increased emphasis on naval operations in support of the land battle, attention focused again on command in the Atlantic. Reaction to the British proposal for the Doublestar/Speedway/Bullmoose command organization in the Atlantic (see figs. 2.14 and 2.15) formed the basis of an American counterproposal made while the Crosspiece/Galloper discussions were ongoing. The important features of the British proposal included relegating strategic direction (not control) of the Atlantic to the U.S. Chief of Naval Operations with command delegated to a British CinC North Atlantic and a U.S. CinC Central/South Atlantic, both of which would have integrated staffs. In the British view, the Atlantic should be divided at 42° north latitude and command should be split there.

The U.S. view of the British proposal was articulated by CinCLANT, Adm. W. H. P. "Spike" Blandy, through Adm. Louis Denfield, the CNO.[20] The most striking thing about the internal reaction was its rather frank assessment of the British position: "The proposed British command organization is based upon political aspects and an attempt to retain British prestige and not upon the fundamental military or strategic principles involved.... I further recommend it be indicated to the British in definitive terms that except for minor adjustments the U.S. proposal is final and that the British naval organization in the Atlantic necessarily will have to conform thereto...."[21]

Furthermore, Blandy rejected the notion of one strategic director for the Atlantic and favored one overall commander. The actual U.S. counterproposal contained softer language and emphasized the need for one overall ASW commander instead of a single commanding authority for the whole area. Second World War experience, according to Denfield, "demonstrated the need for continuity of action against the enemy regardless of area boundaries. It is essential that antisubmarine operations continue to follow the same pattern in the future...."[22] In accordance with the developing Crosspiece/Galloper concept, which emphasized the development of a base area in North Africa, U.S. convoys on their way to that base area were to be routed much further south than they had been during World War II. The better weather, improved sonar conditions, and distance from enemy bases were appealing to the U.S. Navy.[23]

The American planners also sought to avoid the wartime COMNAVNAW controversy. In their view, the Atlantic was to be commanded by a theater commander in chief responsible to a body similar to the CCS or Standing Group. Tasks would include the coordination of convoy routes and command over offensive ASW force deployments. This position was to be held by a U.S. Navy officer with an integrated staff. The Atlantic would then have two area commanders, one for the Western Atlantic who would be American and one for the Eastern Atlantic who would be British (see figs. 3.3 and 3.4). Each of these would have an integrated staff. In the U.S. view, operational control over all naval forces (including all offensive task forces and submarines) was to be delegated by the allied Atlantic CinC to

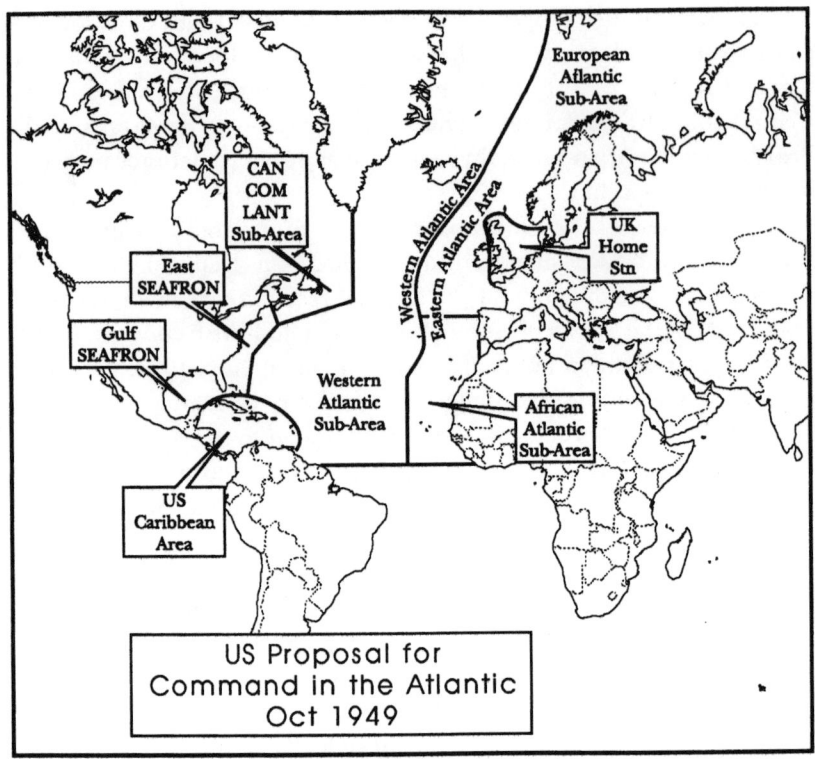

Fig. 3.3.

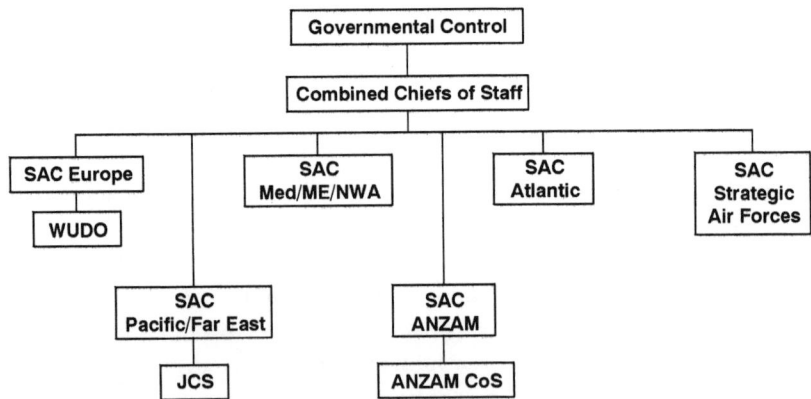

Fig. 3.4. Proposed U.S. command organization for the Atlantic, October 1949

the area commanders. Under the area commanders there were to be several sub-area commanders. The U.S. positions would be Commander, Western Atlantic Sub-area; Commander, African Atlantic Sub-area; and Commander, Eastern Sea Frontier. The British would have Commander, European Atlantic Sub-area, and the Canadians were to supply Commander, Canadian Atlantic Sub-area. Island bases such as the Azores and Iceland were to be responsible to their area commanders. For air cover each sub-area was to have one air commander, subordinated to the sub-area commander.[24]

There were many advantages to the U.S. proposal. Convoys remaining in a particular sub-area for the duration of their run would remain under the command of that sub-area. There was only one CHOP in the Atlantic theater, thus simplifying command and control. National inshore waters remained under the command of their own staffs, and boundaries would not affect operations.[25]

The British, however, clung steadfastly to the Doublestar/Speedway/Bullmoose view of command organization in the Atlantic, pointing out that the problems of national prestige and the complexities of coordinating air operations were too substantial. In fact, the British attempted to redirect attention toward organization in the Mediterranean instead of going head-to-head with the Americans over the Atlantic at this point; and as a result, the impasse was not resolved.[26] A detailed examination of Mediterranean command arrangements will be deferred to chapter 5.

Interim NATO Command Arrangements

The bilateral U.S.–British discussions on command organization were overtaken by events yet again. The North Atlantic Defence Committee determined that, after the establishment of NATO's organization in September 1949, the alliance required a long-term strategic concept for the defense of the North Atlantic area. The Military Committee was then ordered to prepare a strategic concept that would be valid from 1953 to 1955. The Medium Term Defence Plan (MTDP) was essentially a schedule of force requirements that member nations were to use as a guide in determining their national military establishments from 1950 to 1955. War was considered likely around 1954; the regional planning groups were ordered by the Military Committee to develop detailed plans to act as templates for scheduling defense mobilization in the event of a war with the Soviet Union between 1953 and 1955. The general guidance for the MTDP was approved on 28 March 1950, and the RPGs set out to create their force requirements.[27]

At the same time, bilateral U.S.–British communication on war planning debated the position of their strategy vis-à-vis NATO strategy. In a memo to the JCS the Chief of Naval Operations, Adm. Forrest Sherman, stressed the need to firmly establish such a relationship. From the U.S. point of view, the position of NATO planning relative to U.S.–British planning was analogous to the place of RPGs in the context of the overall NATO MTDP—that is, NATO planning was seen as a subset of U.S.–British planning. The British were in full agreement with this and consistently emphasized that NATO was not "a world wide planning agency."[28] How this was transmitted to the Military Committee is not clear. Although the United States and Britain came to an understanding on this topic, the conciliation did not extend to command organization discussions.

The NATO area had been loosely established as the territory of North American or European NATO members (Canada, the United States, Great Britain, Norway, Denmark, the Netherlands, Luxembourg, Belgium, France, Italy, and Portugal), including island dependencies in the Atlantic and the Mediterranean, French North Africa, occupation forces in Germany, and the Atlantic Ocean north of the Tropic of Cancer.[29] Naturally, the issue of colonies and ex-colonies caused some problems. The defense of such territories lay outside the purview of NATO unless they were located in the NATO area. Although the west coast of North America was technically in the NATO area, arrangements for its defense rested in bilateral Canadian–U.S. planning that was linked to NATO.

The importance of RPGs in the development of command organization is considerable. They provided the operational and organizational basis for the NATO commands that would be established from 1951 to 1953. It should be kept in mind that in late 1949 and early 1950, the efforts of the RPGs were directed primarily toward satisfying the MTDP requirements. In this connection it will be useful to examine the status of the RPGs vis-à-vis planning and organization.

The Western European Regional Planning Group (WERPG) had the most straightforward job. Utilizing the existing WUDO framework, the WERPG focused on the land and air battle for the central region while the Northern Europe Regional Planning Group (NERPG) similarly looked at the defense of Norway and Denmark. The division of responsibility between these two RPGs would complicate the development of SACEUR's AFNORTH command in 1950 and affect the establishment of the Channel Command in 1952. The Western Mediterranean/Southern Europe RPG prepared for the land and air defense of Italy and Greece.[30]

The Canada–U.S. Regional Planning Group (CUSRPG) was among the least muddled of NATO's RPGs. The experience gained through the Permanent Joint Board on Defense (PJBD) boded well for both parties as they sought to reconcile the CUSRPG with the PJBD precedent. There were some minor problems, however. In the U.S. view, the Joint Canadian–U.S. Military Coordinating Committee (MCC) that had been established in 1946 should simply adopt the title of Canada–U.S. Regional Planning Group. The Canadian viewpoint appears to have been much more Machiavellian: the establishment of CUSRPG at the international level within the NATO framework was thought by the Canadian Chiefs of Staff Committee to provide more direct access to the U.S. JCS in matters relating to the defense of North America than would a circuitous route that involved other Canadian ministries. Surprisingly, the United States acceded to the Canadian view. The U.S. members of the MCC were double-hatted as CUSRPG representatives for all intents and purposes. Strangely, the MCC was not required to share information with the CUSRPG even though some members served on both committees. It is possible that both parties were concerned that such a "special relationship" could become the object of jealousy among other NATO members and thus a point of contention. The Americans did not want to duplicate such a relationship with all of their real and potential allies because it would be cumbersome.[31]

Located in Washington, the CUSRPG was tasked to "develop and recommend to the Military Committee through the Standing Group plans for the defense of the Canada–U.S. region" and to "cooperate with the other Regional Planning Groups . . . [to] ensure harmony among the various regional plans."[32] Its primary task appears to have been reconciling updated versions of the Joint Canadian–U.S. Basic Security Plan with the NATO strategic concept.[33]

In effect, the JCS and the Canadian Chiefs of Staff Committee provided guidance to a joint regional planning committee that had as its mandate the establishment of military requirements and the preparation of plans for the defense of Canada and the United States. The CUSRPG was, essentially, a "front organization" to shield the MCC from other NATO members while allowing it to coordinate with the North Atlantic Ocean Regional Planning Group. It also had the added advantage of offering more and better access by the Canadian Chiefs of Staff to their American counterparts in planning matters and allowing the defense of North America to continue under NATO auspices.[34]

Additionally, the CUSRPG allowed the United States to share intelligence information affecting the defense of North America with Canada through a direct link between the JCS and the Canadian Chiefs of Staff. Keeping in mind the necessity of North America remaining a secure industrial and mobilization base for NATO, it is not surprising that the scenario of a Soviet outpost in Alaska providing a base for atomic-armed TU-4 aircraft or V-2 type missiles had a direct impact on NATO planning, pointing to the need for CUSRPG. On the Atlantic side, no real boundary was ever set between the CUSRPG and the North Atlantic Regional Planning Group (NAORPG), although for planning purposes Canadian coastal waters were considered to be part of the CUSRPG area.[35]

NAORPG, however, inherited the problem of preparing for a future battle of the Atlantic and all the international and historical baggage that this task entailed. It was convened on 31 October 1949 and set out developing a Short Term Defence Plan (similar to the Anglo-American emergency defense plans) as well as contributing to the overall Medium Term Defence Plan. Since NAORPG was essentially the predecessor to the SACLANT command, a brief foray into NAORPG's status in 1950 will be useful. Notably, the first U.S. representative to the planning group was Adm. Lynde McCormick, who would become the first Supreme Allied Commander, Atlantic in 1952.[36]

The NAORPG Short Term Plan's estimate of the threat was based conceptually on Crosspiece/Galloper, and the group was given its own copy of this plan in order to retain continuity in strategy while the Short Term Plan was being developed. The strategic concept used for NAORPG was rooted firmly in NATO's principles of collective defense, the coordination of the military resources of all members, and combined planning, training, intelligence exchanges, research, and infrastructure development. As with earlier war plans, the United States, Canada, and Britain were tasked to provide SLOC defense.[37]

The main problem that developed during the creation of the NAORPG Short Term Plan was the issue of naval control of shipping outside of NAORPG's area of responsibility. How were convoy protection operations to be conducted between the NATO area and other areas of national responsibility? The British and the Americans came to a consensus that the NAORPG was not meant to exercise worldwide naval control of shipping; however, NAORPG would coordinate directly with national NCS organizations for operations south of the Tropic of Cancer. The use of national infrastructure outside the NATO area would result from bilateral discussions. The Short Term Plan was finalized in February 1950 as NAORPG Defense Plan 1-50, and NAORPG set out to determine force requirements for both that plan and the MTDP even though a proper command organization was not in place.³⁸

It was clear to those involved that determination of NAORPG's force structure for the Short Term Plan was to be based on the economic capability of the members to provide forces rather than the particular threat to the NAORPG area. However, the MTDP was prepared at the Standing Group and Military Committee level without regard to any such limitations and reflected a lack of coordination among the RPGs on the issue of medium-term planning. As a result, the Standing Group was saddled with the job of coordinating all of these efforts and had to delay development of the MTDP.³⁹

NAORPG planning progressed within the MTDP, unlike that of other RPGs. An additional problem in the creation of the short-term plan, however, was the complete lack of any formalized command organization for the RPGs. This was noted by a number of American participants, and they recommended that steps be taken to fill this gap at the earliest possible opportunity.⁴⁰

Wartime command organization thus became the focus of more U.S.–British discussions. At a meeting in London in March 1950 the First Sea Lord, Lord Fraser of North Cape, and the U.S. CNO, Adm. Forrest Sherman, were unable to come to an agreement over a U.S.–British general command plan; it was clear to the participants that the complexity of any command arrangements in the North Atlantic precluded any easy solution.⁴¹ The land and air defense of Western Europe, at the very least, could utilize the World War II–based WUDO command organization if war broke out, but NAORPG had no such precedent. Thus, the development of a command plan for NAORPG was stalled. As Admiral Blandy noted, the international prestige of the U.S.–British leadership of NATO was on the line: "If the Canadians or the French or the Dutch should inquire about progress, it could force the issue. If nothing is done at all before the next Chief of Staff meeting, and we produce a Short Term Plan still without touching the command plan, some very embarrassing questions could be asked and the U.S. as chairman and the British would certainly have to come down with some sort of explanation."⁴² Analyzing the situation from a more pragmatic stance, the British concluded that "NATO, with its multiplicity of regions and committees, although adequate for planning purposes in peacetime having regard for their need for safeguarding national sovereignties which no nation would abrogate except under the impact of war, would be quite unworkable in war...."⁴³

Throughout May 1950, NAORPG labored to produce a wartime command organization. The only concrete proposal emanated from the Americans, who provided a variant of their earlier position in the bilateral U.S.–British talks of 1949. Stressing the need for continuity of action necessary for an offensive ASW campaign, the Americans once again pushed for one overall commander for the Atlantic, this time conceding the requirement for an integrated staff at all levels. In substance, however, the British proposal in May 1950 did not differ significantly from the U.S. proposal tabled in the October 1949 discussions over Crosspiece/Galloper's command organization. The physical division of the Atlantic and the nationalities of the commanders did not change significantly.[44] Events in the second half of 1950 would intervene, and these issues would be superceded by the decision to establish formal NATO commands.

THE CREATION OF SACEUR

While discussions over command in the Atlantic continued, North Korean troops crossed the 38th parallel on 25 June 1950 and initiated the Korean War. The effects of this event on the development of NATO command organization and planning were considerable and fell into two phases. In the first, which lasted from June to October 1950, there was increased interest in grafting a hastily developed wartime command organization onto the existing RPGs' Short Term Plan organizations. However, the Chinese escalated the situation by invading Korea and attacking UN troops in November 1950. In this second phase, formal NATO military command organizations were established throughout 1951–52. These steps were fueled by the legitimate fear within NATO that the Korean situation was a feint to distract the Western nations from a Soviet invasion of Western Europe. Notwithstanding the serious situation in Korea, NATO was the strategic priority.[45]

The debate over command organization in the second half of 1950 not only touched on the continuing drama over the higher direction of war but highlighted the problem of command in the Atlantic in a more urgent fashion. As Britain's First Sea Lord, Lord Fraser of North Cape, stated in August 1950, "The time has come when we must face this difficult problem of high command for a global war. The international situation is tense, but except for Western Union, no agreement exists among the Allies for wartime command or control of any theater. . . ."[46] In fact, NATO was examining several options for the higher direction of a coalition war and had presented these options to the U.S. JSPC and the British JPS. The principles that such an organization had to live by to be acceptable to NATO included the ability to move quickly from a peacetime to a wartime posture and the recognition that command organization should undergo continuous review.[47]

During preliminary discussions aimed at a possible revision of the Crosspiece/Galloper strategic concept, the British and the Americans both recommended that the RPGs be phased out and replaced with military command organizations that would have operational control over forces assigned to them in wartime as well as continuing the planning functions already established by the RPGs.[48] The political aspects of the RPGs would be assumed by the North Atlantic Defence Committee. However, the JSPC noted that "not all of the functions now assigned to the European regional planning groups can appropriately be transferred to the commanders under the Standing Group. These functions of the present regional planning groups not suitable for transfer to commanders under the Standing Group . . . should be assumed by the Standing Group. . . ."[49] As a result, the JSPC suggested that the Northern European Regional Planning Group, Western European Planning Group, Western Mediterranean Regional Planning Group, and WUDO be replaced with an integrated command.

The tentative but agreed-upon October 1950 NATO command organization for war followed figure 3.5. The resemblance to the Doublestar/Speedway/Bullmoose command organization is evident. The authority for the

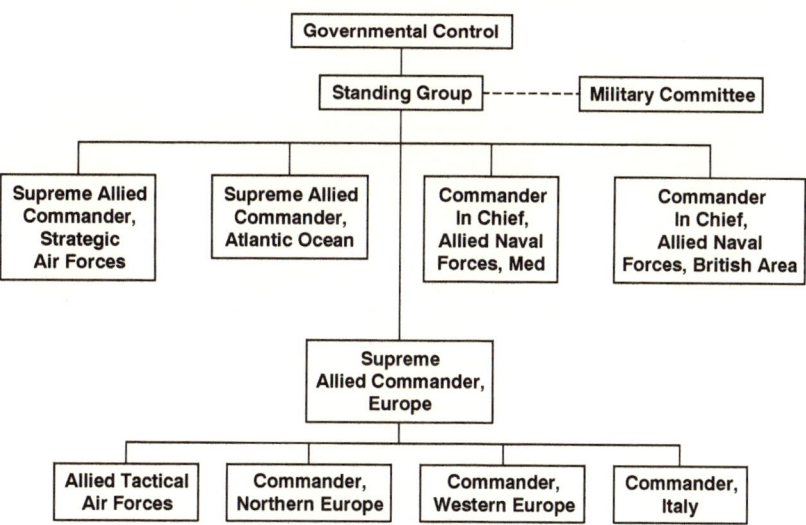

Fig. 3.5. Tentative NATO command organization for war, October 1950

higher direction of war was embodied in the Standing Group, with the national commands providing the operating forces. The supreme commands for this tentative organization included a Supreme Allied Commander, Strategic Air Forces; a Supreme Allied Commander, Atlantic; a Supreme Allied Commander, Europe, with four subordinate commands; a Commander in Chief, Allied Naval Forces, Mediterranean; and a Commander in Chief, Allied Naval Forces, British Area, which appears to be a predecessor to the Channel Command (to be discussed in chapter 4).[50]

As early as the July 1950 meetings, proposals for a global coalition command organization had been put forth. Six alternatives were examined, with the final version resembling the October organization. In all six, the Standing Group was replaced with a British-American-French Combined Chiefs of Staff based on the Second World War model. The world was divided into six supreme commands, none necessarily a specific NATO command. These included Europe, Mediterranean/Middle East/Northwest Africa, Atlantic, Pacific/Far East, Australia/New Zealand, and a Strategic Air Command (see fig. 3.6).[51]

The first concept for command in Europe simply divided the continent in two, with a Supreme Allied Commander, North and a Supreme Allied Commander, West. SAC West handled operations in the Mediterranean basin and in Germany-France, while SAC North was responsible for operations in Norway and Denmark. Both commands were tri-service in nature and based on a unified command system. Alternative number two was similar but split the Mediterranean off into a separate Supreme Allied Commander, Italy.[52]

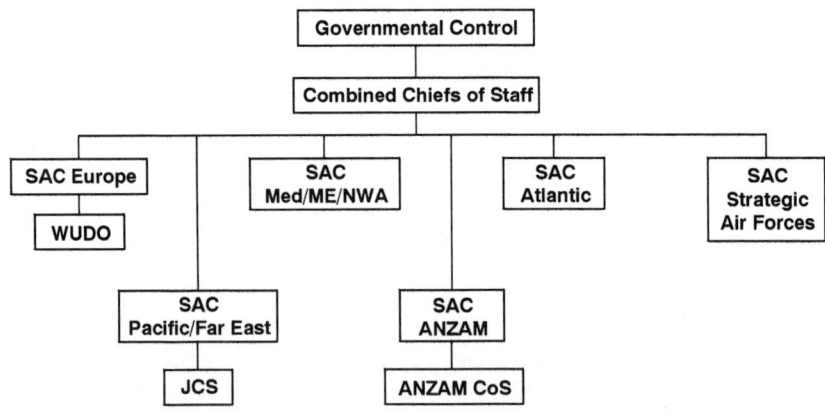

Fig. 3.6. Proposed global coalition command organization, July 1950

These first two alternatives failed to consider in a detailed manner the inclusion of the Middle East. Under the third alternative, SAC Italy was replaced with a Supreme Allied Commander, Northwest Africa/Mediterranean/Middle East. Under this proposal, this SAC NWA/MED/ME had his own land, air, and naval commanders in chief to advise him directly, while operating forces reported to three theater commanders from Northwest Africa, Italy, and the Middle East. Each of these theater commanders in turn had his own air and land commanders in chief plus a Flag Officer, Middle East and an Admiral, Italy to conduct the actual operations—not unlike the British joint staff system. A variant of this proposal had three commanders in chief, one from each service, handling the operations of that service in the entire NWA/MED/ME theater.[53]

Some British planners considered the NWA/MED/ME theater to be too large for one supreme commander to handle, given the distances and the differing political problems in the Middle East. The fifth alternative recommended dividing the areas into a Supreme Allied Commander, Northwest Africa/Mediterranean and a Supreme Allied Commander, Middle East, both on par with a supreme allied commander in Europe (see fig. 3.7). The need for continuity of naval operations throughout the entire region was addressed by creating a Commander in Chief, Navy in the Mediterranean and having him coordinate with a Flag Officer, Levant. A variant of the proposal made a Commander in Chief, Navy subordinate to both supreme commanders; this, of course, had obvious complications.

A temporary consensus was reached in August 1950. The agreed-upon interim command organization for war in Europe had a Combined Chiefs of Staff consisting of the French, British, and Americans (see fig. 3.8) and four supreme commanders: SAC Northern Europe, SAC Western Europe, SAC Mediterranean/Northwestern Africa, and SAC Middle East. The naval command for the Mediterranean and Middle East areas was to be responsible to both SAC MED/NWA and SAC ME. This was done to ensure continuity of operations in the entire area.[54]

The North Atlantic Council (NAC) conducted its fifth session on 15 September 1950 and reaffirmed the concept of forward defense embodied in the Crosspiece/Galloper plans. The NAC also called for the revision of the MTDP and agreed to examine in detail the possibility of setting up NATO military commands.[55] The attraction of the military commands was obvious given the NATO doctrine of collective defense. This resolution was given further impetus by the Chinese intervention in Korea in November 1950. By 18 December 1950, the NAC agreed that "an integrated force should be constituted under the Supreme Command of an

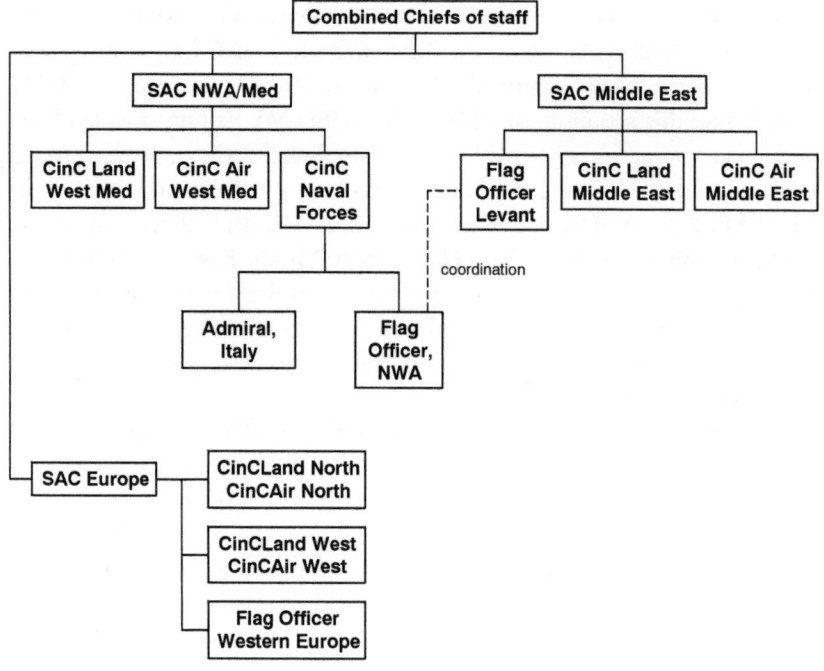

Fig. 3.7. Proposal no. 5, July 1950

American officer," since the preponderance of forces that would eventually be operating in theater were to be American.[56] This first integrated NATO command would be Supreme Allied Commander, Europe (SACEUR) with its own headquarters, Supreme Headquarters, Allied Powers Europe (SHAPE).

With these proposals as background, the events of November 1950 established the need for a permanent command organization in NATO. A communication from the Military Committee to the Defence Committee in December 1950 noted that not only was the existing command organization for the defense of Europe inadequate, but no infrastructure such as air and logistical bases, pipelines, or roads existed beyond normal national economic requirements. The reserve systems were disorganized and underequipped, and the RPGs lacked coordinated planning. The recommended solution was the establishment of centralized command and control organizations to be responsible for all of these matters.[57]

The Military Committee recommended that three commands be formed. The first was the European Command, which would assume

Crusade in Europe Revisited ➤ *105*

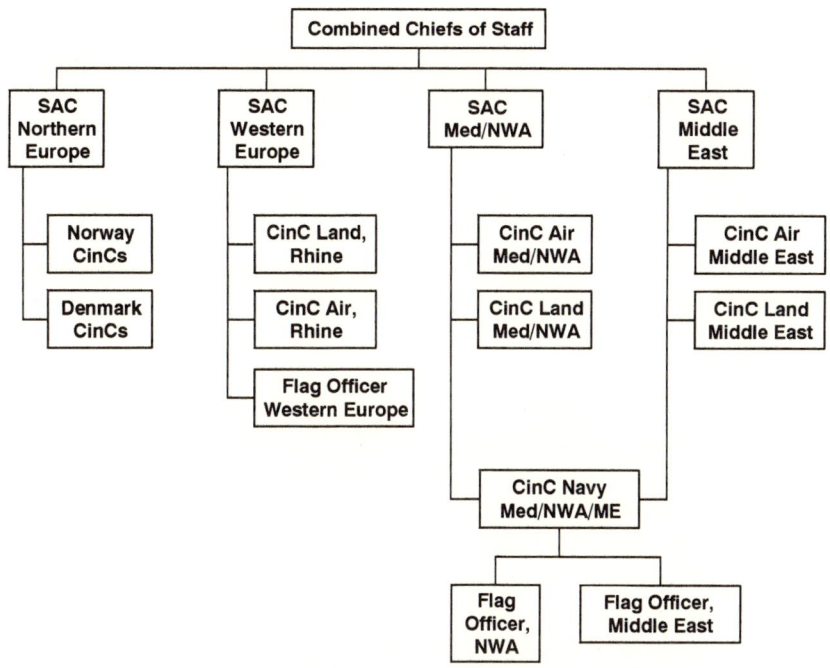

Fig. 3.8. Temporary consensus, August 1950

responsibility for the area occupied by the Western European RPG, the Northern European RPG, and the Western Mediterranean RPG. The flank areas, north and south, were physically separated from the main defense for Western Europe in the central region and as a result had special command requirements. So both north and south were to have complete joint commands, and the whole package would be subordinated to the Supreme Allied Commander, Europe.

The second command recommended by the Military Committee was Allied Naval Forces, Mediterranean. Because the naval requirements in the Mediterranean included more than just amphibious, air, and gunfire support, a separate command was warranted. Finally, it was clear to the Military Committee that the Atlantic Ocean should have a supreme commander because of its geographic detachment from Europe proper. The Military Committee noted: "The relationship of the UK Home Station and of the Southern North Sea and Channel Approaches in the North Atlantic Treaty command structure will be determined by the Military Committee in the near future. A Supreme Allied Commander, Atlantic should be appointed as soon as possible after the appointment of a Supreme Allied Commander, Europe...."[58] For the time being, the Military Committee also suggested that the U.S.–Canadian relationship continue in the form of the CUSRPG.

The terms of reference for the Supreme Allied Commander, Europe were straightforward. As established by the Military Committee, SACEUR's responsibility was to "ensure that, if an emergency comes, the North Atlantic Treaty Organization forces made available by nations for the defense of Western Europe will be organized, equipped, trained and ready to implement agreed war plans...."[59] Expanding on the view of the Military Committee, the JCS emphasized that SACEUR had "overall strategic direction and conduct of operations in war within his area, except as specifically excluded.... [SACEUR's mission is] the defense of the land and sea areas of the North Atlantic Treaty nations in Europe to include West Germany; control of sea lines of communications within the area of his command include the conduct of naval control of the movement of the movement of merchant shipping."[60]

The issue of naval forces and SACEUR's possible command over them had to be resolved or at least clarified before the command itself could be established. The working concept for SACEUR's command organization in January 1951 did not at first examine naval involvement in great detail (see fig. 3.9). This concept was quite similar to the SHAEF model of World

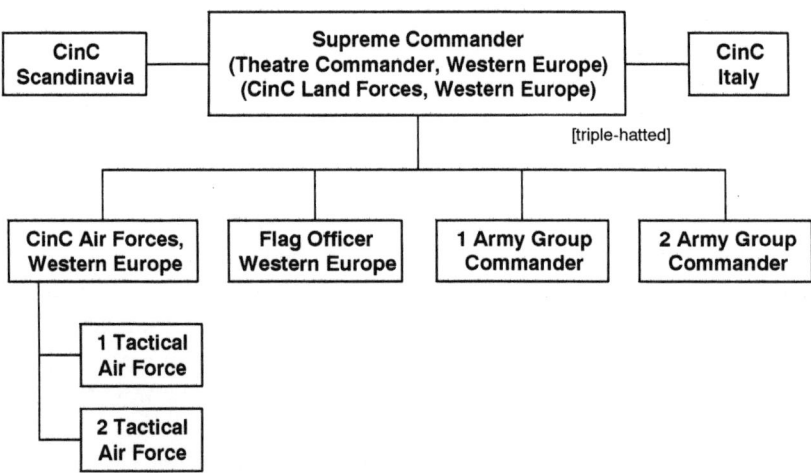

Fig. 3.9. Working concept for SACEUR, January 1951

War II with the addition of a Commander in Chief, Scandinavia and a Commander in Chief, Italy. This similarity was not surprising, since Gen. Dwight Eisenhower was nominated for the position of SACEUR on 20 December 1950.[61]

One particular problem with the working concept was noted immediately. The command organizations for the flanks in Scandinavia and Italy were rather vague with regard to naval and air activity. The Second World War model did not offer a solution for this problem because operations in and around Norway had been essentially a British responsibility, while Italy had been under SACMED. The British Chiefs of Staff suggested that these flank commands be organized as a joint staff, with the land commanders reporting to SACEUR directly (see fig. 3.10); another concept recommended that SACEUR have three functional deputy commanders for his entire region, with Scandinavia and Italy becoming separate theaters (see fig. 3.11).[62] Again, most of these concepts were quite general and did not consider the need for SACEUR to interact with commands that would be established later, particularly SACLANT, CHANCOM, and AFMED.

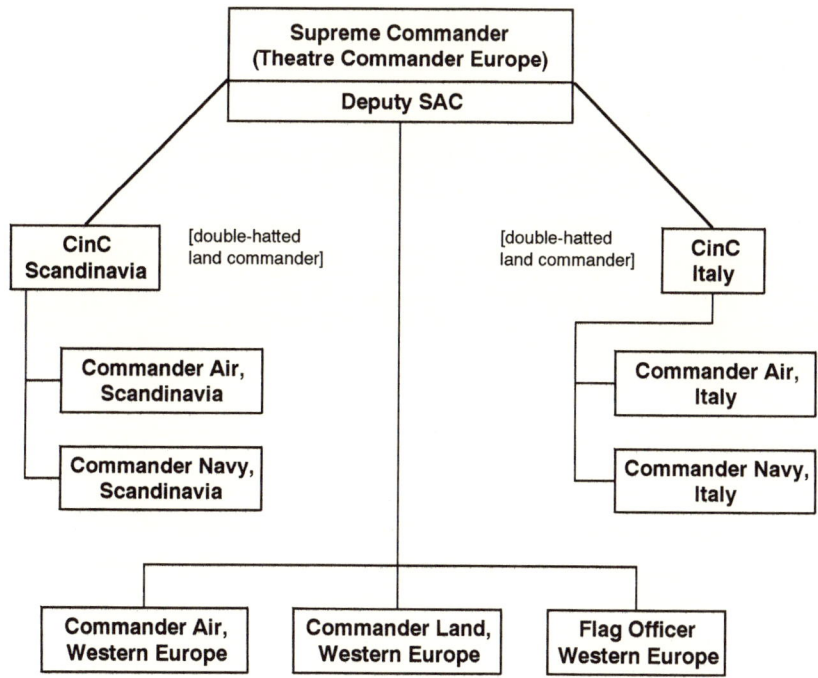

Fig. 3.10. British SACEUR proposal, January 1951

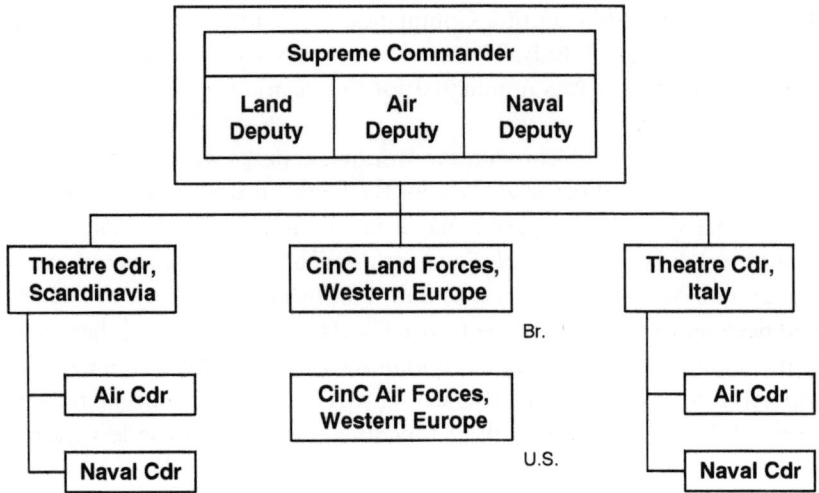

Fig. 3.11. Alternate British SACEUR proposal, January 1951

Eisenhower, however, had his own ideas on how SACEUR should be set up. He focused on the type of campaign he envisioned being fought in each geographic area. The central area in Western Europe would clearly be contested in a land battle with a great deal of tactical air support. A single commander would be needed for this battle, with an air deputy and a naval adviser. The northern and southern regions were of secondary importance and more air- and naval-oriented, the stress being on carrier-based airpower to support smaller ground operations. This in turn dictated that two unified commands be established, both reporting to SACEUR but having operational control over their own assigned forces (see fig. 3.12).[63]

The northern flank commander in Eisenhower's plan was to be a British naval officer with elements of the Home Fleet under his command. Eisenhower was quick to note that this did not mean SACEUR was assuming responsibility for the naval defense of Britain. For the southern flank, Eisenhower wanted Admiral Carney, who at the time was CinCNELM, the U.S. unified commander in the Mediterranean and Near East. The southern flank and the Mediterranean command situation will receive closer examination in chapter 5.[64] At this point, the position of Flag Officer, Western Europe (FOWE) had not been fleshed out in any form; in fact, the whole problem of naval support to SACEUR still had to be addressed. No naval forces had been specifically allocated to SACEUR as

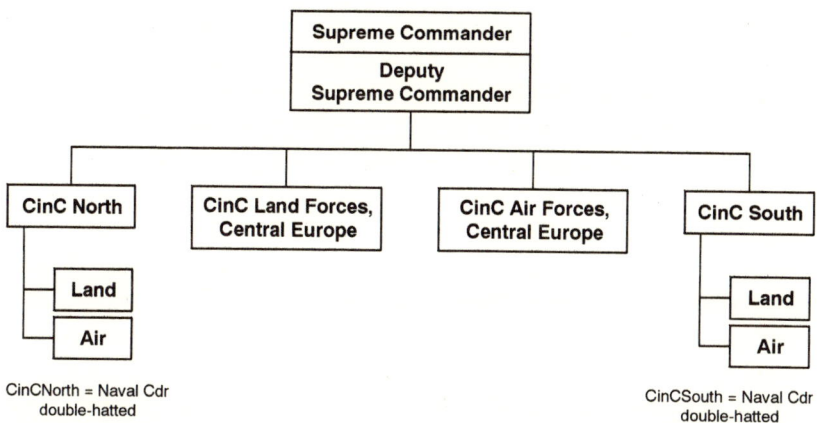

Fig. 3.12. Eisenhower's view of command organization in Europe, January 1951

an interim measure. FOWE's job was to provide SACEUR with a close liaison with the British CinC Home Fleet, since the English Channel was temporarily under British national command.[65]

On 22 March 1951, Eisenhower transmitted his first message as SACEUR: "It is my intention at 2359Z hrs 1 Apr 1951 to formally assume the command responsibilities of SACEUR which have been entrusted to me by the North Atlantic Treaty powers. I have recommended and the Standing Group has approved that my subordinate command arrangements on the continent of Western Europe will include: 1. a Commander in Chief, Land Forces; 2. a Commander in Chief, Air Forces; and 3. a Naval Flag Officer. All are responsible directly to me for the defense of the Central Region...."[66] SACEUR replaced the WUCoS, and WUDO finally retreated into the background for the time being. SACEUR's command included the British Army of the Rhine and RAF, Germany; elements of the U.S. unified command, U.S. EUCOM; as well as elements of the armed forces of the WUDO nations. Notably, Britain retained national responsibility for the aerial and land defense of its islands and refused to place these national forces under NATO command (this will be examined in chapter 4).

One addition to Eisenhower's command was the U.S. Navy's Sixth Fleet in the Mediterranean. Admiral Sherman placed this important carrier striking force under SACEUR for a variety of reasons. He recognized that interservice bickering over roles and missions left gaps that could be exploited by other nations within the coalition—specifically, Great Britain.

By subordinating the Sixth Fleet to Eisenhower, Sherman accomplished three things. First, there would be a united front in dealing with the British or anyone else over NATO command organization in Europe or the Atlantic. With Eisenhower on its side, the navy had more leverage to use against the British. Second, the U.S. Navy gained prestige in the interservice rivalry with the U.S. Air Force by allying itself with the army. Third, assigning aircraft carriers to support SACEUR demonstrated to all involved the usefulness of carrier airpower; this was also targeted at air force critics. Placing the Mediterranean carriers under SACEUR, however, would have divisive effects on the development of the Mediterranean command organization.[67]

In the final measure, NATO's Allied Command, Europe under the leadership of SACEUR and his headquarters, SHAPE, was organized according to figure 3.13. Eisenhower was SACEUR, with Montgomery as his deputy. Allied Forces, Northern Europe (AFNORTH) was under the command of Admiral Brind (RN), who had a joint staff relationship with the land com-

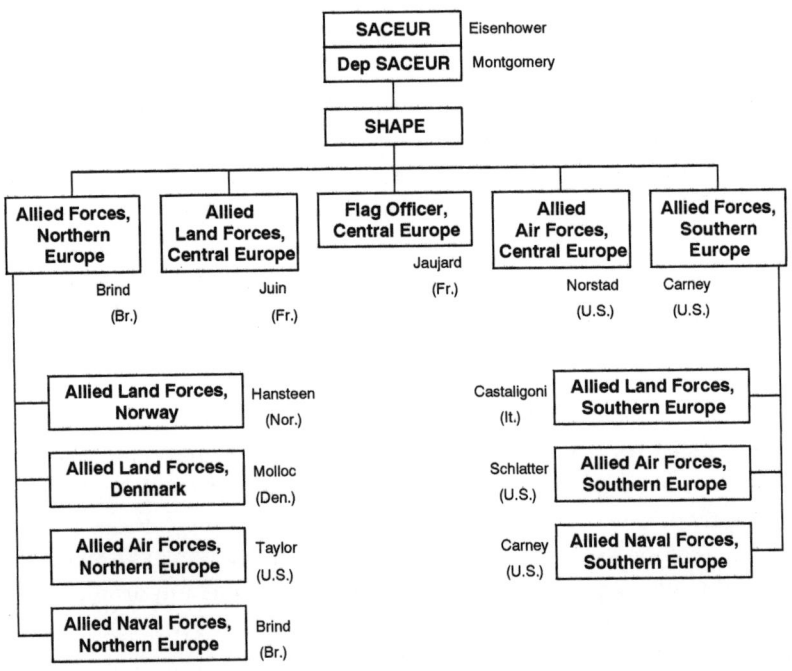

Fig. 3.13. Allied command in Europe, November 1951

manders in Norway and Denmark and the commander of Allied Air Forces, Northern Europe. Allied Forces, Southern Europe (AFSOUTH), under the unified leadership of Admiral Carney, consisted of Allied Land Forces, Southern Europe under Italian General Castaligoni; Allied Air Forces, Southern Europe under Major General Schlatter (USAF); and Allied Naval Forces, Southern Europe under Admiral Carney, who was double-hatted. The central region commands all reported directly to SACEUR. These were Allied Land Forces, Central Europe under French General Juin; Allied Air Forces, Central Europe, responsible to General Norstad (USAF); and Flag Officer, Central Europe, who was French Rear Admiral Jaujard. The command boundaries were flexible but followed approximately those displayed in figure 3.14.[68]

The position of Flag Officer, Western Europe was expanded beyond the limits envisioned previously. The French, British, and U.S. navies all pos-

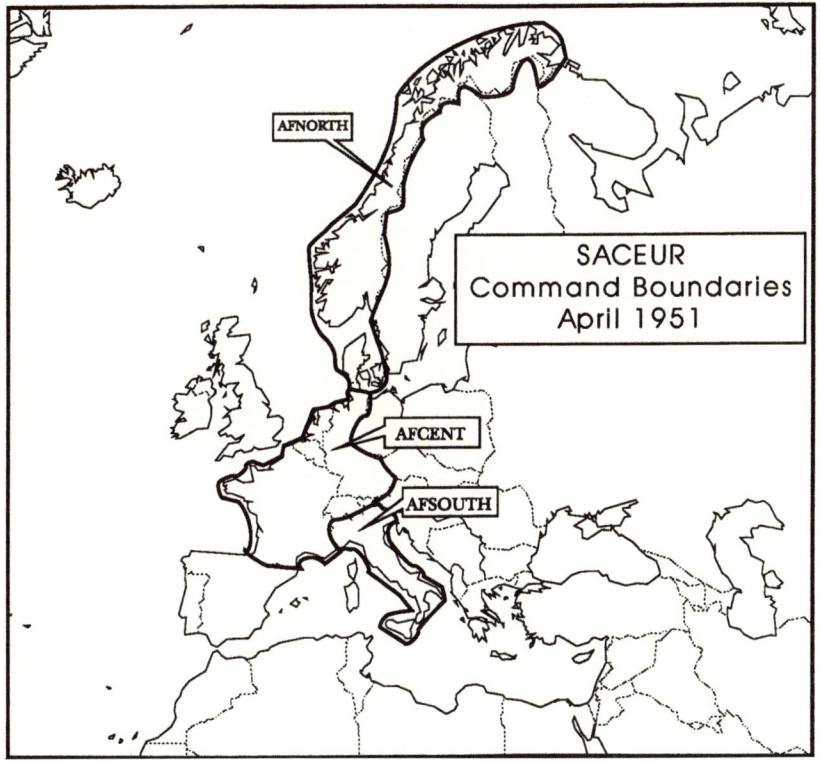

Fig. 3.14.

sessed riverine forces that operated on the major rivers in Western Europe, particularly the Rhine, Ijssel, and Elbe. These forces, the Royal Navy Rhine Flotilla, the U.S. Navy Rhine River Patrol, and the French Forces Maritims De Rhin, were originally established separately during World War II and continued their activities into the 1950s as part of the occupation forces. All three of these riverine units were assigned to the FOWE. Though numerically small, the units' projected role in the event of war was significant given that the Rhine was a great obstacle to enemy land movements. Roles for these riverine units included the provision of port security to Düsseldorf, Duisburg, Wesseling, and other minor ports on the Rhine; the protection of friendly bridges, and the demolition of enemy ones; the destruction of port facilities and Rhine River barge traffic; the evacuation or transport of friendly forces; and the denial of the rivers to the enemy as necessary. Notably, NATO riverine forces under Admiral Jaujard had a significant special operations capability for their demolition role in the form of a Royal Navy Special Boat Service flotilla.[69]

Thus, up to this point, NATO had a slightly revised strategic concept as well as a command organization set up for the defense of Western Europe, which of course was NATO's raison d'être. How that vital theater would be sustained in the event of war was to be resolved by the creation of a NATO command to direct the defense of the North Atlantic.

THE ESTABLISHMENT OF SACLANT

Once SACEUR was firmly established by April 1951, attention turned toward establishing a coalition command for the Atlantic, which had been agreed to in December 1950. Both the United States and Great Britain continued to put forward command organization proposals to NAORPG from August to November 1950. Almost all of these would have an impact on the development of the SACLANT command and should receive some examination. Unlike SACEUR, which had a discernible genealogy dating back to the Mediterranean command organizations and SHAEF of the Second World War, SACLANT was born out of conflict and a five-year series of hypothetical and theoretical command plans, none of which had been agreed upon by the potential participants.

Following the May 1950 Atlantic command organization proposal, which was not much different from the proposal presented in the October 1949 discussions over Crosspiece/Galloper, the unresolved differences in British and American opinion resulted in a radical departure from a command organization based on geographic considerations. In July 1950, a functional command organization proposal emanated from NAORPG's coordinating committee. In this proposal, the concept of a Supreme Allied Commander, Atlantic Ocean (SACAO) was not challenged. Instead of arbitrarily carving up the Atlantic into specific regions, NAORPG recommended that three commanders in chief be created, with each having command over specific types of naval forces (see fig. 3.15). These CinCs included a Commander in Chief, Antisubmarine Warfare, Atlantic, who would command hunter-killer groups and escort groups; he would also provide naval control of shipping. CinCASWA was to be a Royal Navy officer. The Commander in Chief, Offensive Task Forces, Atlantic (CinCOTFA), a U.S. Navy officer, would command submarines, aircraft carrier task forces, some hunter-killer task forces, and presumably amphibious task forces. Finally, the Commander in Chief, Atlantic Maritime Air Forces (CinCAMAF) would be responsible for long-range maritime patrol aircraft in the entire region; he would also be an American. All three were to be headquartered in Britain. The only geographic limitation that these CinCs had to obey in this command concept was an established demarcation line somewhere west of Gibraltar.[70] Regarding national coastal waters,

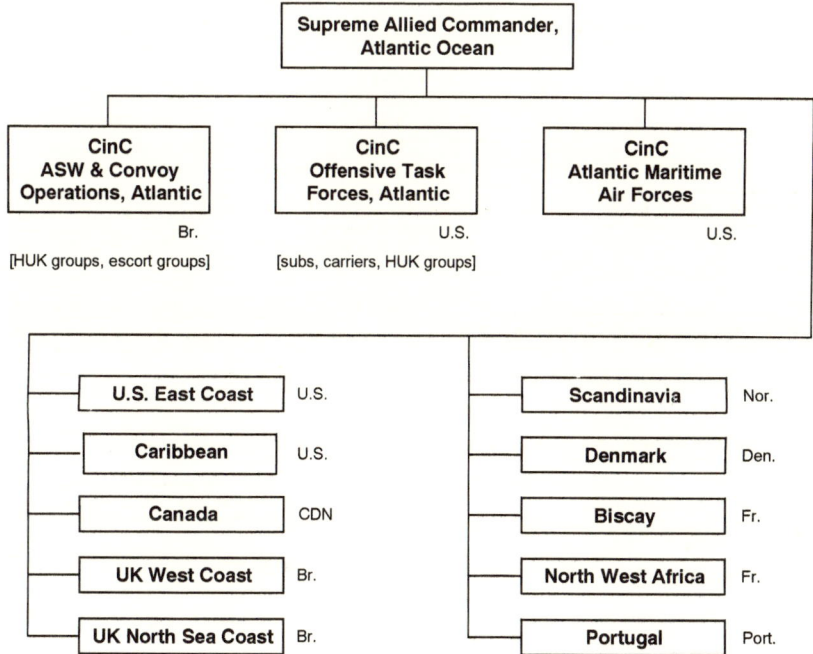

Fig. 3.15. NAORPG's functional command proposal, July 1950

the NAORPG proposal did not specify an exact distance; coastal waters were considered to be national responsibilities.

The advantages of this concept were many. The Atlantic was not arbitrarily divided; the troublesome CHOP lines could be abolished because there was one convoy authority and the offensive forces were extremely flexible. On the down side, the problem of having a single authority over such an extensive area could not be overcome. Force commanders would have to deal with large numbers of subordinates over a huge distance. Anticipated problems with the coordination between different functional commanders operating in the same area, particularly around the British Isles, worked against the proposal. Because of these disadvantages, the NAORPG proposal was shelved.[71]

When NAORPG convened again in August 1950, the Americans noted that "to date, representatives of the British and the United States have been unable to agree on the command arrangements in the Atlantic," and that as a result the U.S. members had modified their position on the matter.[72] Again, as in the previous concepts, a single overall commander in the Atlantic, SACAO, headed the effort (see fig. 3.16). Unlike in previous proposals, the SACAO normally would delegate operational control of offen-

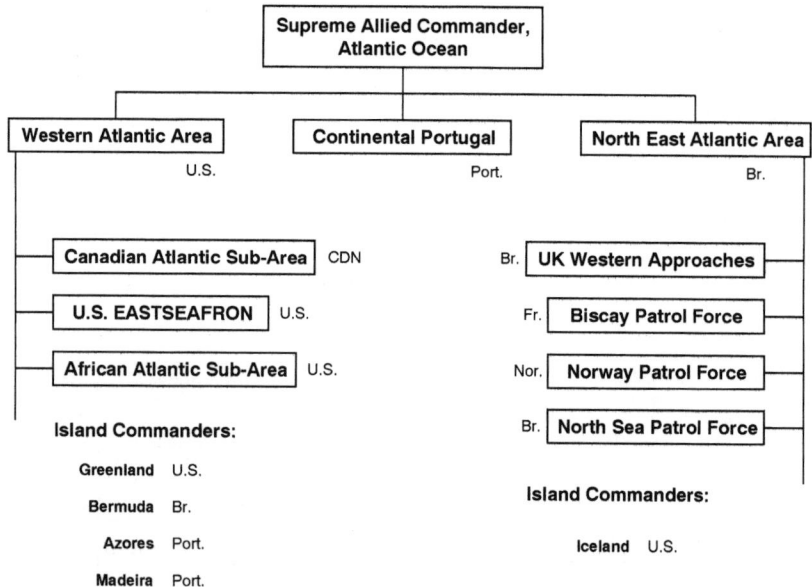

Fig. 3.16. NAOR command organization—U.S. proposal, August 1950

sive and defensive forces to his two area commanders, Western Atlantic Area (U.S.) and Northeastern Atlantic Area (British). The area commanders would handle transoceanic convoys jointly, with a CHOP line running from Greenland to the coast of Portugal. Each area commander controlled several sub-areas (see fig. 3.17). The Western Atlantic Area commander had the Canadian Atlantic Sub-area, the U.S. EASTSEAFRON Sub-area, and the African Atlantic Sub-area, while the Northeastern Atlantic Sub-area commander handled the Western Approaches, a French Biscay Patrol Force, a Norway Patrol Force, and a North Sea Patrol Force. These forces were to be responsible for SLOC protection within their geographic areas, while the sub-area commanders handled local control and protection of shipping. Again, as with the previous U.S. positions, the controversial African Atlantic Sub-area remained in U.S. hands and not subject to a British area commander.[73] Since the Crosspiece/Galloper concept was

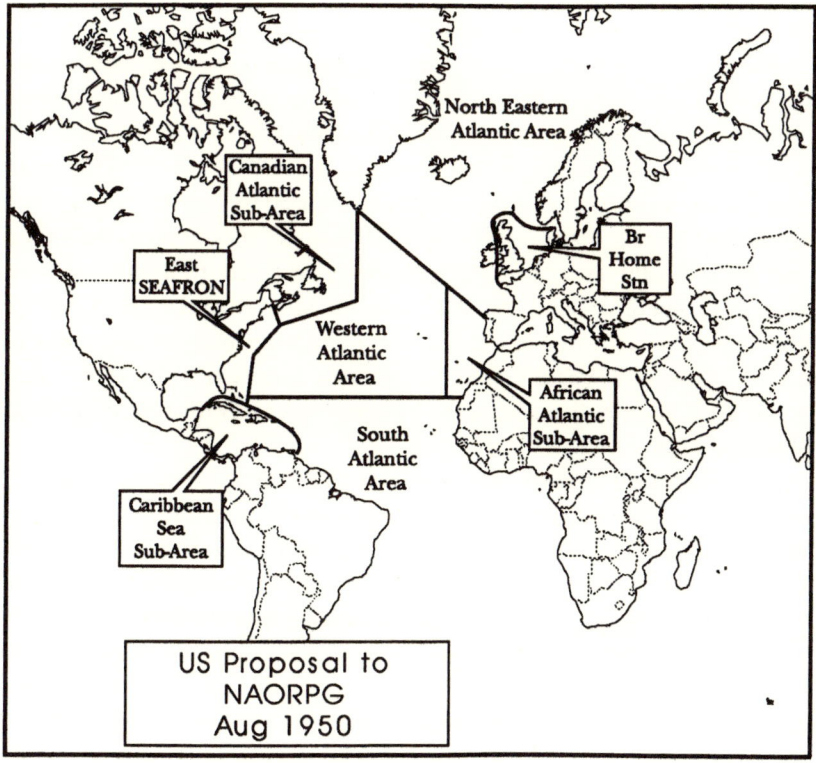

Fig. 3.17.

based on a reinforced fighting withdrawal, the United States required port facilities in Spain, Portugal, and western France to deploy land forces directly into the theater or, in the event of Western Europe being overrun, to Northwest Africa to prepare for a return to the continent. The United States believed that it had to have control over its own troop convoys as it had during World War II.

In comparison to earlier proposals the geographic size of the African Atlantic Sub-area was reduced, with the cast-off portions given to areas under U.S. control. In compensation, the operating area for the British (Northeastern Atlantic) was increased to include Iceland; the Canadian sub-area remained the same as it had since 1943. In terms of command, the South Atlantic and the Caribbean were removed from the auspices of SACAO and were assigned to the U.S. unified command CinCLANT. The inclusion of the French under British command was suspect for political reasons, but this seemed to be indicative of the need to include the newly reconstituted French navy. Unlike in previous proposals, however, U.S. planners did not address how air cover over the Atlantic would be controlled, a serious flaw in any command proposal.

British reaction in August 1950 to this American proposal emphasized some principles for the delineation of areas of command in the Atlantic before developing new proposals. Essentially, the British believed that areas of vital interest to a particular nation should be under the control of that nation, a rule that fit Britain's perceived need to control the sea areas around the British Isles proper. Second, command should go to the nation that deployed the largest number of operating forces to a particular sea area; this sometimes would conflict with the first principle. Third, CHOP lines had to be kept to a minimum and away from areas of concentrated activity, as Second World War experience had demonstrated. Finally, command areas should also conform to the operational radius of long-range maritime patrol aircraft.[74]

With these principles in mind, the British determined that the division of the Atlantic into an Eastern Atlantic area and a Western Atlantic area was still valid (see fig. 3.18), as was the concept of a single Supreme Allied Commander, Atlantic Ocean. However, the British diverged in their view of sub-area commands, and the issue of the African Atlantic Sub-area was disputed again. The British still refused to allow American naval forces to control what they considered to be the two most vital SLOCs (North America to Britain and the Mediterranean to Britain). Any such concession would also abrogate Britain's relationship with its traditional ally Portugal, which owned one of the most important island bases, the Azores.[75]

Crusade in Europe Revisited 117

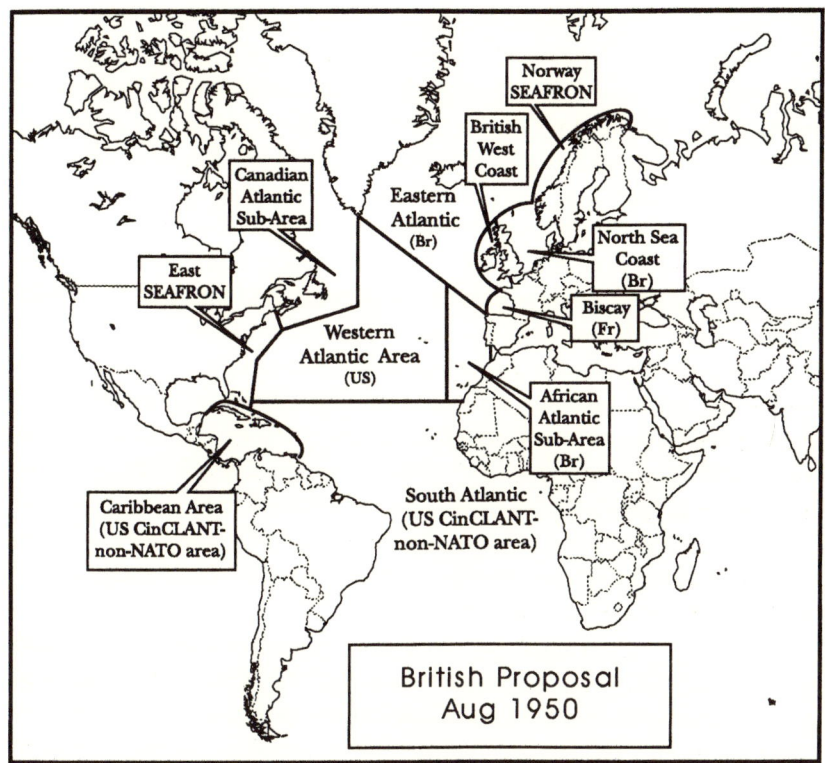

Fig. 3.18.

The British proposal also rectified the problem of air cover over the Atlantic area. Based on the World War II experience, this plan would have given the Eastern Atlantic area commander a NATO air counterpart called the Air Commander in Chief, Eastern Atlantic; this was to be the Commander in Chief, RAF Coastal Command, double-hatted. Subordinate commands would have included Air Commander, African Atlantic; Air Commander, UK West Coast; and Air Commander, UK North Sea Coast. They were to come from whatever RAF Coastal Command Group was already responsible for those sea areas. In the Western Atlantic, the British proposal was rather sketchy, since it lacked an understanding of the American air situation. The Canadian sub-area had its own Air Commander, Canadian Atlantic; there was also an Air Commander, Western Atlantic and an Air Commander, Eastern Sea Frontier, and all were subordinated to an Air Commander in Chief, Western Atlantic, a NATO position double-hatted to the appropriate American air commander.[76] In fact, such a commander would have come from the U.S. Navy, which, as a result of the Unified Command Plan and the Key West Agreement discussed in chapter 2, had control over all fixed-wing long-range patrol aircraft on the Atlantic coast. The problem over the USAAF Antisubmarine Bomber Command would not be repeated in 1950, because the navy now owned all such aircraft and the air force was preoccupied with providing strategic nuclear forces.

The issue of command boundaries in the Atlantic and command over the African Atlantic Sub-area was so divisive that Admiral Sherman, Admiral Douglas-Pennent of the British Joint Staff Mission, Washington, and Admiral Grant of the Royal Canadian Navy met in Washington on September 1950 to come to some accommodation. Agreement was reached on the broad division of the North Atlantic into two areas of responsibility by a line running due west from the Spain-Portugal border to 20° west longitude and then to Cape Farewell. However, no agreement could be reached on the African Atlantic issue without detailed study because of the conflicting U.S. requirement to move troops through it and the British requirement to sustain trade.[77]

The participants decided that there were four alternatives. The African Atlantic Sub-area could be assigned to either the Western Atlantic Area or the Eastern Atlantic Area, or it could become a separate area of command under SACAO. The advantage of this last idea was that one commander could be responsible directly to SACAO. This would be useful if there was a lot of activity in the region, as it would not distract the other area commanders; on the down side, there would be more CHOP lines to cross. The fourth possibility was for the African Atlantic Sub-area to become a sub-area of the still-developing NATO Mediterranean command, with the advantages of having only one CHOP line to cross and expanding the authority of the Flag Officer, Gibraltar to include more maritime air forces. However, it was clear to the participants that any supreme commander in the Mediterranean would be overworked because of his large operating area.[78]

Douglas-Pennent informed the gathering that Britain's favored option was the inclusion of the African Atlantic Sub-area into the Eastern Atlantic Area; failing that, the British would push for a separate command under SACAO, hoping that it would fall under British control in the process. In responding to this, Sherman stated that if it could be demonstrated that the volume of north-south shipping in a war situation would be greater than the volume of east-west shipping through the African Atlantic Sub-area, he would favor incorporation of the sub-area into the Eastern Atlantic

Area. Until such an accounting took place, the temporary solution would be to place the sub-area directly under SACAO. This became known as the "Gentleman's Agreement."[79] The only other significant outcome of the meeting was the British concession to allow SACAO to assume responsibility for Caribbean–British Isles SLOCs. Britain would remain responsible for the internal security of its colonial territory in the Caribbean through the national command organizations already established there.[80]

Following the September meeting, Douglas-Pennent corresponded with Sherman regarding Atlantic command organization in preparation for the North Atlantic Defense Council meeting in Washington in October 1950. Essentially, the British wished to have the ability to influence any American SACAO's decisions by adding a Deputy SACAO; this was similar to the SACEUR arrangement. For practical purposes, the Deputy SACAO was the British CinC America and West Indies, double-hatted only during wartime but with a small peacetime staff co-located with SACAO (see fig. 3.19). One of these staff members was to be SACAO's chief of staff. In his

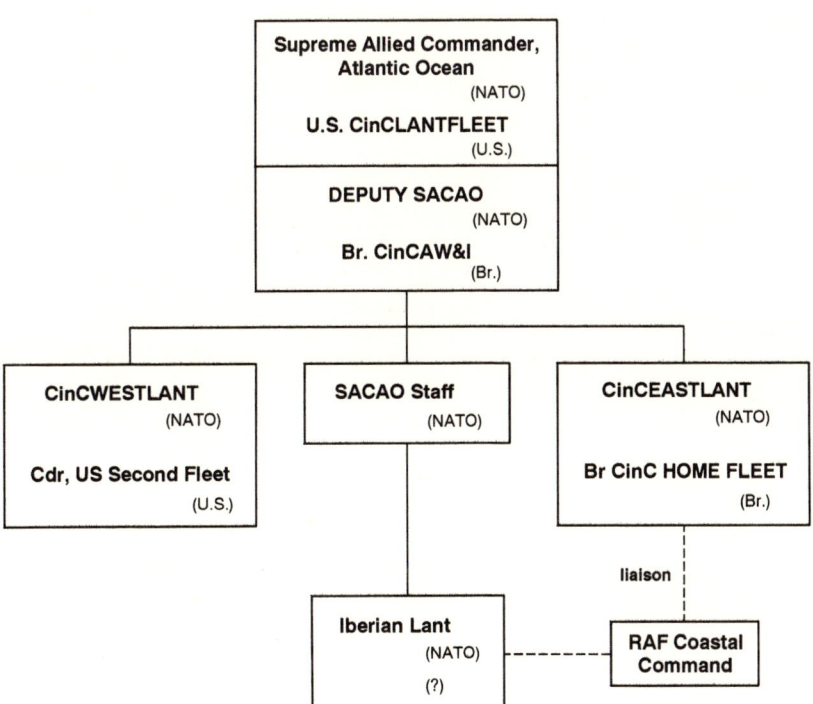

Fig. 3.19. British view of SACLANT organization, October 1950

NATO role, CinCAW&I was to act as a liaison officer between the British CinC Home Fleet and the American CinCLANT, which was SACAO's American position anyway. To retain close planning links between the NATO WESTLANT commander (an American) and the British Home Fleet, the Deputy SACAO would be provided with a senior planning officer. Regarding the Iberian Atlantic (the renamed African Atlantic) command situation, Douglas-Pennent left room for future discussions as necessary.[81] In the British view, then, if SACAO could not be British by nationality, influence could be applied through a coalition staff stacked with British officers.

The October 1950 meeting of the North Atlantic Defense Council was quite significant. In addition to preparing the ground for the establishment of SACEUR, the NADC also approved a command organization for the Atlantic based on an NAORPG recommendation.[82] Although the contents of the decisions that came out of this meeting, DC 24/2 and 24/3, were not available as of this writing, the outline of this recommendation appears to have followed the lines of figure 3.20, which is quite similar to figure 3.16. The obvious problem here is the placement of the Iberian Atlantic (formerly the African Atlantic Sub-area; hereafter IBERLANT) under the WESTLANT commander—a move that was at variance with the Gentleman's Agreement, which would continue to cause problems between the British and the Americans through 1951 and 1952.

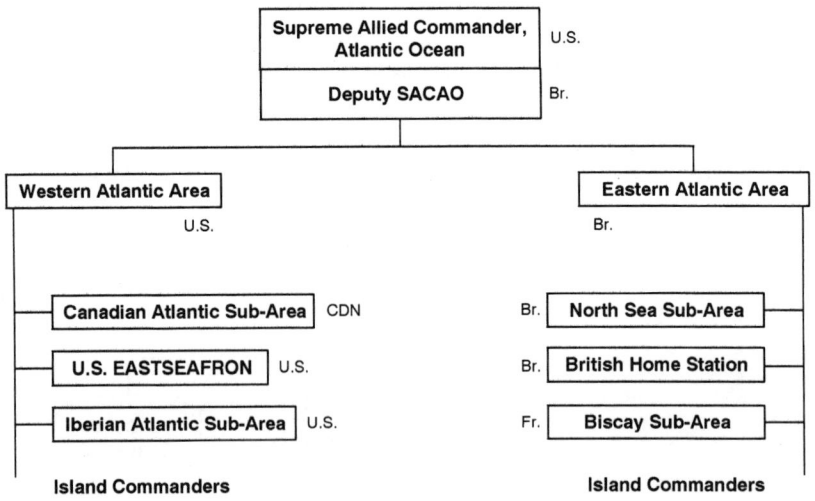

Fig. 3.20. NAORPG recommendation to the NADC, October 1950

Whatever potential problems existed, the Atlantic command issue simmered on the back burner throughout November 1950 as the Americans and the British focused on responding to the Chinese intervention in Korea. While preparing for the sixth meeting of the North Atlantic Council scheduled for December 1950, Admiral Sherman made a series of recommendations to the JCS regarding command organization. Given the pressing need to focus on the establishment of SACEUR in order to provide a collective deterrent against the vast Soviet land-force threat, Sherman believed that a Supreme Allied Commander, Atlantic (hereafter SACLANT instead of SACAO) should not be appointed yet.[83] He did, however, believe that it was prudent to designate a commander and a small staff to organize preliminary planning. In this vein, he also stressed that "it is intended that the North Atlantic Regional Planning Group continue as an agency for international representation" in the Atlantic theater, and that it should be used as much as possible to review SACLANT plans until the headquarters of Supreme Allied Commander, Atlantic was actually set up.[84] Since Admiral Fechteler was already the U.S. CinCLANT commander and the leading American representative to NAORPG, Sherman recommended that he be named the designated SACLANT. On 22 December 1950, the North Atlantic Council approved the appointment of Admiral Fechteler (who would later replace Blandy as U.S. CinCLANT) to the SACLANT position once it was formally established; this was not publicly announced at the time for various political reasons. The debate then turned to SACLANT's terms of reference and his responsibilities vis-à-vis the other NATO commands in SACEUR; this inevitably became a point of contention between the American and British naval leadership.[85]

The American secretary of defense, Louis Johnson, had by 11 January 1951 accepted the Fechteler appointment. Both the proposed terms of reference for SACLANT and the designation of Fechteler were sent to the British through the SG for their input. In the American view, SACLANT should have a coalition staff made up of NAORPG members, and he should have absolute command responsibility for all air, naval, and land forces assigned to him from the national governments operating in the NAORPG region. SACLANT would for all intents and purposes replace NAORPG. Whereas NAORPG had a planning role but no command role, SACLANT would be a military command under the SG responsible for "the overall direction and conduct of wartime operations within his area. He will be responsible directly to the Standing Group for the general formulation and dissemination of policy, the assignment of forces, missions and operations to his subordinate commanders and for the development of operational plans. He will, consistent with his other responsibilities, support the operations of SACEUR...."[86]

In effect, SACLANT's primary responsibility was to support SACEUR; however, the word "support" was deliberately not clarified and left flexible. It could mean direct support of SACEUR's land battle by carrier air strikes, naval gunfire support, or amphibious operations; in another sense, SACLANT's support of SACEUR's land battle could be more indirect, as in the close protection of shipping or attack-at-source operations to eliminate a naval surface or subsurface threat. Peacetime responsibilities for SACLANT would necessarily include organization, collective training, and administration—notably, logistical support would be a national responsibility.[87] The Americans also understood the necessity of clear delineation between SACLANT and SACEUR's areas to avoid confusion: "The matter of responsibility for naval operations in the Northern North Sea and approaches to the Baltic in support of missions in Europe of the SACEUR will be arranged between SACLANT and SACEUR. The resolution of these arrangements, particularly as regards the provision of forces in this area, will be dependent in some degree upon the relation of the British Home Command to NATO when this subject is clarified...."[88] This problem could not be resolved until SACLANT was established and the British and American positions within the command finalized.

The appointment of Admiral Fechteler was well received by the British Chiefs of Staff. However, they believed that his terms of reference as SACLANT required further study.[89] The British were prepared to accept most of the U.S. position on SACLANT terms of reference with some exceptions. The American proposal to the SG had allowed for special powers that would give SACLANT the right to inspect all national fleets that had units assigned to SACLANT in wartime. To the British, this was a clear violation of sovereignty: "We are unable to accept [these powers] in their present form since we are not prepared to give SAC Atlantic unrestricted command over British forces in peacetime...."[90]

The agreed-upon version of SACLANT's terms of reference closely followed the American proposal. SACLANT would have a coalition staff consisting of members from the U.S., British, Canadian, Norwegian, Danish, French, Dutch, and Portuguese navies. National coastal waters were to be under the command of respective national entities, while SACLANT remained "responsible for the overall direction and conduct of wartime operations within his area . . . to the Standing Group...."[91] Instead of having extensive inspection powers, one of SACLANT's peacetime responsibilities included "the organization and conduct of international combined training of national forces earmarked for his command in war which can be made available in order to insure that they can operate as effective forces, integrated as necessary."[92] Thus, SACLANT's mission and powers were defined and agreed upon by British and American planners by the end of February 1951; however, they had not yet been ratified by the NAC. The actual creation of the SACLANT command and its geographic delineations posed political problems and prevented the establishment of SACLANT at this time.

These political problems emanated from Britain. Winston Churchill was, at the time, leader of the opposition against Clement Attlee's Labour government. In February 1951, Churchill attempted to take down the Attlee government with a vote of no confidence. One arrow in the Conservative Party's quiver was a sustained attack on Attlee on defense issues. Basically, at issue were the small size of the army, the lack of an atomic bomb and the means to deliver it, and the belief that "far too little was being done to meet the danger from Soviet submarines."[93] Churchill also attacked Attlee on the appointment of a U.S. admiral to the SACLANT position after the Danes leaked the name and nationality of SACLANT to the news media.[94] Even though the attempt to remove Attlee failed, British defense policy came increasingly into the limelight as a political issue in 1951.

British political opinion was closely monitored by the Americans, particularly Eisenhower in his role as SACEUR: "Another concern has been centered on the fight in the British parliament over the announcement of Admiral Fechteler's command. I have a very deep suspicion that none of us has really learned the lessons from World War II. . . . Among other things, the super sensitiveness of the British public to anything and everything naval is one of the factors that apparently we have not thought through carefully. . . ."[95] At a meeting with Sherman and Carney in early March 1951, Eisenhower expressed his grave concern over British public opinion and determined that the British must receive a command in the Mediterranean or the Atlantic at least equivalent in prestige to SACEUR in order to compensate.[96] Sherman agreed with this in principle, but Carney did not:

> It is difficult to conceive of our relinquishing, or abdicating, the post–World War II American leadership which we have built up by vast economic and moral support. If we are leaders, it is on the basis of actual accomplishment and current future capability for accomplishment; by the

same token, military prestige can not be legislated but must be based on capabilities for accomplishment—forces—as well as tradition. It is difficult to see how British prestige can be enduringly synthesized by the device of titles unless we are ready to credit to British leadership the accomplishment and potentiality of American contribution.[97]

The three agreed to relay a compromise proposal in which the title of SACLANT would be changed to commander in chief. (Other considerations discussed at this meeting regarding the Mediterranean will be dealt with in chapter 5.) Later, in a meeting between SACEUR, the CNO, CinCNELM, and the British Chiefs of Staff (at that time consisting of Field Marshal Slim, Marshal of the RAF Slessor, and First Sea Lord Fraser), the compromise was flatly rejected. During this meeting, the Americans had also pushed for Carney (in his position as NATO CinCAFSOUTH) to become the primary naval commander in the Mediterranean.[98] To the British, the prospect of all the prestigious NATO commands being led by Americans was politically unacceptable. In the British view, SACLANT should have only the ability to allocate forces rather than absolute control over them; Sherman rejected this, suggesting that SACLANT's power would be too diluted to be of any use.

As a result of this impasse, Sherman recommended that the Fechteler appointment be delayed and that resolution of the SACLANT problem be deferred until command arrangements in the Mediterranean were resolved.[99] In the end, the Allied Forces, Mediterranean (AFMED) command would not be established until March 1953, long after SACLANT was finally established in January 1952.

Perceiving that SACLANT was now a public political football, Minister of Defence A. V. Alexander ordered the British planners to demonstrate the need for a SACLANT and the need for an American to command it. The resulting document, "The Reasons for the Appointment of a Supreme Allied Commander, Atlantic," was to be the basis for Labour's defense of the concept in the House of Commons Defence Committee. The JPS paper traced the history of the SACA/SACAO/SACLANT idea from 1948, pointing out that the British Ministry of Defence agreed to the establishment of the command and the selection of an American officer at the NATO Defense Council meeting in October 1950. The arguments for having a SACLANT were almost identical to previous U.S. positions on the concept. These included the familiar economy of force argument: "In the last war there was no command organization to ensure such economy of force as between the British Navy and the USN and the Air Forces. Consequently, the deployment of available resources was not coordinated by a Supreme Commander and could only be done by the CCS...."[100] To support this, the JPS included two examples of Second World War problems: the distribution of long-range maritime patrol aircraft, and the U.S. response to the Paukenschlag offensive in early 1942.[101] Other echoes from past U.S.–British arguments included the need for international coordination of more than two navies, the need for unity of operations (particularly convoy routing), and the need for advance planning. In an appendix, the JPS had a simplified chart drawn from Jane's demonstrating the preponderance of U.S. naval strength vis-à-vis the Royal Navy. The members of the JPS definitely understood their adversary's previous arguments and committed this information to memory well.

Other preparations for the defense of the SACLANT concept from Conservative assault included providing members of the House with an aide-mémoire in case the media asked awkward questions. It was hoped the voting public would be reassured that Britain was not about to give up naval supremacy by a series of virtual nonanswers such as:

> Media question: Why is SACLANT not a British Admiral?
> Answer: There are twelve nations involved, so it is not just a matter between the United States and Britain. From that point of view, the appointment of an American was clearly right and this was the unanimous decision of the twelve nations concerned.[102]

Ironically, arguments similar to those in the JPS paper would be used by the Americans to support their position on the issue in later bilateral U.S.–British meetings with Churchill when he pushed for a British SACLANT in October 1951.

In an attempt to move the deadlocked command issue, Admiral Sherman met informally with the British Chiefs of Staff. All agreed that the SG and NATO bureaucracy was at least as responsible for slowing down the establishment of NATO commands as any political problem, and that informal measures among themselves could be used to speed things up. The primary difficulties with this approach were that (1) few problems were purely naval, so other services' participation was required, and (2) "the susceptibilities of the minor powers were liable to be hurt."[103] Regarding the Atlantic, Sherman was not happy with his headquarters arrangements in the United States, noting the distance between Virginia and EASTLANT. He also launched a trial balloon on changing the name of SACLANT to NATO CinCLANT. The problem of location was seized upon by the British, hoping to arm-twist Sherman into putting the SACLANT HQ in London while at the same time suggesting that it was too late for a name change.

The ongoing IBERLANT problem—that is, the NADC's placement of IBERLANT under an American naval officer—was discussed extensively as the British again made a bid for the command. The British position continued to emphasize the need to cover the Atlantic approaches to Gibraltar and to exert continuous command through the Mediterranean and into the Atlantic; this could easily be accomplished by redrawing the EASTLANT/WESTLANT boundary farther south and eliminating IBERLANT completely (see fig. 3.21). Sherman, however, fell back on the Gentleman's Agreement made between Douglas-Pennent and Fechteler that deferred solving the problem until after the Mediterranean had been conclusively sorted out, and very little was resolved beyond informal understandings.[104]

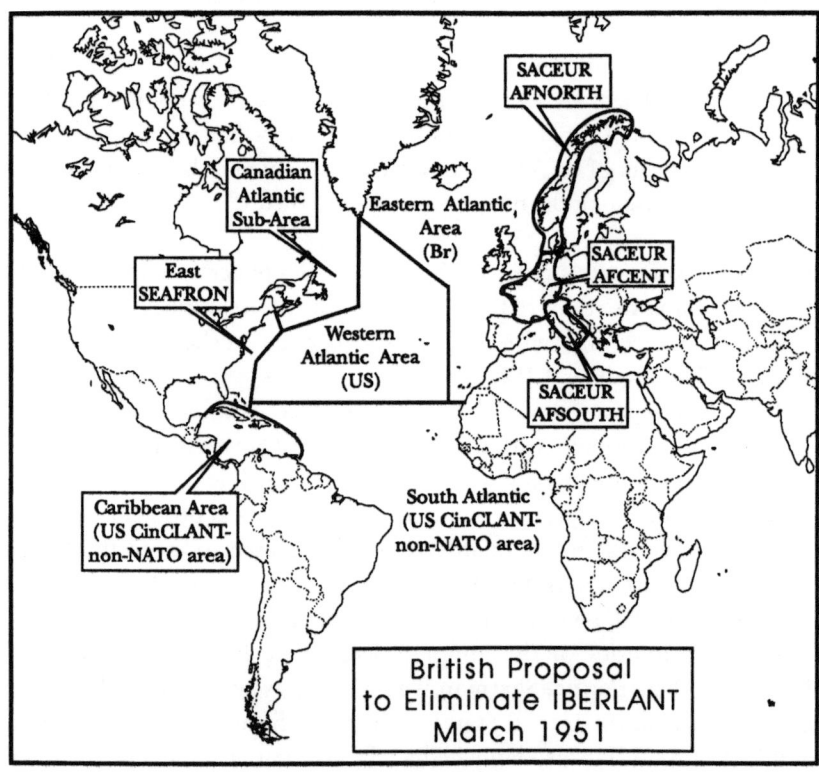

Fig. 3.21.

Meanwhile, back in the British political arena, Attlee's new foreign secretary, Herbert Morrison, was demanding information about what exactly Britain had agreed to when it conceded SACLANT to the Americans.[105] The primary concern of the Labour government ministers was that Churchill would continue to take them to task on this issue. They determined that they could be attacked on two points: first, there had been no SACLANT during World War II, and second, if the position were somehow necessary now, why had there been no public debate? To counter these criticisms, the British Chiefs of Staff briefed the foreign secretary and suggested that some mechanisms could be factored into SACLANT's power structure to guarantee British influence, mostly along the lines of Douglas-Pennent's communications with Sherman in October 1950. This could be done either by firmly emplacing a liaison officer in SACLANT's HQ or by exerting influence through the SG. However, the chiefs noted that they "were professionally convinced of the necessity for a Supreme Allied Commander, Atlantic in some form for a future war. The First Sea Lord has never wavered in his conviction on this point or in his own acceptance of an American for the appointment. . . . It was pointed out that although it would clearly be inexpedient to say so publicly, we were likely to gain far more than we should lose from the appointment of an American Admiral."[106] In the end, the chiefs believed that the issue was not as serious as the politicians believed it to be. This belief was primarily based on the understanding that reinforcements to EASTLANT would come under EASTLANT's control and that the operational and tactical battle for the Atlantic in EASTLANT would be a British responsibility.[107] In fact, members of the BJSM in Washington favored inserting an escape clause into SACLANT's terms of reference that would allow for lower-echelon commanders to communicate directly with their national governments if they felt maltreated.[108]

Thus, by the end of March 1951 the status of command organization within NATO was stalled. SACEUR and SHAPE were established, but no official announcement had been made regarding the appointment of SACLANT—and the Mediterranean command problem had not been solved.

The IBERLANT issue was a serious one in British military circles. Even though the British agreed to Fechteler as SACLANT, some members of the Chiefs of Staff worried that he might make some sort of unauthorized announcement on the IBERLANT command. In order to stave off any such attempt, the BJSM was instructed to inform the JCS that the positions of SACLANT and EASTLANT were confirmed and that "any announcement of an American commanding IBERLANT would have considerable political repercussions in the United Kingdom."[109] Fortunately, no such announcement took place to test the resolve of the British Chiefs of Staff.

While the command issue simmered once again, the British used the time to develop their EASTLANT command arrangements.[110] Essentially, the problem revolved around the interaction between EASTLANT and SACEUR, and the need for the British to retain control in the EASTLANT area of offensive operations and naval control of shipping (NCS) and not have such control diluted by SACEUR or IBERLANT.

The British Commander in Chief, Plymouth, Sir Rhoderick McGrigor (who would become First Sea Lord in 1951), examined the situation from an NCS point of view and suggested that the old Second World War command, Commander in Chief, Western Approaches, be reestablished as a separate command under SACLANT but on the same level as EASTLANT or IBERLANT. CinCWA would be a NATO command that was functional in nature. Offensive operations involving submarines and carrier task forces in the EASTLANT area (refer to fig. 3.16 for area boundaries) would come under the operational control of British CinC Home Fleet, who was double-hatted as EASTLANT anyway, while NATO CinCWA would handle NCS and convoy protection duties within the EASTLANT and IBERLANT areas (see fig. 3.22). In this way, Britain would retain control over vital convoys coming in from the Mediterranean, and the

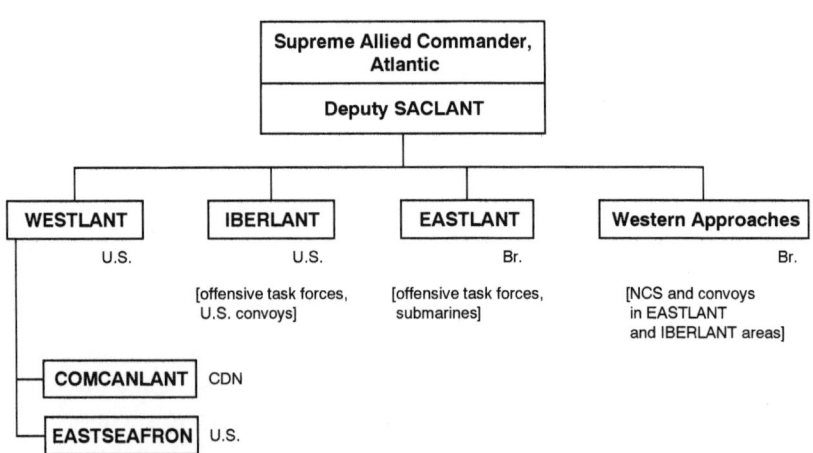

Fig. 3.22. The McGrigor proposal, April 1951

Americans would have control over their troop convoys heading for Spain and Portugal.[111]

This idea was immediately shot down by the First Sea Lord. His main criticism was that coordination between EASTLANT and NATO CinCWA would have to be done by a U.S. admiral (SACLANT) who was located in Norfolk, Virginia, thus allowing the SACLANT to micromanage everyday operations in the EASTLANT area. In World War II, the Admiralty coordinated operations between the British CinCWA and the British CinC Home Fleet or between CinCWA and the U.S. Western Atlantic. If a NATO CinCWA were set up under SACLANT, the French would probably push for a separate command of their own in the Bay of Biscay; as the French had apparently made clear to the British and the Americans in the SG, "they would not serve under an allied commander who had less than half of the Atlantic under his command."[112]

Regarding interaction between EASTLANT and CinCAFNORTH, the command situation was still ill defined at the SG level; however, since the British held both positions, they set about developing their own understanding. CinCAFNORTH, a British admiral leading a joint command under SACEUR, had responsibility for coastal convoys moving between Norway and Denmark, mine countermeasures operations off these coasts, and naval operations in the Baltic and northern Norway up to ten miles off these coasts. CinCAFNORTH also had functional control over naval forces being used to support land operations in Scandinavia, which would be allocated through EASTLANT by SACLANT; the task force commander would remain responsible for the specifics of the operation. CinCEASTLANT, on the other hand, would be made responsible for the protection of SLOCs in the EASTLANT area instead of a NATO CinCWA. CinCEASTLANT would control offensive task forces allocated to him by SACLANT for attack-at-source, counteramphibious, and countersurface operations.[113]

The First Sea Lord, Fraser of North Cape, spelled out to his planning staff exactly what he believed to be the command relationships within EASTLANT so that there would be no confusion. The protection of sea communications and the organization of convoys was a CinCEASTLANT responsibility. CinCEASTLANT would delegate this responsibility for convoys in the Northern European Sub-area (essentially the area labeled Norway Sea Frontier in fig. 3.18) to the British command, Admiral, Rosyth; CinCAFNORTH was not concerned with the movement of convoys except as a reception authority so that he could coordinate his coastal and mine countermeasures forces. As for the movements and operations of offensive carrier task forces, these would remain a CinCEASTLANT responsibility. CinCAFNORTH would apply to CinCEASTLANT for support of the land battle; if such support were allocated, CinCAFNORTH would select the targets while the task force commander conducted the actual operation.[114]

At this point in April 1951 the First Sea Lord felt that he should reexamine the need for an Atlantic command, so he convened a meeting of his naval commanders in chief and sea lords. In blunt language, Fraser stated that the command situation in the Atlantic duplicated too much effort and was confusing. The introduction of a SACLANT was a further complication and an unnecessary command link—the Admiralty could function just as well as SACLANT for the coordination of operations in the EASTLANT area. EASTLANT itself controlled both offensive and defensive forces; why not bring back a functional ASW command like CinCWA and let EASTLANT handle offensive operations?[115] The First Sea Lord's solution was to push the SG for the devolution of SACLANT and the reestablishment of bilateral U.S.–British naval links along Second World War lines.

It appears that Fraser's wavering on the command issue was either not passed on to the Chiefs of Staff or quashed at the political level, and therefore it was not transmitted to the SG or the Americans. The Americans were still monitoring the Atlantic command situation closely and noted that "there is evidence that the British government is apprehensive of U.S. global policies and is not wholeheartedly supporting them. The British government is opposing certain U.S. policies in the far east and toward Spain. The British people have evidenced dissatisfaction regarding certain proposals concerning NATO command arrangements. . . ."[116] This American observation was fueled by none other than Churchill, who Fechteler believed was being manipulated by a "group of retired British Admirals who kept feeding him propaganda."[117] During a House of Commons debate over defense issues in April 1951, Churchill spoke out against the concept of a SACLANT commanded by an American and poured gasoline on an already raging fire: "To take control of this process [ASW and SLOC protection to Britain] out of Admiralty hands, would I am sure be a grave and perhaps a fatal injury not only to ourselves but to the common cause. . . ."[118] Churchill did, however, believe that the concept of a SACEUR led by an American was sound, since the defense of Europe depended on the use of large numbers of American reinforcements. Control of the Atlantic was by tradition a British responsibility, and the British had the experience at the higher level of directing such a campaign.

The command organization situation remained stalled from March to May 1951 and was continually discussed in the British media.[119] One possible explanation, apart from the more conventional political and military reasons, was personal. Because of his tight schedule, Fraser apparently did not meet with Sherman on at least two occasions when Sherman visited London and toured the Mediterranean. This, combined with misinterpreted public statements by Sherman to the U.S. Congress, estranged the two men at a critical juncture. Sherman wrote:

> I would be less than candid if I denied that Fraser's failure to meet me in March indicated to me that he placed less importance on our previous relationship than I did. . . . More recently I have been criticized by the British for my testimony under oath before a senate committee and my remark concerning decreased capabilities quoted out of context which showed I was defending [the] British rather than criticizing them. Former Minister of Defence Alexander recently went so far as to call on Radford to say I had slandered the Royal Navy. . . . If I have been reserved in my recent attitude it has been because of my determination to uphold the dignity of the United States Naval Service and withdraw it as far as possible from a controversy which has an international political basis and which [is] inevitably damaging to both navies. I intend to visit Europe some time this month but shall not visit England unless specifically asked by Fraser. If I were asked, I would come.[120]

Carney assisted in healing the rift:

> An earlier apparent loss of contact between Fraser and myself has been repaired and Fraser is exerting himself to keep alive a continuing close and friendly relationship with me. . . . He is greatly perturbed over an apparent lack of frank camaraderie between himself and [the] CNO. He fears that he has offended you and considers that his absence from London during your visit and his failure to make contact in the Med may be contributing factors but states that news of your itinerary came too late to permit any change in plans. . . . I believe this concern is genuine and I think that some token of friendly regard from you might set his mind at rest. . . .[121]

At a meeting of the British Chiefs of Staff Committee in May 1951, Field Marshal Slim set the agenda by urging that "every effort should be made to resolve the present deadlock on command organization without delay"—probably because the Korean situation was deteriorating once again.[122] In a position counter to that of the committee, Sir Pierson Dixon (the Foreign Office representative) suggested that British insistence on a NATO command on the same level as SACLANT or SACEUR might not necessarily be desirable and would not promote a solution to the problem. In order to resolve the stalemate, Dixon believed that the British position should allow for the establishment of SACLANT under Admiral Fechteler and the acceptance of Admiral Carney as NATO CinCAFSOUTH, which would include command over all naval activity in the Mediterranean. The military members of the committee must have thought that this was incredibly naive and an effort to relinquish British position within the NATO community.[123]

NATO was left in a paradoxical position. The SACLANT problem could only be solved after the Mediterranean had been sorted out, and IBERLANT (which was part of the SACLANT problem) could not be put to rest until the Mediterranean command had been resolved. The American position on the command issue was blunt and simple: because they were providing the majority of forces in all theaters and had set their planning estimates high enough to do so, they naturally wished to have control over the entire situation. The British view was based on prestige and experience, backed by a willingness to protect what they perceived to be their vital interests: control over the survival of the British Isles and their destiny in any conflict.[124]

The first steps toward breaking the deadlock had, strangely enough, occurred back in February 1951 when Churchill launched his attack on Labour's defense policies. Although the defense issue was not the driving force behind the downfall of the Attlee government, the noticeable decline in Britain's position that had occurred under Attlee struck a discordant note in the public domain. Apparently, the NADC understood the relationship between the SACLANT issue and the election and chose not to attempt to resolve it during the campaign.[125] Winston S. Churchill once again became prime minister on 26 October 1951.

Privately, Churchill called for an immediate reassessment of the SACLANT concept in November 1951 and was surprised to find out that the NADC had approved SACLANT's organization and nationality back in December 1950. Churchill then attempted to block the acceptance of SACLANT's terms of reference (which still had not been ratified) in NATO's Military Committee. The committee, however, approved the terms of reference that the British had agreed to the previous February; the British member of the committee, Marshal of the RAF Slessor, did make it perfectly clear that there were some aspects of the terms of reference that would still have to be discussed.[126]

Slessor was instructed to explain to the Military Committee that the terms of reference that had been agreed to in February were believed by the British to be hypothetical in nature, if and when the appointment had been approved by the Military Committee at that time (that is, in February 1951). If this ploy failed, the British representative to the NADC would voice strong British disapproval at the upcoming NADC meeting in Rome in November. As a last resort, Churchill decided that he would take up the matter himself with the U.S. president.[127]

All British efforts in late 1951 to block SACLANT did not succeed, including a threat to withdraw from any Atlantic command arrangement. As a result, Churchill had to resort to a direct meeting with President Truman. It should be noted that the January 1952 summit was not strictly geared toward resolving the SACLANT issue; other items on the British agenda included economic aid, the provision of military material, and possibly atomic bomb information.[128] However, the Americans definitely wanted to discuss the Atlantic command problem and set as one of their objectives "the establishment of a SACLANT and the designation of a United States Naval officer as SACLANT without further delay."[129] This said, Eisenhower and Fechteler were not prepared to be entirely cavalier with their British allies, as Eisenhower noted: "I am quite ready to admit that Britain has a particular sensitivity to this problem because of its threatened position [in antisubmarine warfare] and the added fact that in the waters surrounding that nation, including the North Sea, may possibly be fought out a question of Britain's survival. . . . In this particular spot, we must be quite considerate of their views and anxieties. . . ."[130]

Prior to the summit, Slim, McGrigor, and Ismay urged Churchill to accept SACLANT based on the belief that the First Sea Lord would be able to exercise real command in the Atlantic through other means such as restrictive terms of reference or escape clauses. Churchill did not agree with these tactics any more because principle and accountability were now at stake: "I realize that England is a broken and impoverished power, which has cast away a great part of its Empire and of late years has misused its resources; but these fellows [the Americans] bungled the U-boat war and had to come to us for help. America may know far more than our navy does about combined 'ops' in the Pacific between their navy and air force but she knows very little of U-boat warfare. You have urged me to do this fake without any explanation to public or parliament. I will not do that. It must all come out publicly. . . ."[131]

Churchill was true to his word. On 7 January 1952, the first engagement over command in the Atlantic was joined. U.S. Secretary of Defense Lovett presented the U.S. position as tactfully as he could, cognizant of the personification of courage seated in front of him. According to Lovett, the NADC had already agreed to SACLANT, with the exception of the British, and the "problem was being too widely publicized in the press and had become a serious issue." It was clear to the Americans that one commander was needed since the Soviet Union had over six times the number of submarines available than the Germans had at the start of World War II.[132]

Churchill told Lovett that he never had been convinced of the need for a supreme commander in the Atlantic, even during the Second World War. The informal contacts between the First Sea Lord and the U.S. CNO had served the alliance well then; why would they not work in 1952? Should the survival of the British people not be in the hands of the British people?[133] In an effort to preempt the point that NATO consisted of more than two powers and as a result was more unwieldy in terms of command, Churchill recommended that a naval adviser become part of the Standing Group, so that he could mediate between the CNO and the First Sea Lord in war; if this adviser could not mediate, irreconcilable problems could continue up to the political level for a solution.[134]

This was unacceptable for Truman, who wanted a unified command in the Atlantic. Using the U.S. Pacific experience in World War II, Truman pointed out that twelve nations in the Atlantic were still too many, and almost all had shipping interests that had to represented somewhere. Falling back on the force-size argument, Churchill asked how many of the twelve had sizable fleets and could really be expected to retain input?[135]

Admiral Fechteler redirected the argument by pushing attack at source as an ASW strategy; this, he argued, had different command and control requirements, and the nature of the contemporary ASW problem was different from that of the World War II experience. Fechteler conceded that the British could and should have absolute control over shipping reception in the EASTLANT area and that one solution could be to form a United Kingdom Home Command separate from SACLANT.[136]

At this point the debate became extremely heated and threatened to go out of control. Churchill calmed it down and stated that he wanted out of the previous commitment made by the Attlee government regarding SACLANT, suggesting that Attlee's people forgot that Britain had great experience in ASW and mine countermeasures warfare. Fechteler replied that it was not within the United States' power to abrogate the understanding; it had been agreed to by the NADC, and if the issue was not resolved now, it would go back to the NADC. This meeting ended, and both sides retreated and regrouped.[137]

The next day, Churchill faced off with Truman at the Pentagon, where Churchill gave, according to Dean Acheson, U.S. secretary of state, one of his most moving speeches. Unfortunately, only a portion of that speech remains: "For centuries England has held the seas against every tyrant, wresting command of them from Spain and then from France, protecting [the Western] hemisphere from penetration by European systems in the days of [American] weakness. Now, in the plenitude of [American] power, bearing as [the Americans do] the awful burden of atomic command and responsibility for the final word of peace or war, surely [the Americans] could make room for Britain to play her historical role 'upon that Western sea whose floor is white with the bones of Englishmen'."[138] Other matters were resolved that day, and the issue of command in the Atlantic was delayed until after Churchill returned from a side trip to Ottawa.

When Churchill queried Canadian views on command in the Atlantic, Lester B. Pearson, the Canadian secretary of state for external affairs, replied that he did not believe it mattered one way or another but that the Royal Canadian Navy people supported the SACLANT idea for reasons of technology and standardization.[139] This was borne out in a special meeting of the Canadian Chiefs of Staff, and Churchill left empty-handed.

On Churchill's return to Washington, Truman, Acheson, and Fechteler sought compromise on the issue of SACLANT. Elements of that compromise included U.S. support of a recommendation to NATO that the United Kingdom Home Command be expanded geographically and that absolute control over this area be exclusively British. (This would evolve into NATO's Channel Command, which will be discussed in chapter 4.) Second, control by SACLANT of operations in the EASTLANT area would be flexible and subject to discussion. Third, Churchill would be allowed to make modifications via NATO if certain elements of the command remained unacceptable to the British. Finally (and most important from a domestic political point of view), if Churchill agreed to the establishment of SACLANT the press release would note that he still objected to the concept in principle so that Churchill would be spared public wrath. According to Acheson, Churchill looked at the proposal for about one minute and signed it, thus ending the command deadlock.[140] Later, Churchill approached Fechteler's wife at a reception and remarked: "I surrendered to your husband this afternoon but we went down with the band playing, the colours flying and the Marines at present arms!"[141] On 30 January 1952, after a virtual cesarean section, SACLANT was born.

Admiral Fechteler would not become SACLANT: the impasse of the previous year had seen him through his last days as U.S. CinCLANT, and he was posted to command the Naval War College. In his place Truman nominated Adm. Lynde McCormick, who had extensive experience in NAORPG affairs. The NADC approved McCormick's nomination on 30 January 1952.[142] From the date of his nomination until 10 April, when SACLANT headquarters was finally in place, McCormick went on an extensive inspection tour before putting together a provisional command organization.

This tour highlighted the multitude of problems McCormick would have to deal with, particularly those involving the delineation between SACLANT and the newly established Channel Command. Suffice it to say that SACLANT's provisional organization was similar to that shown in figure 3.23. Note that there was no IBERLANT command; McCormick deliberately chose not to deal with boundary issues early on. Essentially, the provisional organization followed the North Atlantic Ocean Regional Planning Group's October 1950 recommendation to the NADC.[143]

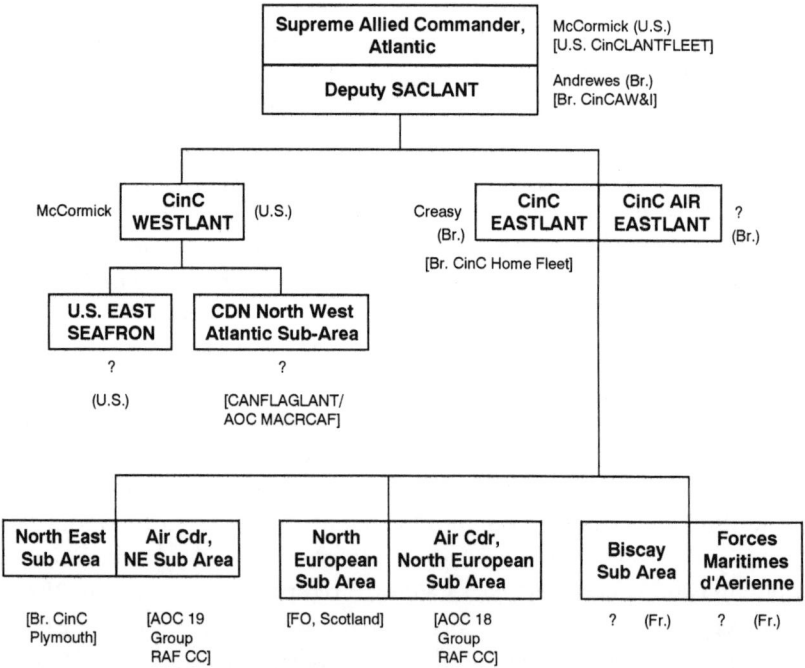

Fig. 3.23. SACLANT's provisional organization, February 1952

The evolution of NATO command organization throughout 1950–51 was an arduous one. The formalization of an Anglo-American strategic concept that took into consideration NATO requirements was a significant step, followed by interim arrangements and the creation of the regional planning groups as entities for international planning coordination. Following the threat of worldwide hostilities emanating from the Korean situation, the decision to create NATO supreme commands in peacetime in preparation for war is not surprising. The SACEUR command had a wealth of historical experience behind it, the added advantage of having Eisenhower at its head, and a fair amount of international compromise in its makeup. SACLANT had no such formative experience, and its creation was the result of acrimonious debate, high-level political interference, and prolonged stalemate; personalities as well as national prestige, survival, and capabilities were the primary factors in the resolution of the Anglo-American dispute. Even after SACLANT was in place, problems did not cease. Once SACLANT was established as a command agency, it had to undergo a shakedown stage to finalize its exact composition and to develop ways and means of coordinating with the naval elements of SACEUR's decentralized command structure. That is the subject of chapter 4.

4 ➤ From the Ditch to the Pillars of Hercules

Command Organization in the Channel, STRIKEFLEETLANT and IBERLANT, 1951–1953

The maxim that the command of the sea depends on the battle-fleet is then perfectly sound so long as it is taken to include all the other facts on which it hangs. The true function of the battle-fleet is to protect cruisers and the flotilla at their special work. The best means of doing this is of course to destroy the enemy's power of interference. The doctrine of destroying the enemy's armed forces as the paramount object here reasserts itself, and reasserts itself so strongly as to permit for most practical purposes the rough generalization that the command depends upon the battle-fleet. . . .
—Corbett, *Some Principles of Maritime Strategy*

England does not love coalitions.
—Benjamin Disraeli

The new level of tension between the West and the Soviet Union established after November 1950 continued into 1951. It did not slacken significantly from 1951 to 1953. In Europe, incidents in Berlin and the loss of several NATO members' reconnaissance aircraft to Soviet fighters served to maintain it. Elsewhere, the seesaw war across the 38th parallel in Korea continued, as did French efforts in Indochina and British attempts to prevent Malaya from falling into the Chinese sphere. The Dutch also continued to have problems in Indonesia. Notwithstanding Stalin's attempt at a "peace offensive" in early 1952, which included the bizarre concept of having the Soviet Union actually join NATO, Soviet subversion and espionage operations in Western Europe continued unabated. The most important consequence of these events was the creation of the NATO commands SACEUR and SACLANT.

Despite the obvious threats to Western interests, the state of the NATO alliance in late 1951 and early 1952 remained uncertain. Attempts to bring a federal German republic into NATO and integrate its armed forces into the organization caused political problems with the French, while discussion continued over the incorporation of Greece and Turkey into NATO and the exact delineation of the NATO area in the Mediterranean and the Middle East. In terms of command organization, the newest NATO commands, SACLANT and Channel Command (CHANCOM), went through a developmental period while the problem of strategic command in the Mediterranean basin was under review. The inclusion of the Mediterranean into NATO and its relationship to SACLANT were points of contention between not only the Americans and the British but the French as well. The specific problems of the Mediterranean will be dealt with in chapter 5. This chapter will examine the continuing strategic debate over defense of the NATO area in 1951 and 1952, the establishment of the Channel Command in early 1952, SACLANT's developmental period, and the IBERLANT command problem from 1951 to 1953.

Strategic Concepts

The strategic concepts guiding NATO from 1951 to the early part of 1953, MC 14 and MC 14/1, were virtually identical to the Crosspiece/Galloper concept examined in detail in chapter 3.[1] This concept envisaged a massive Soviet land and air campaign against Western Europe, Britain, and Scandinavia, with secondary thrusts at Turkey and the Persian Gulf, followed by a heavy anti-SLOC campaign in the Atlantic as well as limited land or subversive operations against the North American continent and the use of TU-4 aircraft equipped with atomic weapons against targets in Europe, the United States, and Canada.[2] Masthead, the "U.S. Joint Emergency War Plan for a War in 1952," and Binnacle, its closest British counterpart, were code names for the Anglo-American Emergency War Plan for a global war against the Soviet Union in the 1951–52 time frame. These were almost identical to Crosspiece/Galloper. For Masthead/Binnacle's purposes, the land and tactical air forces available to the Soviet Union were not considered to be any different in quantity than previous estimates had suggested. In terms of naval forces, the predominant threat was still considered to be the Type XXI submarine clone (see appendix 1) and a small surface fleet "in being" (see appendix 2). The Soviet strategic air threat estimates from

1951 to 1953 differed slightly from Crosspiece/Galloper in that the Soviets were thought to have 800–1,000 TU-4 Bull strategic bombers and 700 IL-28 Beagle intermediate-range bombers. The Soviet atomic stockpile was estimated to include 50–100 kiloton-sized bombs similar to the U.S. Mk III (22 kt) and was assumed to be targeted on North America and Europe.[3]

The NATO response in Masthead/Binnacle was also similar to Crosspiece/Galloper—that is, a fighting withdrawal to the Rhine and, if necessary, the Pyrenees. Relying on Britain, Spain, or North Africa as a base area and with aircraft carrier task forces providing support, the allies would counterattack while an Anglo-American strategic air offensive rained atomic and conventional bombs down on the Soviet heartland. In an improvement on previous capability, from 1951 to 1953 the American Strategic Air Command (SAC) and the U.S. Navy had access to a total of 788 atomic-capable aircraft, RAF Bomber Command had eighty-seven atomic-capable aircraft, and there was an American stockpile of 1,000 kiloton-size weapons.[4]

The concept of a conventional forward defense (fighting the early stages of a land campaign in Germany rather than in France) was reiterated in NATO planning in early 1951, although it appeared to be at variance with the Anglo-American strategic concept. Eisenhower's concept for the defense of Western Europe was based on having fifty to sixty divisions available, arranged into three heavily defended areas: Denmark/Netherlands, Italy, and a center that would withdraw to the Rhine to form a pocket. Two simultaneous flank attacks from the fortified zones would occur, supported by aircraft carrier–based aviation, to destroy the Soviet onslaught.[5] Clearly, such a strategic concept would require vast naval support—not only direct involvement in the land battle but in reinforcing and supplying it. The size of NATO's combined naval potential was more than adequate for these varied tasks (see appendix 2). However, the gap between force requirements embodied by the NATO Medium Term Defence Plan (MTDP) and the actual forces available from NATO members prevented SACEUR from realizing his minimal force goals for the defense of Western Europe; attempts to develop an integrated European army also came to naught. SACEUR thus had to rely on the original gloomy plans involving a fallback to Spain.[6]

Interestingly, a meeting of the North Atlantic Council in October 1952 perused the current NATO strategic concept and force-level situation and concluded that NATO had two options: defend the central region, or withdraw to defended peripheral bases and reenter Europe. The Standing Group (SG) continued to support the former option and ratified the decision to plan for the defense of Western territory right on the border of the

From the Ditch to the Pillars of Hercules ➤ *141*

Iron Curtain.[7] This again flew in the face of the force-level situation, but the political ramifications of anything less were just too great.

Unlike previous war plans, Masthead/Binnacle contained some discussion of command organization. In a clear departure from Crosspiece/Galloper, the allied planners included current and projected NATO commands within a global command organization (see fig. 4.1). Later versions of the U.S. Joint Outline Emergency War Plan such as the 1953 version included the Channel and Mediterranean organizations. In real terms, then, the Masthead/Binnacle concepts valid for the 1951–53 period were not very different from the Crosspiece/Galloper concepts of the 1949–50 period. The only changes made recognized the increased capability to deliver atomic weapons from land bases or from aircraft carriers.[8]

THE CHANNEL COMMAND

In order to conduct the defense of Western Europe, NATO command organization at sea had to adapt to SACEUR's clarification of his concept

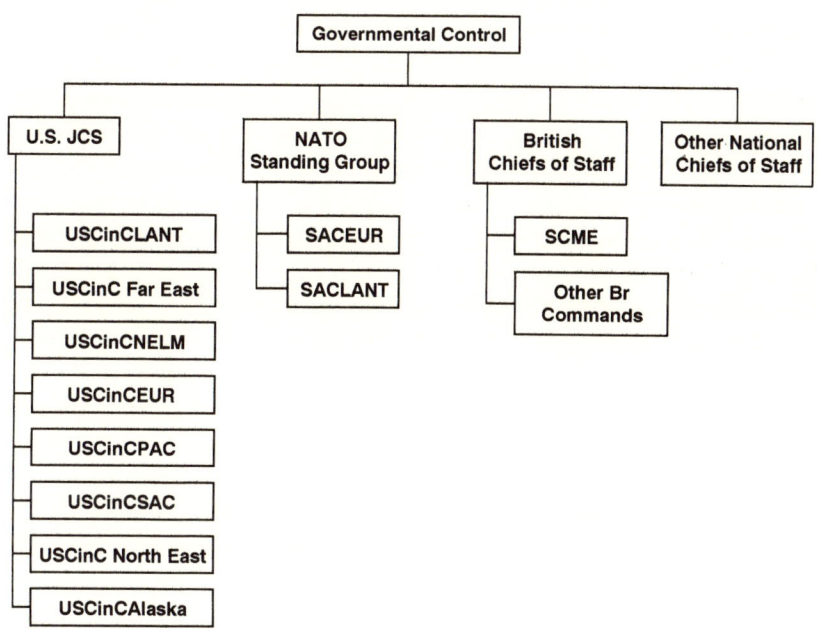

Fig. 4.1. Masthead/Binnacle command organization for the higher direction of war

of operations and the projected needs for naval support to it. One consequence of this was the development of the Channel Command (CHANCOM). During the January 1952 summit in Washington, Churchill received a concession that allowed Britain control over sea areas out to the 1,000-fathom line from the British Isles—and by inference, operational control over the forces operating in the English Channel and the North Sea. However, the need to clarify the overlap between operations on continental Europe and in the Atlantic was noticed long before SACLANT and SACEUR were actually established.

As noted in chapter 1, World War II naval operations in the Channel and the North Sea were a British responsibility exercised through the Area Combined Headquarters (ACHQ) system. The relevant ACHQs in this case were Chatham, whose senior naval officer was called Admiral, Nore; Plymouth, whose senior naval officer was called Admiral, Atlantic Coast; and Rosyth, whose senior naval officer was called Admiral, Rosyth. The operating forces handled by the ACHQs included coastal convoys, mine countermeasures (MCM) operations, and coastal patrol craft, as well as air support for these activities. The larger naval units such as aircraft carriers and battleships remained under the control of British CinC Home Fleet. This system worked fairly well during the Second World War, but it should be kept in mind that the enemy frontier was the German-controlled French-Belgian-Dutch coast, Allied coastal traffic was restricted to one British controlling authority, and the operating forces were predominantly British.[9]

In the 1950s, the situation was quite different. There was no single authority for the control of coastal traffic. There were in fact six: Great Britain, France, Belgium, the Netherlands, Denmark, and Norway, each with its own operating forces and all answering to the Western Union Chiefs of Staff Committee separately through national commands. An expedient was implemented by the British in November 1950 while they were sorting out their national air and sea defense overlap with the projected SACEUR command. The British initially saw the Channel and North Sea areas as coming under the command of the projected Supreme Allied Commander Atlantic's Eastern Atlantic Area commander, with a liaison officer co-located with SACEUR's Flag Officer, Western Europe (see fig. 4.2). Assuming that the Eastern Atlantic commander was British (and was in fact the CinC Home Station "double-hatted"), the British planners placed their ACHQs under him. In a general sense, the planners predicted that the French would have their own ACHQ in the Bay of Biscay based on the French coastal area command, Premar II, with the French Premar I and

From the Ditch to the Pillars of Hercules ➢ 143

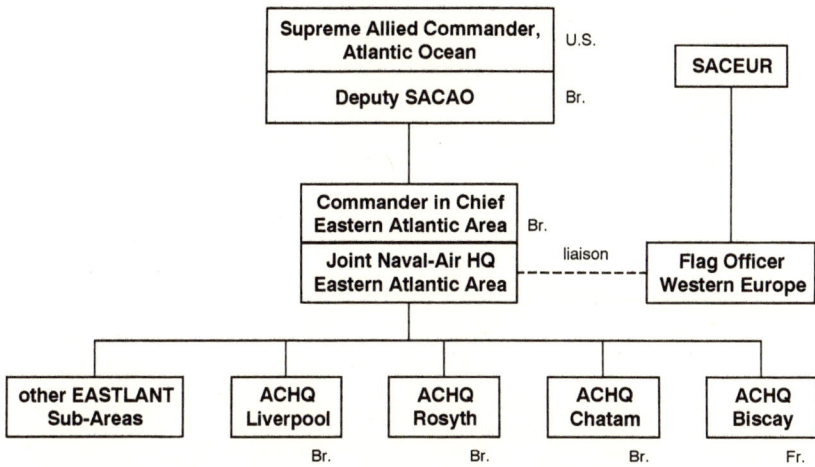

Fig. 4.2. British concept for command in the Channel area, November 1950

the Belgian and Dutch sea frontier commanders under the control of the Chatham and Rosyth ACHQs. Norwegian forces and their area would presumably be subject to ACHQ Rosyth (see fig. 4.3). These arrangements were logical given that the proposed SAC Atlantic Ocean's terms of reference were under consideration by the NATO Military Committee in November–December 1950 and that SACLANT's primary responsibility was naval and air support to SACEUR.[10]

The British understanding of command in the Channel area was further clarified by the First Sea Lord, Admiral Fraser of North Cape, to the British Chiefs of Staff Committee while the debate over SACAO continued in early 1951. Fraser saw that, under the North Atlantic Ocean Regional Planning Group's scheme for the establishment of sub-areas under the Eastern Atlantic Area commander, two of his national commands (Admiral, Atlantic Coast and Admiral, Rosyth) would be double-hatted as NATO Eastern Atlantic sub-area commanders, confusingly labeled UK Atlantic Coast Sub-area and UK North Sea Coast Sub-area. Although this was needless duplication, operating forces were actually allocated to the British ACHQs pending their acknowledgment as NATO SACAO sub-areas.[11] This state of affairs, while clarifying the situation in the approaches to the Channel, did not bring the Channel under NATO command as yet. This still remained the bailiwick of the British national command ACHQ Chatham; Admiral, Nore; and his associated RAF Coastal Command maritime air group.

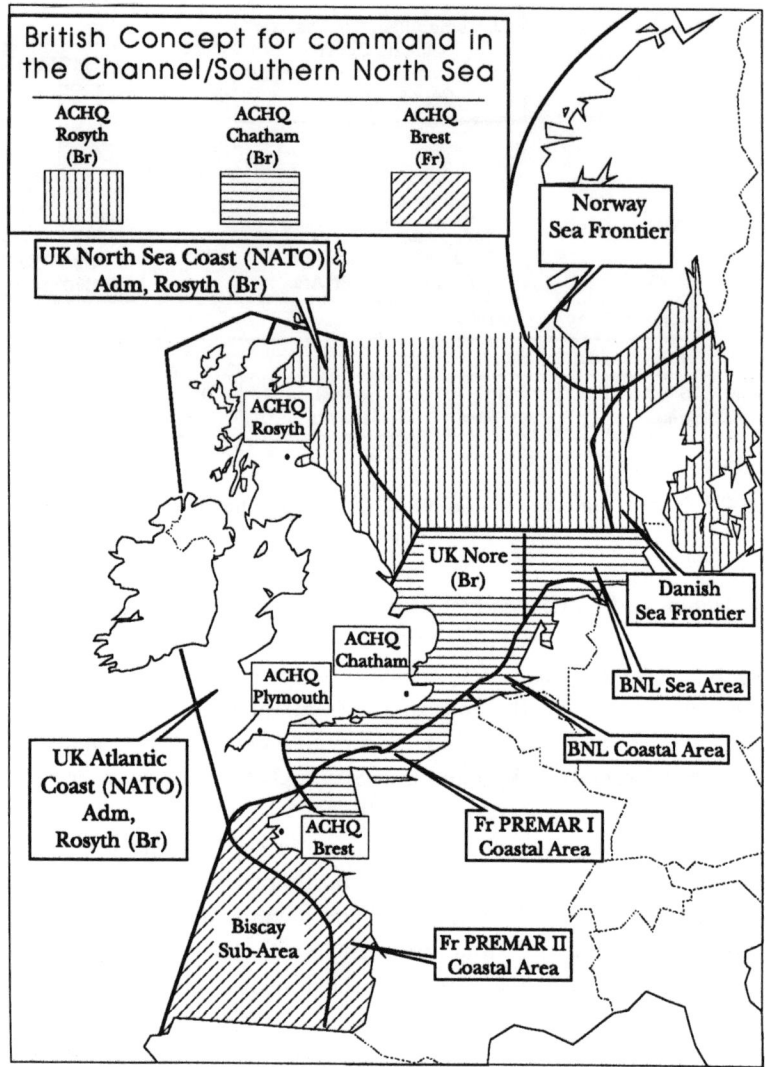

Fig. 4.3.

These arrangements were pared slightly by the SG while it was preparing emergency command organizations in February 1951. In the interim, the SG decided that the British would control the area if war broke out and that the general command plan they would follow would come from SACAO once he was appointed at the beginning of the war (see fig. 4.4). Instead of the cumbersome NATO nomenclature for the

From the Ditch to the Pillars of Hercules ➢ *145*

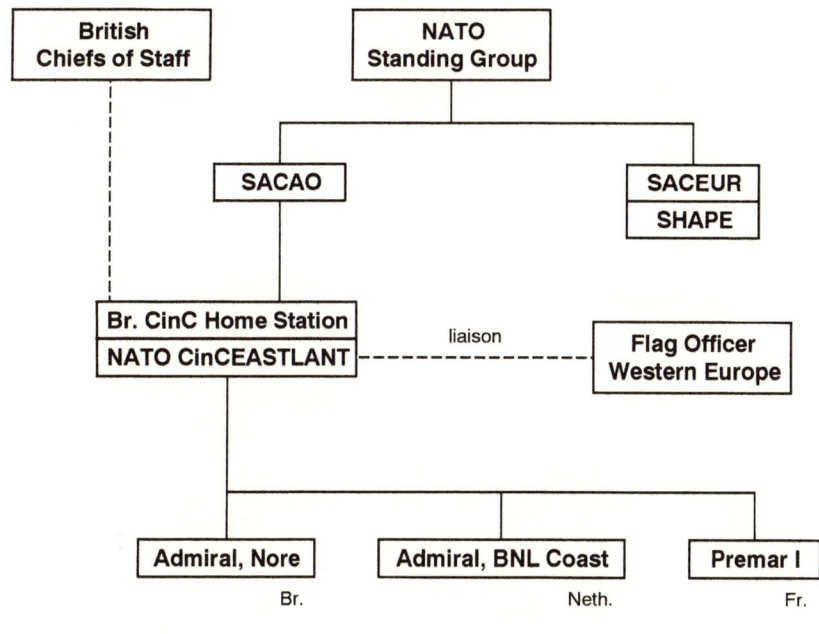

Fig. 4.4. Standing Group's interim arrangement for command in the Channel, February 1951

various national coastal area commands, the SG merely subordinated Admiral, Nore, Premar I, and a Dutch admiral, Belgium/Netherlands Coast, to NATO CinC EASTLANT, who was a double-hatted British CinC Home Station.[12]

With the issue of disbanding the Western Union Chiefs of Staff in 1951 came a further review by NATO of command in the Channel. The Dutch had noted that if and when WUCoS was disbanded, the Netherlands, France, and Belgium would have no representation in any Channel command. Furthermore, the Dutch suggested that the area become a separate command subordinate to the SG, much as SACEUR was and SACAO would be, since the Channel area was not only the busiest shipping zone in the world but also had a central role in reinforcing Europe. The result of the Dutch proposal was the creation of the Channel Committee in February 1951 to evaluate the problems of command in the Channel and Southern North Sea. The committee was composed of naval members from Britain, France, the Netherlands, and Belgium.[13]

The British seized upon this opportunity to review the situation in more detail and overhaul the interim proposal. The options for command over the Channel area fell into three categories. Either the area became subordinate to SACEUR, subordinate to SACAO, or a separate command. The arguments against the Channel being part of SACEUR were quite compelling: the European members believed that most of the convoys moving through the area would be supporting the civilian needs of the member nations in war, while SACEUR had different priorities, such as reinforcement convoys. As such, if SACEUR had control over escort protection and schedules, the needs of the civilian populations would be lower on the priority scale. On the other hand, if SACAO were responsible for the region, EASTLANT would wind up being overworked; he would have to create separate staffs anyway to deal with the distracting and intricate coastal convoy NCS problems.[14]

As such, the establishment of a separate command made sense, and there was complete agreement on the tasks that any commander in the Channel would have to face. These included escort of cross-Channel convoys, aerial ASW operations, air defense of convoys, MCM operations, and NCS duties. But a decision on the matter would have to wait, because the SG was preoccupied throughout early 1951 with other command matters.[15]

If the Channel and Southern North Sea were to become a separate command, the relationship between it and SACEUR's AFNORTH had to be clarified as well. As we saw in chapter 3, AFNORTH and EASTLANT jointly handled naval operations in support of the land battle within SACEUR's area, while AFNORTH was responsible for MCM and coastal convoys within the immediate coastal waters of Denmark and Norway. However, in a conflict in which Norway would be supported, who was to be responsible for UK–Scandinavia convoys: a Channel and Southern North Sea command, SACEUR, or SACAO? Previously, under the regional planning group system, the Western European RPG (SACEUR's predecessor) controlled the entire North Sea up to the Shetland Islands. With the expanded influence over carrier operations and the larger area of operations that was projected for SACAO, this could no longer be the case, so SACEUR's area shrunk to include the coastal areas around only Norway and Denmark. To supplant the already existing conflict of interest between SACAO and SACEUR, any new command would have to resolve its differences with those two.[16]

One point of contention between SACEUR and the proposed new command was over air cover to the Channel and Southern North Sea region. The British had, so far, been successful in preventing SACEUR from acquir-

The primary threat to NATO sea lanes of communication in the 1950s included the Soviet Whiskey (*top*) and Zulu classes of submarines. *U.S. Navy photos*

The formation of a Supreme Headquarters, Allied Powers, Europe under a Supreme Allied Commander, Europe was a critical step in the creation of NATO's system of deterrence. The first SACEUR, Gen. Dwight D. Eisenhower, is shown here at Fountainebleau, France, with his subordinate commanders (*left to right*): Gen. Alphonse Juin (French Army), Gen. Alfred M. Greunther (U.S. Army), Vice Adm. Robert Jaujard (French Navy), and Lt. Gen. Lauris Norstad (U.S. Air Force). SACEUR's deputy, Field Marshal Bernard L. Montgomery (British Army), is not present.
U.S. Army photo

SHAPE was originally located at Marly, France.
U.S. Army photo

The January 1952 summit between Prime Minister Churchill and President Truman was instrumental in breaking the deadlocked SACLANT command issue. *U.S. Navy photo, courtesy Harry S. Truman Library*

Adm. Lynde McCormick (USN), NATO's first Supreme Allied Commander, Atlantic. *U.S. Navy photo*

The culmination of World War II experience and five years of bilateral discussions, NATO's Supreme Allied Commander, Atlantic was established in 1952. Admiral McCormick presided over the opening of SACLANT headquarters in Norfolk, Virginia, on 10 April 1952. *NATO SACLANT photo*

Held in September 1952, Exercise Mainbrace was the first large-scale multinational naval exercise conducted by NATO in the Atlantic. Mainbrace was also instrumental in the creation of SACLANT's Striking Fleet, Atlantic. Forming up in the Firth of Clyde, the nuclear strike carriers USS *Midway* *(below, left)* and USS *Franklin D. Roosevelt (below, right)* lie alongside HMS *Eagle*. Other forces participating in Exercise Mainbrace included *(at right)* USS *Wright*, HMS *Eagle*, and HMS *Illustrious*. *U.S. Navy photos*

The introduction of nuclear-capable aircraft into the U.S. Navy complicated NATO command arrangements in both the Mediterranean and the Atlantic. Initially deployed to land bases along the Mediterranean, the AJ-1 Savage also operated from aircraft carriers off northern Norway. *U.S. Navy photo*

Adm. Sir Arthur Power, NATO's first Commander in Chief, Channel. *Royal Navy photo*

HMCS *Magnificent* operated as part of a multinational ASW support group during Mainbrace. *Canadian National Defence photo*

Adm. Robert Carney (USN), SACEUR's Commander in Chief, Allied Forces Southern Europe. Carney fought to retain control over American resources allocated to NATO. Some thought that Carney's Irish background was an obstacle to improving Anglo-American naval relations in the Mediterranean. *U.S. Navy photo*

Channel Command, first headed by Admiral Power of the Royal Navy, is responsible for mine countermeasures along this highly congested shipping route. Although this photograph was taken in the 1970s, MCM vessels from Britain, France, Belgium, and the Netherlands have cooperated under CHANCOM since 1952 to safeguard SACEUR's reinforcement by sea. *NATO CHANCOM photo*

NATO's southern flank was the responsibility of SACEUR's Allied Forces Southern Europe, headquartered in Naples, Italy. *NATO AFSOUTH photo*

Adm. Lord Louis Mountbatten of Burma, SACEUR's Commander in Chief, Allied Forces Mediterranean. Many believed that he was appointed primarily to enhance British prestige along NATO's southern flank. *U.S. Navy photo*

After a great deal of deliberation, SACEUR's Allied Forces Mediterranean headquarters was established at Malta in December 1952. *NATO photo*

ing control over the air defenses of Great Britain, and they went to great lengths to retain control over long-range maritime patrol aircraft as well. On the SACEUR side of the coin, the Americans were adamant that the operational control of air tasks in the Channel/North Sea area "is not intended to include any control whatsoever of air operations in the subject area other than those required for the immediate accomplishment of the tasks and missions assigned to CinC British Home Command. . . ."[17] In other words, the Americans did not want their aircraft assigned to SACEUR "misused"; since Channel Command would not be responsible for the air defense of its area, some coordinating agency had to be found. This problem raised the specter of having to coordinate air operations among SACEUR (central region), CHANCOM, RAF air defenses in Britain, and the joint command of AFNORTH, which itself was under SACEUR's command. This problem would remain unresolved throughout 1951.

The Channel Committee met in October 1951 to establish terms of reference for the projected Allied Commander, Channel and Southern North Sea and to resolve its relationship with the projected SACLANT command. Essentially, the problem was resolved in functional terms. SACLANT, through his EASTLANT commander, would control offensive carrier, ASW hunter-killer, or amphibious operations if they happened to be within the geographic bounds of the Channel Command. CHANCOM in turn would be responsible for local convoy protection, MCM, and coastal craft operations.[18]

This having been resolved, NATO went ahead and created Channel Command in February 1952 (see fig. 4.5). The Channel Committee remained the dispute-resolving entity and was subordinated to the SG. Allied Commander in Chief, Channel (Adm. Sir Arthur Power, RN) and Allied Air Commander in Chief, Channel (Air Marshal Stevens, RAF) were in command of the operating forces; ACinCCHAN was also the British CinC Portsmouth, while his air counterpart was triple-hatted as CinC RAF Coastal Command and NATO CinCAIREASTLANT, a subordinate of SACLANT. There were five geographic sub-area commands (see fig. 4.6): BENECHAN Sub-area, led by a Dutch naval officer; Commander, Nore Sub-area and Commander, Plymouth Sub-area and their associated maritime air group commanders, who were both British and double-hatted to ACHQ positions; Premar I, a French naval commander, with his associated Forces Maritimes D'Airienne; and Premar II, who worked with Premar I for some operations in the Channel within his national geographic area. The actual CHANCOM area was extended slightly to the west after a meeting between SACLANT and CinCCHAN

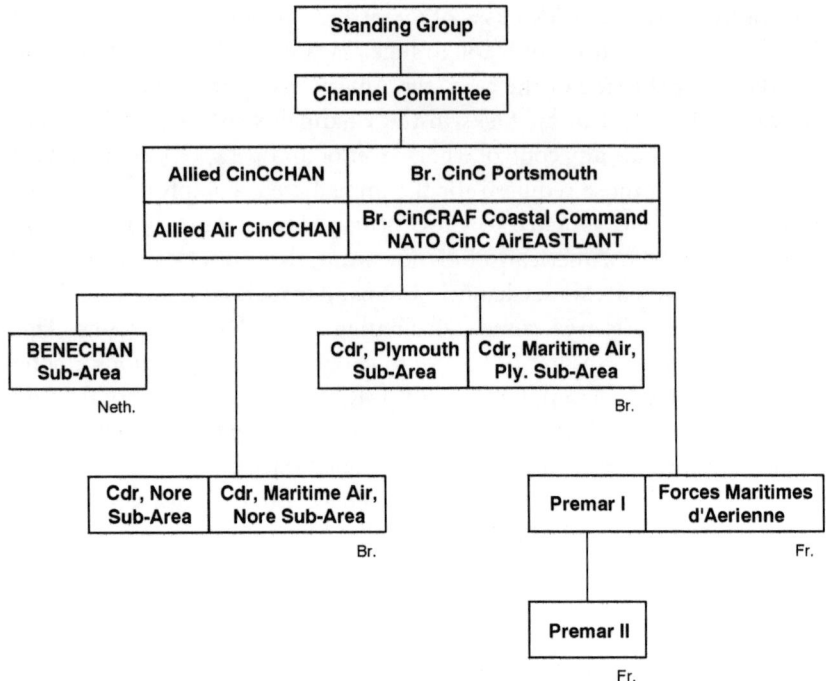

Fig. 4.5. Channel Command, February 1952

in March 1952. AFNORTH remained responsible for the coastal waters of Denmark and Norway under SACEUR.[19]

CHANCOM took its place with the other NATO command organizations in 1952 and started to create its own war plans; its unique geographic position was reconciled with the functional nature of its operating forces and those of SACLANT and SACEUR.[20] Although it may appear as though CHANCOM was deemed to be a British responsibility after the January 1952 summit, its roots did in fact go back much farther. In any case, it probably would have remained a British-influenced area since the preponderance of forces available for operations within the area would be British (see appendix 2).

SACLANT Shakes Out

After the establishment of SACLANT under Adm. Lynde McCormick (USN) in January 1952, the next twenty-four months were essentially a developmental period. Although SACLANT had a specific mission within the

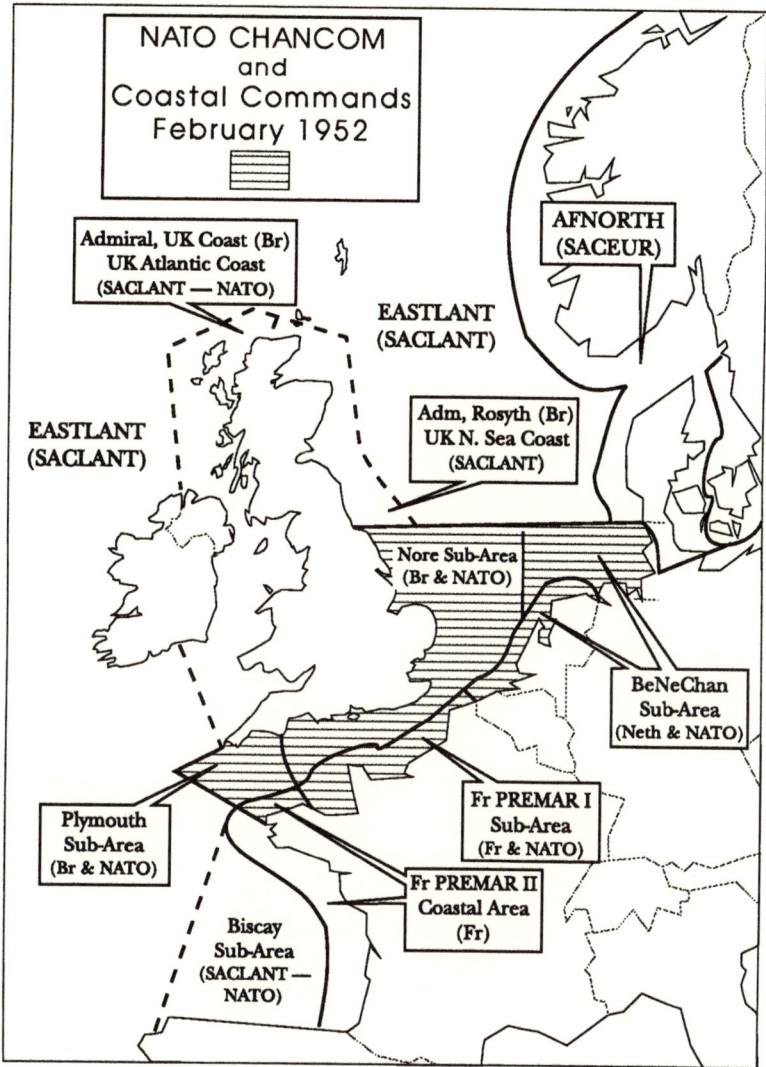

Fig. 4.6.

strategic concept and a provisional organization, a detailed and finalized command organization was necessary before planning could continue.

As we have seen, the British already had a detailed national organization for their side of the Atlantic and had worked out coordination arrangements with SACEUR and, later, CHANCOM. Only official NATO titles and positions needed to be added to these national commands. These included NATO CinCEASTLANT, who was Adm. Sir George Creasy, British CinC Home Station; NATO CinCAIREASTLANT, Air Marshal Stevens, CinC RAF Coastal Command; and Deputy SACLANT, Vice Adm. Sir William Andrewes, British CinC America and West Indies Station. EASTLANT's initial sub-areas included the Northeast Sub-area, Northern Europe Sub-area, and Biscay Sub-area, the latter being a French command under Admiral Nomy. What about the other side of the Atlantic?

Before finalizing his command arrangements, Admiral McCormick embarked on a tour of the SACLANT area from 24 February to 20 March 1952. He noted that, in all cases, actual area boundaries had yet to resolved. After a visit to Norway, however, McCormick publicly reiterated the previous NAORPG recommendation that coastal waters remain a national responsibility and that command in the Atlantic be decentralized at the area and sub-area level as much as possible. Other earlier decisions (such as one made by the Military Committee in November 1951) allowed for the broad division of sea areas into Ocean Areas under NATO command, Coastal Areas under national command, and Island Bases under national command. The rationale for this was the mobility of naval units and the international and legal aspects of the high seas.[21]

When McCormick arrived in Ottawa on 18–19 March, the Canadian piece of the SACLANT puzzle fell smoothly into place. The proposed and interim command organizations for the Atlantic dating from 1947 all had geographically expanded the Second World War–era Canadian Northwest Atlantic Command eastward to the tip of Greenland but had paid little attention to the actual command organization that would exercise control over it. The Canadians had set up a modified ACHQ system during World War II for both the Canadian Atlantic coast and for Newfoundland, which at the time was not a part of Canada (see chapter 2). The Canadian Northwest Atlantic Command was in charge of convoy operations, ASW, and LRMPA activity within its area. Command was exerted through CinCCNA and his subordinate coastal commands, Joint Services Committee, Atlantic Coast (JSCAC) and Joint Services Subcommittee, Newfoundland (JSSC); larger fleet units such as carriers and battleships remained under national British or American operational control. After 1945 CinCNA was disbanded, and the previous Canadian commands, Commanding Officer, Atlantic Coast (COAC) and JSCAC, were reestablished in 1946. There was no need for JSSC Newfoundland once Newfoundland joined Canada in 1949.[22]

The Joint Services Committee, Atlantic Coast in its post-1945 incarnation resembled a British ACHQ and consisted of the commanders of two geographic commands, Flag Officer, Atlantic Coast (Navy) and General Officer Commanding, Eastern Command (Army). Air operations were commanded by the Air Officer Commanding, Air Defence Command (RCAF; later AOC Maritime Group) in a functional capacity. The terms of reference for the JSCAC were limited to local defense planning and coordination between the services; it was not permitted to deal with any other national command unless authorized to do so by the Canadian Chiefs of Staff Committee.[23]

The potentially confusing problem of command boundaries between the NAORPG (and later SACLANT) and the Canada–U.S. Regional Planning Group (which was not dissolved when the other regional planning groups were) was the topic of discussion when McCormick visited Ottawa in March 1952. Previously, no exact boundary between CUSRPG and NAORPG existed because "the same operational authority will be responsible for both the ocean area and coastal area of the eastern Canadian and U.S. coast."[24] By 1952, however, the delineation between CUSRPG and the North Atlantic area was finalized. CUSRPG was responsible for coordinating the defense of harbors and inland waterways, coastal and inland MCM operations, land coastal defenses, the defense of airspace, and NCS for coastal convoys. NAORPG/SACLANT remained in control of oceangoing convoys, offshore ASW operations, and other high seas naval operations.[25]

The Canadian executive agency for the seaward defense of the CUSRPG area was the Canadian FOAC (Rear Adm. R.E.S. Bidwell, RCN), who in turn exercised his CUSRPG function through a Coastal Defense Commander (see fig. 4.7). FOAC handled his SACLANT function through his headquarters and remained under WESTLANT, who was actually a triple-hatted SACLANT (NATO SACLANT, NATO WESTLANT/U.S. CinCLANT, and U.S. CinCLANTFLEET, unified). Thus FOAC, a Canadian national command, headed the NATO Canadian Atlantic Sub-area as COMCANLANT under WESTLANT/SACLANT and was responsible to the CUSRPG for coordination of his coastal operations, using the Canadian JSCAC as the mechanism for operational control of the operating forces. The Canadian national command AOC Maritime Group was responsible for all LRMPA operations within the entire Canadian Atlantic Sub-area, be they coastal or oceanic. In effect, the entire Canadian naval effort on the Atlantic coast was subordinate to NATO WESTLANT and under a Canadian commander, much like it had been in the Second World War.[26]

The Americans, on the other hand, had placed all LRMPAs under naval command back in 1949. The commander of the U.S. Eastern Sea Frontier

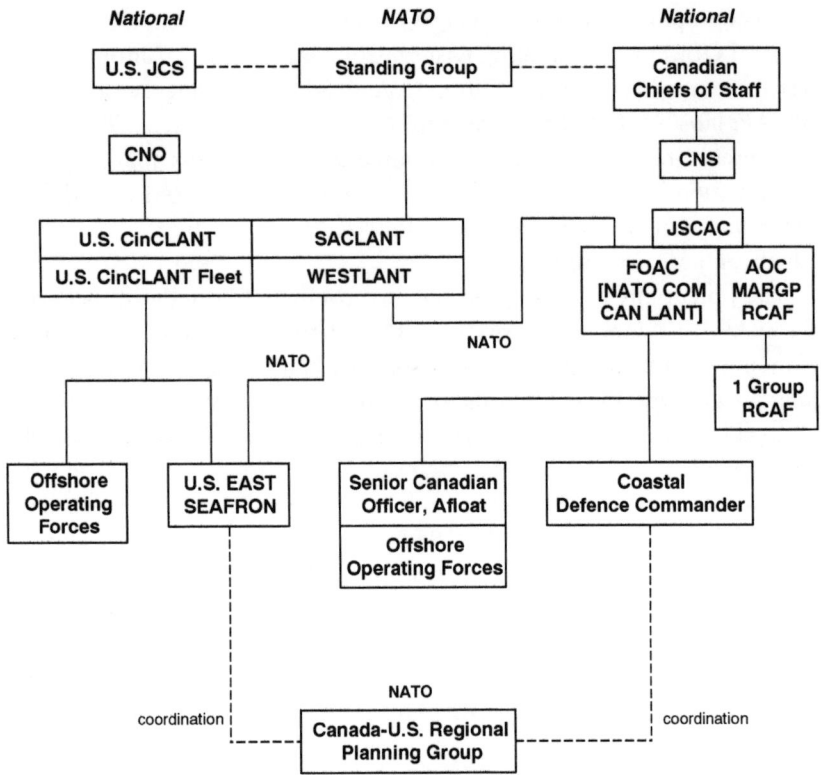

Fig. 4.7. Command organization for the Canadian Atlantic Sub-area and its relationship to SACLANT, March 1952

(EASTSEAFRON), the U.S. national command for coastal operations, was the equivalent of the Canadian JSCAC minus the army command. The U.S. EASTSEAFRON commander, Vice Admiral DuBose (USN), was directly responsible to Chief of Naval Operations Admiral Fechteler for MCM operations, harbor defense, and coastal NCS; again, like the JSCAC, DuBose had a dual responsibility to CUSRPG for coordination of continental defense efforts as well as a responsibility to SACLANT/U.S. CinCLANTFLEET for coordination with offshore ASW operations. Air defense of the U.S. coast was under a separate command, Continental Air Defense Command (CONAD). Operations in the Caribbean were, by mutual agreement with the British, under the command of McCormick in his capacity as U.S. CinCLANTFLEET, while the southernmost limit of

SACLANT's command was established at the Tropic of Cancer.²⁷

Reporting back to the North Atlantic Council after he had completed his tour, McCormick explained the status of his command and its limitations. The most critical item on his staff's agenda was an Emergency Defense Plan for the immediate defense of the North Atlantic area with the resources at hand in 1952. McCormick specifically stated that this planning could not go ahead until SACLANT's command organization was more or less firmly established. In assembling the plan, he had to rely on the precedents and general planning done by the NAORPG in 1950 and 1951. So far, the EASTLANT and WESTLANT organizations were developing without difficulty; the prime exception was IBERLANT, which McCormick again deferred to a later date.²⁸

In terms of the threat to the North Atlantic area in 1952, SACLANT estimated that the primary naval problem would come from mines, submarines, surface raiders, and guided missiles; he also stated that "it would be unwise to assume that the USSR submarine fleet [is] anything but efficient."²⁹ Convoying would not be a problem: McCormick assured the NAC that an organization would be in place on D-day. A major concern was the use of atomic bombs against infrastructure such as port facilities. To test the organization that was in place, McCormick informed the NAC that the first exercise held by SACLANT in the North Atlantic area, Exercise Mainbrace, would take place in September 1952, notwithstanding the still unsurmounted problems of intelligence sharing, standardization, and communications.³⁰

One element of SACLANT's command organization deserves special mention. In July 1952, SACLANT proposed to the Standing Group that a coalition submarine command be established under SACLANT to coordinate and control friendly submarine activity within his area. Surprisingly, given the American proclivity for secrecy regarding submarine operations, SACLANT recommended that such a command, if established, should be subordinate to EASTLANT and led by a British naval officer with a U.S. deputy and a coalition staff.³¹ The objective of Commander Submarines, Eastern Atlantic Area (COMSUBEASTLANT) would be to "ensure effective direction of the submarine effort in the Eastern Atlantic and coordination between Sub Force Eastern Atlantic and Air Forces, Eastern Atlantic. . . ."³² Apparently, the concern over the possibility of targeting LRMPAs on friendly submarines was paramount, and COMSUBEASTLANT was needed to coordinate with CinCAIREASTLANT. The British rapidly concurred, and the proposal was approved by the SG sometime in August 1952, prior to Exercise Mainbrace. The first COMSUBEASTLANT was Rear Adm. George Simpson (RN), who was double-hatted in his national position of Flag Officer, Submarines.[33]

Just prior to the groundbreaking Exercise Mainbrace, the problem of IBERLANT became the focus of Anglo-American discussion again. Why this issue was raised at this time is unclear, but it appears to have been a British initiative. The British took great pains to demonstrate that allowing IBERLANT to become a separate command on par with EASTLANT under an American commander was as absurd as the second option, placing IBERLANT under WESTLANT—which amounted to the same thing anyway. Keeping in mind that the IBERLANT issue involved conflicting British and American shipping interests (north-south shipping to support Britain from the Far East versus east-west troop convoys to the Iberian Peninsula to reinforce the fighting withdrawal), the British Chiefs of Staff actively pushed for the subordination of IBERLANT to EASTLANT, with a local headquarters in Gibraltar.[34]

Admiral Fechteler, who had succeeded Adm. Forrest Sherman as CNO of the U.S. Navy when the former died tragically in July 1951, actually supported the British position in private conversations with Adm. Sir Rhoderick McGrigor, the First Sea Lord, and was clearly in favor of the Gentleman's Agreement previously established under Fechteler and Douglas-Pennent that allowed for the IBERLANT settlement to follow the establishment of a naval command organization in the Mediterranean. McCormick as SACLANT, meanwhile, stuck to his conviction that IBERLANT should become a separate command led by an American under SACLANT on par with EASTLANT. In the end the British were again successful, possibly with Fechteler's help, in delaying the creation of IBERLANT and retaining the status quo that allowed EASTLANT to command the area in the event of war.[35]

Thus, prior to Exercise Mainbrace in September 1952, the status of SACLANT's command was more firmly established than it had been when McCormick assumed command in January 1952 (see fig. 4.8). SACLANT in August 1952 retained its traditional EASTLANT/WESTLANT division, with IBERLANT to be set up in the event of war as a sub-area under EASTLANT. The British, French, and Canadians each had some form of ACHQ system to handle air-sea cooperation within their areas, while the Americans had previously solved this problem by removing the LRMPA mission from the air force and giving it to the navy. Geographically SACLANT's command boundaries were not very different from the British proposal of August 1950 (see fig. 4.9).

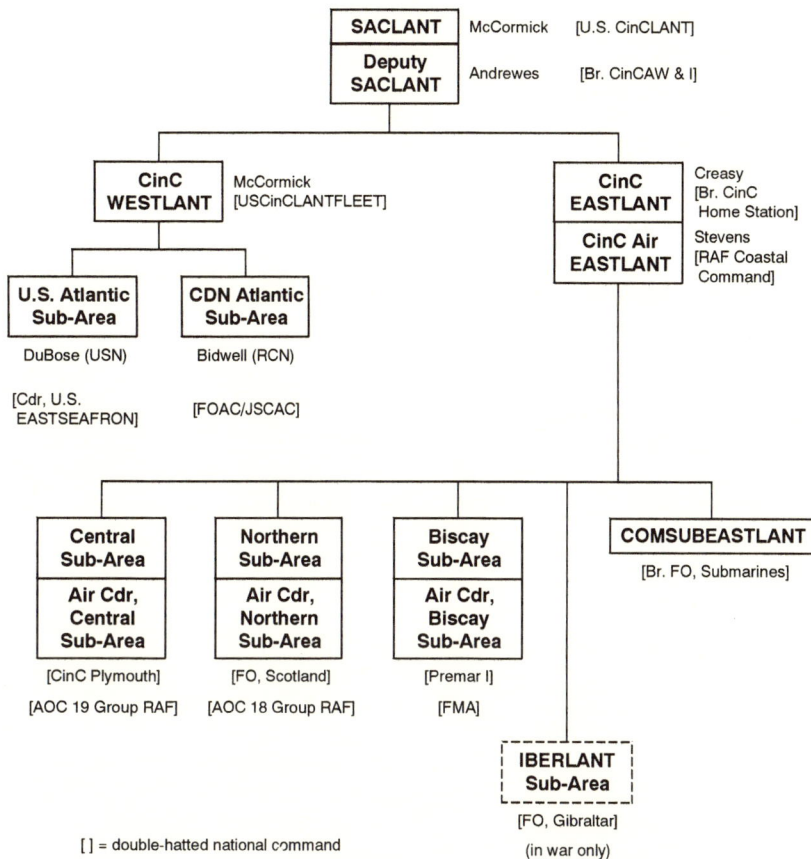

Fig. 4.8. SACLANT organization, August 1952

Striking Fleet Atlantic

The significance of Exercise Mainbrace regarding SACLANT command organization was considerable. In effect, Mainbrace, which took place from 15 to 25 September 1952, tested the command organization of EASTLANT in its capacity to provide direct naval support to SACEUR's AFNORTH and AFCENT regions as well as SLOC protection within the EASTLANT area in the face of strong submarine and LRMPA opposition. Notwithstanding the geographic scope of Mainbrace, the forces deployed for it were considerable and reflected impressive NATO commitment and cooperation. All types of naval operations were conducted during Mainbrace, including MCM, escort of convoy, hunter-killer, antisurface,

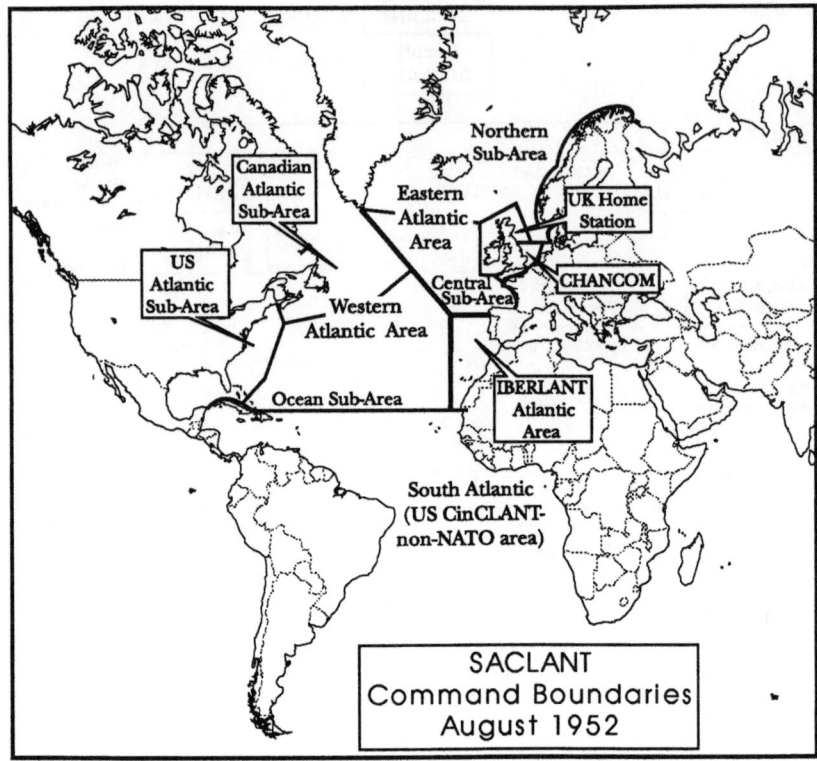

Fig. 4.9.

and carrier air support of the land battle; an Orangeland task force even sortied from the Baltic. The command organization followed that laid down for SACLANT and SACEUR: Adm. Sir George Creasy (RN) was EASTLANT and Admiral Brind (RN) served as CinCAFNORTH.[36]

Exercise Mainbrace was considered by all participants to be a complete success. Even the Americans were impressed: "It is considered that the nature and magnitude of this exercise were such as to provide the Joint Chiefs of Staff with information which could be of considerable assistance in future joint and combined planning. . . . The results of the exercise could be indicative of the effectiveness of plans for SACLANT to support SACEUR. . . ."[37] The most important consequence of Mainbrace was SACLANT's request for the establishment of a NATO Carrier Striking Force in the Atlantic directly subordinate to SACLANT. During the exercise EASTLANT had under his operational control a Carrier Striking Force consisting of four U.S. and two British fleet aircraft carriers, and a

Carrier Support Force consisting of two British and one Canadian light carriers. These formations provided much of the air support to SACEUR's land forces during the exercise, consistent with the NATO strategic concept. In an actual protracted conflict, however, a similar Carrier Striking Force consisting primarily of U.S. aircraft carriers armed with nuclear weapons would be tasked to prosecute the attack-at-source strategy. How would this organization be controlled if operations were, by geographic definition, conducted within the EASTLANT area? The World War II experience demonstrated a reluctance on the Americans' part to allow operational control over major fleet units such as aircraft carriers to pass to other navies; the rather restrictive American laws regarding nuclear weapons added a new wrinkle to this problem.[38]

To deal with the projected Soviet submarine threat (see appendix 1), both the British and the Americans planned defensive and offensive measures. During the Second World War, antisubmarine operations included attack at source (destruction of U-boats and their port facilities in the same location by bombing, minelaying, or both); offensive hunter-killer groups, each consisting of a CVE and several destroyers; the use of signals intelligence to reroute convoys around areas of U-boat activity; and close escort of convoy by ships and LRMPAs.

All of these measures would be employed in the event of a war with the Soviet Union in the 1950s, though there was perhaps an overemphasis on offensive hunter-killer and attack-at-source operations in American thinking. In an oversimplified way, American ASW doctrine in the 1950s focusing on attack at source and hunter-killer groups has been categorized as offensive and therefore aggressive in nature, while the British emphasis on close escort of convoy and offensive minelaying was derided by some Americans as defensive and therefore passive. In actuality, both the British and the Americans planned offensive and defensive measures to complement each other during both the Second World War and the Cold War. The Americans did have a large number of escorts in the Atlantic theater in World War II that were in fact used for close escort of convoy, while the British used RAF Bomber Command in an attempt to destroy German submarine bases and construction facilities. The sheer number of destroyer escorts and frigates kept in the reserve fleets of the Royal Navy and the U.S. Navy, as well as the planning estimates in the various war plans, indicated that escort of convoy operations were still a priority.[39]

Even though hunter-killer, close escort of convoy, and other operations were vitally important in securing SLOCs, the advent of the atomic bomb and the means to deliver it from an aircraft carrier made attack at source seem more efficient. Arguably, the use of atomic weapons became merely an extension of strategic bombing doctrine, insinuating itself into the naval mind after World War II and during interservice debates over budgetary considerations. This thinking did not significantly alter from 1945 to 1953 and would not until the development of the hydrogen bomb, the British Global Strategy Paper, and the American "New Look" in the 1953–55 time frame.[40]

The U.S. Navy had been promoting attack-at-source doctrine since 1946, and its success in the 1947–49 interservice debates against the air force allowed for the creation of an atomic strike force based on aircraft carriers. The ability of the navy to conduct sustained atomic operations in a war existed only after the AJ-1 Savage aircraft became available in October 1950 and a substantial atomic stockpile was built up in 1950–51. The relatively limited U.S. atomic arsenal, the small numbers of interim P2V3C Neptunes, and their inability to be recovered by an aircraft carrier precluded any real naval atomic attack-at-source operation before 1951. Even after the Savage became operational, only five U.S. aircraft carriers could store and service atomic weapons by 1952. For a variety of reasons, the British atomic bomb project did not mature until October 1952, when their first atomic bomb was tested; the design was not weaponized until November 1953, with the RAF as its primary recipient. Since the Royal Navy would not have an atomic-capable carrier aircraft until the Supermarine Scimitar was deployed in 1958, attack at source from the sea remained an American prerogative in the early 1950s. No other navy appeared to be capable of delivering atomic weapons.[41]

Another confusing factor that exists in any discussion of attack at source with atomic weapons in the 1950–53 time frame is the distinction between strategic and tactical uses of such weapons. Today, nuclear weapons are measured by their yield in kilotons or megatons, as well as by how they are employed; generally, weapons in the 15–50 kt range are classed as tactical nuclear weapons. The situation in the early 1950s was quite different. The primary U.S. Navy atomic bomb from 1949 to 1952 was the Mark IV, a large, bulky bomb with a yield in excess of 50 kt. At the time, there was no clear distinction between tactical and strategic nuclear weapons due to the limited number of bombs available. These early weapons planned for use in the attack-at-source role were classed as strategic weapons because the targets in attack-at-source operations were those whose destruction affected the Soviets' long-term ability to wage a naval war. After 1952, improved atomic weapon technology allowed smaller U.S. carrier aircraft (such as the F2H2 Banshee, FJ Fury, and AD-

4B Skyraider) to carry kiloton-size nuclear weapons—no longer would specialized aircraft such as the AJ-1 Savage be needed for all operations involving atomic weapons. Range was a limiting factor, however: the F2H2, FJ, and AD-4B could fly less than half as far as the AJ-1 when loaded with a special weapon. Also, these other aircraft could carry only one Mark VII or Mark VIII weapon, while the AJ-1 could carry several.[42]

Weapons deployed by the U.S. Navy in 1952–53 included the Mark VII, which allowed users to select a yield between 10 and 70 kt, and the Mark VIII, a 15–20 kt device designed specifically to penetrate concrete before detonating. These weapons not only offered greater flexibility in targeting at the strategic level but gave U.S. aircraft carriers the ability to support the land battle tactically in a realistic way. High-speed jets instead of slower propeller-driven aircraft were preferable for such operations. On the down side, the existence of these weapons helped contribute to the blurring of tactical and strategic definitions and targeting policy.[43]

In sum, the U.S. Navy had the doctrine, the aircraft, and the weapons by 1952 and were fully capable of conducting attack at source using atomic weapons. CinCLANTFLEET had an atomic strike plan, but this was not passed on to the SACLANT staff.[44] Since the attack-at-source mission was considered by the Americans to be a key factor in winning any future Battle of the Atlantic, the fleet units involved in such operations had to be coordinated or commanded by NATO command organizations.

The largest obstacle in the command problem regarding U.S. aircraft carriers and atomic weapons was the McMahon Act, which prohibited the sharing of atomic weapons, atomic weapon design data, and by inference targeting information.[45] It was interpreted by some American planners in strict terms: "Only in the U.S. command channels is there a clear cut line of both authority and responsibility from politicians to military leaders who order/execute atomic attack. No commander of atomic forces can be responsible to both U.S. and NATO authority. . . ."[46]

The existing RAF/USAF strategic air targeting arrangement provided no panacea for the problem of an atomic-armed striking fleet operating under a British commander. Since Britain possessed a comparatively small and conventionally armed strategic air force, coordination between RAF Bomber Command the U.S. Air Force's SAC was accomplished through informal links. There was no reason for the Americans to transmit specific atomic targeting information to the RAF, only the need to coordinate air movements—and then only for a limited time. With the deployment of aircraft carriers equipped with atomic weapons, the need to coordinate movements at sea was more complex given the sustained activity and variety of surface, subsurface, and air movements within the area of EASTLANT where such ships would be operating.

The American organization for the command of major fleet units in the Atlantic was the Second Task Fleet (later changed to Second Fleet). The organization of the U.S. Navy for control of operating forces consisted of the Chief of Naval Operations, who was subordinate to the JCS, and five commanders in chief: Far East, Western Pacific, Atlantic, East Atlantic and Mediterranean, and the Fleet Marine Force (see fig. 4.10). Forces were assigned to either the Atlantic Fleet or the Pacific Fleet, which acted as holding and administrative bodies for the actual ships. CinCLANTFLEET not only was under command for U.S. Navy operations in the Atlantic but was a U.S. unified command (see chapter 3) under the JCS, having operational control over U.S. Air Force or Army units assigned to its geographic area. The Second Fleet was the actual operational control body for units operating in the Atlantic under CinCLANTFLEET and was initially activated only for exercises or war (this later changed, and the Second Fleet became more or less permanent). Thus,

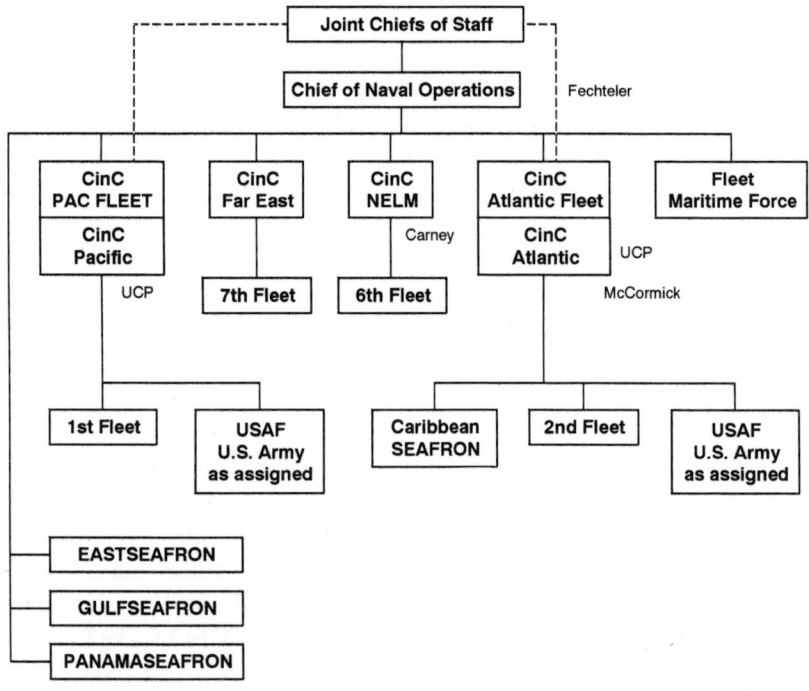

Fig. 4.10. U.S. Navy organization, 1951

U.S. aircraft carrier task forces operating in the Atlantic were part of the Second Fleet, which was subordinate to CinCLANTFLEET—who in turn was Admiral McCormick, whose NATO "hat" was SACLANT. The unified commander for CinCLANTFLEET thus retained command over Second Fleet units equipped with atomic weapons and had a direct chain of command to the JCS so that he could secure release of such weapons in an expedient fashion.[47]

The conflict between American legislation for the control of atomic weapons and the NATO command organization resided in the decentralized nature of the SACLANT command. To conduct attack-at-source operations with atomic bomb–equipped Savage aircraft operating from carriers in the North Atlantic, carriers would have to operate in the EASTLANT area, which was under the command of Adm. Sir George Creasy of the Royal Navy. If SACLANT attempted to give operational control of these carriers to EASTLANT, he would violate American law. If he did not pass over operational control, the coordination of operations between SACLANT and EASTLANT posed problems. Despite these legal issues, many U.S. admirals simply did not want the British to exercise any control over major fleet units, for a variety of prestige- and doctrine-oriented reasons.[48]

The Admiralty feared that any attempt to form a striking fleet for attack-at-source operations or to support the land battle in AFNORTH would leave EASTLANT in the dark as to the fleet's movements. In addition, half of the striking fleet's carriers would initially be British, and to have them under the direct operational control of an American was unacceptable because an American had strategic direction of the theater and was by agreement supposed to delegate command authority to EASTLANT, who was British.[49]

The ensuing debate over the matter resulted in an informal meeting between McGrigor and McCormick after Mainbrace. McCormick reassured the First Sea Lord that if a striking fleet was organized, it would come under EASTLANT's operational control for air and sea movement coordination even though U.S. elements of it would at times be conducting operations involving atomic weapons—"tactical" with F2H2 Banshees, or "strategic" with AJ-1 Savages. When such operations were under way (that is, the actual launching and recovery of an atomic strike), SACLANT would in effect change hats to become U.S. CinCLANTFLEET and assume control of the striking fleet for the duration of that particular operation. SACLANT did not have an Atomic Strike Plan in place or any coordination with SACEUR on this matter until Adm. Jerauld Wright became SACLANT in 1954.[50]

While McCormick was placating the British, the problem of NATO command over the proposed striking fleet was exacerbated by the ongoing friction between the U.S. Air Force and the U.S. Navy over the strategic bombing and targeting role. This debate, which can be traced back to the 1920s, revolved around the utility of airpower and seapower in the broader context of warfare, and the addition of the atomic bomb served as a catalyst for more U.S. and even British interservice rivalry.[51] This spilled over into the NATO arena when SAC, RAF Bomber Command, and tactical air units assigned to SACEUR had to form some mechanism to coordinate strategic targeting.

The air force questioned the strategic bombing role of U.S. aircraft carriers frequently in JCS debates and continued to do so while the JCS was examining SACLANT's Emergency Defence Plan in 1952. The gist of the its argument was put forth by the Chief of Staff of the Air Force, Hoyt Vandenberg: "I do not in any manner indorse [sic] the concept that operations of offensive carrier task forces are vital to military success against a land mass power. Rather, I accept the large aircraft carrier as a temporary expedient capable of providing a degree of support to SACEUR in the absence of sufficient land based tactical air power...."[52] Regarding the planned use of carriers in the attack-at-source role, Vandenberg believed that there would not be enough carriers available both to conduct attack-at-source operations and to provide critical support to SACEUR in the early stages of a Soviet offensive. His solution was to remove the carriers from the attack-at-source mission and leave the job for SAC, arguing that most of the Soviet submarine force would be at sea immediately and that on their return for replenishment or repair would be caught in their bases and destroyed.[53]

Admiral Fechteler, the U.S. CNO, defended the Navy's position eloquently. Citing recent experience in the Korean conflict, Fechteler noted:

> A fleet operating from a central position, capable of moving to the area in which its power is most needed, equipped with modern weapons, including carrier aircraft and responsible for furnishing direct support to SACEUR forces, as well as for controlling and exploiting the seas, is the only means by which SACLANT's responsibility can be met with the maximum economy of force.... SACLANT's fleet is neither a single purpose force nor is it built around a single weapon, but carrier attack forces are vital to the striking power ... and are indispensable to the accomplishment of SACLANT's mission.... Should this capability be denied to SACLANT's forces by the removal of his carrier attack forces, the capability to support SACEUR will be denied by the same action and SACEUR's forces will inevitable face defeat....[54]

For Fechteler, the war in Korea was SACEUR's problem in microcosm. Naval forces secure the flanks to the playing field; amphibious forces, carriers, and battleships support the land battle; while merchant shipping supplies the entire effort.[55]

The fundamental point left unanswered by the air force staff was how air operations in Europe could be conducted on a sustained basis without secure SLOCs or secure base areas, which essentially was similar to a problem encountered in World War II. The narrow and parochial U.S. Air Force view focused strictly on a comparison of carrier-based air to land-based air and completely ignored other critical naval operations that SACLANT could provide to SACEUR like naval gunfire support and amphibious operations.

If the air force could not remove the navy from its strategic attack role, it would try to dominate the targeting process within NATO. In July 1952, two organizations were established under SACEUR to coordinate air operations within that geographic area. These were the Special Air Staff and Group Able (see fig. 4.11). The operating forces available to SACEUR included elements of SAC, RAF Bomber Command, SACLANT's striking fleet, and the U.S. Air Force's 49th Air Division. Since SACLANT's mission was to support SACEUR with carrier-based air, some liaison had to be set

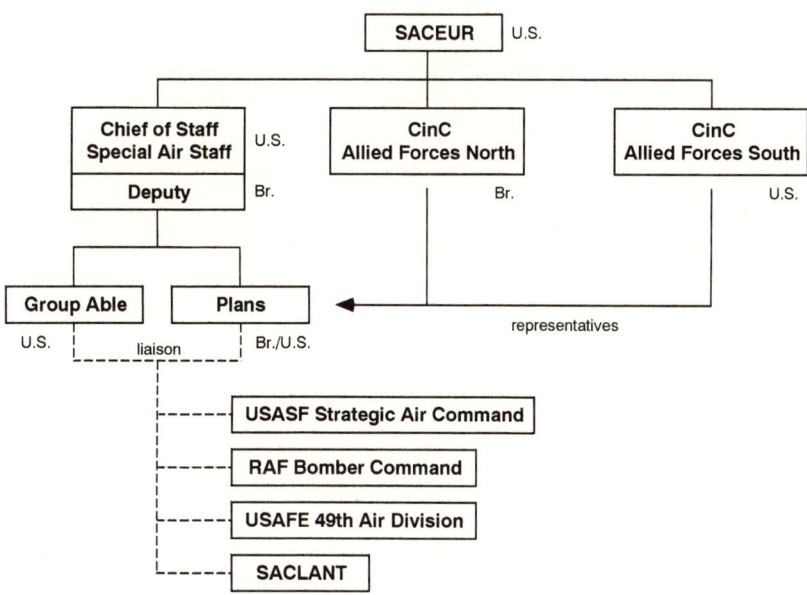

Fig. 4.11. SACEUR's Special Air Staff, July 1952

up to avoid redundancy; this was the Special Air Staff. Group Able was responsible for atomic targeting within the SACEUR area. Captain Lambrecht (USN), SACLANT's liaison officer to SACEUR, firmly believed at the time that, since the Special Air Staff and Group Able were almost completely controlled by USAF and RAF officers, these organizations would be used to overshadow the capabilities inherent to carrier-based airpower that could be of use to SACLANT. This effort was staved off by SACLANT's efforts to place liaison officers at all levels of the planning process within the Special Air Staff. The already cordial relations between SACLANT and AFNORTH (Admiral Brind) via EASTLANT were conducive to this endeavor.[56]

IBERLANT

SACLANT's STRIKEFLEETLANT proposal had survived attempts to dilute its viability when the French proposed a solution to the IBERLANT impasse in October 1952. Though still numerically small and in the process of expansion (see appendix 2), the French navy still had a national role in maintaining SLOCs between French Morocco, Algeria, and metropolitan France and was quite naturally concerned about having some input into the SACLANT command organization in the Atlantic area. The French considered the concept of a British IBERLANT commander located at Gibraltar unacceptable because it placed the French Moroccan sea command under British control. The French proposal recommended dividing the existing IBERLANT area into two more sub-areas, North IBERLANT and South IBERLANT, both subordinate to EASTLANT (see fig. 4.12). In the French view, South IBERLANT would become an extension of the French Moroccan sea frontier and act as the NCS organization for the sub-area. Also, the French may have wanted to control all of IBERLANT so as to maintain continuity in shipping from French Morocco and other African colonies to the Biscay Sub-area, and to bolster French prestige.[57]

There was much to be said for the French concept. It would eliminate the need for more troublesome CHOP lines for British ships coming in from the Mediterranean. This interested the British, who gave their support to the proposal. In addition, this plan could allow the British to extend the North IBERLANT Sub-area eastward to encompass Gibraltar, which would assist the British in maintaining their shipping continuity. It also would allow the French some political frontage within SACLANT. Unfortunately, the IBERLANT issue became embroiled in a renewed

From the Ditch to the Pillars of Hercules

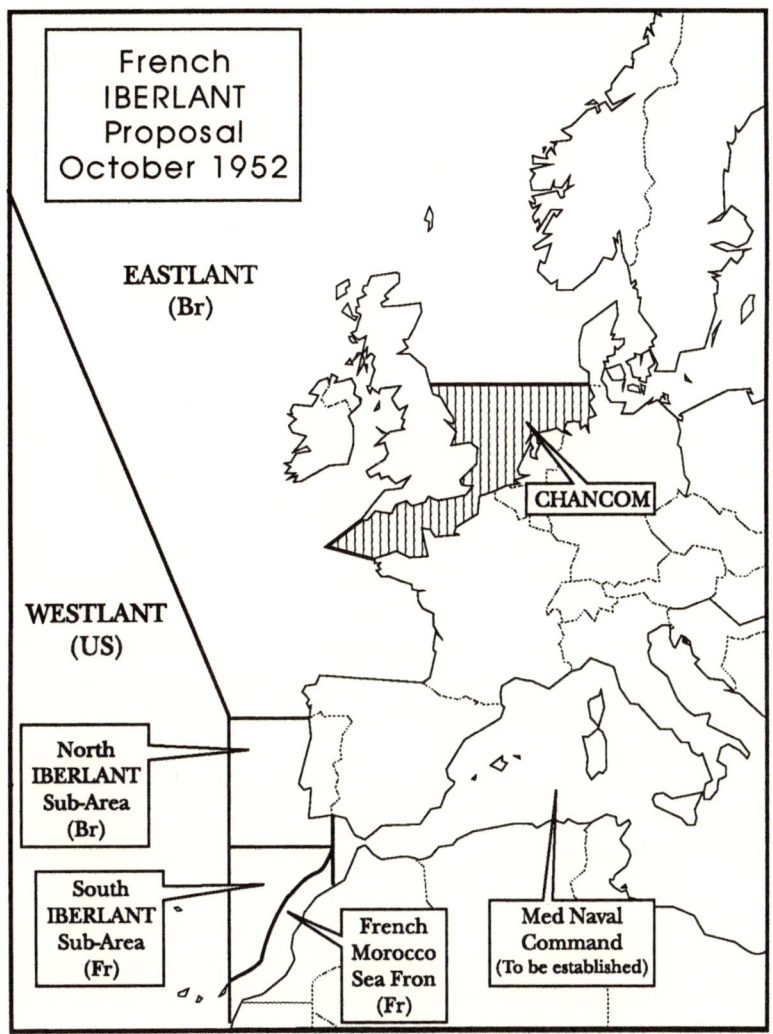

Fig. 4.12.

Anglo-American argument over the establishment of the STRIKE-FLEETLANT.

At some point in October elements within the U.S. Navy, apparently disenchanted with the STRIKEFLEETLANT status quo, raised the issue again internally. This attitude appears to have been influenced by the appearance that, under existing SACLANT command arrangements, the navy had no commands on SACLANT's front line—that is, on a coast projected to be occupied by the Soviet Union. The British had EASTLANT and CHANCOM, and this seeming imbalance appeared to place 90 percent of U.S. Navy forces assigned to NATO under British operational command.[58] In fact, McCormick and his staff were frequently queried by some naval personnel, "How much of the Navy are you giving away today?" with little regard for less glamorous but still important operations in the South Atlantic, Caribbean, or WESTLANT.[59] Regarding the delegation of U.S. carriers to British operational control, the British believed that "[the] U.S. position on these matters is firm. They objected to handing over task forces comprising mainly U.S. units to British control when they were of the opinion that, first, we did not know how to operate them, secondly, we attached more importance to the defense of sea communications than to the support of land operations, a point of view in direct conflict with their own...."[60] This was essentially the old World War II problem of operational control over CVEs reiterated all over again.

This attitude, as well as the success of the first American hydrogen bomb test on 1 November 1952 and with it the promise of a weapon with a highly increased destructive capability, may have been instrumental in forcing McCormick to raise the issue of STRIKEFLEETLANT with the British once again.[61] He offered a new concept that envisioned the creation in wartime of a separate STRIKEFLEETLANT consisting of British, Canadian, and American aircraft carriers (some armed with atomic weapons) directly subordinated to SACLANT and not delegated to EASTLANT at all.

The British Chiefs of Staff Committee response was quite scathing:

> Since the inception of NATO we have been continually forced to accept, through American pressure, command organizations which we knew to be unsound; in every case we have so far given way solely in the interests of Anglo-American solidarity. The time has now come when we must stand firm on what we know to be the correct solution to the various outstanding naval problems, since SACLANT's proposals for the IBERLANT command and for the Striking Fleet commander undermined the whole basis on which we had to agree to the establishment of the Atlantic Command. Should no agreement be possible with the Americans at the military level, the matter should be raised to the Prime Minister–Presidential level....[62]

The Americans were once again using their legislation regarding atomic weapons to make their case for SACLANT's control over the STRIKE-

FLEETLANT. The British, still not appeased by the success of their own atomic bomb test in October, were incensed and insisted that it was "patently absurd to suggest that, because a particular striking force was attacking a target with special weapons that the operational command of that force must necessarily be vested in an American. . . ."[63] The British Chiefs of Staff asked the Foreign Office to research the legal problem.

The debates over NATO naval commands preoccupied the British Chiefs of Staff throughout November 1952. Apart from operational control over U.S. aircraft carriers, there was a real need to sort out airspace management and ship movements in the AFNORTH and EASTLANT areas since the McCormick-McGrigor status quo was in jeopardy. The Americans continued to fall back on legal difficulties and used the superficial treatment given by the current SACLANT Emergency Defence Plan to argue for STRIKEFLEETLANT's position directly subordinate to SACLANT. Under the 1952 plan, SACEUR's subordinate commander AFNORTH was permitted by SACEUR to coordinate directly with SACLANT through the Special Air Staff for STRIKEFLEETLANT targeting; furthermore, the STRIKEFLEETLANT commander merely had to inform EASTLANT of his ship movements instead of relaying air movements as well. The problem of coordination among long-range bombers belonging to SAC or RAF Bomber Command, U.S. Navy attack-at-source missions, LRMPA activity, land- and CVE-based fighter protection to convoys, fighter intercept aircraft, transport aircraft supporting Norway, and sea-air rescue planes was immensely complex. There was no immediate solution, and as a result another Anglo-American deadlock occurred.[64]

The Americans refused to give any ground whatsoever regarding STRIKEFLEETLANT; they had in the past given way on many issues, such as the nature of the AFNORTH command (joint staff system under a British commander) and certain command issues in the Mediterranean, which will be discussed later. In their assessment of the deadlock, the British Chiefs of Staff—with Churchill's careful guidance—decided that their primary concerns in the naval command situation were the need to retain British control over the shipping-reception side of the Atlantic and the integrity of the SLOC through the Mediterranean to the British Isles. As a result, the British chose to maintain the status quo regarding IBERLANT (under EASTLANT command in war), hope for concessions in the Mediterranean command organization, and give in on the STRIKEFLEETLANT issue.[65]

By the end of 1952, the organization of SACLANT was more or less finalized in a form that would be recognizable today (see fig. 4.13; note the

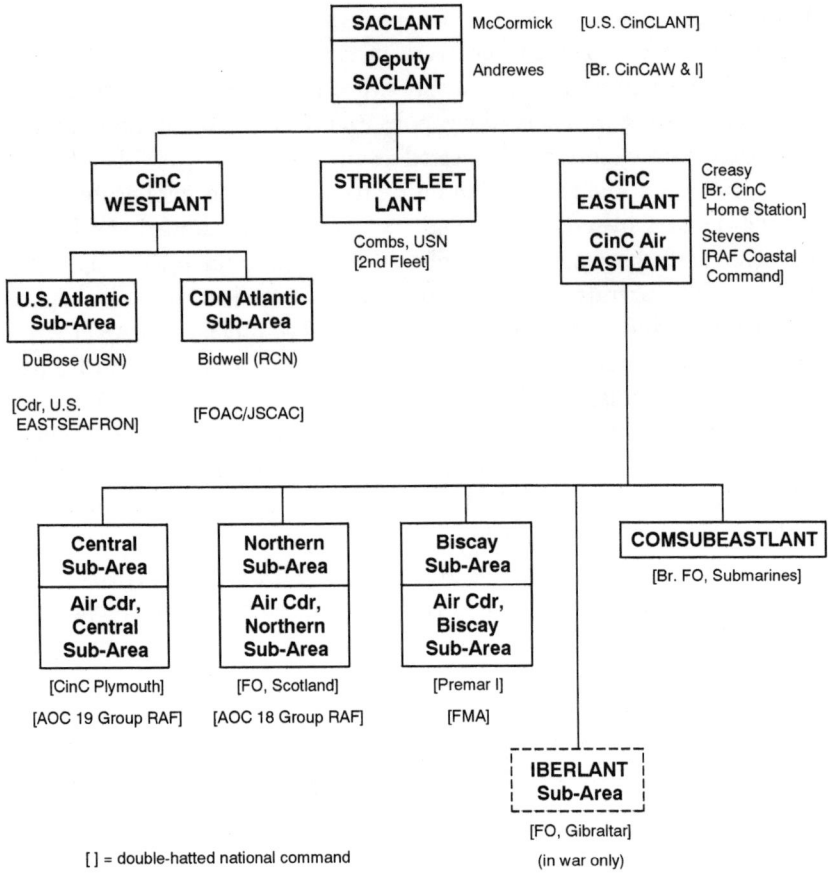

Fig. 4.13. Finalized SACLANT organization, 1952–53

close resemblance to fig. 4.8). The only changes were the addition of the STRIKEFLEETLANT under SACLANT; the subordination of the French Maritime Forces, Morocco to EASTLANT; and the placement of IBERLANT as a sub-area commanded by the British Flag Officer, Gibraltar but subordinate to EASTLANT. Although it is outside of the scope of this study, it is worth noting that the Americans finally got IBERLANT under an American commander subordinated to SACLANT in the 1970s.[66]

The development of the CHANCOM and SACLANT command organizations demonstrates the process of compromise within a coalition and must be seen within the framework of conflicting British and American strategic needs and wants. The American legal need for command and control over atomic weapons, coupled with the need to satisfy the U.S. Navy's penchant for offensive action and the strategic need to deploy American land forces throughout the IBERLANT area, had to be balanced with Britain's need to retain control over what it perceived to be its destiny: the survival of Britain via a tenuous line of communication. Although the British were able to retain control over waters adjacent to the British Isles, their longer view encompassed control over a lifeline extending from the British Isles through the IBERLANT area and ultimately into the Mediterranean. This eventually proved to be unrealistic within the NATO context. In addition, the clear deficiency in British offensive capability relative to the Americans' and the need to coordinate air and naval activity within EASTLANT made the concept of unrestrained British control over American offensive forces (embodied by STRIKFLEETLANT) operating within its area unrealistic. These problems also received wide play in the creation of a NATO command organization in the Mediterranean, which is the subject of chapter 5.

5 ➢ The Struggle for the Mediterranean

The Development of CinCAFMED, 1951–1954

Circumstances have caused the Mediterranean Sea to play a greater part in the history of the world, both in a commercial and a military point of view, than any other sheet of water of the same size. Nation after nation has striven to control it and the strife still goes on....
—Alfred T. Mahan, *The Influence of Sea Power on History*

The biggest problem [with command organization] in the Mediterranean was that every member assigned to the Southern flank of NATO had been at war with everybody else at least once.
—Adm. Robert Carney

The final naval command to be established by NATO in the early 1950s was Commander in Chief, Allied Forces Mediterranean (CinCAFMED). CinCAFMED was the product of similar factors encountered in the debates over the SACLANT and SACEUR commands, including the issue of carrier support to the land battle, the need for equal division of labor between the British and the Americans, and the relative importance of the SLOCs running through the Mediterranean Sea to Britain. The resolution of the Mediterranean command problem was therefore closely linked to the debates over the Atlantic command discussed in chapters 3 and 4. In addition, the need to link NATO with strategic concerns in the Middle East was instrumental in focusing attention on the Mediterranean basin, and the situation must be set against the long-standing British interests in the region dating back to the Second World War and the continuing Soviet threat to Western Europe. This chapter will focus on the

The Struggle for the Mediterranean ➢ *171*

development of CinCAFMED, its historical precedents, and its relationship to SACEUR and SACLANT.[1] The degree of international political activity over the Mediterranean and Middle East was considerable and complex; as in previous chapters, these factors will be examined only insofar as they affect the creation of NATO command organizations.

Command of the Mediterranean area during World War II was invested in the Supreme Allied Commander, Mediterranean (SACMED), which was subordinate to the Combined Chiefs of Staff and had three commanders in chief for air, naval, and land units. The Middle East remained separate under the supervision of a British Commander in Chief, Middle East as part of the Middle East Command, which exercised command through the Senior Naval Officer, Persian Gulf and Headquarters, RAF Middle East.

After the Second World War, the pre-NATO organization for the Anglo-American Broiler/Doublequick strategic concept in 1948 allowed for a Supreme Allied Commander, Mediterranean/Middle East under a projected Combined Chiefs of Staff. In wartime, this SACMEDME was theoretically responsible for the defense of everything south and east of the European coastline; the strategic concept in 1948 placed great emphasis on the Middle East as a base area for the prosecution of the land and air campaign against the Soviet Union.[2]

This thinking was reaffirmed by Broiler/Doublequick's replacement concept, Doublestar/Speedway/Bullmoose, which remained in effect until 1949. With the creation of NATO in 1949 and the shift to regional planning groups, the decision was made to exclude the Middle East area from NATO defense planning. The region once again became primarily a British and French concern, while the Mediterranean came under the Southern Europe/Western Mediterranean Regional Planning Group. In war, arrangements were made to allow for a single naval commander for the Mediterranean and Middle East theaters; this was merely a paper concept, however. Under the Crosspiece/Galloper concept in effect from 1949 to 1951, the base area required for the U.S. strategic bombing offensive was moved from the Middle East to North Africa, while the British continued to plan for the land defense of the Middle East region to guarantee access to petroleum resources and to protect the SLOC to remaining British possessions in the Far East.[3]

As discussed in chapter 3, with the establishment of SACEUR under Eisenhower, the southern European coastline of Italy and France—including naval units supporting the land battle in the western Mediterranean—all became subject to SACEUR's subordinate command, Commander in Chief, Allied Forces South (CinCAFSOUTH or AFSOUTH) in 1951 (see figs. 5.1 and 5.2). This was in accordance with the strategic concept that

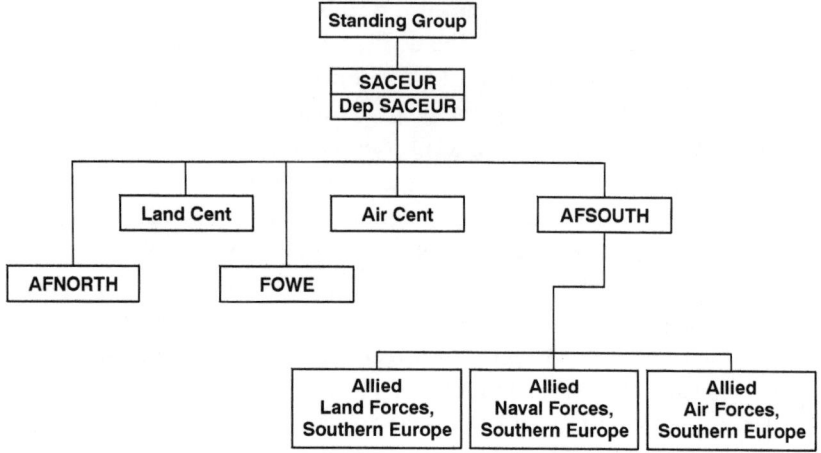

Fig. 5.1. NATO CinCAFSOUTH organization, January 1951

envisioned Italy as the southern flank "hedgehog" from which a flanking attack against a Soviet assault on Western Europe could be launched. AFSOUTH's subordinate commands included Allied Land Forces Southern Europe, Allied Air Forces Southern Europe, and Allied Naval Forces Southern Europe. AFSOUTH's commander was Adm. Robert Carney (USN), who was double-hatted as Allied Naval Forces, Southern Europe and triple-hatted in his national position of Commander in Chief, U.S. Naval Forces, Eastern Atlantic and Mediterranean (CinCNELM). CinCNELM's primary operational force in the Mediterranean was the U.S. Sixth Fleet—essentially the Mediterranean counterpart of CinCLANTFLEET's Second Fleet. The Sixth Fleet consisted primarily of offensive carrier task forces (four carriers, four cruisers, twenty-four destroyers) that had a full range of capabilities including the ability to deliver atomic weapons. As such, the restrictions of the McMahon Act that applied to the Second Fleet regarding the need for a clear U.S. chain of command also applied to the Sixth Fleet. This posed problems for the creation of any Mediterranean command organization in much the same way that it had for SACLANT, since the primary job of the task forces inevitably was to support SACEUR while control of atomic weapons by law had to rest with an American commander.[4]

The exact delineation of AFSOUTH's boundaries was not firmly established in January 1951, and the function of Allied Naval Forces, Southern Europe appeared to conflict with Britain's national command, Commander

The Struggle for the Mediterranean ➢ 173

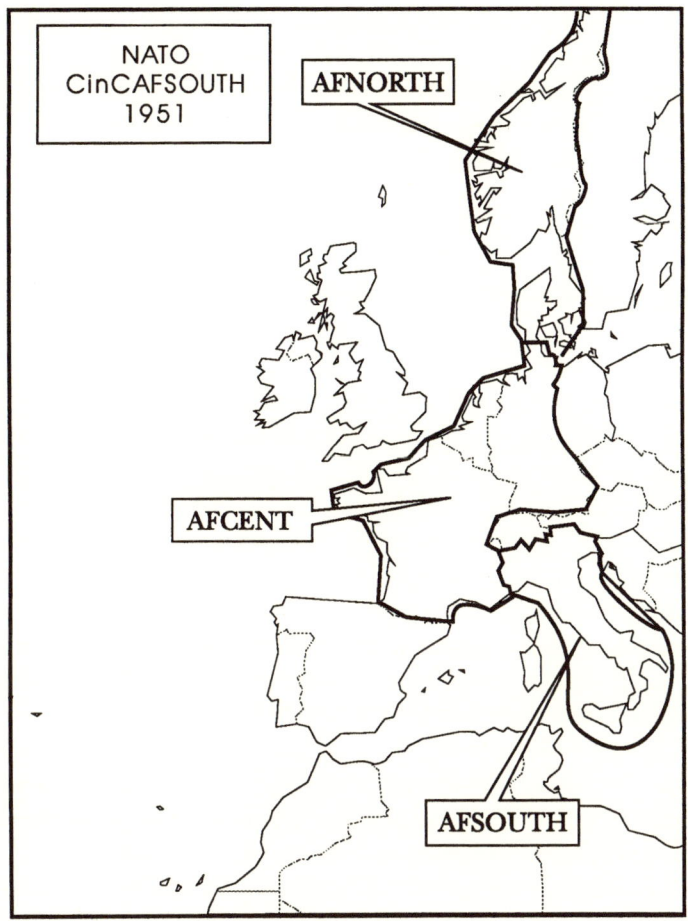

Fig. 5.2.

in Chief, Mediterranean. CinCMED, which predated World War II, and (as we saw in chapter 1) SACMED handled all naval activity in the Mediterranean during that conflict, and the British government had strenuously objected to placing their vital SLOCs in the Mediterranean under SACEUR.[5] Relations between the British CinCMED (Admiral Edlesten, RN) and CinCAFSOUTH (Admiral Carney, USN) were somewhat strained from the beginning. Initially, CinCAFSOUTH had no physical headquarters and thus lacked secure communications facilities. When, as an apparently friendly gesture, Edlesten offered Carney the use of British communications facilities on Malta, Carney replied, "I'm not about to play Faust to your Mephistopheles through the medium of communications!"⁶ This set the tone for Anglo-American naval relations in the Mediterranean for some time.

As early as February 1951, Eisenhower in his position as SACEUR had noted that many naval operations in the Mediterranean such as SLOC protection and MCM operations were beyond the purview of SACEUR, and he suggested that a separate NATO naval command in the Mediterranean be established to deal with these operations.⁷ Believing it would have Eisenhower's support in the matter, the British Joint Staff Mission in Washington was instructed to push the Americans for the creation of a new SACMED based on the Second World War organization. This proposal reflected the British view that all naval forces operating in the area needed to be subordinated to one commander for coordination purposes.⁸

A meeting between the U.S. CNO Admiral Sherman, Admiral Carney, Admiral Creasy, Air Marshal Slessor, and Field Marshal Slim in March 1951 provided the perfect venue for discussing the Mediterranean since the naval command organization in the Atlantic was under review. According to Eisenhower, the purpose of the meeting was "to alleviate the bitterness of British popular opinion to the recent announcement of Fechteler as the Supreme Allied Commander for the North Atlantic," which, as was discussed in chapter 3, became the subject of a vicious backlash in British public opinion.⁹

The British Chiefs of Staff saw a clear need for a British NATO supreme commander in the Mediterranean. The inevitable result, however, would be the existence of two navies in the area: one under the proposed SACMED and one under SACEUR, which would support the land battle. Additionally, according to the strategic concept Masthead/Binnacle, it could be argued that North Africa fell into SACEUR's sphere. Other problems that would delay the creation of a SACMED included the coordination of air operations in such a relatively small area, the allocation of U.S. aircraft carriers from the Sixth Fleet, and the difficulties of coordinating AFSOUTH with SACMED and whatever command organization was developed for the Middle East.¹⁰

In Sherman's ideal view, the Mediterranean would be controlled by a "SACMEDSEA," with subordinate land, air, and naval commanders to handle the entire area as well as operations in the Middle East, Iran, and the Persian Gulf. The land and air campaign in Italy would remain under SACEUR. This view was heartily endorsed by Creasy, Slessor, and Slim, and the meeting shifted to more pressing items such as command in the Atlantic.¹¹

Carney did not agree at the time, but he held his fire until he could communicate with Eisenhower informally. As CinCAFSOUTH, Carney understood SACEUR's concept of operations and strongly believed that the Mediterranean should be under SACEUR, with an American in command of Mediterranean naval forces. In Carney's view, the numbers of naval forces in the Mediterranean were disproportionately American: "It is over these predominantly American forces that the British advocate British command. The sensitiveness of British pride is understandable but the immutable fact is that the British Navy is not only smaller than the USN but it also lacks the comprehensive inventory of weapons and techniques possessed by the USN...."[12] The latter was a less than veiled reference to the employment of atomic bomb–equipped aircraft from carriers attached to the Sixth Fleet in the land support role. He was correct in his evaluation: the proportion of Mediterranean forces in being was on the order of 40 percent American, 20 percent British, 15 percent French, 12 percent Italian, 5 percent Greek, and 8 percent Turkish.[13] Carney then suggested that the undeveloped Middle Eastern command be used to placate the British instead of the Mediterranean: "We should never be unmindful of Britain's right and responsibility to nourish the Middle East theater. We have always recognized the soundness and propriety of the British controlling a line of communication through the Mediterranean to the Middle East and the command scheme which for some time was mutually acceptable to the U.S. and the Royal Navy envisaged such a line of communication . . . under British command."[14] Underlying Carney's argument was the apparent U.S. view that there were "too many Brits in control" of NATO commands, a view that later permeated the debate over SACLANT's STRIKEFLEETLANT in 1952.

Eisenhower, however, continued to support the creation of a British NATO supreme command. Although the Mediterranean, Middle East, and Atlantic commands were not really part of SACEUR's direct concern, the political impact on the NATO alliance was not to be underestimated: "The announcement of [an American as SACLANT] has created such reactions throughout the United Kingdom that some way should be found to give to the British the type of command and command title that would help ameliorate their obvious resentment...."[15] Eisenhower's only concerns as SACEUR were that the ability of the Sixth Fleet to support AFSOUTH not be interfered with and that the SLOCs in the Mediterranean be protected to keep Britain secure. He was not interested in the specifics of the arrangements so long as the British were given their due: "Aren't we big enough and strong enough to be magnanimous and to be generous? The British need a gesture of this sort."[16] To this Carney replied: "I'm not in a position to judge that, nor am I in a position to implement any such generous and altruistic view. I am a servant of the United States in spite of the fact that I am a NATO commander. I am given to the NATO organization by the United States and I do not feel that it is up to me to permit personal generosity to dilute the interests of the United States and I think it would be very definitely against the interests of the United States for the British to have control of the Sixth Fleet...."[17]

An informal follow-up meeting between Sherman and the British Chiefs of Staff reviewed the concept of a supreme command in the Mediterranean and the Middle East. Sherman once again proposed that a Supreme Commander, Middle East (who would be British) be established, with a British Naval CinCMEDME who would command naval forces protecting the Gibraltar–Suez–Red Sea and Persian Gulf SLOC; SACEUR would retain the U.S. Sixth Fleet under CinCAFSOUTH. If later circumstances warranted, Sherman would not object to the Naval CinCMEDME becoming a NATO command.[18]

The British reaction to Sherman's idea was mixed. The biggest problem was the complicated division of the Mediterranean both functionally and geographically. In effect, the Mediterranean would be divided north-south, with the north under CinCAFSOUTH and the southern Mediterranean SLOC under a British national command not linked to NATO except through a circuitous route from the British Chiefs of Staff to the Standing Group and then down to SACEUR and CinCAFSOUTH. Second, the functional arrangement posed a problem similar to that of STRIKEFLEETLANT in the Atlantic whereby the offensive orientation of the carrier task forces conflicted with the need for defensive and NCS SLOC protection forces. Additionally, the British noted that the French and the Italians would be left out in the cold because no consideration had been given to their shipping needs.[19]

The American position was formalized by the Joint Chiefs of Staff in a communication to the British Chiefs of Staff in April 1951 (see fig. 5.3). If a Supreme Allied Commander, Middle East (SACME) were established under British national command, four liaison links would exist, probably instituted through the exchange of liaison officers at these levels. The American proposal envisaged that SACME would be a mirror image of SACEUR, with three CinCs: Land, Air, and CinC Allied Naval Forces, Middle East (CinCANFME). Under CinCANFME, British SLOC protection forces in the Mediterranean would be placed under a Commander, Gibraltar-Alexandria LOC Forces, while the offensive carrier task forces

The Struggle for the Mediterranean ≻ 177

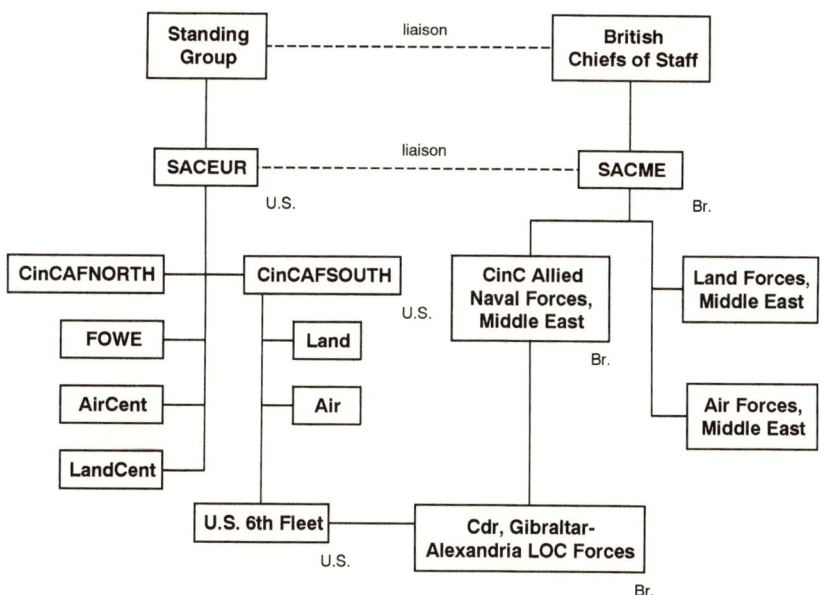

Fig. 5.3. SACEUR and the proposed relationship to SACME—U.S. view, April 1951

remained under CinCAFSOUTH and SACEUR: "The control of lines of communications and supply to the Middle East, being of primary British concern and outside the purview of NATO, should be under British Command. The same sea communications must also serve the NATO forces in the Mediterranean area. Therefore the interwoven NATO and United Kingdom interests regarding shipping control, protection of convoys, submarine operations etc. can be expected to be solved through close coordination between CinC Southern Europe and CinC Allied Naval Forces, Middle East."[20]

Geographically, the U.S. proposal would have resulted in a situation similar to the later STRIKEFLEETLANT problem, with EASTLANT being analogous to CinCANFME and the U.S. Sixth Fleet analogous to the Second Fleet for functional purposes; the exact boundaries were ill defined at this point (see fig. 5.4). The proposal would examine the problem of SLOC protection between France and French North Africa and the exact area of SACME at a later time.[21]

In their usual pragmatic way, the British found disadvantages in the U.S. position. To them, the SACME position was almost confined to a high-level coordination role, while operational control over most forces

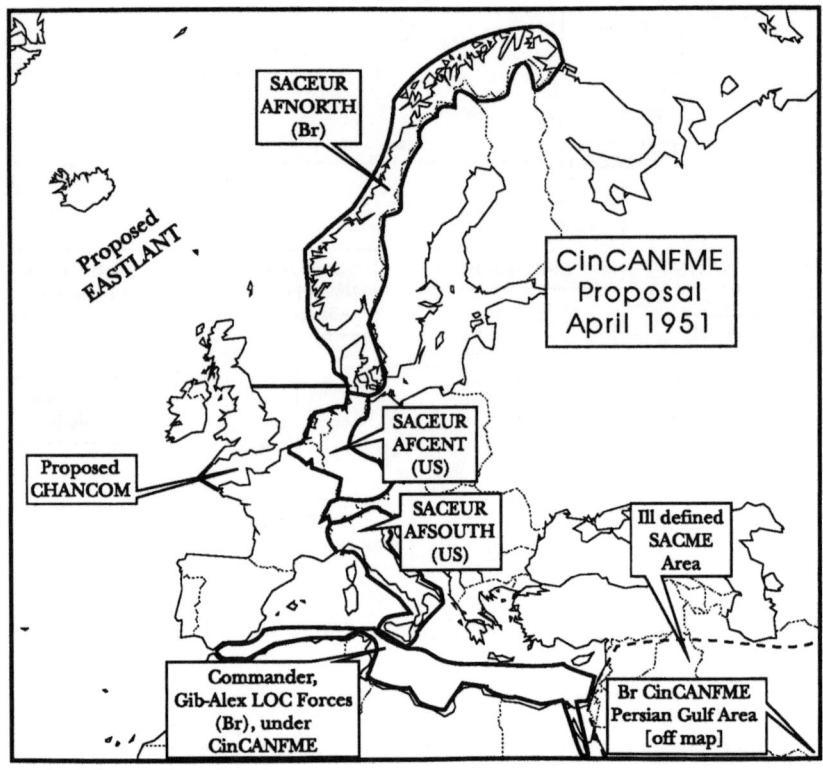

Fig. 5.4.

in the Mediterranean would remain under American control if the Americans wished to force their operational emphasis on offensive support operations over defensive SLOC operations. The British understanding of the American view revolved around the belief that CinCANFME controlled only the SLOC protection forces in the Mediterranean and not Britain's base facilities, which would come under CinCAFSOUTH. This was unacceptable to them. In addition, the British believed that the Americans lacked the experience of operating in the Mediterranean; the only U.S. Navy units operating in the Mediterranean during the Second World War were part of the Eighth Fleet, an amphibious support fleet that was subordinated to the British SACMED through his naval CinCMED commander.[22]

Air Marshal Slessor, the Chief of the Air Staff, took great pains to convince the British Chiefs of Staff Committee that Sherman's proposal was a big step forward by the United States to meet British requirements in light of the SACLANT appointment and that the British military leadership should not dismiss the U.S. view out of hand. Slessor pointed out several advantages. Basically, it was unwise for one man to be both supreme commander of the Middle East area and a CinC in the Mediterranean since the area was so large. With modifications, however, the plan still met the British need for a supreme command somewhere. Politically, the British thought that the creation of SACME would encourage the United States to become more involved with the defense of the region. Another potential spin-off of the debate was the possibility that the IBERLANT command under SACLANT might become redundant and thus that a continuous SLOC from Britain to the Far East would be under exclusively British command within the NATO structure.[23] Other possible resolutions to the command problem in the Mediterranean included creating a U.S. deputy for the Mediterranean Naval Commander in Chief so that the Sixth Fleet could be brought under British control, but this was rejected out of hand by the Joint Chiefs of Staff.[24]

American planners also recognized the need to incorporate the French into a detailed Mediterranean command organization. The French considered Algeria to be part of metropolitan France, and the SLOCs running to it as constituting one sea frontier; this was recognized by NATO. As a result, the JCS modified its position and planned for liaison links with the proposed SACME Commander, Gibraltar-Alexandria LOC Forces and the French Mediterranean naval command, as they geographically overlapped the NATO commands (see figs. 5.5 and 5.6). Once the war in Algeria started in 1954, the political need for a separate French naval command

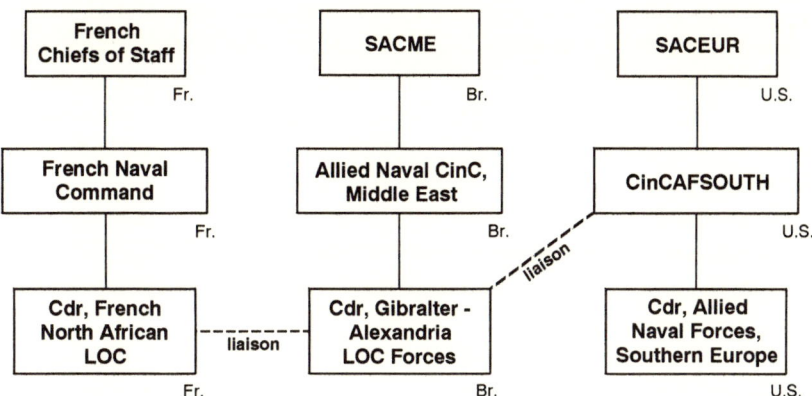

Fig. 5.5. Incorporation of French area into Mediterranean command plan

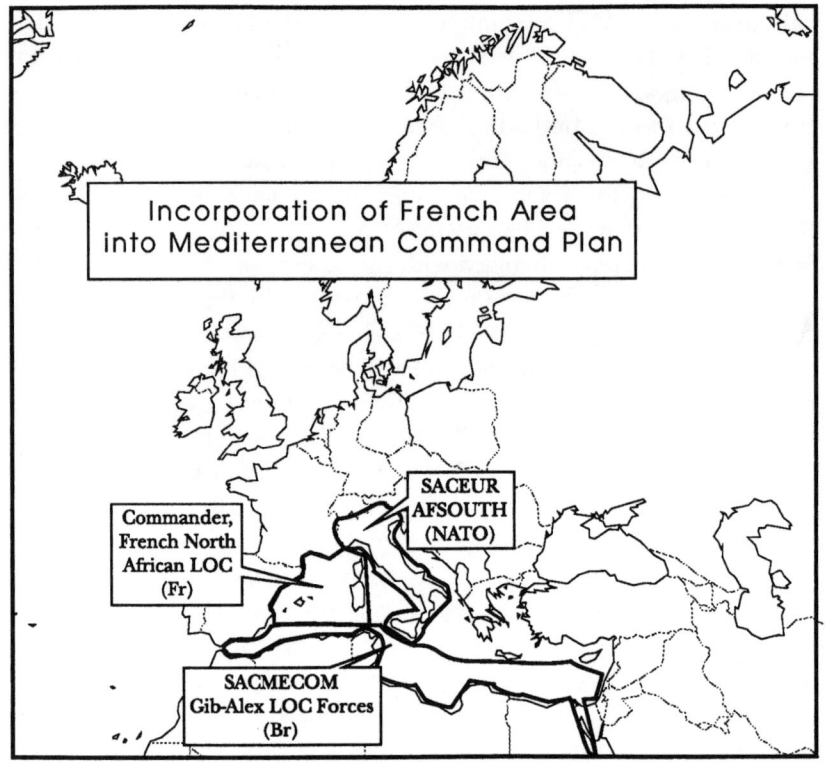

Fig. 5.6.

outside of NATO became apparent when French naval units provided air and gunfire support to land operations.[25]

By May 1951, debate over other command issues such as SACLANT stalled attempts to set up NATO commands in the Mediterranean and Middle East region. At this point, both Greece and Turkey had requested formal admittance to NATO. This exacerbated the situation, since both the United States and Britain sought the entry of these two powers into some form of defensive alliance to protect the eastern flank of SACEUR, the Bosporus, and the Middle East. Unfortunately, Canada, Norway, and Denmark objected to this—particularly to the idea that the Middle East or Middle Eastern countries should become part of NATO. The result was the complete dissociation of the Middle East from NATO.[26]

At a Chiefs of Staff Committee meeting in May 1951, the British reassessed the command situation. The primary British requirements in the region continued to be control of the Mediterranean SLOC and the

The Struggle for the Mediterranean ➤ *181*

formalization of some arrangement with the French. Significantly, some members thought that insisting on a supreme commander who was British to balance the prestige lost by the appointment of an American as SACLANT was a mistake and that the deadlock could be broken if the British backed down on the specific title of the command—that is, accepting a CinC instead of a SAC. Some also felt that SACEUR's AFSOUTH command should be contested as vigorously as possible so that some concessions might be received from the Americans for the creation of a Middle East command with Greece and Turkey as participants. As a compromise, the British would accept a north-south split of the Mediterranean (see fig. 5.7), with the SLOC protection forces under British command and naval units supporting AFSOUTH under NATO command, while pushing for a SACME with a British commander under NATO.[27]

Due to other pressing matters, the JCS reply to the British position did not come until June 1951 when the JCS and the British Chiefs of Staff

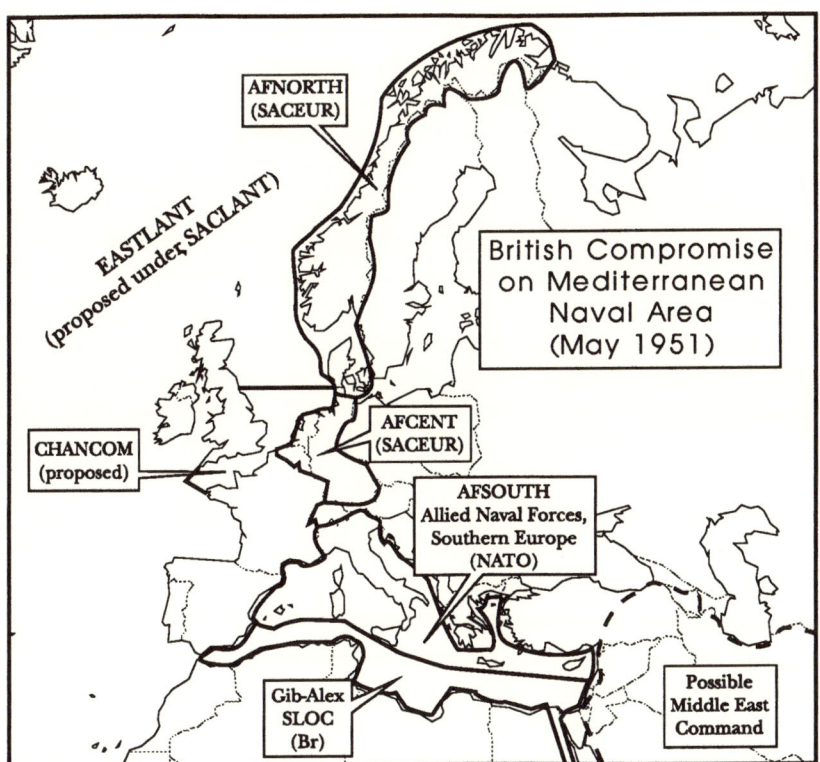

Fig. 5.7.

conducted a formal meeting. Some common ground was established at this meeting, particularly the recognition on both sides that the Mediterranean and Middle East command situation could not be solved separately and that a sense of urgency was necessary in order to accommodate the Greeks and the Turks. However, all that came of the meeting was a series of proposals to rename the Middle East area as the Allied Eastern Command and to change the proposed Gibraltar-Alexandria LOC Forces to CinC, British Naval Forces, Mediterranean.[28]

By the end of October 1951, the intent to establish a Middle East Command (MEC) outside of NATO was publicly announced jointly by the United States, Britain, France, and Turkey. The MEC's stated task was to assist and support member nations in defending themselves, to handle regional planning, and to make material available to the members; in effect, it was similar to the earlier NATO regional planning groups.[29] Although the Middle East region was outside the established NATO area, the impact of the MEC was felt in early attempts to bring Turkey into NATO's command organization.

In a series of talks in Ankara and Paris, the problem of setting up a command organization for the Mediterranean and Middle East and the express need to incorporate the new members occupied all participants. SACEUR believed that the incorporation of Greece into AFSOUTH was feasible but that Turkey extended SACEUR's flank too far eastward. Eisenhower favored a split in the Aegean, with Greece under AFSOUTH and Turkey under the proposed SACME; the Greeks supported this view. Turkey, on the other hand, indicated that placement under AFSOUTH was an absolute prerequisite for its entry into NATO. Furthermore, the Turks emphasized that they considered themselves to be a European and not a Middle Eastern state and that they would not serve under any British command.[30]

The British ignored the Turkish prerogative and proposed the creation of separate Turkish and Greek commands under a British Supreme Allied Commander, Eastern Mediterranean (SACEM) (see figs. 5.8 and 5.9).[31] This organization made sense militarily, but the out-and-out refusal of the Turks disqualified it from the start.

The American representatives disregarded not only Eisenhower's view (he was wearing his NATO hat for the conference) but also reality. They proposed establishing a separate unified Greek-Turkish command subordinate to CinCAFSOUTH, which was a unified command subordinate to SACEUR. Frustrated with the impasse and probably goaded on by Churchill, the British threatened to withdraw from the conference and

The Struggle for the Mediterranean ➤ 183

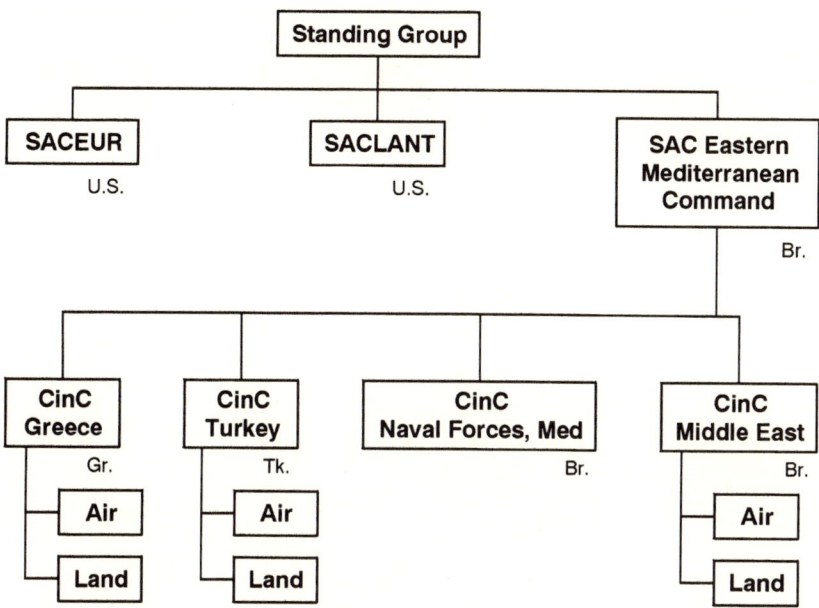

Fig. 5.8. British proposal for an eastern Mediterranean command, November 1951

even suggested that pending British approval of the appointment of an American as SACLANT would be hotly contested.[32]

As the talks on Mediterranean–Middle East command arrangements devolved into confusion, a U.S. Joint Strategic Survey Committee study of the eastern Mediterranean and the Middle East concluded that Soviet domination of Greece and Turkey did in fact expose SACEUR's flank and threaten the Mediterranean SLOC by giving the Soviets the ability to base long-range aircraft in Greece.[33] This base area could also be used to threaten Malta with airborne attack and thus close the eastern Mediterranean completely. The study's conclusions were that Greece and Turkey were part of Europe, that bringing them into NATO lessened the chance of this worst-case scenario actually happening, and that debate should continue to find a solution to the command problem.

In preparation for the Rome meeting of the North Atlantic Council and the Military Committee at which the command issue and the entry of Turkey and Greece would be discussed, the JCS asked the Joint Strategic Planning Committee to examine all current or planned alternatives for the successful resolution of the Mediterranean and Middle East command problem. Boiled down, no alternative examined by the JSPC solved all the

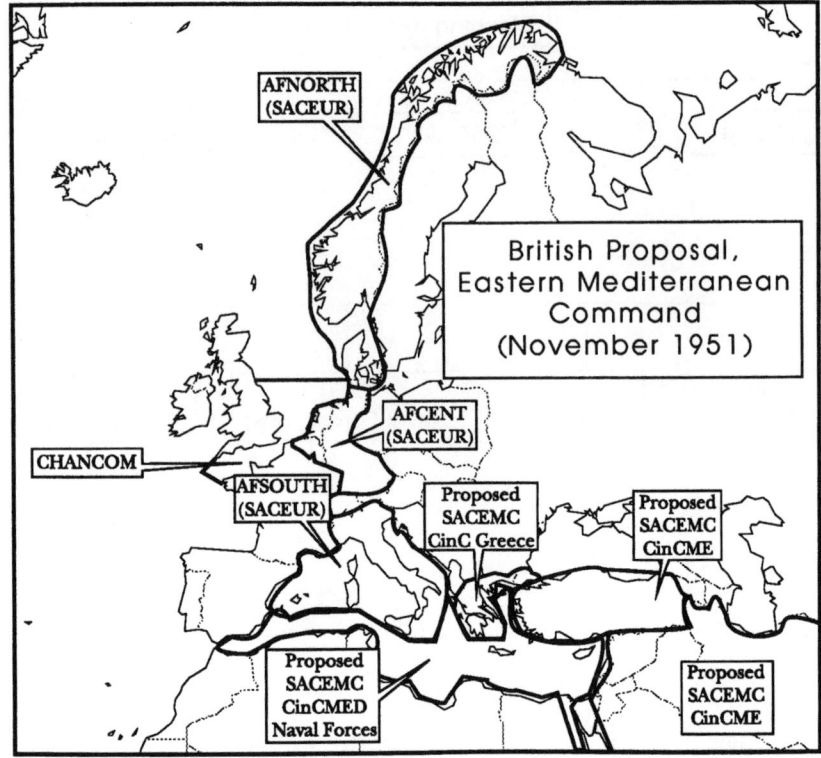

Fig. 5.9.

problems associated with command in the Mediterranean region, although the JCS favored a plan that divided the naval forces in the Mediterranean into SLOC protection forces under a British commander and carrier task forces under an American.[34] The British requirements included command over the Mediterranean SLOC and some link with the Middle East. The Turks refused to serve under the British, and the Greeks wanted to be part of SACEUR.

The United States not only needed a clear chain of command to the Sixth Fleet because it carried atomic weapons on its aircraft carriers but also had SACEUR's needs to contend with. Only some form of compromise could end the stalemate.

By the end of December 1951, the JCS had decided that "the establishment of a Middle East Command is a matter outside the cognizance of the North Atlantic Council." Since coordination of the defense of the Middle East could not occur without the creation of a Middle East

The Struggle for the Mediterranean ➢ *185*

Command and the Mediterranean command could not be created until Greece and Turkey entered NATO, the Americans decided to force the issue at the next North Atlantic Council meeting scheduled for February 1952.[35] In preparing for this meeting, the Americans' plan of action had three stages. First came arrangements for the integration of Greece and Turkey into NATO command organizations, followed by the establishment of a Middle East command outside NATO. Only then could coordination between NATO and the Middle East defenses occur.[36]

The Americans came to the February talks with a detailed concept for a Middle East command organization that bore a stunning resemblance to SACEUR (see fig. 5.10). SACME's naval influence ended at the Red Sea, and the Commander, Land Forces Middle East encompassed the area from Egypt to Iran—but not Turkey. For the Mediterranean, the Americans preferred a variant of their previous alternative B; coordination between the two organizations was supposed to be effected by liaison among the

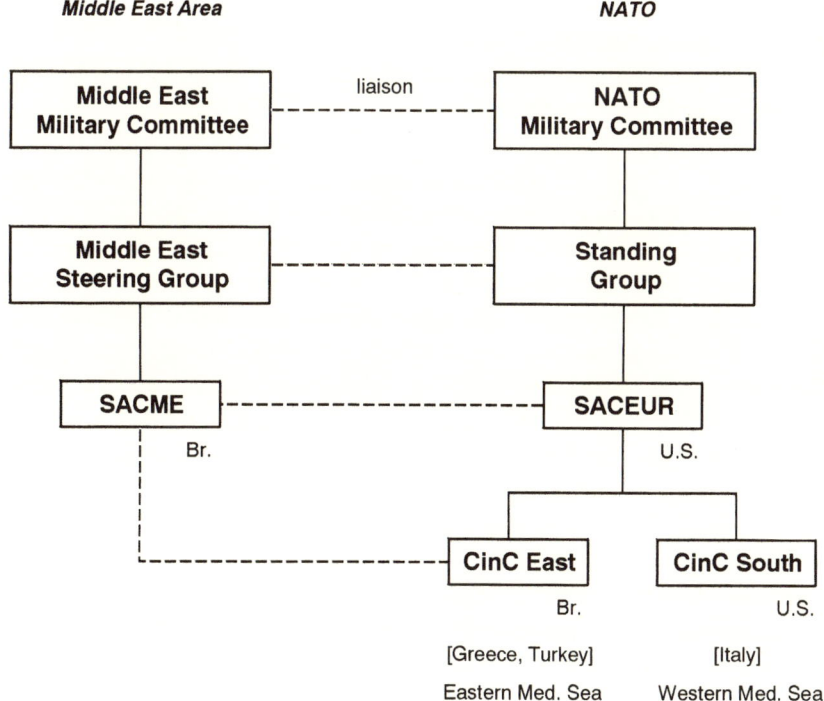

Fig. 5.10. U.S. proposal for command organization in the Mediterranean and Middle East, December 1951

NATO Military Committee and the proposed Middle East Military Committee, the NATO Standing Group and the Middle East Steering Group, and SACME and SACEUR.[37] This proposal would bear fruit at a later time.

The Churchill-Truman summit in January 1952 marked another milestone in the creation of a NATO command in the Mediterranean. The British delegation noted that the primary British interest in the region was the protection of the Suez Canal and that the creation of a Middle East Command would facilitate this. However, "Churchill . . . stressed that a British commander of the Middle East Command must not be considered as compensation for British 'losses' elsewhere [i.e., SACLANT]. . . ."[38] Acheson, the U.S. secretary of state, concurred and recommended that the Middle East Command be set up in March or April 1952. He emphasized that the MEC ought to be kept completely separate from NATO and that Greece and Turkey should become part of SACEUR. The problem of how to effect such an incorporation remained unsolved.[39]

The British position on command in the Mediterranean hardened after Churchill's meeting with Truman in January 1952 and their agreement that SACEUR's AFSOUTH command was too big for one man to handle.[40] The political need for a NATO supreme command under a British officer came to the fore once again: "We consider that having gained the principle of a unified command in the Mediterranean under an allied naval commander who would be British, we should press . . . for all naval forces in the Mediterranean to be placed unreservedly under the allied naval commander, who would be parallel in status with SACLANT and directly responsible to the Standing Group."[41] The new British scheme revolved around the idea that the British national commander CinCMED could easily be double-hatted as a NATO Allied CinCMED, whose deputy could be an American in order to satisfy the McMahon Act. Targeting activity could also be conducted by a separate cell of Americans subordinate to the deputy (see fig. 5.11). Under this proposal, the Allied Naval Commander, Mediterranean was also the British CinCMED, who was responsible to SACME.[42] The obvious problem here was the Americans' categorical refusal to place the U.S. Sixth Fleet under SACME—or, for that matter, under a British commander at all.

American planners were also frustrated in their attempts to set up a command organization since "none of the NATO Mediterranean–Middle East area command organizations proposed to date by the Standing Group, a nation or SACEUR has proven acceptable to all concerned. . . . "[43] Again, the JSPC opted for a proposal that split the Mediterranean naval forces

The Struggle for the Mediterranean ➤ *187*

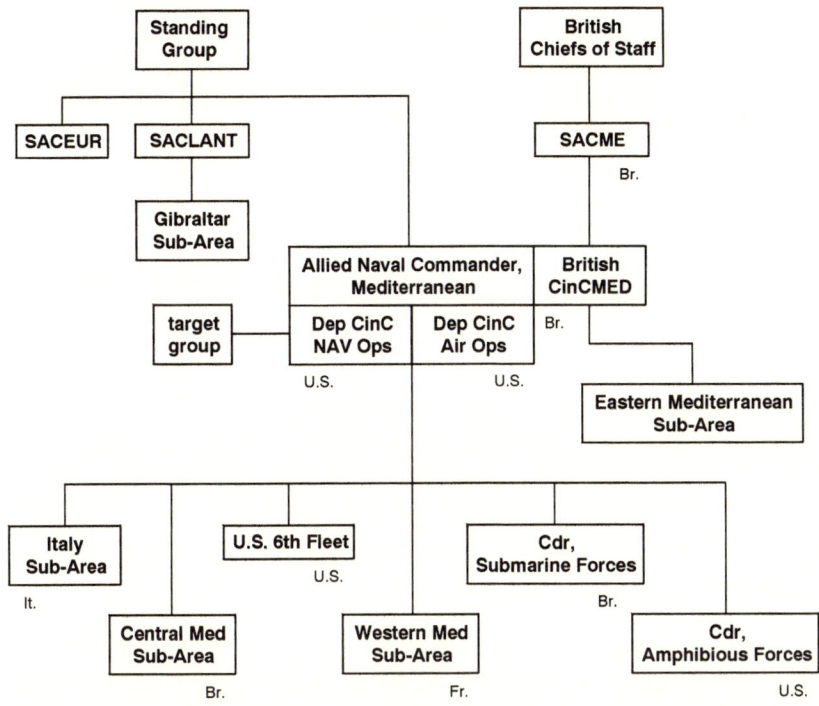

Fig. 5.11. British proposal for command organization in the Mediterranean, January 1952

into two commands: a CinC Naval Forces, Mediterranean under a British commander who would handle SLOCs and a Commander, Naval Striking Forces, Mediterranean who would be a U.S. officer and have control over the Sixth Fleet (see fig. 5.12).[44] To add fuel to the fire, the JCS liaison officer to SHAPE reported to the JCS that "many of the nations are extremely sensitive to any U.S.–UK agreement on matters of importance and general concern which are reached without their active participation. I hope that there will be no 'leaks' as to the extent of your discussions and that any announcements made clearly indicate that NATO command arrangements are not matters for bilateral negotiation but must be worked out by established NATO agencies."[45]

Driven by the need to keep the Mediterranean and Middle East SLOC under one commander, the British also attempted to reconcile NATO and non-NATO commands. In the words of the British planners, "In any event, a command in the Middle East exists and has existed since long before NATO was thought of. In war, the distinction between NATO and non-

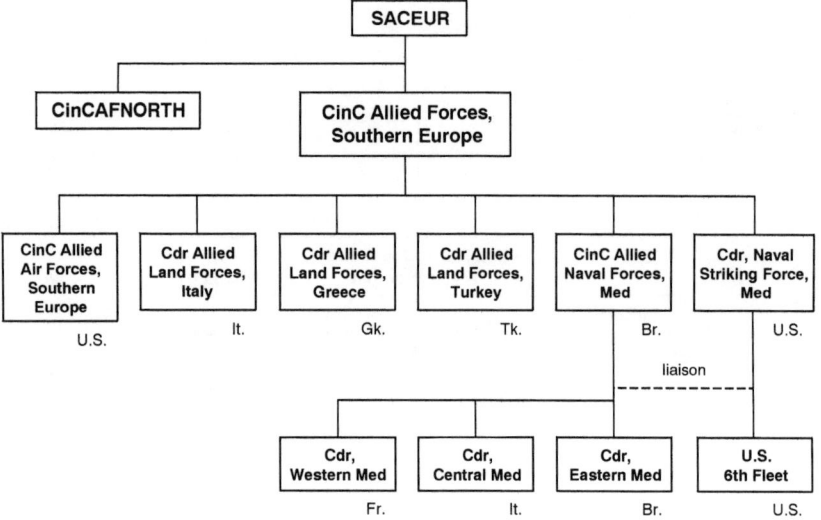

Fig. 5.12. U.S. proposal for command organization in the Mediterranean, January 1952

NATO becomes meaningless—all the forces of the Western Alliance in the Mediterranean Sea and in the area around its shores will then be allies facing a common enemy."[46] Not willing to hand the region to SACEUR and under pressure to split the Mediterranean and the Middle East into two distinct theaters, the British suggested placing the naval commander for the Mediterranean directly under the Standing Group on par with SACEUR and SACLANT so that coordination between SACME could be achieved via this command, with the SG as the coordinating agency.[47]

The Americans were quick to point out what they saw as serious flaws in British thinking. Foremost on the American agenda was the familiar argument over "unity of command" of all naval forces operating in the same geographic area—a staple of the SACLANT debate. Similarly, the problem of air coordination haunted any proposed organization in the Mediterranean, and the British had not provided an acceptable solution.[48]

The publicity surrounding the announcement of the Middle East Command in February 1952 temporarily overshadowed the Mediterranean command problem. The Middle East Command Organization (MECO) was established under a British supreme allied commander, which would be designated in peacetime and would take over MECO in war. The objective of MECO in peace was to plan, coordinate, and provide liaison among the nations in the Middle East, and its organization in

The Struggle for the Mediterranean ➢ 189

war closely followed that suggested by the Americans in December 1951. The exact relationship between MECO and NATO remained unclear during the time frame of this study.[49] But the new command signaled the end to any NATO dabbling east of the Suez Canal.

At the Lisbon meeting at the end of February 1952, the Americans offered the Standing Group a new solution to the Mediterranean command problem. Their recommendation was to dump COMNAVSOUTH and replace it with a British CinC Allied Naval Forces Mediterranean; an American Commander, Allied Carrier Task Forces Mediterranean; and an American Commander, Allied Amphibious Task Forces Mediterranean. This was similar to their January proposal but included a more detailed division of the Mediterranean Sea area to accommodate the French, Italians, Greeks, and Turks, as well as a functional division of offensive forces from the SLOC protection forces (see fig. 5.13). The Commander,

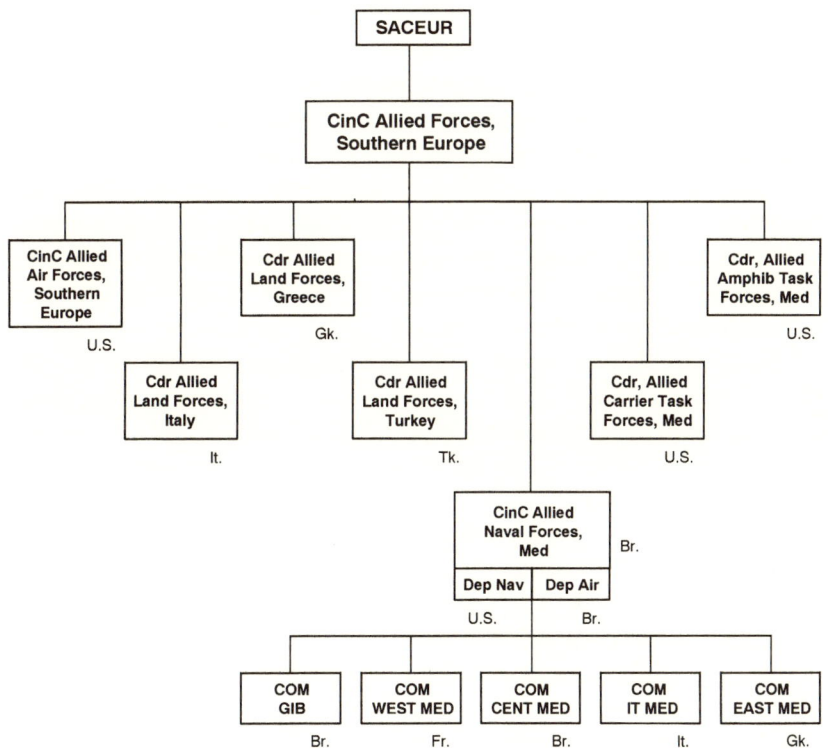

Fig. 5.13. U.S. proposal to the Standing Group at the Lisbon meeting, January 1952

Allied Carrier Task Forces Mediterranean was to be an American naval officer with access to the Sixth Fleet.[50] CinC Allied Naval Forces Mediterranean would have a deputy that handled maritime air operations and coordinated with the carrier task forces; this was promising since the problem of air management over the Mediterranean had not really been addressed in a command organization since World War II, and even the wartime precedent was a poor one.

A meeting between the British Chiefs of Staff Committee (Slim, Slessor, and McGrigor) and the U.S. CNO (Fechteler) and CinCNELM designate (Wright) attempted to resolve the issue outside of NATO auspices in May 1952. In a lengthy and heated meeting, all gloves were off. The British were quite upset with Carney. Slessor stated that Carney was "bulling in, asking too much and assuming too much responsibility."[51] Fechteler, on the other hand, caused a stir when he informed the British that the eastern Mediterranean was now a NATO area under SACEUR's and thus CinCAFSOUTH's control now that Greece and Turkey were in the alliance. McGrigor, flushed, emphatically denied this, arguing that if the Mediterranean were now under CinCAFSOUTH, then Admiral Brind, as CinCAFNORTH, should be SACLANT.[52]

The British were legitimately concerned with the status of the Middle East vis-à-vis NATO planning. In fact, Slim believed that "the Mediterranean naval commander would cease to be a NATO commander on D-day and become a commander under the agency set up to direct a global war, such as the Combined Chiefs of Staff and, that NATO would be a nice tight little compartment within that global set up. Admiral Fechteler said such would not necessarily be so. . . . "[53]

What would the Italians and French have to say about the Mediterranean? The British maintained that the Italians were only involved for local reasons and were not really "players." The French on the other hand, were in a different situation. The Americans were quick to note that Admiral Nomy, the French naval commander, had been quoted as saying that "if he put French naval forces under other than Carney's command, the French Government would throw him out of his job and if they didn't, the French people would throw the Government out. . . ."[54] Slim's response was typically British: "If we have to depend on the desires of the French politicians as to the soundness of the military organization we are in a sad position."[55]

Slessor, ever the pragmatist, noted that "if it were not for public opinion it wouldn't make much difference what command organization were decided upon and announced."[56] The problem remained unresolved. The

Americans wanted the Mediterranean under CinCAFSOUTH, while the British wanted a separate organization on par with SACEUR and SACLANT.⁵⁷ Significantly, Admiral Carney was replaced as CinCNELM by Adm. Jerauld Wright, a future SACLANT; Carney remained CinCAFSOUTH, however. Eisenhower at the time believed that one man could not handle both jobs.⁵⁸ This change still allowed Carney to receive operational control over Sixth Fleet carrier task forces from CinCNELM if necessary.

The only positive result to emerge from Lisbon regarding command in the Mediterranean was the acceptance of Greece and Turkey into the NATO command organization without any detailed discussion about how they would fit in. While the Mediterranean command issue stagnated throughout the spring and summer, Allied Land Forces, Southeastern Europe was created as a subcommand to CinCAFSOUTH in August 1952. This was primarily a land and tactical air command consisting of Greek and Turkish land forces with its headquarters in Ibiza. Its formation had been anticipated by the Americans at the Ankara-Paris talks in 1951. This solved some problems by making it appear that CinCAFSOUTH delegated authority to the new subcommand and probably would not interfere in day-to-day or operational matters during a war.⁵⁹

The British also conducted a change of command in May 1952 when the First Sea Lord announced that Louis, Earl Mountbatten of Burma would take over from Admiral Edlesten as British Commander in Chief, Mediterranean. Noting that the Sixth Fleet received wide media coverage, Mountbatten immediately embarked on a public relations tour in his area with the express objective of increasing British influence in the Mediterranean. The purpose of Mountbatten's deployment to command CinCMED was not lost on Carney, who initially believed that he was ultimately there to take over AFSOUTH: "[It was obvious that] Mountbatten's prestige was being utilized to maintain a position in the Mediterranean since the British were hurting there; they obviously were playing second fiddle to the Sixth Fleet in its imposing strength, its numbers and also its popularity. . . . The British were [still] feared by some and disliked by others in the Mediterranean. . . ."⁶⁰ Needless to say, the relationship between CinCAFSOUTH and CinCMED continued to be strained once Mountbatten took over.

Mountbatten also had to contend with individuals within the British government who instructed him "not to put himself into any position which might give the impression that Carney was [his] superior."⁶¹ In fact, some believed that CinCMED should not even participate in NATO exercises in the Mediterranean in order to avoid such a situation. Mountbatten beat back such attempts to hamper NATO naval cooperation and continually fought to maintain the British position. The Soviets even attempted to exploit this Anglo-American division for propaganda purposes.[62]

As was demonstrated in chapter 4, many unresolved Anglo-American naval command issues rapidly came to a head in November 1952, and the Mediterranean situation was no exception. In preparation for a Standing Group meeting scheduled for late November, the British Chiefs of Staff Committee met with Mountbatten to plan its argument. In his report, Mountbatten informed the committee that CinCAFSOUTH and particularly the U.S. Sixth Fleet lacked vital communications and logistical facilities. In his view, the British were in a position to conduct a naval war in the Mediterranean by themselves with their current infrastructure and base network, which was considerable. Even CinCAFSOUTH was surprised at the size of it. In addition, the British possessed the only naval control of shipping organization in the Mediterranean.[63] In Mountbatten's opinion, CinCAFSOUTH could not exercise command and therefore could not assume control over the entire Mediterranean. CinCAFSOUTH also had no air movements coordinator (a situation regarded by Mountbatten as "completely chaotic"), no procedures for centralization of information, and no command facility linked to CinCAFSOUTH headquarters.[64] To add insult to injury, Mountbatten told the committee that Carney's assertion that no other nation would accept British control was absolute nonsense: he had personally contacted the French and the Italians, who were more than willing to operate under the British within a NATO framework. This contradicted what Admirals Nomy (France) and Ferrari (Italy) had told Fechteler.[65]

The British presentation to the Standing Group was a success and broke the deadlocked Mediterranean command issue. The Standing Group determined that there would be a NATO Mediterranean naval command under a single NATO CinCMED, subordinated to SACEUR but having double-hatted Middle East responsibilities if necessary. This organization would be under the command of a British naval officer, with a coalition staff. The position of the Sixth Fleet, however, remained protected, and its employment would be similar to that of STRIKEFLEETLANT. In return, British naval and air bases in the Mediterranean would be at the disposal of NATO, and Gibraltar would become jointly responsible to EASTLANT and CinCMED to simplify NCS.[66] Privately, some British naval officers planned to prohibit the use of carriers in the confined waters of the Mediterranean in wartime and rely instead on land-based air.

Implicitly, this would strengthen British control over operations in the area if the Americans used the STRIKEFLEETLANT "excuse" again.[67]

An actual, working organization and clear delineation of geographic areas was still needed. British planners conveniently had a proposal at hand in late November 1952 (see fig. 5.14). NATO CinCMED, a British naval officer, would have two deputies, a U.S. Navy officer and an RAF officer, as well as five areas: Central, Eastern, Gibraltar, French, and Italian. Commander Striking Force South (COMSTRIKEFORSOUTH) was to be an American, who would have the Sixth Fleet under command; the problem of atomic weapons would be addressed by CinCMED's U.S. deputy to SACEUR.[68] NATO CinCMED's responsibilities in war included the protection of SLOCs; the provision of support to adjacent commands of SACEUR, SACLANT, and the Middle East; and the coordination of logistics, MCM operations, submarine operations, and offensive ASW operations.[69] It should be noted that the British still had the ability to influence Mediterranean strategy through SHAPE. SACEUR's deputy was British, as was his air deputy, his plans and operations chief of staff, and his assistant chief of staff for organization.

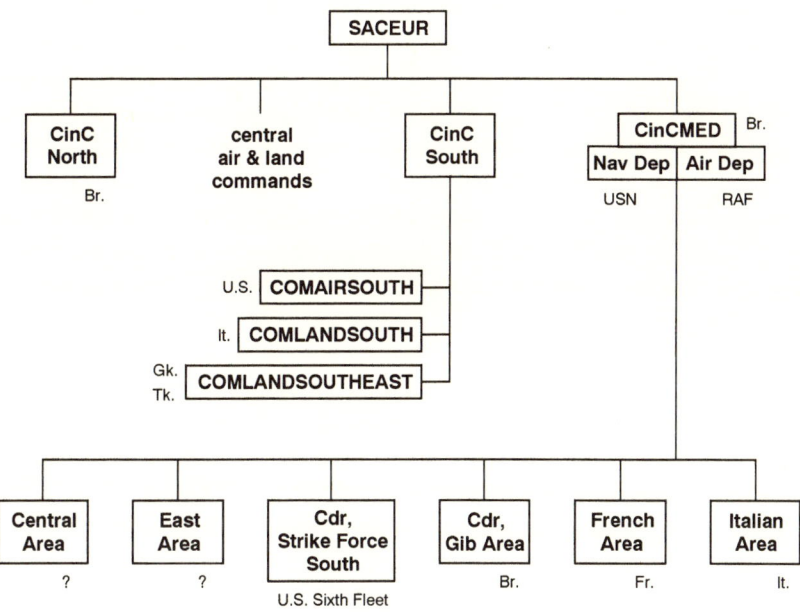

Fig. 5.14. British proposal for naval command organization in the Mediterranean, November 1952

As palatable to the British as these arrangements were, some modifications took place. The title of the command was changed to NATO Commander in Chief, Allied Forces Mediterranean (NATO CinCAFMED), and his command was extended to include the Black Sea. In a concession to the Americans, Churchill recommended the removal of STRIKEFORSOUTH from CinCAFMED's command and left it under CinCAFSOUTH's command; its operating arrangements were similar to those developed for SACLANT's STRIKEFLEETLANT.[70] This concession followed naturally from the resolution of the STRIKEFLEETLANT problem in the Atlantic.

Not surprisingly, Mountbatten (British CinCMED) was double-hatted as NATO CinCAFMED and chose to establish HQ, NATO CinCAFMED in Malta. This process lasted from December 1952 to March 1953. An unfortunate problem developed when Carney delayed transferral of the submarine and amphibious command organizations from Naples to Malta. Mountbatten believed that Carney was attempting to establish a rival naval headquarters (Headquarters, STRIKEFLEETSOUTH) under CinCAFSOUTH. This was quickly resolved by a meeting of the Standing Group in Paris in March. Later, Admiral Fechteler replaced Carney as CinCAFSOUTH, and this brought peace to the Mediterranean.

CinCAFMED developed over the next few months into a more or less finalized organization that remained in place until 1967 (see figs. 5.15 and 5.16). Headquarters, CinCAFMED (HALFMED) was a coalition command consisting of the NATO CinCAFMED, who was Mountbatten; Admiral Fife (USN) as Deputy CinCAFMED; and a staff from Italy, France, Greece, Turkey, Britain, and the United States. CinCAFMED had nine commands—six geographic and three functional. The geographic commands were similar to the British ACHQ system, with a naval commander and an air commander. These included the Gibraltar Mediterranean Command (GIBMED) under the British Flag Officer, Gibraltar; Mediterranean Occidentale (COMEDOC) under Admiral Sala of the French navy; Central Mediterranean Area (COMMEDCENT) under Admiral Girosi of the Italian navy; Southeast Mediterranean Area (COMSOUEAST) under Admiral Reid, British CinCMED's second in command; Eastern Mediterranean Command (COMMEDEAST) under Admiral Lappas of the Royal Hellenic Navy; and Northeast Mediterranean Command (COMNOREAST) under Admiral Altican of the Turkish navy. The functional commands included Commander, Submarines Mediterranean (COMSUBMED), who was the British Commander, Submarines, Mediterranean; Submarines, Mediterranean Northeast under the Turks; and Commander, U.S. Patrols,

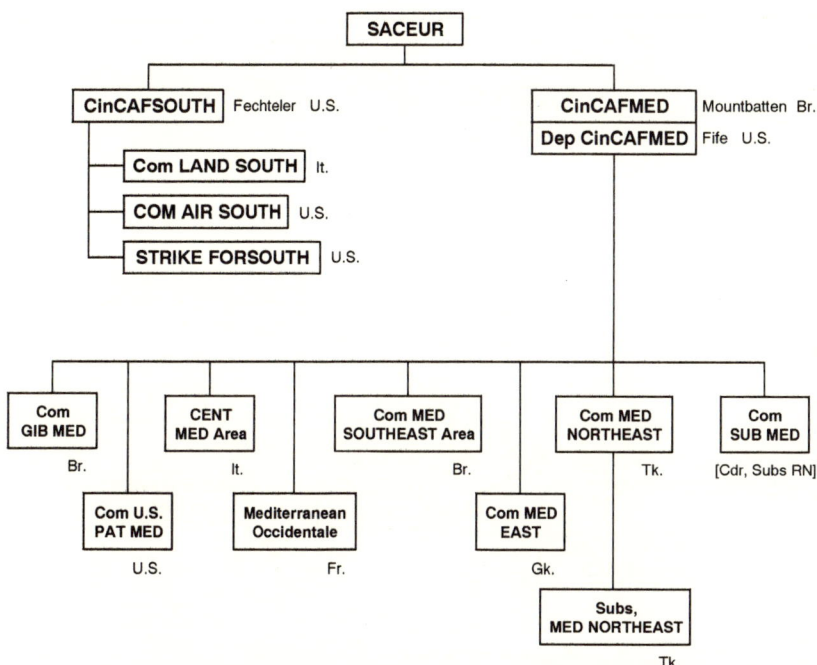

Fig. 5.15. Final NATO CinCAFMED organization

Mediterranean (COMUSPATMED), which was the holding organization for naval LRMPAs allocated to CinCAFMED in wartime. The exact boundary between COMMEDCENT and COMDOC remained undefined throughout the 1950s due to a long-standing Franco-Italian dispute.[71]

In conclusion, the creation of a NATO naval command organization in the Mediterranean resulted from a process similar to that which the Atlantic command went through; it was also intimately related to the resolution of the Atlantic situation. The similarity between the STRIKEFLEETLANT debate and the STRIKEFORSOUTH problem resided in the American legal need to retain operational control over forces equipped for atomic delivery. In addition, the conflict between Britain's need to retain a SLOC to sustain itself in war and the American strategy of supporting the land battle with sea-based forces in the Mediterranean also paralleled the Atlantic problem. But the political problems of Greece and Turkey and their incorporation into NATO had no parallel, nor did the problem of geography embodied by the Suez defile and the separation of the Mediterranean and Middle East into two separate commands. Finally,

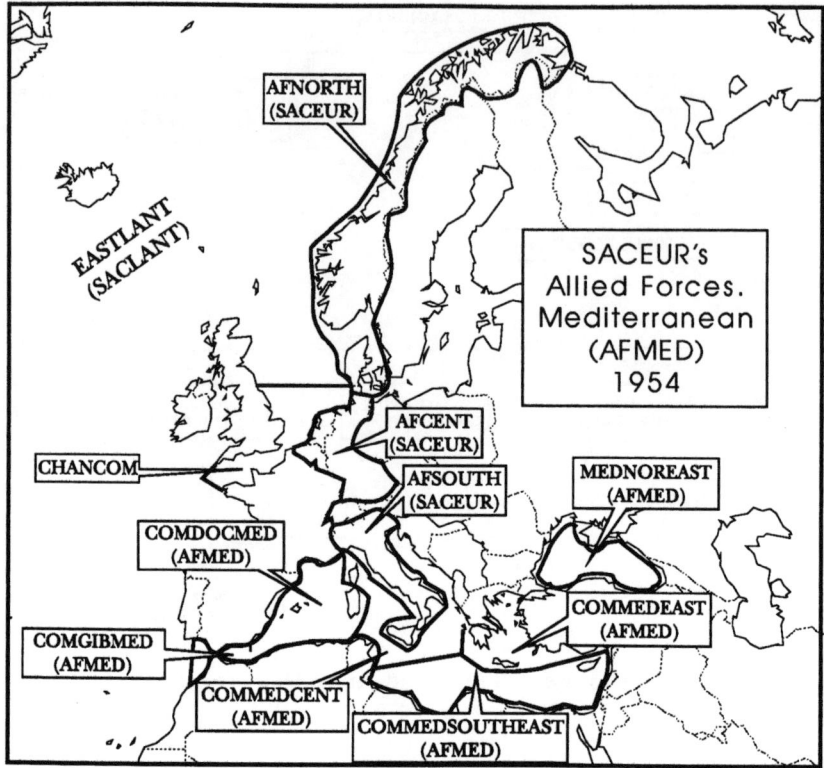

Fig. 5.16.

the decrease in the size and composition of British operating forces in the Mediterranean was a key factor in the reduction of British command and influence in the region. This corresponded with the decline of British power worldwide, and thus the CinCAFMED fight could be considered a rearguard action meant to preserve at least some British prestige. In the words of one journalist, "The delays [in Mediterranean command organization] have been caused partly by the hope that a wider treaty and a wider military command might be organised in and beyond the Eastern Mediterranean. But there has been no progress and until there is, that project ought not to stand in the way of proper arrangements with the allies we have. Mark Antony was beaten on the Nile when his attention was divided. His is not the example to follow."[72]

➤ Conclusion

The World War II command structure, led by Great Britain and the United States, was set up to prosecute coalition war against the Axis powers. Inevitably, the organizations in the Atlantic, Europe, the Mediterranean, and the Middle East were established under the stress of global conflict. After the war was over, coalition command was limited to bilateral command arrangements between the United States and Great Britain, and between the United States and Canada. Europe was the responsibility of the Western Union Defense Organization, led by the French and the British. The Berlin crisis in 1948 provided the catalyst for the melding of these arrangements into the North Atlantic Treaty Organization, thus providing higher direction for the new collective security system in the event of conflict with the Soviet Union. With the Korean War, tension in 1950–51 escalated; one important result was the creation of the NATO military commands Supreme Allied Commander Europe, Supreme Allied Commander Atlantic, Channel Command, and Allied Forces Mediterranean, organizations that matured throughout 1951–53.

Debate over NATO command organization did not end after the creation of AFMED in 1953. As has been demonstrated, the NATO structure was an outgrowth of several factors, including the formulation of changing strategic concepts. On 1 November 1952, the United States tested its first thermonuclear device; the Soviet Union tested its on 12 August 1953, and both were "weaponized" by the end of 1953. By 1954–55, the Soviets were producing jet bombers

197

such as the TU-16 Badger and the MYA-4 Bison, both of which were capable of reaching North America on two-way missions. In addition, the Soviets were testing submarine-launched cruise and ballistic missiles. The vast increase in destructive power offered by the hydrogen bomb had been anticipated by both the Americans and the British. Both nations convened investigative bodies to redefine military policy in light of this new and apocalyptic capability. In essence, the argumentative extremes during this debate ranged from the complete abandonment of conventional forces, with the future emphasis placed on the Vulcans, Victors, and Valiants of the Royal Air Force's V-Force or the B-47s and B-52s of USAF's Strategic Air Command, to the maintenance of the ability to conduct warfare at all magnitudes of conflict, be it limited, cold, or global. It should be noted that as yet there was not the clear differentiation among conventional, tactical nuclear, or strategic nuclear war that is so familiar today, and the concept of flexible response was in an embryonic state.[1]

The conclusion of both bodies was that the United States and Britain should retain the ability to conduct war at all levels; as a result, the NATO command organization did not undergo vast changes in response to these new strategic imperatives. In fact, the belief that the Soviets would soon have submarine-launched missiles equipped with nuclear warheads made SACLANT more important to NATO. Given North America's role as a vast mobilization and resource base from which war with the Soviet Union could be sustained, some organization had to limit the Soviets' ability to place submarines off the Atlantic seaboard. The logical candidate was SACLANT. To deal with submarine-launched missiles, the Americans developed a "barrier strategy" that envisaged several layers of ASW forces—including hunter-killer submarines, hunter-killer carrier groups, and LRMPAs—extending from northern Norway to the east coast of North America. These barrier forces were to be tied into a joint Canadian–U.S. network of underwater detection sensors called SOSUS, which would be under the operational control of the Commander, Oceanographic Systems, Atlantic (a U.S. CinCLANT command) with some duties handled by the Canadian FOAC.[2] This essentially added another important task to SACLANT: the continental defense of North America.

However, there were other contenders for the function of continental defense. In 1954 the USAF had organized the Continental Air Defense Command (CONAD) and was once again attempting to gain control over U.S. Navy carrier aircraft, this time in the interest of air defense of the United States. There was even another debate over who had command

Conclusion ➢ 199

over new U.S. Navy airborne early warning aircraft operating as extensions to the radar network located in Canada for defense against air attack. Efforts in this sphere resulted in the Canadian–U.S. bilateral agreement creating the North American Air Defense Command (NORAD) in 1958. This occurred outside NATO and is thus beyond the purview of this study.[3]

The British were greatly dismayed by NORAD because they believed the threat to North America to be exaggerated and thought that any such barrier would not encompass the British Isles. Noting that the early sound detection systems did not work as well as expected and probably would not for the present, the British continually emphasized attack at source (even to the point of allocating scarce V-Force resources to the task), offensive mining, and forward-deployed hunter-killer submarines.[4] The Vice Chief of the Naval Staff even noted that "if the Russians only knew how much effort [the Americans] were proposing to lock up already, I am sure that it would pay Malenkov to build a few guided weapons submarines and publicize them to the maximum. . . ."[5]

Nonetheless, NATO naval command organization survived not only the technological onslaught of the H-bomb but fissures within the alliance caused by the Suez crisis in 1956. Even though U.S. Navy units were ordered to interfere with the Anglo-French amphibious task force heading for Egypt after Dulles publicly condemned the adventure,[6] Adm. Arleigh Burke, the U.S. Chief of Naval Operations, sent this message to First Sea Lord Mountbatten via a back channel: "The United States Navy has noted with interest and admiration the speed and efficiency with which the Royal Navy has been able to undertake and perform its many additional tasks within the last week or so. The present Suez situation demonstrated once again that, when the chips are down it is the navy who must first act and continue to carry out its naval tasks in order for any other action to be possible. . . ."[7]

There was also some gnashing of teeth at SACLANT. Adm. Jerauld Wright (USN) complained that he had not been consulted when the British redeployed the aircraft carriers *Eagle, Bulwark, Ocean,* and *Thesus* and a substantial force of amphibious ships to the Mediterranean in August and September 1956. The British view on this point was that since EASTLANT had not been consulted when the Americans sent STRIKEFLEETLANT carriers to the Far East during the Quemoy-Matsu crisis of 1954, SACLANT was not entitled to be upset when British STRIKEFLEETLANT carriers were redeployed for national reasons at short notice.[8]

To focus solely on these examples would be misleading. Relations between the U.S. Navy and the Royal Navy steadily improved after 1954.

The British Joint Staff Mission, Washington, attributed this to several factors: new personalities, new and closer contacts, the increased awareness of the Americans that they were getting more mileage out of the British than from any other nation, and the Korean experience.[9]

The cooperation of the U.S. Navy and the Royal Navy in Korea was almost a test case, much in the way Fechteler viewed it as the NATO strategic problem in microcosm. The naval command organization was a smaller version of SACLANT and is worth brief examination (see fig. 6.1). The supreme commander was the United Nations Commander in Chief, who inevitably was MacArthur. National naval forces allocated to UNCinC were placed under the UN Commander, Naval Forces Far East (COMNAVFE), who was Vice Adm. C. Turner Joy (USN). COMNAVFE's operating forces came from the British Commander in Chief, Far East Fleet, and the American Commander in Chief, Pacific, who also controlled the Seventh Fleet. COMNAVFE included Task Force 77, which was essentially a

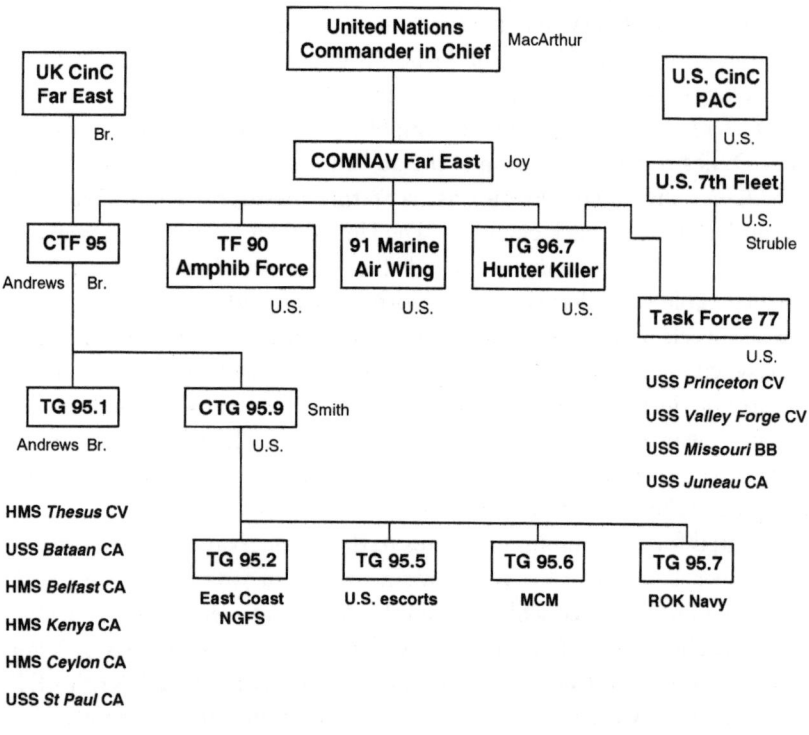

Fig. 6.1. Naval command organization for the Korean War, February 1951

STRIKEFLEETLANT doppelgänger consisting of two U.S. carriers, a battleship, and a cruiser. Offensive ASW hunter-killer operations, an amphibious force, and a USMC Air Wing also were subordinate to COMNAVFE. The largest subunit of COMNAVFE, however, was CTF-95, the UN Blockade and Escort Force under Vice Adm. W. G. Andrews (RN). CTF-95's TF-77 equivalent was Task Group 95.1, which included one British carrier, one U.S. carrier, three British cruisers, and a U.S. cruiser. The blockading force was also multinational, including U.S. escorts, British destroyers and MCM vessels, and the entire Republic of Korea navy.[10]

From all accounts, this organization performed extremely well and undoubtedly served as a model for U.S. Navy–Royal Navy cooperation. All operations conceivable under the NATO strategic concept (except, of course, the use of atomic weapons) including submarine, hunter-killer, air support to land forces, naval gunfire support, and escort of convoy were successfully conducted during the Korean War.[11]

The apparent American dominance in the Korean command organization was symptomatic of Britain's decline, and it should not be surprising that this trend continued after 1956. Whereas the Second World War command hierarchy was fairly split between the United States and Great Britain, the number and importance of British-controlled coalition commands in the 1950s noticeably decreased. In fact, NATO naval command organization in the 1980s reflected the abrupt decline of Britain's influence in the world arena after the 1950s (see fig. 6.2).[12] The IBERLANT problem, which had proved to be such a thorn in everybody's side in 1951–53, was resolved as a separate area under SACLANT in 1967. AFMED was disestablished in 1967 as well and replaced by Naval Striking and Support Forces, South; the area came under SACEUR's CinCAFSOUTH. With the increased importance of submarine operations involving the U.S. submarine-launched ballistic missile force, COMSUBEASTLANT was placed under a functional command, COMSUBLANT, which handled submarine operations for the entire Atlantic. A standing multinational naval force called STANAVFORLANT was created in the 1960s. Other than these changes, the basic NATO command structure created between 1949 and 1953 has remained sound for almost forty years. Only in 1991 were significant changes made when CHANCOM was absorbed by SACEUR's AFNORTH to form AFNORTHWEST.[13]

Decisions over which nation controls which coalition command appear to have been based on two primary factors. First and most important, control usually is vested in the nation with the largest number of operating

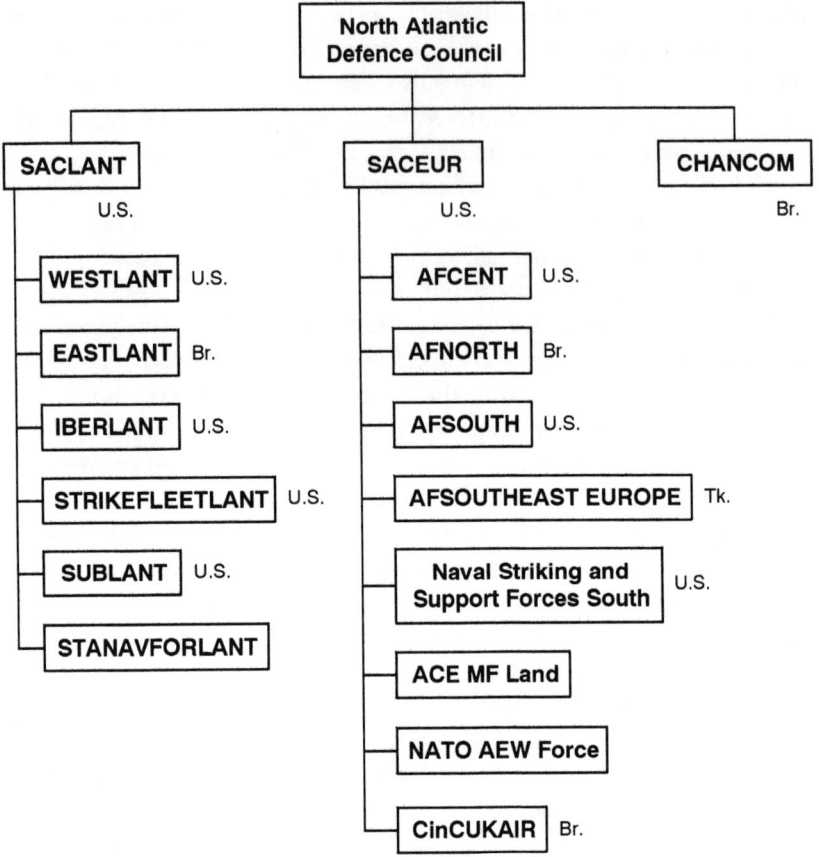

Fig. 6.2. NATO commands, 1990

forces either available or allocated to that command area in the event of war. Examples include CHANCOM and SACLANT. Second, the American need for a legal chain of command in order to exert positive control over American nuclear weapons appears to have been the deciding factor in the issues of STRIKEFLEETLANT and AFMED. This is confirmed by the disestablishment of COMSUBEASTLANT as an independent EASTLANT command once the Americans deployed submarine-launched ballistic missiles in the 1960s. In the clash between command styles, the Americans also won out by eventually falling back on their chain-of-command requirement as well as demonstrating the superior numbers available to them. Although the British joint committee system is superior to the American unified command system, the latter was incorporated into NATO commands. National

Conclusion ➣ 203

prestige was initially an issue here, but hard military considerations were the priority. There is a definite process, however, in the formulation of command arrangements. Disputes initially were mediated at the military level and then escalated to the political level if the issue was perceived by one party as affecting vital national interests; this was evident in the resolution of the SACLANT, AFMED, and IBERLANT problems.

In summary, then, the creation of a viable command structure for the West was accomplished with the appointment of SACLANT in 1952 and the finalizing of NATO lines of authority by 1954. This process was influenced by two main concerns: the legacy of the Second World War Anglo-American command for global war, and the comparative decline of Britain as a world power in relation to the United States.

The actual state of Western collective security after World War II was threatened by deep divisions during the formative period of the NATO alliance from 1949 to 1953. The problem of NATO naval command organization in the Atlantic and the Mediterranean contributed to these divisions, which almost reached a critical point when Britain threatened to remove itself from the Atlantic command. Since Britain was one of only two nations with substantial resources capable of supporting allies in their defense against the Soviet Union during this period, and since the NATO alliance was constructed on the groundwork of the Anglo-American defense relationship, such a rift would have further encouraged the Soviets to use any or all means to exploit the divisions in the alliance and destroy its deterrence value. This, thankfully, did not happen. The establishment of a stable command structure was central to effective deterrence.

The impact of the Second World War command organization on NATO was also profound. The problems involving the coordination of Canadian, British, and American services in the Battle of the Atlantic were definitely a catalyst for the creation of SACLANT. SACEUR's formative experience as SHAEF and his earlier Mediterranean incarnations had a definite impact on the creation of a NATO command for Europe; certainly, personalities helped here. Similarly, the development of SACMED and its division from CinCME during World War II was replayed when SACME was separated from AFSOUTH and AFMED in the 1950s. In addition, it is interesting to see the COMNAVNAW controversy from the Second World War continue into the 1950s as the IBERLANT problem.

The state of the Anglo-American relationship as a whole was not a good one in the late 1940s and early 1950s, despite the rhetoric. The American decision not to allow Britain access to nuclear information forced Britain to spend an inordinate amount of scarce resources to duplicate the effort during a period of economic instability. This had far-reaching effects on command organization, since the numbers of British conventional forces had to decrease and the delay in deploying British nuclear weapons gave the Americans the upper hand in targeting policy and control over forces equipped with nuclear weapons. The problems with the declining number of British operational forces in relation to the United States are seen when the United States consistently reminds Britain that the country providing the preponderance of forces to a given coalition command has traditionally controlled it. Even in the area of command organization philosophy, the American unified command system is applied to several NATO commands while the British principle of joint command is utilized only in those areas controlled by British commanders. Since the establishment of command structures owed much to the level of conventional or nuclear forces that a nation could deploy, the postwar decline of Britain left most major NATO commands—even those of primary interest to the British—in the hands of the Americans.

➤ Appendix 1
Assessing the Soviet Submarine Threat, 1945–1956

Their German scientists are better than our German scientists.
—a common phrase in the 1950s

The Soviet underwater threat to allied SLOCs was the driving force behind naval strategy from 1945 to 1956. However, the personnel supplying the intelligence estimates on which NATO plans were based did not have access to the information that became available in 1991 with the demise of the Soviet Union. The purpose of this appendix is to assess the postwar Soviet underwater threat in light of this new data.

Because of the advanced stage of German submarine development and the fact that the Soviets were in possession of both completed boats and the means to produce more, naval planners in the late 1940s were completely justified in fearing the underwater capabilities of the Soviet navy, and particularly the German Type XXI subs. Unlike the German Types VIIC or IXC, which were essentially submersible torpedo boats that dived for protective purposes, the Type XXI was a true submarine capable of sustained underwater combat activity. Equipped with a proportionally larger battery capacity, a streamlined hull form, and a *Schnorkel* system, the Type XXI could reach speeds of 17 knots underwater, making it faster than most surface escort vessels built during World War II. Moreover, the sonar systems of that period were designed to detect objects moving at slower speeds.

Other innovations of the Type XXI included an analog computer fire control center, high torpedo storage, acoustic- and pattern-running torpedoes, anechoic tiling, and mast-mounted sensor systems. The Type XXI also had the ability to project decoy sounds to confuse sonar. Royal Navy assessments of captured Type XXIs and of 1944–45 state-of-the-art ASW equipment and tactics suggested that these submarines might be unstoppable in large numbers.[1]

The coastal counterpart of the oceangoing Type XXI was the Type XXIII, which utilized the same fire control system as the Type XXI and also had a streamlined shape, *Schnorkel,* and large battery capacity. The primary drawback of this design was its limit of two torpedoes with no reloads.[2]

From 1945 to 1949, the Soviet submarine force included the following captured German submarines: four Type XXIs, two Type IXCs, and five VIICs, all of which were classified as long-range oceangoing boats. According to Royal Navy Monthly Intelligence Reports, the Soviets tested a Type XXIII in the Caspian Sea in 1946; unfortunately it did not resurface, probably because of their lack of familiarity with the sophisticated German technology. This incident apparently slowed Soviet exploitation of the German designs in the late 1940s. Additionally, if the U.S. Navy's experience with its Type XXIs is any indication, the boats were difficult to maintain, even for a nation with advanced naval technology such as the United States.[3]

The state of the Soviet submarine force after the war was decidedly mediocre; most of the types possessed by the Soviets were based on interwar designs. From 1945 to 1950, the Soviets are credited with owning 172 oceangoing submarines: 3 type "N"s, 8 type "B"s, 10 type "K"s, 34 *Stalinetz*es, 8 *Leninetz* series Is, 16 *Leninetz* series IIs, 78 *Shchuka*s and 2 *Pravda*s. The *Leninetz, Stalinetz, Pravda, Shchuka,* and "K" classes (and especially their powerplants) traced their lineage to interwar German technical cooperation and could be considered equivalent to Type VIICs. The Soviets also had 126 coastal types of limited range and endurance; 104 of these were the prewar *Malodki*s, whose nearest equivalent would be the German Type II coastal boat.[4]

The oceangoing boats could reach the equator if they were based in the Baltic or in northern Russia; the *Malodki*s could operate in and around the British Isles. Obviously, if the Soviets were able to overrun Norway and France in a war, that would extend their submarines' ranges considerably.[5]

Thus, by 1950 the Soviets operated 298 submarines. If the standard operational rate of 33 percent is used, they had the ability to put fifty-eight oceangoing types and forty-two coastal types at sea at any one time, numbers that compare favorably with German capabilities in 1940. However, it should be noted that the total number of Soviet boats would have been divided among the Pacific, Northern, Baltic, and Black Sea fleets.

By extrapolating from actual capabilities, one can see that an SLOC campaign in the 1945–50 time frame would have been similar to the 1941–43 phase of the Battle of the Atlantic. Allied ASW technology in 1945 could have dealt adequately with a fair proportion of the Soviet submarines; what the Soviets' four Type XXIs could have accomplished is difficult to ascertain. A combined Anglo-American-Canadian working group on antisubmarine doctrine produced an accurate assessment in 1950 when they concluded that the Soviet submarine force was "imposing but not formidable."[6]

A new submarine construction program was instituted by the Soviet Union in 1951 after a furious debate over naval force structure and roles.[7] This effort resulted in three new classes: the "Whiskey," the "Zulu," and the "Quebec," to use their NATO code names.

At first, Western observers believed the Whiskey to be a Type XXI clone, but this was not the case. As Jan Breemer demonstrates, the Whiskey was really developed out of the *Stalinetz;* in fact, although the class may have incorporated other German advances, no Whiskey was observed to have a *Schnorkel* before 1955. A total of 236 Whiskey-class boats were built between 1951 and 1957; five of these were modified for early warning missions, and a number were modified in 1956 to carry the SS-N-3 "Shaddock" cruise missile.[8]

The Zulu, on the other hand, was a Type XXI derivative and retained many of its predecessor's structural and endurance features. Twenty-six of these were constructed between 1952 and 1957. Six were modified in 1956 to carry two modified SCUD-1a intermediate-range ballistic missiles apiece.[9] Both the Whiskey and Zulu classes were long-range submarines capable of sustained operations in the Atlantic.

The Quebec was a short-range successor to the *Malodki.* It was inspired by the Type XXIII but had four tubes instead of two. Thirty Quebecs were built between 1952 and 1957.[10]

Thus, from 1951 to 1956 an ASW campaign would have had a different character. Since it could be argued that ASW technology had not improved significantly between the end of the war and the early 1950s, the West would have faced a serious SLOC problem—one that might have required an attack-at-source strategy combined with close escort of convoy.

➤ Appendix 2
Fleet Structure and Technological Change, 1945–1956

The U.S. Navy and the Royal Navy were formidable and balanced naval forces in 1950, with very large reserve fleets of war-built craft of every type. Most of the smaller NATO navies except Canada relied on secondhand British and American ships or, in the case of France, captured Axis vessels. NATO forces were structured to take advantage of the mature force projection and SLOC protection doctrines developed during the war.

Soviet naval capability during the 1946–50 period had two elements, coastal submarines and surface units. Long-range aircraft and oceangoing submarines were added to its arsenal by 1955. Before 1946 the primary combat force of the USSR was its army; the navy had a very minimal blue-water role. Soviet naval practice in 1946 was based on traditional Russian defensive strategy. It featured a "fortress fleet" that emphasized coastal defenses, shore batteries, and small patrol combatants, and an embryonic "fleet in being" consisting of cruisers, destroyers, submarines, and eventually aircraft carriers. Stalin wanted a bigger, balanced fleet, but postwar economics precluded such a buildup; as a result, the construction of a large oceangoing submarine force gained priority.[1]

The state of naval technology in 1950 was not substantially different from that of 1945. The vast numbers of ships built during the war still served in all navies. In terms of surface and aerial warfare, there was still a strong emphasis on naval gunnery, unguided torpedoes, long-range maritime patrol aircraft, and propeller-driven carrier aircraft carrying unguided bombs and rockets.[2] ASW technology in 1950 centered on large numbers of long-range patrol aircraft with centimetric radar (mostly based on Second World War–era bombers such as Lancasters and Liberators), primitive homing torpedoes such as Fido and Proctor, Hedgehog and Squid ASW projectiles, and depth charges, all using hull-mounted sensor systems for target acquisition. This level of technology had not closed the "Type XXI gap," so although many paths were being explored (these would bear fruit later in the decade) the difficulties in locating, tracking, and destroying the first true submarines had not been overcome.[3] The main threat to any NATO naval effort to maintain SLOCs would be presented by a mix of Soviet submarine types. The danger from surface forces or from the air was negligible; only if NATO chose to enter Soviet coastal areas would its ships be at risk from these elements.

By 1955 more U.S. and British war-built ships were placed in reserve. Great Britain upgraded its aircraft carriers, and the smaller NATO fleets were "beefed up" with improved or modified U.S. or British ships left over from the war. On the other side, the Soviets drastically increased the size of their submarine fleet and started to replace war-built frigates and destroyers with a larger number of more modern vessels.

While the shape of the world's fleets did not change dramatically between 1950 and 1955, a noticeable shift in technology did take place in almost every area, most significantly in naval aviation and submarine propulsion. U.S. jet aircraft such as F2H Banshee and F9F Panther fighters demonstrated their ability to operate for protracted periods from the decks of *Essex*-class carriers during the Korean War. Linked to the newly developed carrier-based Airborne Early Warning (AEW) aircraft, these advances gave the U.S. Navy the capability to intercept and destroy the new generation of Soviet long-range patrol aircraft. Later, early air-to-air missiles such as the Sidewinder were added to jet aircraft to increase their stand-off lethality against long-range Soviet aircraft, which could threaten convoys and warships alike. The Soviets started to produce four major maritime aircraft types based on bomber aircraft: the TU-4 Bull, the TU-16 Badger, the TU-20 Bear, and the IL-28 Beagle. The TU-16 and IL-28 were jet propelled. When added to the USSR's formidable submarine arsenal, this airpower gave the Soviet naval threat a new dimension.[4]

Nuclear propulsion was developed in the United States in the late 1940s at the instigation of Hyman G. Rickover. By 1955 the world's first SSN, the USS *Nautilus*, was launched, followed by the USS *Seawolf*. These vessels underwent rigorous tests over the next two years. Although their impact would not be felt until the 1960s, their development gave impetus to parallel Soviet developments in this field and triggered a revolution in naval technology that, according to Norman Friedman, was nearly on par with that of the 1860s.[5]

There were many other important technological changes between 1950 and 1955, particularly in the ASW field. The range of ship-mounted ASW weapons had doubled; sensor systems became faster and more sensitive. More important, the two were successfully linked in such systems as the American "Weapon Alfa" and the British "Limbo" ASW mortar. Weapon Alfa was connected to a QHB search sonar and a SQC fire control sonar, while the Limbo was linked to a Type 170 (a similar fire control device), thus cutting the reaction time between spotting a target and attacking it.[6] These weapons replaced the Hedgehog and Squid systems on a number of 1945-era ships. Improved radar was introduced into long-range patrol aircraft such as the P2V Neptune and the Avro Shackelton. Improved homing torpedoes such as the American Mark 37 were also available to NATO fleets. Finally, larger carrier-based ASW aircraft such as the British Gannet and the U.S. Tracker were coming into service, equipped with sonobuoys and a greater weapons load.[7]

The surface and antiaircraft realm in 1955 was still ruled by the "gunnery god." Radar-directed rapid-fire guns dramatically increased kill probabilities, but their range was not significantly greater than that of their World War II counterparts. Surface gunnery was kept alive in NATO fleets because of the large *Sverdlov*-class cruisers that the Soviets were building; in addition, the requirement for naval gunfire support still existed.

Antiship missiles (ASMs) first appeared in 1943 when a German Fritz-X was used to sink an Italian battleship. Two more versions followed, the HS-293 and HS-294; these were radio-controlled glide bombs released from an aircraft and guided terminally onto their targets. An early form of cruise missile appeared: Japan's manned Baka kamikaze aircraft, used against American ships at Okinawa. Thus, the British and the Americans both had some firsthand experience in countering ASMs, and there was little doubt that these weapons could be mass-produced by the Soviets and used in the event of a war with NATO. The first of these was the Komet or ASN-1, which could be launched from a ship or submarine. The cumulative effects of these advances were an increase in the stand-off capability of long-range patrol aircraft and the appearance of a new threat to convoy operations.[8]

The Fleets, 1950 and 1955

The U.S. Navy and the Royal Navy

	U.S. Navy, 1950		Royal Navy, 1950	
	active/reserve	total	active/reserve	total
BB	2/16	18	4/1	5
CV	7/18	25	5/5	10
CVL	3/6	9		
CVE	4/62	66		
CA	25/16	41	15/12	27
CL	44/40	84		
DD	142/199	341	33/65	98
DE/FF	65/179	244	25/129	154
SS	73/94	167	30/31	61
MCM	175/0	175	47/0	47

	U.S. Navy, 1955		Royal Navy, 1955	
	active/reserve	total	active/reserve	total
BB	0/18	18	1/4	5
CV	24/1	25	8/7	15
CVL/CVE	11/12	23		
CA	20/21	41	10/14	24
CL	3/32	35		
DD	245/132	368	32/58	80
DE/FF	127/72	197	30/137	164
SS	117/39	156	43/14	57
MCM	275/0	275	277/0	277

Other NATO Navies

France	1950	1955
BB	2	2
CVL/CVE	2	2
CA	4	4
DD	35	35
SS	12	17
MCM	0	118

Canada	1950	1955
CVL/CVE	1	1
CA	2	2
DD	11	11
DE	15	21
MCM	14	30

Netherlands	1950	1955
CVL/CVE	1	1
CA	0	2
DD	0	5
FF	6	16
SS	6	2
MCM	0	52

Norway	1950	1955
DD	8	9
FF	8	13
SS	5	8
MCM	2	17

Other NATO Navies

Denmark	1950	1955
DD	8	0
FF	13	13
SS	2	3
MCM	40	37

Portugal	1950	1955
DD	0	5
FF	0	8
SS	0	3
MCM	0	12

Italy	1950	1955
BB	4	2
CA	2	3
CL	0	2
DD	20	7
DE	21	38
MCM	16	64

Greece	1950	1955
CA	1	1
DD	10	3
DE	0	22
SS	6	4
MCM	24	14

Other NATO Navies

Turkey	1950	1955
CA	1	0
DD	10	9
SS	10	12
MCM	25	13

Belgium	1950	1955
FF	3	1
MCM	9	30

The Soviet Union

USSR	1950	1955
CA	16	12
DD	15	7
FF	0	18
SS	360	507

➢ Notes

CHAPTER 1 SECOND WORLD WAR COMMAND ORGANIZATION

1. British Combined Operations was similar to today's U.S. Special Operations Command. Essentially it was a collection of special warfare units including commandos, the Special Air Service, raiding parties, and their associated air and naval support. See Seymour, *British Special Forces*, chaps. 1 and 2; Ehrman, *Grand Strategy*, 5:15–16.
2. Ehrman, *Grand Strategy*, 5:16–18; John C. Ries, *Management of Defense*, 70–72; Krulak, *Organization for National Security*, 16–20.
3. Morison, *History of U.S. Naval Operations*, 1:45–48.
4. Ehrman, *Grand Strategy*, 5:19.
5. Pogue, *Supreme Command*, 37.
6. Ehrman, *Grand Strategy*, 5:19; Pogue, *Supreme Command*, 37–39; Matloff, *War Department*, 5–7.
7. Stacey, *Arms, Men, and Governments*, 161–63.
8. Ibid., 166.
9. Matloff and Snell, *War Department*, 165–66.
10. John Terraine, *The Right of the Line: The Royal Air Force in the European War, 1939–1945* (Toronto: Houghlin & Stewart, 1985), 542–45.
11. Pogue, *Supreme Command*, 43; Ehrman, *Grand Strategy*, 5:20.
12. Ibid.
13. Matloff and Snell, *War Department*, 168–69. See also Morton, *War in the Pacific*; Thomas B. Buell, *Master of Sea Power: A Biography of Fleet Admiral Ernest J. King* (Boston: Little, Brown, 1980), 194–95. Apparently, Admiral Halsey once stated that if he heard of any interservice bickering, he would replace all of his commanders' uniforms with coveralls and stamp "South Pacific Fighting Force" on their backsides. See Adm. Robert B. Carney, oral history transcript, Operational Archive, U.S. Naval Historical Center, Washington, D.C. (hereafter cited as USN Op A).

215

14. There was the short-lived ABDA Command (Australian, British, Dutch, and American) under General Wavell, which existed from 28 Dec. 1941 to 25 Feb. 1942. The Allies' first experiment with coalition command, ABDA reported to the CCS. However, due to the lack of resources in the face of the overwhelming Japanese threat, it was disbanded. See Matloff and Snell, *War Department*, 123–24; Marshall, *Encyclopedia of World War II*, 164; Pogue, *Supreme Command*, 41; Slim, *Defeat into Victory*, 168.
15. Molony et al., *Mediterranean and Middle East*, 5:859–60; Roskill, *War at Sea*, 2:312–13; Playfair et al., *Mediterranean and Middle East*, vol. 4.
16. Howe, *Mediterranean Theater of Operations*, 32–33; Roskill, *War at Sea*, 2:313–14, 322.
17. Morison, *History of U.S. Naval Operations*, 2:15–18, 37–41; Playfair et al., *Mediterranean and Middle East*, 4:113–14.
18. Howe, *Mediterranean Theater of Operations*, 354; Morison, *History of U.S. Naval Operations*, 2:254–55, 9:x. The Eighth Fleet was composed primarily of amphibious assault ships and specialized in the planning and execution of amphibious operations.
19. Roskill, *War at Sea*, 2:358–60.
20. Ibid.
21. Matloff, *War Department*, 60–62.
22. Molony et al., *Mediterranean and Middle East*, 5:859–64.
23. Ibid., 862–64.
24. Ibid., 6–8.
25. D'Este, *Bitter Victory*, 162–65, 583.
26. Matloff, *War Department*, 270–73.
27. Molony et al., *Mediterranean and Middle East*, app. 5.
28. See Roskill, *War at Sea*, vol. 3.
29. Pogue, *Supreme Command*, 46–47; Roskill, *War at Sea*, 3:13–17.
30. Roskill, *War at Sea*, 3:20–21. For example, mine countermeasures vessels were from home commands, while battleships came from the Home Fleet.
31. Roskill, *War at Sea*, 2:19, 35–37.
32. This was coordinated in the submarine tracking room at the Admiralty Operational Intelligence Centre; see Patrick Beesly, *Very Special Intelligence* (London: Sphere Books, 1977), chap. 2.
33. Roskill, *War at Sea*, 2:35–37.
34. Milner, *North Atlantic Run*, 12–24.
35. Douglas, *National Air Force*, 2:373–82.
36. See Stacey, *Arms, Men, and Governments*, 327–49; J. L. Granatstein and Norman Hillmer, *For Better or for Worse: Canada and the United States to the 1990s* (Toronto: Copp, Clark & Pittman, 1991); "A Brief History of the Canada–United States Permanent Joint Board on Defence, 1940–1960," 82/820, Directorate of History, Department of National Defence, Ottawa, Canada (hereafter cited as DHIST).
37. Douglas, *National Air Force*, 2:382–83.
38. Ibid., 383–84; Stacey, *Arms, Men, and Governments*, 349.
39. See W.G.D. Lund, "The Royal Canadian Navy's Quest for Autonomy in the North Atlantic," in Boutilier, ed., *RCN in Retrospect*, 141–42.

40. See Douglas, *National Air Force*, 384–87; Stacey, *Arms, Men, and Governments*, 349–51. At this point, the RCAF was divided into western and eastern regional commands. The dividing line was eastern Quebec, with a gap extending to eastern Alberta.
41. Stacey, *Arms, Men, and Governments*, 347–48; Morison, *History of U.S. Naval Operations*, 1:51.
42. Douglas, *National Air Force*, 388.
43. Morison, *History of U.S. Naval Operations*, 1:71; Stacey, *Arms, Men, and Governments*, 311.
44. Stacey, *Arms, Men, and Governments*, 312; Buell, *Master of Sea Power*, 136–41.
45. See Douglas, *National Air Force*, pt. 4.
46. Douglas, *National Air Force*, 380–88.
47. Ibid., 388–89, 485, 530.
48. Milner, *North Atlantic Run*, 187; Richards and Saunders, *Royal Air Force*, 2:100–116, esp. maps after 100, 112. This volume has an obvious bias toward strategic bombing and skirts the issue of aircraft allocation. See also Max Hastings, *Bomber Command* (Toronto: Touchstone, 1989), 179.
49. Buell, *Master of Sea Power*, 152–53, 526–27.
50. Morison, *History of U.S. Naval Operations*, 1:207–8.
51. Michael Gannon, *Operation Drumbeat* (New York: Harper & Row, 1990), chap. 6; Roskill, *War at Sea*, 2:93–99.
52. Morison, *History of U.S. Naval Operations*, 1:206–7.
53. Ibid.
54. Ibid., 237–40.
55. Ibid., 240–44.
56. Roskill, *War at Sea*, 2:108–11; message, 19 Sept. 1942, PRO, ADM 1/16 200; Browning, "Operations and Routing," 31–36.
57. Milner, *North Atlantic Run*, 125–27.
58. Lund, "Quest for Autonomy," 147–51; Milner, *North Atlantic Run*, 229–31; Gilbert Tucker, *The Naval Service of Canada* (Ottawa: King's Printer, 1952), vol. 2, chap. 14.
59. Milner, *North Atlantic Run*, 232–33; Roskill, *War at Sea*, 2:358.
60. Lund, "Quest for Autonomy," 152–53; Milner, *North Atlantic Run*, 233; Roskill, *War at Sea*, 2:358–59; Morison, *History of U.S. Naval Operations*, 9:18–20. Differences of opinion regarding the use of escort carriers in the Atlantic are discussed in Y'Blood, *Hunter-Killer*. The Americans wanted to hunt down wolfpacks with hunter-killer groups, while the British placed their CVEs close to convoys since that was where U-boats would attack.
61. Morison, *History of U.S. Naval Operations*, 10:20–22.
62. Ibid., 23–25.
63. Ibid., 26–29.
64. Richards and Saunders, *Royal Air Force*, 106–7.
65. Ibid., 107.
66. Roskill, *War at Sea*, 2:361.
67. Morison, *History of U.S. Naval Operations*, 10:16.
68. Roskill, *War at Sea*, 2:361–36.

69. Morison, *History of U.S. Naval Operations,* 10:16.
70. Ibid.

CHAPTER 2 AN ATTACK AGAINST ONE IS AN ATTACK AGAINST ALL

1. Some cursory analysis of Soviet intentions was started by the Americans and the British as early as 1944. However, it was not as fully developed as the Pincher series. See, for example, "Postwar Strategic Posture of the U.S. Armed Forces," Strategic Plans Division, box 197, file A-16-1(1), USN Op A; Ross, *American War Plans,* 4–5. U.S. planning for the postwar period was quite advanced in 1945. See Davis, *Postwar Defense Policy;* Sherry, *Preparing for the Next War.* Readers should be skeptical about Michio Kaku and Dan Axelrod, *To Win a Nuclear War* (Boston: South End Press, 1987), which contains many factual errors regarding U.S. postwar planning.
2. The Pincher series consisted of several separate yet related documents and can therefore be confusing. The initial concept of operations and estimate of the situation is entitled Pincher. The other documents provide general strategic guidance for operational planning in specific geographic areas. These were: Broadview, 24 Oct. 1946, defense of the continental United States; Griddle, 15 Aug. 1946, defense of Turkey; Cauldron, 2 Nov. 1946, defense of the Middle East; Cockspur, 20 Dec. 1946, defense of Italy; Drumbeat, 4 Aug. 1947, defense of the Iberian Peninsula; Moonrise, 29 Aug. 1947, defense of the Far East; and Deerland, 30 Sept. 1947, defense of the northeastern approaches to North America. For further details, see Clark and Wheeler, *British Origins of Nuclear Strategy,* 59–62; Geoffrey Till and Eric Grove, "Anglo-American Maritime Strategy, 1945–1960," in Hattendorf and Jordan, eds., *Maritime Strategy.* A unit called the "British Postwar Hostilities Planning Staff" recommended in November 1944 that a "Western European Security Group" be created. See Baylis, *British Defence Policy,* 19–20; Schnabel, *History of the Joint Chiefs,* 1:108–20. The Iran crisis almost led to war in northern Iran as the Soviets provided support to factions that were interested in the removal of British influence from the Persian Gulf region. Soviet armored forces had been deployed in northern Iran and had not been removed as of January 1945.
3. JCS, "Pincher: Concept of Operations," 2 Mar. 1946, p. 1, in U.S. Joint Chiefs of Staff, *Records of the Joint Chiefs of Staff, Part 2, 1946–1953: The United States and the Soviet Union* (Bethesda, Md.: University Publications of America, 1980, microfilm) (hereafter cited as *JCS 1946–53: U.S. and USSR*).
4. JWPC, "Pincher: Overall Strategic Concept and Estimate of Initial Operations," 27 Apr. 1946, p. 6, in *JCS 1946–53: U.S. and USSR.*
5. Ibid., 7.
6. Carroll, *Seventy Years,* 68–72. As late as 1989, Warsaw Pact units in East Germany were on fifteen-minute notice to move. For information on the Royal Navy reserve fleet, see Grove, *From Vanguard to Trident,* chap. 2.

7. Ross, *American War Plans*, 11; JWPC, "Pincher: Overall Strategic Concept," pp. 22–23, in *JCS 1946–53: U.S. and USSR*.
8. JCS, "Pincher: Concept of Operations," pp. 22–23, in *JCS 1946–53: U.S. and USSR*.
9. JWPC, "Pincher: Overall Strategic Concept," p. 24, and JCS, "Pincher: Concept of Operations," pp. 33–35, in *JCS 1946–53: U.S. and USSR*.
10. See, for example, V. I. Achkasov and N. B. Pavlovich, *Soviet Naval Operations in the Great Patriotic War, 1941–1945* (Annapolis, Md.: Naval Institute Press, 1981); JWPC, "Pincher: Overall Strategic Concept," p. 27, in *JCS 1946–53: U.S. and USSR*. The Soviets were still debating the nature of naval warfare within their strategic concepts. See Robert Herrick, *Soviet Naval Theory and Policy: Gorshkov's Inheritance* (Annapolis, Md.: Naval Institute Press, 1988).
11. JWPC, "Pincher: Overall Strategic Concept," pp. 27–29, in *JCS 1946–53: U.S. and USSR*.
12. The utility of seapower against the Soviet Union will be explored in chapter 3. In 1946–47 this was still under debate in both Britain and the United States.
13. Rosenberg, "U.S. Nuclear Stockpile," 26, 30; Hansen, *U.S. Nuclear Weapons*, 122–23; Christopher Andrew and Oleg Gordievsky, *KGB: The Inside Story* (London: Hodder & Stoughton, 1990), 310–14. The bombs in the U.S. arsenal were similar to the one dropped on Nagasaki in 1945.
14. Ross, *American War Plans*, 48.
15. Not to be confused with its British counterpart, the British Chiefs of Staff Committee Joint Planning Staff. Both organizations included members of all the services, and both were charged with creating strategic plans and keeping the U.S. JCS and the British CoS, respectively, apprised of the strategic situation. In 1946 the only formal contact between the two bodies was through the British Joint Staff Mission (Washington). The Canadian equivalent was the Canadian Joint Planning Staff.
16. JSPC, "Discussion Regarding Pincher," 18 July 1946, in *JCS 1946–53: U.S. and USSR*.
17. Dimbleby and Reynolds, *An Ocean Apart*, 176–82; Arnold, *Very Special Relationship*, 6–8. The McMahon Act prohibited the transfer of any atomic information to any foreign country. Ironically, McMahon admitted later that if he had known about the extent of Anglo-American cooperation, he would never have proposed the legislation. Essentially, the act forced Britain to spend scarce resources on a nuclear program. See also "The U.S.–UK–Canadian Collaboration in the Field of Atomic Energy, 1940–1957," PRO, DEFE 7/1517.
18. JSPC, "Discussion Regarding Pincher," in *JCS 1946–53: U.S. and USSR*.
19. Schnabel, *History of the Joint Chiefs*, 1:171–73.
20. Ibid., 184–85; George S. Eckhardt, *Vietnam Studies: Command and Control, 1950–1969* (Washington, D.C.: Department of the Army, 1972), 3–5; "Annual Report to the Chief of Naval Operations," 3 June 1947, Strategic Plans Division, USN Op A; "CNO's Annual Report to the Secretary of the Navy, 1948," USN Op A; Adm. Charles K. Duncan, letters to author, 17 Dec. 1990, 14 Aug. 1991.

21. Palmer, "U.S. Navy and the Mediterranean"; memo, Chief of Naval Operations to Deputy Chief of Naval Operations, "Geographic Responsibility between Operational Commands and Shore-based Commands," Strategic Plans Division, box 242, file A-3-1, USN Op A; "CNO's Annual Report to the Secretary of the Navy, 1948," USN Op A.
22. Royal Navy War Manual, 1947, pp. 20–21, DHIST; Adm. Charles K. Duncan, letter to author, 14 Aug. 1991.
23. Jockel, *No Boundaries Upstairs,* 11; Schnabel, *History of the Joint Chiefs,* 1:383–84.
24. Jockel, *No Boundaries Upstairs,* 15.
25. Schnabel, *History of the Joint Chiefs,* 1:384–86; Louis E. Grimshaw, "On Guard: A Perspective of the Roles and Functions of the Army in Canada" (master's thesis, Royal Military College of Canada, 1984), 218–20; "Defence Policy General Considerations: Joint Planning with the United States," 26 Nov. 1946, in Cabinet Defence Committee Papers, Dec. 1945–Mar. 1947, DHIST 112.3M2 (D125); Canadian Chiefs of Staff Committee, "Canada–U.S. Planning Committees," 13 July 1948, DHIST 112.3M2.009 (D182).
26. James Eayrs, *In Defence of Canada,* vol. 3, *Peacemaking and Deterrence* (Toronto: University of Toronto Press, 1972), 387; "Canada–U.S. Joint Defence," 9 July 1946, in Cabinet Defence Committee Papers, Dec. 1945–Mar. 1947, DHIST 112.3M2 (D125). Though not available to the author, a summary of the Basic Security Plan can be found in "Situation Report by Major General Mann on Canada–U.S. Basic Security Plan, Dec. 47–Dec. 49," DHIST 327.009 (D201); it is unclear how much access the Canadian side of the MCC had to Broadview or Deerland, however.
27. Document 2, Joint Canadian–U.S. Basic Security Plan 5, 5 June 1946, in Eayrs, *In Defence of Canada,* vol. 3.
28. Unpublished memoir, Brooke Claxton Papers, pp. 958–64, MG 32 B5, National Archives of Canada, Ottawa (hereafter cited as NAC); JLPG, "The Logistic Feasibility of ABC 101," 12 Nov. 1948, in *JCS 1946–53: U.S. and USSR.*
29. See Halle, *Cold War as History,* chap. 12; Krulak, *Organization for National Security,* chap. 3; *Command 6923: Central Organisation for Defence* (London: Her Majesty's Stationery Office, 1946).
30. JCS Staff Studies, "Problems Derived from the Concept of Operations from Pincher," 13 Apr. 1946, pp. 13–15, in *JCS 1946–53: U.S. and USSR.*
31. British Chiefs of Staff JPS, "Subjects for U.S.–UK Meetings," 6 Jan. 1948, PRO, DEFE 6/5.
32. Ibid.
33. Ross, *American War Plans,* chap. 3.
34. British Chiefs of Staff JPS, "U.S.–UK Discussions Regarding Joint Planning," 30 Mar. 1948, PRO, DEFE 6/5; memo, British Chiefs of Staff to JPS, 31 Mar. 1948, PRO, DEFE 6/5; British Chiefs of Staff JPS, "Long Term Combined Planning," 30 Apr. 1948, PRO, DEFE 6/5. Doublequick itself remains under security classification unlike its U.S. counterpart.
35. JSPC, "BROILER—Joint Outline War Plan for Fiscal Year 1949," 18 Dec. 1947, pp. 1–5, in *JCS 1946–53: U.S. and USSR.*

36. Ibid., 6.
37. Notably, Broiler considered the internal security problems of the West and anticipated that the Soviets would make all sorts of attempts to internally subvert and infiltrate Western society in order to disrupt economic and wartime production. Interestingly, the JSPC planners also noted that "the extent of Soviet espionage was clearly brought out in the Report of the Royal Canadian Commission Concerning Soviet Espionage Activities in Canada." See Broiler, pp. 22, 80–88.
38. Ibid., 22–23.
39. Ibid., 28–44.
40. It should be kept in mind that only six of the long-range Type IXc's were involved in the first wave of Operation Paukenschlag in 1942 and were able to wreak havoc on unprotected shipping on the East Coast. The Type XXI was considered unstoppable from the close of the Second World War until ASW technology caught up in the 1950s. See Milner, "Dawn of Modern Antisubmarine Warfare," 61–68.
41. Broiler, 6–7.
42. Ibid., 8.
43. Knaack, *Encyclopedia of USAF Aircraft*, 2:494; *Avro Aircraft since 1918* (London: Putnam Books, 1974).
44. Adm. J. T. Hayward, letter to author, 7 Aug. 1991. The capability to do this did not yet exist, however; see Broiler, 67–68.
45. Broiler, 68–69.
46. Ibid., 69; Rosenberg, "U.S. Nuclear Stockpile," 26. As of 30 June 1948 only fifty atomic bombs were in the U.S. stockpile, and only thirty-five B-29s capable of carrying such weapons were available.
47. Memo, JSPC to SecDef, "Emergency Plans," 9 Mar. 1949, in *JCS 1946–53: U.S. and USSR*.
48. Memo, CNO to JCS, "Planning Guidance for Medium Range Emergency Plan," 6 Apr. 1948, in *JCS 1946–53: U.S. and USSR*.
49. Ibid.
50. Ibid.
51. See Schratz, "Admirals' Revolt." This particularly vicious interservice battle would culminate by pitting the B-36 long-range bomber against a planned nuclear-capable supercarrier in a budgetary fight. It was as much a clash of strategic concepts as a contest for dollars. See Adm. J. T. Hayward, letters to author, 13 Nov. 1990, 29 June 1991.
52. See Palmer, *Origins of the Maritime Strategy*.
53. Broiler, 66.
54. "Joint Planning Staff Report on Command Organization," 15 Apr. 1948, PRO, DEFE, 6/6.
55. Ibid.
56. Ibid.
57. Ibid.
58. "Meeting of U.S. and British Planners, October 1948," 4 Nov. 1948, PRO, DEFE 6/7; Condit, *History of the Joint Chiefs*, 2:288–89.

59. Hamilton, *Monty*, 3:699–701; Cook, *Forging the Alliance*, chaps. 5 and 6; British Chiefs of Staff JPS, "CIGS Proposal for WUDO," 9 June 1948, PRO, DEFE 6/6; JPS, "WUDO," 22 June 1948, PRO, DEFE 6/6.
60. See Fursdon, *European Defense Community*, chap. 2; Beufre, *NATO and Europe*; Ismay, *NATO: The First Five Years*, 78. The WUDO estimate of the international situation was similar to that of Broiler/Doublequick; see JPS, "WU Defence Policy: International Relations," 26 June 1948, PRO, DEFE 6/6.
61. Cook, *Forging the Alliance*, 113, 115, 127–31. Interestingly, after the talks were completed, the Berlin crisis of 1948 commenced. Cook also notes that the infamous Donald Maclean was a British participant at the secret talks in Washington.
62. JCS, "Brief of Short Range Emergency Plan DOUBLESTAR," 6 May 1948, p. 33, in *JCS 1946–53: U.S. and USSR*.
63. JCS, "Brief of Short Range Emergency Plan DOUBLESTAR," 6 May 1948, in *JCS 1946–53: U.S. and USSR*.
64. The added emphasis on the use of nuclear weapons in Doublestar reflected the enhanced ability of the U.S. Air Force to deliver its growing stockpile, estimated to be approximately 240 Mk III bombs, using thirty-eight B-29s, eighteen longer-range B-50s, and four B-36s. See Rosenberg, "U.S. Nuclear Stockpile," 26–30; JCS, "Brief of Short Range Emergency Plan DOUBLESTAR," 6 May 1948, pp. 32–33, in *JCS 1946–53: U.S. and USSR*.
65. JCS, "Brief of Short Range Emergency Plan DOUBLESTAR," 6 May 1948, pp. 34, 37, in *JCS 1946–53: U.S. and USSR*. In fact, Doublestar emphasized the use of air-portable Canadian and U.S. forces in the defense of vital areas and nuclear installations.
66. Ibid.
67. Ibid.
68. "Washington Exploratory Conferences on Security," 9 Sept. 1948, PRO, DEFE 11/19. See also Cook, *Forging the Alliance*, 179.
69. Memo, Chief of Staff, USAF to JCS, 30 July 1948, in U.S. Joint Chiefs of Staff, *Records of the Joint Chiefs of Staff, Part 2, 1946–1953: Europe and NATO* (Bethesda, Md.: University Publications of America, 1980, microfilm) (hereafter cited as *JCS 1946–53: Europe and NATO*).
70. JPS, "Western Union Defence Organization," 22 June 1948, PRO, DEFE 6/6.
71. JSPG to JCS, "Command Relationships," 14 July 1948, in *JCS 1946–53: Europe and NATO*.
72. Ibid.; JPS, "WUDO System of Command: Peacetime Organization of Flag Officer Western Europe," 14 Sept. 1948, PRO, DEFE 6/6; JPS, "WUDO Withdrawal Organization," 30 July 1948, PRO, DEFE 6/6.
73. Memo, Chief of Staff, USAF to JCS, "Command Plan for Western Europe, Mediterranean and the Middle East," 4 Sept. 1948, in *JCS 1946–53: Europe and NATO*.
74. "Agreed Final Version of Minutes of Newport Meetings, 20–22 Aug. 1948," p. 9, Double-zero file (1948), USN Op A.
75. "Meeting of U.S. and British Planners, October 1948," 4 Nov. 1948, PRO, DEFE 6/7; nuclear-armed, carrier-based bombers were still under develop-

ment at this time but were factored in for planning purposes. For a discussion of the early efforts of the U.S. Navy, see Hansen, "Nuclear Neptunes."
76. "Meeting of U.S. and British Planners, October 1948," 4 Nov. 1948, PRO, DEFE 6/7; memo, CNO to JCS, "Establishment of the Northeast Command," 30 Nov. 1948, Strategic Plans Division, box 243, file A-16-3(1), USN Op A.
77. "Command Organization for DOUBLEQUICK," 8 Nov. 1948, PRO, DEFE 6/7. At this point, British names had not changed from Doublequick to Speedway in the same way that Doublestar succeeded Broiler.
78. Ibid.; see also Browning, "Operations and Routing," 31–36.
79. "Command Organization for DOUBLEQUICK," 8 Nov. 1948, PRO, DEFE 6/7, esp. app. 2, "Atlantic Command."
80. Ibid.
81. Ismay, *NATO: The First Five Years*, 9.
82. Cook, *Forging the Alliance*, 222.
83. British Chiefs of Staff Committee, "North Atlantic Pact Military Organization," 24 Feb. 1949, PRO, DEFE 11/19; JPS, "Atlantic Pact Military Organization," 19 Feb. 1949, PRO, DEFE 11/19; "British View on North Atlantic Pact Organization," 19 Feb. 1949, PRO, DEFE 11/20.
84. "British View on North Atlantic Pact Organization," 19 Feb. 1949, PRO, DEFE 11/20.
85. Eayrs, *In Defence of Canada*, vol. 4, *Growing Up Allied* (Toronto: University of Toronto Press, 1980).
86. Ibid., 136.
87. Ibid., 136–37.
88. "Atlantic Pact Military Organization," 18 Mar. 1949, PRO, DEFE 11/20; "Problems in Integrating Command Organizations," 5 Mar. 1949, PRO, DEFE 11/20.
89. JSPC to JCS, "Command Arrangements," 6 Apr. 1949, in *JCS 1946–53: Europe and NATO*.
90. JSPC, "Atlantic Pact Military Organization," 11 Apr. 1949, in *JCS 1946–53: Europe and NATO*.
91. Memo, Chief of Staff, USAF to JCS, "Atlantic Treaty Organization," 14 May 1949, in *JCS 1946–53: Europe and NATO;* British Chiefs of Staff Committee, "Atlantic Pact Military Machinery," 20 Apr. 1949, PRO, DEFE 11/21.
92. Ibid.
93. Memo, Chief of Staff, USAF to JCS, "Atlantic Treaty Organization," 14 May 1949, in *JCS 1946–53: Europe and NATO;* JSPC, "Proposed Military Organization under the North Atlantic Treaty," 23 July 1949, in *JCS 1946–53: Europe and NATO;* British Chiefs of Staff Committee, "Views of the Canadian Government on Atlantic Pact Military Machinery," 29 July 1949, PRO, DEFE 11/21; JPS, "British Chiefs of Staff View on North Atlantic Treaty Military Organization," 6 July 1949, PRO, DEFE 11/21.
94. Memo, Chief of Staff, U.S. Army to JCS, "Command Arrangements," 2 Aug. 1949, in *JCS 1946–53: Europe and NATO*.

95. Ismay, *NATO: The First Five Years*, 24–26; "Discussions between VCNS, VCIGS, and VCAS on Command Arrangements," 18 Aug. 1949, PRO, DEFE 11/22; memo, CNO to JPS, "Proposed Military Organization under the North Atlantic Treaty," 2 Aug. 1949, in *JCS 1946–53: Europe and NATO*.
96. JSPC, "U.S. Position on British–U.S. Cooperation for Planning Within the North Atlantic Treaty," 7 Sept. 1949, in *JCS 1946–53: Europe and NATO*; memo, CNO to JCS, 14 Sept. 1949, in *JCS 1946–53: Europe and NATO*.
97. JPS, "British Views on Military Organization," 12 Sept. 1949, PRO, DEFE 11/22.
98. "North Atlantic Council (First Session): Report of the Working Group on Organization as Adopted by the Council on September 17, 1949," PRO, DEFE 7/743.
99. Ibid.
100. Ziegler, "Waiting for JOE-1," 197–229; Holloway, "Entering the Nuclear Arms Race," 159–97.

Chapter 3 Crusade in Europe Revisited and the Third Battle of the Atlantic

1. JPS, "Examination of the U.S. Strategic Concept for War in 1951," 5 Sept. 1949, PRO, DEFE 6/9; JPS, "Emergency Plans," 3 Nov. 1949, PRO, DEFE 6/10.
2. JPS, "Emergency Plans," 3 Nov. 1949, PRO, DEFE 6/10.
3. Trojan was essentially Doublestar with an extensively modified strategic bombing schedule. See Ross, *American War Plans*, chap. 4; Condit, *History of the Joint Chiefs*, vol. 2, chap. 9; JPS, "Status of Emergency Plans," 13 Jan. 1950, PRO, DEFE 6/12; JPS, "Examination of the U.S. Strategic Concept for War in 1951," 5 Sept. 1949, PRO, DEFE 6/9; "Plan GALLOPER," 1 Mar. 1950, PRO, DEFE 6/11; JCS JSPC, "Joint Outline Emergency War Plan CROSSPIECE," 8 Nov. 1949, in *JCS 1946–53: U.S. and USSR*. Galloper is virtually identical to Crosspiece but is less verbose and more logically ordered. Both versions will be used here.
4. JCS JSPC, "Joint Outline Emergency War Plan CROSSPIECE," 8 Nov. 1949, in *JCS 1946–53: U.S. and USSR*.
5. Ibid.
6. Prados, *Soviet Estimate*, 38–40; Murphy, ed., *Soviet Air Forces*, 179; "An Appreciation of the Employment of the Mobile Striking Force in the Defence of Canada," 29 Nov. 1949, DHIST 112.3M2 (D400); "Plan GALLOPER," 1 Mar. 1950, PRO, DEFE 6/11; JCS JSPC, "Joint Outline Emergency War Plan CROSSPIECE," 8 Nov. 1949, in *JCS 1946–53: U.S. and USSR*; JPC to Canadian Chiefs of Staff, "Military Cooperation Committee Planning," 12 Sept. 1950, DHIST 82/196, vol. 8. Canadian planners believed that the Soviet Union had between twenty-five and forty-five bombs that, based on the detected JOE-1 shot, were thought to be almost identical to the U.S. Mark III; see Ziegler, "Waiting for JOE-1";

Ranelagh, *The Agency*, 172–73; Murphy, ed., *Soviet Air Forces*, 166–80. According to Cochran et al., *Soviet Nuclear Weapons*, 228–29, the Tu-4 was not equipped with atomic weapons until 1953. However, Western planners focused on the ability of the delivery system to reach its target, because information on the Soviet stockpile was lacking.

7. "Anti-Submarine Warfare, Canada, Britain and the U.S., 1945–1960," June 1950, and "Estimate of Soviet Submarine Potential," NAC, RG 24 83.84/167, vol. 3734, file 8100.5.
8. Ibid.
9. See Air Vice Marshal S.W.B. Menaul, "The Soviet Air Forces," in *The Soviet War Machine* (New York: Chartwell, 1977), 71–72, 89, 94–95. For a look at how Soviet and Western aircraft performed in Korea, see Hallion, *Naval Air War in Korea*.
10. That is, protect the Western hemisphere and main support areas, secure bases and LOCs, mount a strategic air offensive, stabilize the Soviet offensive, mobilize, provide aid to allies, and wage psychological and unconventional warfare. See JCS JSPC, "Joint Outline Emergency War Plan CROSSPIECE," 8 Nov. 1949, in *JCS 1946–53: U.S. and USSR;* "Plan GALLOPER," 1 Mar. 1950, PRO, DEFE 6/11.
11. "Plan GALLOPER," 1 Mar. 1950, PRO, DEFE 6/11; Knaack, *Encyclopedia of USAF Aircraft*, 2:490–92. The first U.S. Air Force aerial refueling unit, the 97th Air Refuel Squadron, received 116 KB-29 tanker aircraft between September 1950 and December 1951, with deliveries of the larger KC-97 commencing in July 1951; RAF Bomber Command's Lincolns had a range of only 3,750 miles without aerial refueling and required forward basing. See *Avro Aircraft since 1918;* Jackson, *Canberra: The Operational Record*, 9.
12. JCS JSPC, "Joint Outline Emergency War Plan CROSSPIECE," 8 Nov. 1949, in *JCS 1946–53: U.S. and USSR*.
13. Ibid.
14. Ibid.
15. Unlike its predecessor, the P2V3C Neptune, the AJ-1 Savage was recoverable by aircraft carriers. The first Savage-equipped U.S. Navy squadron was VC-5. See Adm. J. T. Hayward, letter to author, 7 Aug. 1991; Scarborough, "Establishing the Heavy Attack Mission," 28–43, and "Launching the Heavy Attack Mission," 16–37.
16. JCS JSPC, "Joint Outline Emergency War Plan CROSSPIECE," 8 Nov. 1949, in *JCS 1946–53: U.S. and USSR;* "Plan GALLOPER," 1 Mar. 1950, PRO, DEFE 6/11. Substantial numbers of U.S. carriers were allocated to Europe and the Mediterranean areas in Crosspiece—seven by D+3 months. See also Till and Grove, "Anglo-American Maritime Strategy," in Hattendorf and Jordan, eds., *Maritime Strategy*.
17. JCS JSPC, "Joint Outline Emergency War Plan CROSSPIECE," 8 Nov. 1949, in *JCS 1946–53: U.S. and USSR;* "Plan GALLOPER," 1 Mar. 1950, PRO, DEFE 6/11.
18. "Plan GALLOPER," 1 Mar. 1950, PRO, DEFE 6/11.
19. JPS, "Command Organization for War in 1951," 5 Sept. 1949, PRO, DEFE 6/10.

20. Memo, CinCLANT to CNO, "Organization of Command in the Atlantic Ocean," 5 Sept. 1949, Strategic Plans Division, box 248, file A-3, USN Op A.
21. Memo, CinCLANT to CNO, "Organization of Command in the Atlantic Ocean," 5 Sept. 1949, in *JCS 1946–53: Europe and NATO*.
22. JPS, "Command Arrangements in War," 15 Oct. 1949, PRO, DEFE 6/11.
23. Ibid.
24. Ibid.
25. Memo, CinCLANT to CNO, "Organization of Command in the Atlantic Ocean," 5 Sept. 1949, in *JCS 1946–53: Europe and NATO*.
26. JPS, "Allied Naval Command Organization (British View)," 18 Nov. 1949, PRO, DEFE 6/11.
27. Extract from minutes of 28th meeting of the Cabinet Defence Committee, 11 Feb. 1947, in Cabinet Defence Committee Papers, Dec. 1945–Mar. 1947, DHIST 112.3M2 (D125); Reardon, *History of the OSD*, 1:481–83.
28. CNO to JCS, "Relationship between North Atlantic Treaty and Global Planning," 23 May 1950, in *JCS 1946–53: Europe and NATO*.
29. Hugh Faringdon, *Strategic Geography: NATO, the Warsaw Pact, and the Superpowers*, 2d ed. (London: Routledge, 1989), 180–81. Certain areas such as the west coast of North America had special defense arrangements. Naturally, the issue of colonies and former colonies caused some problems. It was determined that the defense of such territories lay outside the purview of NATO unless they were within NATO's geographic area.
30. There is little documentation on the regional planning groups. Hamilton, *Monty*, vol. 3, mentions that the WUDO continued work on its assigned task prior to the Korean War. There is not much information on the Western Mediterranean/Southern Europe RPG beyond mention of French and Italian boundary disputes. Apparently, naval planning in the Mediterranean was the bailiwick of U.S. and British planners and was kept separate from WM/SERPG planning. See Wright, "The North Atlantic Treaty Organization."
31. Memo, U.S. section, CUSRPG to JCS, "Organization for CUSRPG Planning," 22 Nov. 1949, in *JCS 1946–53: Europe and NATO*; Canadian Chiefs of Staff Committee minutes, meeting 455, 11 Jan. 1950, DHIST; "MCC Planning," 12 Sept. 1950, DHIST 82/196, vol. 8. It appears that the Americans believed they could control their weaker partner better without outside interference from Britain, which was excluded from such an arrangement.
32. Memo, U.S. section, CUSRPG to JCS, "Organization for CUSRPG Planning," 22 Nov. 1949, in *JCS 1946–53: Europe and NATO*.
33. The Canada–U.S. Basic Security Plan is not yet available in its entirety. For a summary of major points, see "Situation Report by Major General Mann on Canada–U.S. Basic Security Plan, 11 Dec. 1947," DHIST 327.009 (D201).
34. Jockel, *No Boundaries Upstairs*, 97, 112–13; "Canadian and U.S. Communications and Related Boards Concerned with Defence and Related Questions," 8 Feb. 1963, Raymont Papers, file 886, DHIST.
35. Memo, Chief of Staff, U.S. Army to JCS, "Establishment of a Military Requirement for the Defense of Canada–U.S. Area," 5 Jan. 1950, in *JCS 1946–53: Europe and NATO*; Canadian Chiefs of Staff Committee minutes, special meeting, 19 Mar. 1952, DHIST.

36. "Invitation of Action to Convene the Canada–U.S. and North Atlantic Ocean Regional Planning Groups," 20 Oct. 1949, in *JCS 1946–53: Europe and NATO;* memo, CNO to JCS, "NAORPG," 1 Nov. 1949, in *JCS 1946–53: Europe and NATO.*
37. "Tabling of Forces for North Atlantic Treaty Planning Purposes," 31 Jan. 1950, Strategic Plans Division, box 256, file A-16-3(5), USN Op A; JIC, "Intelligence Guidance to North Atlantic Regional Planning," 28 Dec. 1949, in *JCS 1946–53: Europe and NATO;* JCS, "Revised Strategic Concept for the Defense of the North Atlantic Area," 28 Dec. 1949, in *JCS 1946–53: Europe and NATO.*
38. JSPC, "Protection of Shipping Outside the North Atlantic Ocean Region Area," 21 Feb. 1950, in *JCS 1946–53: Europe and NATO;* JPS, "NAORPG Defence Plan," 8 Feb. 1950, PRO, DEFE 6/12.
39. Canadian Chiefs of Staff Committee minutes, special meeting, 16 Dec. 1949, DHIST; JSPC, "NATO MTDP, 1 July 1954," 21 Mar. 1950, in *JCS 1946–53: Europe and NATO.*
40. *JCS 1946–53: Europe and NATO,* 7 Apr. 1959; minutes of meeting, First Sea Lord and CNO, 24 Mar. 1950, PRO, ADM 205, file 74; "Command Problems and NAORPG," 2 May 1950, Strategic Plans Division, box 254, file A-1, USN Op A.
41. "Command Problems and NAORPG," 2 May 1950, Strategic Plans Division, box 254, file A-1, USN Op A.
42. Ibid.
43. JPS, "Allied Organization for Command," 3 May 1950, PRO, DEFE 6/12.
44. "Command Organization in the North Atlantic Region," Strategic Plans Division, box 254, file A-3, USN Op A; for the October proposal, see figs. 3 and 4.
45. Reardon, *History of the OSD,* vol. 1, chap. 16; Stanley R. Sloan, *NATO's Future: Toward a New Transatlantic Bargain* (Washington, D.C.: National Defense University Press, 1985), 9–11.
46. British Chiefs of Staff Committee minutes, meeting 139, 30 Aug. 1950, PRO, DEFE 4/35.
47. JPS, "Allied Organization for Command in a World War," 25 July 1950, PRO, DEFE 6/12.
48. JCS, "British Request for Agreed U.S.–UK Concept of Global Strategy," 18 Sept. 1950, in *JCS 1946–53: Europe and NATO.* The product of these discussions would eventually be U.S. Plan Reaper (later Groundwork and Headstone). The code name of the British counterpart is difficult to determine; the best candidate appears to be Plan Fairfax. See Clark and Wheeler, *British Origins of Nuclear Strategy.*
49. JSPC, "Reorganization of the Structure of NATO and Related Organizations," 12 Oct. 1950, in *JCS 1946–53: Europe and NATO.*
50. JSPC, "Command Structure for Europe," 13 Oct. 1950, in *JCS 1946–53: Europe and NATO;* "Interim Command Arrangements," 16 Oct. 1950, PRO, DEFE 7/743.
51. JPS, "Allied Organization for Command in a World War," 25 July 1950, PRO, DEFE 6/12.

52. Ibid.
53. Ibid.
54. Ibid.; JPS, "Final Version of European Command," 25 Aug. 1950, PRO, DEFE 6/12; British Chiefs of Staff Committee minutes, meeting 132, "Allied Organization in War," 18 Aug. 1950, PRO, DEFE 4/35.
55. Ismay, *NATO: The First Five Years*, 32.
56. Ibid., 35.
57. North Atlantic Military Council to North Atlantic Defense Council, "The Creation of an Integrated European Defense Force, the Establishment of a Supreme Headquarters in Europe, and the Reorganization of the NATO Military Structure," 12 Dec. 1950, in U.S. Department of State, *Foreign Relations of the United States, 1950* (Washington, D.C.: U.S. Government Printing Office, 1977), 3:548–64 (hereafter cited as *FRUS 1950*).
58. Ibid.
59. Ibid.
60. JSPC, "Command Structure for Europe," 5 Oct. 1950, in *JCS 1946–53: Europe and NATO*.
61. Jordan, ed., *Generals in International Politics*, chap 1; British Chiefs of Staff Committee minutes, 12 Jan. 1951, PRO, DEFE 11/25.
62. British Chiefs of Staff Committee, "Problems with the Establishment of Supreme Headquarters, Allied Powers, Europe," 12 Aug. 1951, PRO, DEFE 11/25.
63. Memo, MOD to BJSM, "Talks with Eisenhower Regarding Command Organization," 16 Jan. 1951, PRO, DEFE 11/25; memo, MOD to BJSM, "U.S. Proposed SHAPE Organization," 9 Feb. 1951, PRO, DEFE 11/25; memo from office of Dean Acheson, in *FRUS 1950*, 3:609-10.
64. Memo, MOD to BJSM, "Note on European Command Organization for SHAPE," 10 Feb. 1951, PRO, DEFE 11/25.
65. British Chiefs of Staff Committee, "SHAPE and Naval Commands Eastern Atlantic, Mediterranean and Channel/Southern North Sea," 12 Jan. 1951, PRO, DEFE 11/25.
66. Memo, SACEUR to British MOD, 22 Mar. 1951, PRO, DEFE 7/949.
67. Message, Sherman to Carney, 16 Mar. 1951, CinCSOUTH file 7, USN Op A; Carney, oral history transcript, p. 595, USN Op A; file message, Sherman to Carney, 16 Dec. 1950.
68. See Thursfield, ed., *Brassey's Annual, 1952*, 95–100. In a discussion with Dean Acheson on 15 December 1950, Acheson's secretary noted: "General Eisenhower was very unhappy at what he assumed was an effort on the part of the British and our Navy to remove the Mediterranean forces and the Southern North Sea forces from the command of the supreme commander" (*FRUS 1950*, 3:578).
69. The RNRF, for example, possessed one base ship, six LCTs, six motor launches, and sixteen cutters. See "Rhine Flotilla Strength," 14 June 1950, PRO, DEFE 11/91; "Defence of the Rivers Rhine and Ijessel," 3 June 1952, PRO, DEFE 11/91; Establishment of the Royal Navy Rhine Flotilla," 2 Apr. 1949, PRO, DEFE 11/91; PRO DEFE 11/91 (2 Apr 53) "Royal Navy Requirements for the Rhine and Elbe River Squadrons," 2 Apr. 1953, PRO,

DEFE 11/91. The Special Boat Service flotilla had twelve LCAs and four cutters and consisted of 14 officers and 146 others. See "Addition of Royal Marine Commando Troops for Rhine Squadron," 13 June 1951, PRO, DEFE 11/91. The riverine forces exercised together frequently—during Operation Universe in 1953, for example.

70. JPS, "Command in the Atlantic Ocean," 27 July 1950, PRO, DEFE 6/13.
71. Ibid.
72. JSPC, "NAORPG STDP," 8 Aug. 1950, in *JCS 1946–53: Europe and NATO*.
73. Ibid.
74. JPS, "Organization of Command in the Atlantic Ocean," 12 Aug. 1950, PRO, DEFE 6/12. This was quickly becoming less of a factor. The range of post–World War II maritime patrol aircraft ranges was almost transoceanic; heavier ASW aircraft with greater endurance and load characteristics operated from aircraft carriers.

    1940s:
    B-24 Liberator (Canada/UK/U.S.)   2,800
    PB4Y2 Privateer (U.S.)   2,850
    Lancaster (Canada/France/UK)   2,350
    TBF/TBM Avenger (Canada/France/UK/U.S.)   1,250 (carrier based)

    1950s:
    P2V Neptune (Canada/U.S.)   4,000
    Shackleton (UK)   3,500
    S2F Tracker (Canada/U.S.)   841 (carrier based)
    Gannet (UK)   662 (carrier based)

    1960s:
    Argus (Canada)   +6,000
    P3 Orion (U.S.)   4,800

    Sources: Williams, *Royal Navy Aircraft since 1945*; Sullivan, *P2V Neptune in Action* and *S2F Tracker in Action*; Mackay, *Lancaster in Action*; Scrivner, *TBM/TBF Avenger in Action*; Angelucci and Matricardi, *World War II Airplanes*, vol. 1; Milberry, *Sixty Years*.

75. JPS, "Organization of Command in the Atlantic Ocean," 12 Aug. 1950, PRO, DEFE 6/12.
76. Ibid.
77. In 1950–51 Spain was not a NATO member and had a bilateral relationship with the United States. Under Crosspiece, the United States intended to use Spain as a base and bring troop convoys there to support SACEUR. See Veremis and Valinakis, *U.S. Bases in the Mediterranean*, 43–74; JPS, "Command in the Atlantic Ocean: African Atlantic," 7 Sept. 1950, PRO, DEFE 6/14.
78. JPS, "Command in the Atlantic Ocean: African Atlantic," 7 Sept. 1950, PRO, DEFE 6/14.
79. British Chiefs of Staff Committee minutes, meeting 150, "Command in the

Atlantic Ocean: African Atlantic," 15 Sept. 1950, PRO, DEFE 4/35; "Command in the Atlantic Ocean: African Atlantic," 7 Sept. 1950, PRO, DEFE 6/14.
80. British Chiefs of Staff Committee minutes, meeting 147, "UK Command in the Caribbean," 11 Sept. 1950, PRO, DEFE 4/35.
81. Douglas-Pennent, BJSM (Navy Staff), letter to Sherman, 13 Oct. 1950, Strategic Plans Division, box 251, file EF-13, USN Op A.
82. JSPC, "U.S.–UK Command Arrangements," 29 Jan. 1951, in *JCS 1946–53: Europe and NATO;* "Outline History of the Atlantic Command Idea," 1 Nov. 1951, PRO, DEFE 6/19.
83. Memo, CNO to JCS, "Designation of SACLANT," 30 Nov. 1950, Strategic Plans Division, box 254, file A-3, USN Op A.
84. Memo, CNO to JCS, "Designation of a Prospective Supreme Allied Commander, Atlantic," 1 Dec. 1950, in *JCS 1946–53: Europe and NATO.*
85. Memo, CNO to JCS, "Designation of SACLANT," 30 Nov. 1950, Strategic Plans Division, box 254, file A-3, USN Op A; memo, Chief of Staff, U.S. Army to JCS, "Appointment of the Supreme Allied Commander, Atlantic and Definition of His Missions and Responsibilities." 28 Dec. 1950, in *JCS 1946–53: Europe and NATO.*
86. JCS, "Appointment of the SAC Atlantic: Definitions of His Missions and Responsibilities," 15 Jan. 1951, in *JCS 1946–53: Europe and NATO.*
87. Ibid.
88. Ibid.
89. British Chiefs of Staff Committee minutes, 9 Feb. 1951, PRO, DEFE 4/40.
90. Memo, MOD to BJSM, "Directive for the Supreme Allied Commander, Atlantic," 19 Feb. 1951, PRO, DEFE 6/16.
91. "Terms of Reference for the Supreme Allied Commander Atlantic," 27 Feb. 1951, PRO, DEFE 6/16.
92. Ibid.
93. Gilbert, *Never Despair,* 593.
94. Intelligence Summary, 2 Mar. 1951, Strategic Plans Division, box 261, file A-3, USN Op A; Eisenhower, letter to William Averell Harriman, 2 Mar. 1951, in Louis Galambos et al., *The Papers of Dwight David Eisenhower,* vols. 12 & 13, *NATO and the Campaign of 1952* (Baltimore: Johns Hopkins University Press, 1989), 12:88–90 (hereafter cited as *Eisenhower Papers*).
95. Ibid.
96. Poole, *History of the Joint Chiefs,* 4:231–32; diary entry, 2 Mar. 1951, *Eisenhower Papers,* 12:83–85; Walter Poole, "Organizing NATO's Naval Commands: Anglo-American Rivalry, 1951–1952" (unpublished paper).
97. Carney, letter to Eisenhower, 8 Mar. 1951, in *JCS 1946–53: Europe and NATO.*
98. Letter to George C. Marshall, 12 Mar. 1951, *Eisenhower Papers,* 12:117–23.
99. Poole, *History of the Joint Chiefs,* 4:232–33.
100. JPS, "The Reasons for the Appointment of a Supreme Allied Commander, Atlantic," 3 Mar. 1951, PRO, DEFE 6/16.
101. Ibid.

102. "Notes for Answering Possible Questions from the Media," March 1951, PRO, DEFE 13/3.
103. Record of an informal meeting between the British Chiefs of Staff and Admiral Sherman at 20 Grosvenor Square, 5 Mar. 1951, PRO, DEFE 7/749.
104. Ibid. Strangely, it appears that Sherman was not aware of a U.S. attempt to place IBERLANT headquarters at Gibraltar. The British categorically denied the use of Gibraltar's facilities for IBERLANT unless it was led by a British officer. The British evidently saw this as an attempt to absorb Gibraltar and IBERLANT into a U.S. naval command in the Mediterranean or WESTLANT; see JPS, "Headquarters for IBERLANT," 2 Feb. 1951, PRO, DEFE 6/5.
105. See Allan Bullock, *Ernest Bevin*, vol. 3, *Foreign Secretary, 1945–1951* (London: Heinemann, 1983), chap. 22. Morrison succeeded the redoubtable Bevin in February 1951 and had yet to be brought up to speed.
106. British Chiefs of Staff Committee minutes, meeting 43, "Supreme Allied Commander Atlantic," 7 Mar. 1951, PRO, DEFE 4/40.
107. Ibid.
108. Memo, BJSM to MOD, "Terms of Reference for SACLANT," 26 Mar. 1951, PRO, DEFE 7/949.
109. British Chiefs of Staff Committee, "SACLANT and IBERLANT," 30 Mar. 1951, PRO, DEFE 4/41; Grove, *From Vanguard to Trident*, 104–5.
110. The political and bureaucratic delays can probably be attributed to NATO's need to deal with the German rearmament issue and the European Defense Community; see Fursdon, *European Defense Community*.
111. Memo, DPlans to First Sea Lord, "Atlantic Commands, CinC Plymouth," 4 Apr. 1951, PRO, ADM 205/76.
112. Ibid.
113. Memo, DPlans to First Sea Lord, "Relationship between CinCNORTH, CinCEASTLANT and Admiral, Rosyth," 11 Apr. 1951, PRO, ADM 205/76.
114. Ibid.
115. While there is no clear-cut proof, it appears that Fraser was subjected to some pressure by Churchill for this reconsideration; see Sea Lords and CinCs meeting, "Atlantic Command Situation," 12 Apr. 1951, PRO, ADM 205/76.
116. "Supplementary Study on the 15 January 1951 Review of the Current World Situation and the Ability of the Forces Being Maintained to Meet U.S. Commitments," 13 Apr. 1951, in *FRUS 1950*, vol. 1.
117. Adm. William M. Fechteler, oral history transcript, p. 59, USN Op A.
118. Gilbert, *Never Despair*, 605–6.
119. Letter to William Edward Robinson, 20 Apr. 1951, *Eisenhower Papers*, vol. 12.
120. Message, Sherman to Carney, 7 July 1951, Sherman Papers, box 7, Mediterranean Plans file, USN Op A.
121. Message, Carney to Sherman, 7 July 1951, Sherman Papers, box 7, Mediterranean Plans file, USN Op A.
122. British Chiefs of Staff Committee minutes, 21 May 1951, PRO, DEFE 4/41; see also Hastings, *Korean War*, chaps. 10 and 11.
123. British Chiefs of Staff Committee minutes, 21 May 1951, PRO, DEFE 4/41.
124. Memo, MOD to BJSM, "Command Structure," 17 Apr. 1951, PRO, DEFE 7/744; letter to Sherman, 23 June 1951, *Eisenhower Papers*, 12:376–77.

125. See Kenneth O. Morgan, *Labour in Power, 1945–1951* (London: Oxford University Press, 1985), chaps. 6 and 11; Acheson, *Present at the Creation*, 601.
126. JPS, "Outline History of the Atlantic Command Idea," 1 Nov. 1951, PRO, DEFE 6/19; MOD, "Problems with the SACLANT Terms of Reference," 22 Nov. 1951, PRO, DEFE 13/25.
127. MOD, "Problems with the SACLANT Terms of Reference," 22 Nov. 1951, PRO, DEFE 13/25.
128. JSPC, "Command Organization on Southern European Flank and the Middle East," 9 Nov. 1951, in *JCS 1946–53: Europe and NATO;* Gilbert, *Never Despair*, 669; "U.S. Delegation Minutes of the Second Formal Meeting of President Truman and Prime Minister Churchill, 7 January 1952," in U.S. Department of State, *Foreign Relations of the United States, 1952–1954* (Washington, D.C.: U.S. Government Printing Office, 1986), vol. 6 (hereafter cited as *FRUS 1952–54*).
129. "Approach and Objective for the Churchill Talks, 21 December 1951," in *FRUS 1952–54*, vol. 6.
130. Letter to Fechteler, 17 Jan. 1952, *Eisenhower Papers*, 12:883–85.
131. Lord Moran, *The Struggle for Survival*, 356–58, quoted in Gilbert, *Never Despair*.
132. "U.S. Delegation Minutes of the Second Formal Meeting of President Truman and Prime Minister Churchill, 7 January 1952," in *FRUS 1952–54*, vol. 6.
133. Gilbert, *Never Despair*, 679.
134. "U.S. Delegation Minutes of the Second Formal Meeting of President Truman and Prime Minister Churchill, 7 January 1952," in *FRUS 1952–54*, vol. 6.
135. Ibid.
136. Ibid.
137. Ibid.
138. Acheson, *Present at the Creation*, 602.
139. "U.S. Delegation Minutes of the Second Formal Meeting of President Truman and Prime Minister Churchill, 7 January 1952," in *FRUS 1952–54*, vol. 6; Pearson, *Mike*, 2:79; Lester B. Pearson, letter to Acheson, 15 Jan. 1952, Papers of Dean Acheson, Harry S. Truman Library, Independence, Mo.; Canadian Chiefs of Staff Committee minutes, special meeting, 15 Jan. 1952, DHIST.
140. Acheson, *Present at the Creation*, 602; "U.S. Delegation Minutes of Meeting between President Truman and Prime Minister Churchill, 18 January 1952," in *FRUS 1952–54*, vol. 6.
141. Fechteler, oral history transcript, p. 91, USN Op A.
142. Truman, letter to McCormick, 29 Jan. 1952, and memo, Truman to CinCLANT (McCormick), 30 Jan. 1952, Adm. Lynde McCormick Papers, Library of Congress Manuscript Division, Washington, D.C.
143. Memo, Canadian Delegation, North Atlantic Council to Chairman, Canadian Chiefs of Staff Committee, Raymont Papers, file 266, DHIST; Royal Navy Monthly Intelligence Reports, "British NATO Appointments," 1 Apr. 1952, PRO, ADM 223. *The NATO Handbook, 1952* has no organizational chart for SACLANT, as later editions would.

Chapter 4   From the Ditch to the Pillars of Hercules

1. According to Poole, *History of the Joint Chiefs,* vol. 4, in mid-1952 U.S. JCS planners shifted to a new planning system that eliminated code names. This new system produced three types of plans that were continually updated. These included the Joint Strategic Capabilities Plan (JSCP), which replaced the Joint Outline Emergency War Plan Masthead for the current year; the Joint Strategic Objectives Plan (JSOP), which replaced the Joint Medium Range War Plan Headstone for the three-year time frame; and the Joint Long Range Strategic Estimate (JLRSE), which was the successor to Dropshot for the ten-year planning cycle. See also Watson, *History of the Joint Chiefs,* vol. 5, chap. 4.
2. See "Plan GALLOPER," 1 Mar. 1950, PRO, DEFE 6/11; JCS JSPC, "Joint Outline Emergency War Plan CROSSPIECE," 8 Nov. 1949, in *JCS 1946–53: U.S. and USSR.*
3. Also known as "JOEWP for a War Beginning 1 July 1952." See British Chiefs of Staff Committee, "Preparation of War Plans," 14 Aug. 1951, PRO, DEFE 4/46; JSPC, "Guidance for a Strategic Estimate for a New JOEWP," 25 Oct. 1951, in *JCS 1946–53: U.S. and USSR;* JCS JSPC, "Directives for the Implementation of the JOEWP," 27 June 1952, in *JCS 1946–53: U.S. and USSR.* See also Poole, *History of the Joint Chiefs,* 4:308; Rosenberg, "Origins of Overkill," 23; Cochran et al., *Soviet Nuclear Weapons,* 228; JIC, "Soviet Atomic Capabilities Against Central Europe," 17 Apr. 1952, in *JCS 1946–53: U.S. and USSR.* The range of the TU-4 "Bull" was 3,450 miles, while the IL-28 "Beagle" had a range of 1,100 miles.
4. See "Plan GALLOPER," 1 Mar. 1950, PRO, DEFE 6/11; JCS JSPC, "Joint Outline Emergency War Plan CROSSPIECE," 8 Nov. 1949, in *JCS 1946–53: U.S. and USSR.* Aerial refueling was still maturing at this point. These aircraft included 180 B-29 Superfortresses (range 4,000 miles), 300 B-50 Improved Superfortresses (range 4,000 miles), 96 B-45 Tornados (range 1,500 miles), 176 B-36 Peacemakers (range 6,000 miles), 30 AJ-1 Savages (carrier based, range 1,450 miles), and 6 P2V3C Neptunes (carrier based, no return, range 2,000 miles). See Knaack, *Encyclopedia of USAF Aircraft,* vol. 2; Hansen, "Nuclear Neptunes," 262–68; Standard Aircraft Characteristics, NavAer 13358, *North American AJ-1* (1 Mar. 1951) and *Lockheed P2V2 "Neptune"* (1 Nov. 1949), Naval Aviation Historical Office, U.S. Naval Historical Center, Washington, D.C. There were also eighty-seven B-29 Washingtons, British B-29s used to supplement the eighteen squadrons of Avro Lincolns. The Lincoln was not atomic-capable, and it has never been demonstrated conclusively that the Washingtons were the Silverplate version of the B-29. Five squadrons of Canberra jet bombers were available to the British in 1952–53 and could have been armed with atomic weapons in a pinch if made available to the British by the Americans. For information on Canberra operations, see Jackson, *Canberra: The Operational Record,* 11–13, 19. The British would not have their own atomic weapons until 1952; see Rosenberg, "Origins of Overkill," 23; Arnold, *Very Special Relationship.*

5. White House meeting, 31 Jan. 1951, in U.S. Department of State, *Foreign Relations of the United States, 1951* (Washington, D.C.: U.S. Government Printing Office, 1979–81), 3:449–58 (hereafter cited as *FRUS 1951*), as quoted in Trachtenberg, *History and Strategy,* 160.
6. Of course, this all predated the New Look and the development of a NATO strategic concept that included widespread tactical nuclear weapon use and force structures. See Condit, *History of the OSD,* 2:369–71; Poole, *History of the Joint Chiefs,* 4:307; Fursdon, *European Defense Community.*
7. Poole, *History of the Joint Chiefs,* 4:307–8.
8. JSPC, "Revision of the Command Plan in Support of the JOEWP," 18 Feb. 1953, in *JCS 1946–53: U.S. and USSR.*
9. Cooper, *Buccaneers,* 49–80. There was the exception of Exercise Tiger in May 1944, when several U.S. LSTs were sunk by German torpedo boats while participating in an invasion exercise on the southern coast of Britain. At that time, it was unclear who exactly had operational control over the British escorts to the convoy; see Lewis, *Channel Firing.*
10. JPS, "Coordination of Naval and Air Command in the Eastern Atlantic," 10 Nov. 1950, PRO, DEFE 6/14; memo, Chief of Staff, U.S. Army to JCS, "Appointment of the Supreme Allied Commander, Atlantic and Definition of His Missions and Responsibilities," 28 Dec. 1950, in *JCS 1946–53: Europe and NATO.*
11. JPS, "Naval and Air Coordination between EASTLANT and Home Station," report to the Chiefs of Staff approved by the First Sea Lord, copy to NAORPG, 24 Jan. 1951, PRO, DEFE 6/16.
12. Ibid.
13. JPS, "Command in the Channel and Southern North Sea," 7 Feb. 1951, PRO, DEFE 6/15; JPS, "Naval/Air Command in the Channel and Southern North Sea Area," 21 Feb. 1951, PRO, DEFE 4/40.
14. JPS, "Naval/Air Command in the Channel and Southern North Sea Area," 21 Feb. 1951, PRO, DEFE 4/40.
15. Memo, Secretary General, WUDO to Ministry of Defence, "NATO Reorganization of Defence Machinery," 29 Mar. 1951, PRO, DEFE 7/949.
16. First Sea Lord to Director, Plans, "Relationship between CinCNORTH, CinCEASTLANT and Admiral, Rosyth," 11 Apr. 1951, PRO, ADM 205/76; CNO to JCS, "Division of Command Responsibility between SACEUR and SACLANT in the North Sea Area," 16 May 1951, in *JCS 1946–53: Europe and NATO;* JSPC, "Terms of Reference for the Allied Commander, Channel and Southern North Sea," 7 Nov. 1951, in *JCS 1946–53: Europe and NATO.*
17. Memo, Chief of Staff, USAF to JCS, "Proposal for NATO Command in the Channel and Southern North Sea Area," 3 July 1951, in *JCS 1946–53: Europe and NATO.*
18. JSPC, "Terms of Reference for Allied Commander, Channel and Southern North Sea," 26 Oct. 1951, in *JCS 1946–53: Europe and NATO;* Ismay, *NATO: The First Five Years,* 77–78.
19. The area of CHANCOM shown by the map was extended westward after a meeting between SACLANT and CinCCHAN. See "Log of SACLANT Visit

to the Atlantic Area, 24 Feb.–20 Mar. 1952," Adm. Lynde McCormick Papers, Library of Congress Manuscript Division, Washington, D.C.; "SACLANT and CHANCOM Boundaries," 22 Feb. 1951, Strategic Plans Division, box 272, file A-3, USN Op A; Ismay, *NATO: The First Five Years*, 77-78; Palmer, "Channel Command"; Monthly Intelligence Reports, UK appointments to NATO commands, 1 Feb. 1952, PRO, ADM 223. In 1963, the South Norway and Denmark coastal areas would be extended eastward into the Baltic and become Baltic Approaches Command (COMBALTAP) under SACEUR; see Sokolsky, "Seapower in the Nuclear Age," 89.
20. JSPC, "Channel Command War Plan," 19 Dec. 1952, in *JCS 1946–53: Europe and NATO*.
21. "Log of SACLANT Visit to the Atlantic Area, 24 Feb.–20 Mar. 1952," Adm. Lynde McCormick Papers, Library of Congress Manuscript Division, Washington, D.C.; intelligence summary, Canadian Minister, Oslo to Secretary of State for External Affairs, 17 Mar. 1952, Raymont Papers, file 266, DHIST; JSPC, "Division of Responsibility Between National Territorial Commanders, SACLANT and his Subordinate Commanders," 20 Aug. 1952, in *JCS 1946–53: Europe and NATO*.
22. Memo, CinCLANTFLEET to CNO, "The Organization of the U.S. Fleet Forces in NATO," 22 Mar. 1955, Strategic Plans Division, box 313, file A-3, USN Op A; Canadian Chiefs of Staff Committee, "Joint Services Committee: Pacific and Atlantic Coasts Proposed Reorganization," 4 May 1946, DHIST 193.009 (D53).
23. Canadian Chiefs of Staff Committee, "Organization and Role of the Joint Services Committees, Atlantic and Pacific Coasts," 3 Oct. 1952, DHIST 193.009 (D53).
24. Canadian Chiefs of Staff Committee minutes, special meeting, 19 Mar. 1952, DHIST 193.009 (D53).
25. Ibid.
26. Ibid.; Gilbert Tucker, *The Naval Service of Canada* (Ottawa: King's Printer, 1952), vol. 2, chap. 14; "SACLANT Visits Canada," *Toronto Telegram*, 19 Mar. 1952, in Adm. Lynde McCormick Papers, Library of Congress Manuscript Division, Washington, D.C.
27. Memo, CinCLANT to CNO, "Division of Responsibilities in Wartime between the CinCWESTLANT Area, CinCLANTFLEET and Commander, U.S. EASTSEAFRON," 3 Mar. 1953, Strategic Plans Division, box 279, file A-3, USN Op A. For example, U.S. Navy radar picket destroyers (DDRs) and radar picket aircraft remained under U.S. national command through CinCLANTFLEET; see JSPC, "Planning by SACLANT Relative to the Ocean Area South of the Tropic of Cancer," 14 Oct. 1953, in *JCS 1946–53: Europe and NATO*.
28. SACLANT, speech to North Atlantic Council, 28 May 1952, Adm. Lynde McCormick Papers, Library of Congress Manuscript Division, Washington, D.C.
29. Extract from report of Canadian representative to the North Atlantic Council to Canadian Chiefs of Staff, 30 May 1952, Raymont Papers, file 266, DHIST.

30. NATO's Planning Board for Ocean Shipping was established in May 1950 to recommend to the Standing Group "an appropriate shipping control organization of a civilian character for the mobilization and allocation of merchant shipping on a worldwide basis in time of war and emergency." This organization was to be called the Defense Shipping Authority (DSA); its organization included a Defense of Shipping Council and a Defense Shipping Executive Board with offices in London and Washington, D.C. The DSA would have been the ocean naval control of shipping organization for NATO in wartime. The plan was approved by the NAC in September 1951 but was not set up until October 1953—apparently, national entities were considered superior to such a coalition organization. See JSPC, "Annex 1 to SACLANT EDP 1-52," 30 Oct. 1953, in *JCS 1946–53: Europe and NATO;* SACLANT, speech to North Atlantic Council, 28 May 1952, Adm. Lynde McCormick Papers, Library of Congress Manuscript Division, Washington, D.C.; extract from report of Canadian representative to the North Atlantic Council to Canadian Chiefs of Staff, 30 May 1952, Raymont Papers, file 266, DHIST.
31. This has always been a difficult area to get information on, probably because of the prodigious use of submarines for intelligence gathering operations in the 1950s. See, for example, Richelson, *American Espionage,* chap. 6. For a report on one joint U.S.–British submarine intelligence-gathering operation, see memo, Director of Naval Intelligence to First Sea Lord, 19 Oct. 1956, PRO, ADM 205/110.
32. JSPC, "Submarine Command Organization in the Eastern Atlantic Area of SACLANT's Command," 30 July 1952, in *JCS 1946–53: Europe and NATO.*
33. Exercise Mariner file, Adm. Lynde McCormick Papers, Library of Congress Manuscript Division, Washington, D.C.
34. Adm. Charles K. Duncan, oral history transcript, vol. 1, pp. 381–82, USN Op A; British Chiefs of Staff Committee, "IBERLANT Command," 5 Sept. 1952, PRO, DEFE 4/56.
35. Palmer, *Origins of the Maritime Strategy,* 72; British Chiefs of Staff Committee, "IBERLANT Command," 5 Sept. 1952, PRO, DEFE 4/56; JPS, "IBERLANT," 18 Sept. 1952, PRO, DEFE 6/22.
36. Thursfield, ed., *Brassey's Annual, 1953,* 157–65; Grove, *From Vanguard to Trident;* Royal Navy Monthly Intelligence Reports, "NATO Exercise MAINBRACE," September 1952, PRO, ADM 223.

EASTLANT:	
Carrier Striking Forces	6 CVs (2 UK, 4 U.S.)
Heavy Support Unit 1	2 BBs & 4 CAs (Canada, UK, U.S.)
ASW Screen	28 DDs (Netherlands, Norway, UK, U.S.)
Amphibious Force	6 amph., 4 DDs & 1 USMC bn.
Carrier Support Force	3 CVLs & 1 CA (Canada, UK, U.S.)
Heavy Support Unit 2	2 CAs & 8 DDs (UK, U.S.)
HUK Force	2 FFs, 5 DDs & 1 CVL (UK, U.S.)
Convoy Escort Group	5 DDs & 1 FF (France, Netherlands, UK)
MCM Group	24 MCMs (Belgium, Netherlands, UK)

AFNORTH:
MCM Group	6 MCMs (Norway)
TF 152	4 DDs, 8 FFs & 2 SSs (Denmark, Norway, UK)
TF 153	2 DDs, 2 FFs & 2 SSs (Denmark)
Enemy Force:	
Submarine Group	14 SSs (Denmark, Netherlands, Norway, UK)
Raider	1 CA (Canada)
Baltic Group	4 DDs, 6 FFs & 1 SS (Denmark, Norway, UK)

37. Memo, Chief of Staff, USAF to JCS, "Exercise MAINBRACE," 15 Oct. 1952, in *JCS 1946–53: Europe and NATO*.
38. British Chiefs of Staff Committee, "Command Organization of SACLANT: Striking Fleet Commander," 11 Sept. 1952, PRO, DEFE 4/56; Thursfield, ed., *Brassey's Annual, 1953*, 165; Y'Blood, *Hunter-Killer*, app. 3.
39. Interservice problems over the use of RAF Bomber Command in the attack-at-source role preclude any attempts to measure success. See Terraine, *Business in Great Waters*, 354–56; "Plan GALLOPER," 1 Mar. 1950, PRO, DEFE 6/11; JCS JSPC, "Joint Outline Emergency War Plan CROSSPIECE," 8 Nov. 1949, in *JCS 1946–53: U.S. and USSR*; Grove, *From Vanguard to Trident*, chap. 2, app. B.
40. In the early 1950s the RAND Corporation projected the creation of nuclear deterrence theory. See, for example, Digby, *Strategic Thought at RAND*; Bernard Brodie and Eilene Galloway, eds., *The Atomic Bomb and the Armed Services* (Washington, D.C.: Library of Congress, 1947); Trachtenberg, *Development of American Strategic Thought*, vol. 2.
41. The U.S. Navy also deployed two fleet support vessels, the USS *Albemarle* and the USS *Curtis*, to the Mediterranean to act as atomic bomb storage and assembly ships in 1952. "Storage of Atomic Weapons Overseas," 22 Jan. 1952, RG 218, CCS 471.6, sec. 28, USNARA; "Overseas Storage of Atomic Weapons," 30 July 1952, RG 218, CCS 471.6, sec. 31, USNARA; memo to CNO, "Storage on AEs," 27 Mar. 1953, RG 218, CCS 471.6, sec. 37A, USNARA; "CNO's Annual Report to the Secretary of the Navy, 1952," USN Op A.
42. The AJ-1 Savage could cover a radius of 725 miles; the F2H Banshee, 737.5 miles; the AD-4B Skyraider, 673.5 miles; and the FJ-4B Fury, 500 miles. The performance of the F2H, AD-4B, and FJ-4B would have been reduced considerably while carrying atomic weapons—perhaps down to 60 percent of their normal range. See Hallion, *Naval Air War in Korea*, 313–17; Jim Mesko, *FJ Fury in Action* (Carrollton, Tex.: Squadron/Signal Press, 1990); Sullivan, *Skyraider in Action*; Hansen, *U.S. Nuclear Weapons*, 125–29, 131–41.
43. Adm. J. T. Hayward, letter to author, 8 July 1991; Hansen, *U.S. Nuclear Weapons*, 134–41; memo, CNO to JCS, "Evaluation of Navy Atomic Capability," 6 and 19 Sept. 1951, and memo, JSPC to JCS, "Nuclear Weapons Utilization Planning in NATO," 30 Mar. 1954, in U.S. Joint Chiefs of Staff, *Records of the Joint Chiefs of Staff, Part 2, 1946–1953: Strategic Issues, Part 1* (Bethesda, Md.: University Publications of America, 1980, microfilm) (hereafter cited as *JCS 1946–53: Strategic Issues 1*).

44. Adm. Francis D. Foley, oral history transcript, pp. 615–19, USN Op A; Palmer, *Origins of the Maritime Strategy*, chap. 3; Op Nav 503-P1003, "Aircraft Allowances of the Navy, 1 Oct. 1950," Naval Aviation Historical Office, U.S. Naval Historical Center, Washington, D.C. The first deployment of atomic-capable aircraft by the U.S. Navy actually occurred in February 1951; see Rosenberg, "American Postwar Air Doctrine," 265; Adm. J. T. Hayward, letter to author, 8 July 1991; "CNO's Annual Report to the Secretary of the Navy, 1952," USN Op A. These were aboard the USS *Franklin Delano Roosevelt*, USS *Midway*, USS *Coral Sea*, USS *Kearsarge*, and USS *Oriskany*. Seven more carriers were scheduled for conversion by 1953; see Arnold, *Very Special Relationship*, chap. 3; Blakeway and Lloyd-Roberts, *Fields of Thunder*; Williams, *Royal Navy Aircraft since 1945*. Scimitar carrier trials took place in 1953, and deployment commenced in 1958. The first British carriers modified for nuclear weapon storage were the HMS *Eagle* and HMS *Victorious*, this was not until 1958; see "Nuclear Weapons and Aircraft Carriers," 24 Feb. 1959, PRO, DEFE 7/1676; Friedman, *British Carrier Aviation*, 324–25.
45. Memo, ACoS Plans CinCLANT to SACLANT, 24 Nov. 1953, Strategic Plans Division, box 279, file A-3, USN Op A; Ball and Richelson, eds., *Strategic Nuclear Targeting*, chap. 5.
46. Memo, ACoS Plans CinCLANT to SACLANT, 24 Nov. 1953, Strategic Plans Division, box 279, file A-3, USN Op A.
47. Duncan, oral history transcript, vol. 2, pp. 1041–42, USN Op A; "CNO's Annual Report to the Secretary of the Navy," 1947, 1948, 1950, and 1952, USN Op A; Bracken, *Command and Control*, 193–98; memo, CNO to JCS, "Allocation of Atomic Weapons," 23 July 1953, in *JCS 1946–53: Strategic Issues 1*.
48. Foley, oral history transcript, USN Op A; memo, Op30 to Op09, "Comments on SGM 2538-52," 15 Nov. 1952, Adm. Arleigh Burke Papers, personal file no. 46, USN Op A; Wright to Fechteler, "Naval Support of the Land Battle in Europe," 6 Apr. 1952, OO file 1953, Admiral Fechteler's personal file.
49. British Chiefs of Staff Committee, "Command Organization of SACLANT: Striking Fleet Commander," 1 Sept. 1952, PRO, DEFE 4/56.
50. Foley, oral history transcript, USN Op A; minutes of meeting, First Sea Lord and SACLANT, 19 Sept. 1952, PRO, DEFE 4/56; memo from Headquarters, Second Fleet, 23 Nov. 1953, Strategic Plans Division, box 279, file A-3, USN Op A.
51. It is not my intention to delve into the fine details of airpower versus seapower except where it affects the debate over NATO naval command organization in the Atlantic. Suffice it to say that my maxim when studying these issues has always been to dispute any theorist who suggests that any one weapon system or service arm has the answer that will deliver victory in war. On American "air-mindedness," see Mike Sherry, *The Rise of American Airpower: The Creation of Armageddon* (New Haven: Yale University Press, 1987). On the supercarrier vs. B-36 hearings, see Schratz, "The Admirals' Revolt," 64–71; Reardon, *History of the OSD*, vol. 1. For a British perspective, see Baylis, *British Defence Policy*, chap. 4; Clark and Wheeler, *British Origins of Nuclear Strategy*.

52. Memo, Chief of Staff, USAF to JCS, "SACLANT EDP," 20 Nov. 1952, in *JCS 1946–53: Europe and NATO*.
53. Ibid.
54. Memo, CNO to JCS, "SACLANT EDP," 28 Nov. 1952, in *JCS 1946–53: Europe and NATO*.
55. Ibid.
56. The 49th Air Division was a special unit equipped with thirty B-45 Tornado jet bombers and one hundred F-84G Thunderjet fighters configured for atomic bomb delivery. Its aircraft were equipped with the Mark VII bomb. Its chain of command ran from U.S. Air Forces, Europe to the unified command, U.S. CinCEUR, to the JCS, a situation similar to that in the Atlantic from Second Fleet to CinCLANTFLEET to the JCS; memo, SACLANT liaison officer, SACEUR to SACLANT/CinCLANT, 3 June 1953, Strategic Plans Division, box 279, file A-3, USN Op A. For technical information, see Hansen, *U.S. Nuclear Weapons*, 135–36; Knaack, *Encyclopedia of USAF Aircraft*, 1:37; JSPC, "Information for NATO Commands Concerning Atomic Weapons," 23 Mar. 1953, in *JCS 1946–53: Strategic Issues 1*; JSPC, "Revision of Information for General Ridgeway on Availability of Atomic Weapons," 6 May 1953, in *JCS 1946–53: Strategic Issues 1*.
57. British Chiefs of Staff Committee, "SACLANT Command Arrangements," 21 Oct. 1952, PRO, DEFE 4/57; Beufre, *NATO and Europe*, 38–39.
58. Memo, First Lord of the Admiralty to the Prime Minister, 6 May 1953, PRO, DEFE 13/224.
59. Duncan, oral history transcript, vol. 3, pp. 1482–83, USN Op A.
60. British Chiefs of Staff Committee, "SACLANT Command Arrangements," 21 Oct. 1952, PRO, DEFE 4/57.
61. This was Ivy Mike, the first U.S. hydrogen device. It would not be weaponized until October 1953, two months after the announcement of the first successful Soviet H-bomb test. See Hansen, *U.S. Nuclear Weapons*, 58–61; York, *The Advisors*.
62. British Chiefs of Staff Committee, "Naval Command Problems," 7 Nov. 1952, PRO, DEFE 4/57.
63. Ibid.; see also Arnold, *Very Special Relationship*; Blakeway and Lloyd-Roberts, *Fields of Thunder*.
64. JSPC, "SACLANT EDP," 29 Oct. 1952, in *JCS 1946–53: Europe and NATO*; "Problems in Command Relations—CinCEASTLANT and COMSTRIKFLEETLANT," 12 Nov. 1952, PRO, DEFE 13/224.
65. Memo, Churchill to Chiefs of Staff Committee, 10 Dec. 1952, PRO, DEFE 13/224; memo, Ministry of Defence to Churchill, 24 Nov. 1952, PRO, DEFE 13/224; memo, Minister of Defence to Churchill, 12 Dec. 1952, PRO, DEFE 13/224.
66. See *The NATO Handbook, 1956*, and the Exercise Mariner file, Adm. Lynde McCormick Papers, Library of Congress Manuscript Division, Washington, D.C. Mariner essentially validated SACLANT's organizational concept. See also Thursfield, ed., *Brassey's Annual, 1954*, 285–89; Sokolsky, "Seapower in the Nuclear Age," 206.

Chapter 5 The Struggle for the Mediterranean

1. Due to the complex nature of Middle East politics, complete details of U.S., British, French, and other nations' political interactions in the region are outside the scope of this study.
2. JPS, "Command in the Mediterranean," 8 Dec. 1950, PRO, DEFE 6/15.
3. Ibid.; Sanders, *Losing an Empire*, 65–66. See also Young, *Churchill's Peacetime Administration*.
4. Grove, *From Vanguard to Trident*, 104; Carney, letter to Eisenhower, 25 Jan. 1952, Carney file no. 1, Pre-Presidential Papers, Eisenhower Library.
5. Memo, British Embassy, Paris to Ministry of Defence, 8 Feb. 1951, PRO, DEFE 11/25.
6. Carney, oral history transcript, p. 577, USN Op A.
7. As was the case earlier (see chapter 3), this was the result of U.S. Navy maneuvering within the U.S. defense organization; see "Eisenhower and Command Organization," 8 Feb. 1951, PRO, DEFE 11/25.
8. Memo, Ministry of Defence to British Joint Staff Mission, Washington, D.C., 1 Mar. 1951, PRO, DEFE 13/3.
9. Diary entry, 2 Mar. 1951, *Eisenhower Papers*, 12:83–85.
10. Record of an informal meeting between the British Chiefs of Staff and Admiral Sherman at 20 Grosvenor Square, 5 Mar. 1951, PRO, DEFE 7/949.
11. Ibid.
12. Letter, CinCNELM to SACEUR, 8 Mar. 1951, in *JCS 1946–53: Europe and NATO*.
13. Memo, Anderson to CoS Plans, Policy, and Operations, 25 Feb. 1952, Fechteler file, Pre-Presidential Papers, Eisenhower Library.
14. Letter, CinCNELM to SACEUR, 8 Mar. 1951, in *JCS 1946–53: Europe and NATO*.
15. Letter, Eisenhower to Marshall, 12 Mar. 1951, *Eisenhower Papers*, 12:117–23. The situation so distressed Eisenhower that he wrote to his former boss to seek advice.
16. Carney, oral history transcript, pp. 630-631, USN Op A.
17. Ibid.
18. Record of meeting, Air Marshal Tedder and Admiral Sherman, CNO, 27 Mar. 1951, PRO, DEFE 6/17.
19. Ibid.
20. "U.S. Position on Command Arrangements for the Mediterranean Area," 6 Apr. 1951, in *JCS 1946–53: Europe and NATO*.
21. Ibid.
22. British Chiefs of Staff Committee, "Command in the Mediterranean," 9 Apr. 1951, PRO, DEFE 4/41.
23. Ibid. For a variety of political reasons the U.S. position in the Middle East had changed since 1948, and the United States now saw North Africa as a preferred base area.
24. Report, CNO to JCS, "U.S. Position on Command Arrangements for the Mediterranean Area," 18 Apr. 1951,
25. "U.S. Position on Command Arrangements for the Mediterranean Area," 6 Apr. 1951, in *JCS 1946–53: Europe and NATO;* report, CNO to JCS, "U.S.

Position on Command Arrangements for the Mediterranean Area," 18 Apr. 1951, in *JCS 1946–53: Europe and NATO*; Horne, *Savage War of Peace*, 312–13, 475. See also Furniss, *France: Troubled Ally*, 278.
26. British Chiefs of Staff Committee meeting, 21 May 1951, PRO, DEFE 4/41; Pearson, *Mike*, 2:85.
27. British Chiefs of Staff Committee meeting, 21 May 1951, PRO, DEFE 4/41.
28. JSPC, "Command in the Mediterranean and the Middle East," 9 July 1951, in *JCS 1946–53: Europe and NATO*.
29. Memo, JSSC to JCS, "Middle East Command," 2 Nov. 1951, in *JCS 1946–53: Europe and NATO*.
30. JCS, "Command Organization in Europe: Southern Flank and in the Middle East," 7 Nov. 1951, in *JCS 1946–53: Europe and NATO*.
31. Ibid.
32. Ibid.; JSSC, "Strategic Study of the Eastern Mediterranean and Middle East Areas in Relation to the Admission of Greece and Turkey into NATO," 9 Nov. 1951, in *JCS 1946–53: Europe and NATO*.
33. JCS, "Command Organization in Europe: Southern Flank and in the Middle East," 7 Nov. 1951, in *JCS 1946–53: Europe and NATO*; JSSC, "Strategic Study of the Eastern Mediterranean and Middle East Areas in Relation to the Admission of Greece and Turkey into NATO," 9 Nov. 1951, in *JCS 1946–53: Europe and NATO*.
34. JCS, "Command Organization on Europe's Southern Flank and in the Middle East," 19 Nov. 1951, in *JCS 1946–53: Europe and NATO*.
35. JSPC, "Command Arrangements in Europe, Mediterranean and Middle East," 27 Dec. 1951, in *JCS 1946–53: Europe and NATO*.
36. Ibid.
37. Ibid.; JCS, enclosure D to 28 Jan. 1952, "NATO Command Organization in Mediterranean and Middle East Area," 3 Jan. 1952, in *JCS 1946–53: Europe and NATO*.
38. "Minutes of the Third Formal Meeting of President Truman and Prime Minister Churchill, 8 January 1952," in *FRUS 1952–54*, vol. 6.
39. Ibid.; Condit, *History of the OSD*, 2:366.
40. "Minutes of the Third Formal Meeting of President Truman and Prime Minister Churchill, 8 January 1952," in *FRUS 1952–54*, vol. 6.
41. JPS, "Unified Command in the Mediterranean," 23 Jan. 1952, PRO, DEFE 6/20.
42. Ibid.
43. JCS, "NATO Command Organization in the Mediterranean–Middle East Area," 28 Jan. 1952, in *JCS 1946–53: Europe and NATO*.
44. Ibid.
45. Ibid.
46. "Allied Command in the Mediterranean Sea: The British View," n.d., PRO, DEFE 13/224.
47. Poole, *History of the Joint Chiefs*, 4:312; "Allied Command in the Mediterranean Sea: The British View," n.d., PRO, DEFE 13/224.
48. Memo, CNO to JCS, "NATO Command Organization in the Mediterranean–Middle East Area," 5 Feb. 1952, in *JCS 1946–53: Europe and NATO*.
49. JSPC, "Allied Middle East Command," 25 Feb. 1952, in *JCS 1946–53: Europe and NATO*. MECO evolved into the Middle East Defense Organi-

zation and was the predecessor to the Baghdad Pact, which was formed in February 1955. This later became the Middle East Treaty Organization (METO) involving Pakistan, Iran, Iraq, Turkey, and Great Britain, with the United States as an observer. Once Iraq left in October 1956, METO became the Central Treaty Organization (CENTO); it faded into obscurity in the 1960s as the Soviets supported Arab states against Israel. See R. Ernest Dupuy and Trevor N. Dupuy, *The Encyclopedia of Military History*, 2d rev. ed. (New York: Harper & Row, 1986), 1275.

50. British Chiefs of Staff Committee, "U.S. Proposal for a NATO Naval Command Organization in the Mediterranean Area," 2 May 1952, PRO, DEFE 13/224.
51. Other British commanders were not as kind. One suggested that "Carney wants this command [the Mediterranean] purely out of a personal desire to build an empire. On the surface his claims are legitimate . . . the real facts, however, are on our side and we could lick this situation except for this one personality." MacBain, letter to Carney, 17 July 1952, CinCSOUTH file no. 7, USN Op A.
52. Memo for the record, meeting between CNO, CinCNELM, and British Chiefs of Staff, 5 May 1952, CinCSOUTH file no. 8, folder 8, USN Op A.
53. Ibid.
54. Ibid.
55. Ibid.
56. Ibid.
57. Minutes of meeting of British Chiefs of Staff, CNO, and CinCNELM, 28 May 1952, PRO, DEFE 13/224.
58. Memo, CNO to JCS, "Relief of CinCNELM," 6 May 1952, in *JCS 1946–53: Europe and NATO*.
59. The British continued to push for the creation of a SACMED directly subordinate to the Standing Group. See minutes of meeting of British Chiefs of Staff, CNO, and CinCNELM, 28 May 1952, PRO, DEFE 13/224; Ismay, *NATO: The First Five Years*, 73; Gurkan, *NATO, Turkey, and the Southern Flank*.
60. Carney, oral history transcript, p. 628, USN Op A.
61. Grove, *From Vanguard to Trident*, 104; Ziegler, *Mountbatten*, 516.
62. Ziegler, *Mountbatten*, 517.
63. It should be noted, however, that the United States was in the process of using its bilateral links with Spain, which was not in NATO, to secure bases at Rota and was conducting negotiations with Greece; see Veremis and Valinakis, *U.S. Bases in the Mediterranean*. British possessions and bases in the Mediterranean included Gibraltar, Malta, Cyprus, and the Canal Zone; British Chiefs of Staff Committee, "Naval Command Problems," 7 Nov. 1952, PRO, DEFE 4/57.
64. British Chiefs of Staff Committee, "Naval Command Problems," 7 Nov. 1952, PRO, DEFE 4/57.
65. Memo for the record, meeting between CNO, CinCNELM, and British Chiefs of Staff, 5 May 1952, CinCSOUTH file no. 8, folder 8, USN Op A; British Chiefs of Staff Committee, "Naval Command Problems," 7 Nov. 1952, PRO, DEFE 4/57; Ziegler, *Mountbatten*, 516.

66. British Joint Staff Mission, Washington, D.C., to Ministry of Defence, Chiefs of the Air Staff, and First Sea Lord, Subject: Mediterranean Command, 21 Nov. 1952, PRO, DEFE 13/224.
67. MacBain, letter to Carney, 17 July 1952, CinCSOUTH file no. 7, USN Op A.
68. British Joint Staff Mission, Washington, D.C., to Ministry of Defence, Subject: Mediterranean Command, 22 Nov. 1952, PRO, DEFE 13/224.
69. Ibid.
70. Ibid.; First Sea Lord to Prime Minister, Subject: CinCMED, 9 Dec. 1952, PRO, DEFE 13/224.
71. Sokolsky, "Seapower in the Nuclear Age," 208; this section was compiled from four sources and actually represents the finalized organization in 1954. See "Mediterranean Area Commands," 7 Jan. 1954, PRO, DEFE 6/28; Royal Navy War Manual, 1958, DHIST; Mountbatten, "Allied Naval and Air Commands"; Thursfield, ed., *Brassey's Annual, 1953*.
72. "Mediterranean Makeshift," *Manchester Guardian*, 17 July 1952.

Conclusion

1. See Cochran et al., *Soviet Nuclear Weapons*, chap. 1; York, *The Advisors*; Hansen, *U.S. Nuclear Weapons*, chap. 3. Although very important to the understanding of strategy after 1955, these areas will not be explored in great detail here. The British examination of these new issues was conducted by the British Chiefs of Staff Committee, and its product was the Global Strategy Paper of 1952; see Grove, *From Vanguard to Trident*, chap. 3. The American reexamination was embodied in the annual (starting in 1953) "Basic National Security Policy and Programs" paper, which was the basis for what the Americans called "The New Look." See Trachtenberg, *Development of American Strategic Thought*, vol. 1; Freedman, *Evolution of Nuclear Strategy*, 81–90. The terminology of the period was not yet precise regarding different levels of warfare. The Royal Navy War Manual, 1958, does differentiate among global, limited, and cold war; see Bernard Brodie, "Nuclear Weapons: Strategic or Tactical?" and "Unlimited Weapons and Limited War" (both written in 1954), in Trachtenberg, *Development of American Strategic Thought*, vol. 3.
2. "Sound Surveillance System: Plans for Extension in the Canadian Area," 24 Sept. 1958, NAC, RG 24, vol. 89, 83.84/167, vol. 1270 78-1 v. 5; Palmer, *Origins of the Maritime Strategy*, 82; "Project CAESAR," 28 May 1964, Raymont Papers, file 1087, DHIST; "The Report to the President by the Technological Capabilities Panel of the Science Advisory Committee, 14 Feb. 1955" (also called the Killian Report), in Trachtenberg, *Development of American Strategic Thought*, vol. 1; Robert Wells and C. R. Whiting, *Early Warning: Electronic Guardians of Our Country* (New York: Prentice Hall, 1962), 86–99.
3. Memo, CNO to JCS, "CONAD," 22 Jan. 1954, Strategic Plans Division, box 300, file A-16-1, USN Op A; "Vigil over Barren Seas," *National*

Aviation News, May 1957, 1–5; memo, CNO to CinCLANT, "Possible Overcommitment of Forces for NATO Operations," 21 May 1954, Strategic Plans Division, box 300, file A-16-1, USN Op A; Jockel, *No Boundaries Upstairs,* chap. 5.

4. Memo, Hughes-Hallett to First Sea Lord, "Submarines and Guided Missiles against the United States," 7 and 20 Jan. 1954, PRO, ADM 205/102; memo, DPlans to First Sea Lord, "Potential Use of VForce against Sub Bases," 12 Mar. 1954, PRO, ADM 205/102.
5. Memo, Hughes-Hallett to First Sea Lord, "Submarines and Guided Missiles against the United States," 7 Jan. 1954, PRO, ADM 205/102.
6. William B. Garrett, "The U.S. Navy's Role in the 1956 Suez Crisis," *Naval War College Review* 22, no. 7 (1970): 66–78; H. E. Eccles, "Suez 1956—Some Military Lessons," *Naval War College Review* 21, no. 7 (1969): 28–57.
7. Memo, CNO through USCINCNELM to Rear Admiral Luce to First Sea Lord, PRO, ADM 205/122.
8. Memo, Admiralty to Admiral, BJSM (Washington), PRO, ADM 205/122. See also Grove, *From Vanguard to Trident,* chap. 5; Gordon Chang, "To the Nuclear Brink: Eisenhower, Dulles, and the Quemoy-Matsu Crisis," in Sean Lynn-Jones et al., *Nuclear Diplomacy and Crisis Management* (Cambridge, Mass.: MIT Press, 1990), 200–227.
9. Cecil Hughes-Hallett, letter to Rhoderick McGrigor, 1 Feb. 1954, PRO, ADM 205/102.
10. Royal Navy Monthly Intelligence Reports, February and March 1951, PRO, ADM 223.
11. See Hastings, *Korean War;* Hallion, *Naval Air War in Korea.* On submarine operations see, Paul R. Schratz, *Submarine Commander* (New York: Pocket Books, 1988).
12. For a more complete examination, see Kennedy, *British Naval Mastery,* chap. 12; Grove, *From Vanguard to Trident,* chap. 8.
13. See *The North Atlantic Treaty Organization: Facts and Figures* (Brussels: NATO Information Service, 1989), 346–48; "NATO Streamlines Major Commands," *Jane's Defence Weekly,* 21 Dec. 1991.

APPENDIX 1 ASSESSING THE SOVIET SUBMARINE THREAT

1. JWPC, "Pincher: Overall Strategic Concept," pp. 27–29, in *JCS 1946–53: U.S. and USSR;* Friedman, *Submarine: Design and Development,* 57; Eberhardt Rossler, *The U-Boat* (London: Arms and Armour Press, 1981), 76–77; Milner, "Dawn of Modern Antisubmarine Warfare."
2. Rossler, *U-Boat,* 80–81.
3. Royal Navy Monthly Intelligence Reports, July 1949, PRO, ADM 223; Anti-Submarine Warfare, Canada, Britain and the United States, 1945–1960," June 1950, and "Estimate of Soviet Potential," NAC, RG 24 83.84/167, vol. 3734, file 8100.5.
4. Breemer, *Soviet Submarines,* 50–57.
5. Ibid., 78–81.

6. "Estimate of Soviet Potential," June 1950, NAC, RG 24 83.84/167, vol. 3734, file 8100.5.
7. See Robert W. Herrick, *Soviet Naval Theory and Policy* (Annapolis, Md.: Naval Institute Press, 1988), chap. 6.
8. Breemer, *Soviet Submarines*, 83–85.
9. Ibid., 86; Jordan, *Soviet Submarines*, 26–28.
10. Jordan, *Soviet Submarines*, 33–34.

APPENDIX 2 FLEET STRUCTURE AND TECHNOLOGICAL CHANGE

1. Herrick, *Soviet Naval Strategy*, 60–61; Kassell, "1,000 Submarines," 266–75.
2. See Hallion, *Naval Air War in Korea*.
3. Milner, "Dawn of Modern Antisubmarine Warfare," 61–68.
4. See Hallion, *Naval Air War in Korea;* Dossel, "Airborne Early Warning," 24–37; "The Sidewinder Air-to-Air Guided Missile for RCN Banshee Aircraft," 20 June 1950, Raymont Papers, file 147, DHIST; Nowarra, ed., *Russian Civil and Military Aircraft*, 172–80; Higham and Kipp, eds., *Soviet Aviation and Air Power*, 137–66.
5. See Friedman, *Postwar Naval Revolution*.
6. Hackmann, *Seek and Strike*, 46–48; Friedman, *Postwar Naval Revolution*, 75.
7. Friedman, *Postwar Naval Revolution*, 57–58; Siegfried, "Carrier-Based Airborne ASW," 56–75; Williams, *Royal Navy Aircraft since 1945*.
8. Hogg and King, eds., *Secret Weapons*, 95–97; Pocock, *German Guided Missiles*, chaps. 4 and 6; JSPC, "SACLANT Request for Information Regarding New Equipment, Weapons, and Tactics," 24 Mar. 1953, in *JCS 1946–53: Europe and NATO;* Michael McGwire, "The Structure of the Soviet Navy," in McGwire, ed., *Soviet Naval Developments*, 140–41.

➢ Glossary

AASSB   Allied Anti-Submarine Survey Board (1943)

ACHQ   Area Combined Headquarters, British

Administrative commands   A command organization that has control over personnel, construction, logistical support, and other non-combat activities

AFNORTH   CinC Allied Forces, North, NATO SACEUR command

AFSOUTH   CinC Allied Forces, South, NATO SACEUR command

AOC   Air Officer, Commanding, British and Canadian

ASW   Antisubmarine warfare

BB   Battleship

Binnacle   British Emergency War Plan for 1951–52 (U.S.: Masthead)

BJSM   British Joint Staff Mission, Washington, D.C.

BNL   Belgium/Netherlands/Luxembourg

Broiler   U.S. Emergency War Plan for 1948

Bullmoose   Canadian Emergency War Plan for 1949 (UK: Speedway; U.S.: Doublestar)

CA   Cruiser

CCS   Anglo-American Combined Chiefs of Staff (1941–45)

CHANCOM   NATO Channel Command (1952–)

CHOP line   Change of operational procedure line, where the operational control of forces changes from one command to another

CinC   Commander in chief (pronounced "sink")

CinCAFMED   Commander in Chief Allied Forces, Mediterranean, NATO SACEUR command co-equal to AFSOUTH (1953–67)

CinCAIREASTLANT   NATO SACLANT air command co-equal to SACLANT

247

CinCANFME   Proposed Commander in Chief Allied Naval Forces, Middle East

CinCAW&I   Commander in Chief, America and West Indies, a Royal Navy command

CinCEUR   U.S. unified command in Europe

CinCLANT   U.S. unified command in the Atlantic

CinCLANTFLEET   Commander in Chief, Atlantic Fleet, U.S. Navy

CinCME   Commander in Chief, Middle East, a British command (1939–)

CinCMED   Royal Navy command in the Mediterranean

CinCNA   Commander in Chief, Canadian Northwest Atlantic, a Canadian command (1943–45)

CinCNELM   Commander in Chief, U.S. Naval Forces East Atlantic and Mediterranean (1947–60)

CinCUSFLEET   Commander in Chief, U.S. Fleet (1941)

CinCWA   Commander in Chief, Western Approaches, a Royal Navy command (1941–45)

CL   Cruiser, light

CNO   Chief of Naval Operations, U.S. Navy

COAC   Canadian Commanding Officer, Atlantic Coast (1943–45, 1946–)

Coalition command   Two or more armed services from two or more nations operating together under one command

Combined command   British version of U.S. joint command—that is, one consisting of two or more armed services under one commander for a particular operation; in U.S. thinking, combined command exists when two or more services from two or more nations are operating together

COMCANLANT   NATO SACLANT Commander, Canadian Atlantic Sub-area (1952–)

COMINCH   Commander in Chief, U.S. Navy (1941–45)

COMNAVNAW   Commander, U.S. Naval Forces, North African Waters (1943–45)

COMSUBEASTLANT   NATO SACLANT Commander, Submarines Eastern Atlantic Area

Crosspiece   U.S. Emergency War Plan for 1949–51 (UK: Galloper)

CUSRPG   Canada–U.S. Regional Planning Group (1949–)

CV, CVA   Aircraft carrier

CVE   Aircraft carrier, escort

CVL   Aircraft carrier, light

DD   Destroyer

DE   Destroyer escort

Doublequick   British Emergency War Plan for 1948 (U.S.: Broiler)

Glossary

Doublestar   U.S. Emergency War Plan for 1948–49 (Canada: Bullmoose; UK: Speedway)

Dropshot   U.S. Joint Outline Plan for war in 1957

EASTLANT   NATO SACLANT Commander in Chief, Eastern Atlantic Area

EDP   Emergency Defense Plan

FF   Frigate

Fleetwood   Early code name for Doublestar, which was also called Halfmoon

FO   Flag officer

FOAC   Flag Officer, Atlantic Coast, Canadian (1943–45)

FOWE   NATO or WUDO Flag Officer, Western Europe

Functional command   Command organization responsible for a particular type of operating force assigned to a specific mission (for example, ASW forces); may be geographic or nongeographic

Galloper   British Emergency War Plan for March 1950–January 1951 (U.S.: Crosspiece)

Geographic command   Command organization organized to control forces within a defined physical area, whether national or coalition commands

Halfmoon   Early code name for Doublestar, which was also called Fleetwood

IBERLANT   Iberian Atlantic Sub-area, subordinate to SACLANT

JCS   U.S. Joint Chiefs of Staff

Joint command   In British terminology, a joint command consists of a national or coalition geographic command consisting of representatives from all three services (air, naval, and land); in American language, a joint command consists of two U.S. services linked together for a limited operation

JPS   British Chiefs of Staff Joint Planning Staff

JSCAC   Canadian Joint Services Committee, Atlantic Coast (1939–43)

JSPC   U.S. Joint Chiefs of Staff Joint Strategic Planning Committee

JSSC   Canadian Joint Services Subcommittee, Newfoundland (1939–45)

kt   kiloton, measure of the yield of nuclear weapons in thousands of tons of TNT

LRMPA   Long-range maritime patrol aircraft

Mainbrace   NATO SACLANT exercise, September 1952

Mariner   NATO SACLANT exercise, 1953

Masthead   U.S. Emergency War Plan for 1951–52 (UK: Binnacle)

MCC   Canadian–U.S. Military Cooperation Committee of the Permanent Joint Board on Defense

MCM   Mine countermeasures

MEC   Proposed Middle East Command

MECO   Middle East Command Organization (1951)

MED/ME   Mediterranean/Middle East

MEDO Middle East Defense Organization
MTDP NATO Medium Term Defense Plan
NAC North Atlantic Council
NADC North Atlantic Defense Committee
NAORPG North Atlantic Regional Planning Group
NATO North Atlantic Treaty Organization
NCS Naval control of shipping
NERPG Northern European Regional Planning Group
Offtackle Proposed U.S. Emergency War Plan for 1949
Operating forces Ships and aircraft that actually come into contact with the enemy; they are national in character
Operational command As defined by NATO, the authority to assign missions to subordinates, deploy units, reassign forces, and retain or delegate operational control as necessary
Operational control As defined by NATO, the authority delegated to a commander to direct assigned forces so that specific missions or tasks that are limited by function, time, or locations can be carried out
Pincher U.S. strategic planning documents, 1946
PJBD Canada–U.S. Permanent Joint Board on Defense (1941–)
Political command Command organization that consists predominantly of nonmilitary personnel
RAF Royal Air Force
RAFME Royal Air Force, Middle East
RCAF Royal Canadian Air Force
RCN Royal Canadian Navy
RN Royal Navy
RPG NATO regional planning groups
SAC U.S. Air Force Strategic Air Command (1947–92)
SACAO Supreme Allied Commander, Atlantic Ocean; early planning name for SACLANT (1949–51)
SACEUR NATO Supreme Allied Commander, Europe (1951–)
SACLANT NATO Supreme Allied Commander, Atlantic (1952–)
SACME Proposed Supreme Allied Commander, Middle East (1951)
SACMED Supreme Allied Commander, Mediterranean (1943–45)
SCAT Proposed Supreme Commander, Atlantic Theater (World War II)
SEAFRONS Sea frontiers, or national coastal waters
SG NATO Standing Group (1949–55)
SHAEF Supreme Headquarters, Allied Expeditionary Force (1943–45)

Glossary

SHAPE   NATO Supreme Headquarters, Allied Powers Europe (1951–)
SLOC   Sea lines of communication
Speedway   British Emergency War Plan for 1948–49 (Canada: Bullmoose; U.S.: Doublestar)
SS   Submarine
SSG   Submarine, guided missile
STRIKEFLEETLANT   NATO SACLANT Striking Fleet, Atlantic (1952–)
STRIKEFORSOUTH   NATO SACEUR Striking Force, South (1952–67)
Temporary or transitional command   Command organization that sometimes uses both operating forces and geographic commands on a limited basis for the conduct of a particular operation; sometimes geographic commands are superceded for such an operation
TF   Task force
Trojan   Proposed U.S. Emergency War Plan for 1949
UCP   U.S. Unified Command Plan
USAAF   U.S. Army Air Force
USAF   U.S. Air Force
USN   U.S. Navy
WERPG   Western European Regional Planning Group
WESTLANT   NATO SACLANT Commander in Chief, Western Atlantic Area
WUCoS   Western Union Chiefs of Staff
WUDO   Western Union Defense Organization

➤ Bibliography

PRIMARY SOURCES—UNPUBLISHED

CANADA

Directorate of History, Department of National Defence, Ottawa

ADM 1/16200
Chiefs of Staff Committee Minutes
Department of National Defence War Book, 1950
Military Coordinating Committee Records
Naval Board Minutes
Naval General Orders
Naval Policy and Projects Co-ordinating Committee
Naval Staff Minutes
The Raymont Collection
Royal Canadian Navy (RCN) History—General
Royal Navy War Manual, 1947
Royal Navy War Manual, 1958

National Archives of Canada, Ottawa

RG 24: Department of National Defence

ASW: Canada–Britain–United States
Cabinet Defence Committee
Defence of Canada Planning
Royal Canadian Navy Organization and Postwar Policy
Sea-Air Warfare Committee
Senior Officer Minutes

UNITED KINGDOM

Public Record Office, Kew

ADM 204 Admiralty Research Laboratory Files
ADM 205 First Sea Lord's Records
ADM 223 Monthly Intelligence Reports
DEFE 4 Chiefs of Staff Committee Minutes, 1947–57
DEFE 6 Chiefs of Staff Committee Joint Planning Staff Documents, 1947–59
DEFE 7 NATO—General, 1949–53
DEFE 11 Chiefs of Staff Committee Registered Files, 1946–64
DEFE 13 Private Office Papers, 1950–65

UNITED STATES

Interviews and Correspondence

Duncan, Adm. C. K., USN (Ret.). Letters to author.
Hayward, Adm. J. T., USN (Ret.). Letters to author.
Scarborough, Capt. W. E., USN (Ret.). Telephone conversation with author.

Library of Congress Manuscript Division, Washington, D.C.

Adm. Lynde McCormick Papers

U.S. Naval Historical Center, Washington, D.C.

Naval Aviation Historical Office

Department of the Navy, Bureau of Aeronautics. *Narrative History of the Requirement and Development of the A2J Heavy Attack Aircraft.* 17 December 1957.
Standard Aircraft Characteristics, NavAer 1335A. *Lockheed P2V2 "Neptune."* 1 November 1949.
Standard Aircraft Characteristics, NavAer 1335A. *North American AJ-1.* 1 March 1951.
Standard Aircraft Characteristics, NavAer 1335A. *North American AJ-2 "Savage."* 1 July 1952.

Operational Archive

Annual Reports to the Secretary of the Navy, 1946–55
Adm. Arleigh Burke Papers
Carney, Adm. Robert B., USN. Oral history transcript.
CinCSOUTH files
CNO-Double Zero Files, 1946–50
Duncan, Adm. Charles K., USN. Oral history transcript.
Fechteler, Adm. William M., USN. Oral history transcript.
Fife, Adm. James, USN. Oral history transcript.
Foley, Adm. Francis D., USN. Oral history transcript.

Loughlin, Rear Adm. Charles Elliott, USN. Oral history transcript.
NWP 10 *Naval Warfare*, 1954
NWP 36 *Employment of Restricted Weapons*
OpNav Instruction 5430.2A: Organizational Manual, 1950
OpNav Instruction 5430.2A: Organizational Manual, 1952
OpNav Instruction 5430.2A: Organizational Manual, 1954
Adm. Forrest Sherman Papers
Strategic Plans Division, 1945–55
Thatch, Adm. John S., USN. Oral history transcript.
USF 1 *Principles and Applications of Naval Warfare*, 1947

Primary Sources—Published

Galambos, Louis, et al. *The Papers of Dwight David Eisenhower*. Vols. 12 & 13, *NATO and the Campaign of 1952*. Baltimore: Johns Hopkins University Press, 1989.

North Atlantic Treaty Organization. *SACLANT Information Pamphlet*. Norfolk, Va., n.d.

North Atlantic Treaty Organization. Information Service. *The NATO Handbook, 1952*. Bosch, Netherlands, 1952.

———. *The NATO Handbook, 1953*. Bosch, Netherlands, 1953.

———. *The North Atlantic Treaty Organization, 1956*. Bosch, Netherlands, 1956.

———. *The North Atlantic Treaty Organization, 1959*. Bosch, Netherlands, 1959.

United Kingdom. Ministry of Defence. *Command Paper 6923: Central Organisation for Defence*. London: Her Majesty's Stationery Office, 1946.

———. *Command Paper 7883: Collective Defence under the Brussels and North Atlantic Treaties*. London: Her Majesty's Stationery Office, 1950.

———. *Command Paper 7894: Mutual Defence Assistance Agreement*. London: Her Majesty's Stationery Office, 1950.

———. *Command Paper 8214: The System of Command Established within the North Atlantic Treaty Organisation*. London: Her Majesty's Stationery Office, 1951.

U.S. Department of State. *Foreign Relations of the United States, 1950*. Vol. 1, *National Security Affairs; Foreign Economic Policy*. Washington, D.C.: U.S. Government Printing Office, 1977.

———. *Foreign Relations of the United States, 1950*. Vol. 3, *Western Europe*. Washington, D.C.: U.S. Government Printing Office, 1977.

———. *Foreign Relations of the United States, 1951*. Vol. 1, *National Security Affairs; Foreign Economic Policy*. Washington, D.C.: U.S. Government Printing Office, 1979.

———. *Foreign Relations of the United States, 1951*. Vol. 2, *The United Nations; The Western Hemisphere*. Washington, D.C.: U.S. Government Printing Office, 1979.

———. *Foreign Relations of the United States, 1951.* Vol. 3, *European Security and the German Question, Part 1.* Washington, D.C.: U.S. Government Printing Office, 1981.
———. *Foreign Relations of the United States, 1952–1954.* Vol. 2, *National Security Affairs, Parts 1 and 2.* Washington, D.C.: U.S. Government Printing Office, 1986.
———. *Foreign Relations of the United States, 1952–1954.* Vol. 6, *Western Europe and Canada.* Washington, D.C.: U.S. Government Printing Office, 1986.
U.S. Joint Chiefs of Staff. *Records of the Joint Chiefs of Staff, Part 2, 1946–1953: Europe and NATO.* Bethesda, Md.: University Publications of America, 1980. Microfilm.
———. *Records of the Joint Chiefs of Staff, Part 2, 1946–1953: Strategic Issues, Part 1.* Bethesda, Md.: University Publications of America, 1980. Microfilm.
———. *Records of the Joint Chiefs of Staff, Part 2, 1946–1953: Strategic Issues, Part 2.* Bethesda, Md.: University Publications of America, 1980. Microfilm.
———. *Records of the Joint Chiefs of Staff, Part 2, 1946–1953: The United States.* Bethesda, Md.: University Publications of America, 1980. Microfilm.
———. *Records of the Joint Chiefs of Staff, Part 2, 1946–1953: The United States and the Soviet Union.* Bethesda, Md.: University Publications of America, 1979. Microfilm.

Secondary Sources

Acheson, Dean. *Present at the Creation.* New York: W. W. Norton, 1969.
Angelucci, Enzo, and Paolo Matricardi. *World War II Airplanes.* Vol. 1. New York: Rand McNally, 1976.
Arnold, Lorna. *A Very Special Relationship: British Atomic Weapons Trials in Australia.* London: Her Majesty's Stationery Office, 1987.
Ball, Desmond, and Jeffrey Richelson, eds. *Strategic Nuclear Targeting.* Ithaca: Cornell University Press, 1986.
Barry, Donald. "The British Navy in the Nuclear Age." *U.S. Naval Institute Proceedings* 83 (1957): 1069–77.
Baylis, John. *The Anglo-American Defence Relationship, 1939–1984.* London: Macmillan, 1983.
———. *British Defence Policy: Striking the Right Balance.* London: Macmillan, 1989.
Beebe, Robert P. "The Vital Key West Agreement." *U.S. Naval Institute Proceedings* 87 (1961): 35–41.
Beufre, Andre. *NATO and Europe.* London: Faber & Faber, 1966.
Bitzinger, Richard A. *Assessing the Conventional Balance in Europe, 1945–1975.* Santa Monica, Calif.: RAND Corp., 1989.
Blakeway, Denys, and Sue Lloyd-Roberts. *Fields of Thunder: Testing Britain's Bomb.* London: George Allen & Unwin, 1985.
Borowski, Harry R. *A Hollow Threat: Strategic Air Power and Containment Before Korea.* Westport, Conn.: Greenwood Press, 1982.

Boutilier, James A., ed. *RCN in Retrospect, 1910–1968.* Vancouver: University of British Columbia Press, 1982.
Bracken, Paul. *The Command and Control of Nuclear Forces.* New Haven: Yale University Press, 1986.
Breemer, Jan. *Soviet Submarines: Design, Development, and Tactics.* London: Jane's, 1989.
Brookes, Andrew. *V-Force: The History of Britain's Airborne Deterrent.* London: Jane's, 1982.
Browning, M. R. "Operations and Routing of Modern Convoys." *Military Review* 27, no. 7 (1947): 31–36.
Burns, Thomas. *The Secret War for the Ocean's Depths.* New York: Rawson Associates, 1978.
Butler, J.R.M. *Grand Strategy.* Vol. 2, *September 1939–June 1941.* London: Her Majesty's Stationery Office, 1957.
Carroll, Warren H. *Seventy Years of the Communist Revolution.* Manassas, Va.: Trinity Communications, 1990.
Carver, Lord. "Continental or Maritime Strategy? Past, Present, and Future." *RUSI Journal* (1989): 61–69.
Cave Brown, Anthony. *Dropshot: The U.S. Plan for War with the Soviet Union in 1957.* New York: Dial Press, 1978.
Clare, R.A.G. "Maritime Strategy: National and NATO Requirements." *Naval Review* 79 (1987): 313–21.
Clark, Ian, and Nicholas J. Wheeler. *The British Origins of Nuclear Strategy, 1945–1955.* Oxford: Clarendon Press, 1989.
Cleveland, Harlan. *NATO: The Transatlantic Bargain.* New York: Harper & Row, 1970.
Cline, Ray S. *The War Department, Washington Command Post: The Operations Division.* Washington, D.C.: Office of the Chief of Military History, 1951.
Cochran, Thomas B., et al. *U.S. Nuclear Forces and Capabilities.* Cambridge: Ballinger, 1984.
———. *Soviet Nuclear Weapons.* Cambridge: Ballinger, 1989.
Cole, Alice, et al., eds. *The Department of Defense: Documents on Establishment and Organization, 1944–1978.* Washington, D.C.: Office of the Secretary of Defense, Historical Office, 1978.
Coletta, Paolo. *The U.S. Navy and Defense Unification, 1947–1953.* Newark: University of Delaware Press, 1980.
Compton-Hall, Richard. *Submarine versus Submarine: The Tactics and Technology of Underwater Confrontation.* Toronto: Collins, 1988.
Condit, Doris M. *History of the Joint Chiefs of Staff.* Vol. 2, *The Joint Chiefs of Staff and National Policy, 1947–1949.* Wilmington, Del.: Michael Glazier, 1979.
———. *History of the Office of the Secretary of Defense.* Vol. 2, *The Test of War, 1950–1953.* Washington, D.C.: U.S. Government Printing Office, 1988.
Cook, Don. *Forging the Alliance: NATO, 1945–1950.* New York: Arbor House, 1989.
Cooper, Bryan. *The Buccaneers.* London: MacDonald and Co., 1970.

Corbett, Julian S. *Some Principles of Maritime Strategy.* Annapolis, Md.: Naval Institute Press, 1988.
Cottrell, Alvin, and Stanley L. Harrison. "Alliances: The Ties That Bind." U.S. Naval Institute *Proceedings* 94 (1968): 26–35.
Crowe, W. J. "Policy Roots of the Royal Navy, 1945–1963." Ph.D. diss., Princeton University, 1965.
Cuthberson, Brian. *Canadian Military Independence in the Age of the Superpowers.* Toronto: Fitzhenry & Whiteside, 1977.
Danis, A. L. "Offensive ASW: Fundamental to Defense." U.S. Naval Institute *Proceedings* 83 (1957): 583–89.
Davis, Brian L. *NATO Forces: An Illustrated Reference to Their Organization and Insignia.* London: Arms & Armour Press, 1988.
Davis, Vincent. *Postwar Defense Policy and the U.S. Navy, 1943–1946.* Chapel Hill: University of North Carolina Press, 1962.
De Huszar, George B., ed. *Soviet Power and Policy.* New York: Thomas Crowell, 1955.
Delgado, James P. "What's Become of Sara?" U.S. Naval Institute *Proceedings* 116 (1990): 45–50.
D'Este, Carlo. *Bitter Victory: The Battle for Sicily, 1943.* London: Fontana Books, 1988.
Digby, James. *Strategic Thought at RAND, 1948–1963: The Ideas, Their Origins, Their Fates.* Santa Monica, Calif.: RAND Corp., 1990.
Dimbleby, David, and David Reynolds. *An Ocean Apart: The Relationship between Britain and America in the Twentieth Century.* New York: Vintage, 1988.
Dossel, C. W. "Airborne Early Warning." *The Hook* (1983): 24–31.
Douglas, W.A.B. *The Creation of a National Air Force: The Official History of the Royal Canadian Air Force.* Vol. 2. Toronto: University of Toronto Press, 1986.
———, ed. *The RCN in Transition, 1910–1985.* Vancouver: University of British Columbia Press, 1988.
Dziuban, Stanley W. *Military Relations between Canada and the United States, 1939–1945.* Washington, D.C.: Office of the Chief of Military History, Department of the Army, 1959.
Eayers, James. *In Defence of Canada: Growing Up Allied.* London: University of Toronto Press, 1980.
Eliot, George F. "Sea-Borne Deterrent." U.S. Naval Institute *Proceedings* 82 (1956): 1143–53.
Ehrman, John. *Grand Strategy.* Vol. 5, *August 1943–September 1944.* London: Her Majesty's Stationery Office, 1956.
Fahey, James C. *The Ships and Aircraft of the U.S. Fleet.* 6th, 7th, and 8th eds. Annapolis, Md.: Naval Institute Press, 1988.
Fairhall, David. *Russian Sea Power.* Boston: Gambit Press, 1971.
Freedman, Lawrence. *The Evolution of Nuclear Strategy.* 2d ed. New York: St. Martin's Press, 1989.
Friedman, Norman. *British Carrier Aviation: The Evolution of the Ships and Their Aircraft.* Annapolis, Md.: Naval Institute Press, 1988.

———. *The Postwar Naval Revolution*. Annapolis, Md.: Naval Institute Press, 1986.
———. *Submarine: Design and Development*. Annapolis, Md.: Naval Institute Press, 1984.
———. *World Naval Weapons Systems*. Annapolis, Md.: Naval Institute Press, 1989.
Furniss, Edgar S. *France: Troubled Ally*. New York: Harper & Brothers, 1960.
Fursdon, Edward. *The European Defense Community: A History*. New York: St. Martin's Press, 1980.
Gaddis, John Lewis. *Strategies of Containment: A Critical Appraisal of Postwar American National Security Policy*. London: Oxford University Press, 1982.
Gilbert, Martin. *Never Despair: Winston S. Churchill*. Vol. 3, *1945–1965*. London: Minerva, 1988.
Greenwood, John T. "The Emergence of the Postwar Strategic Air Force, 1945–1953." *Air Power and Warfare: Proceedings of the Eighth Military History Symposium*. Colorado Springs, Colo.: Office of Air Force History, 1978.
Grove, Eric J. *Vanguard to Trident: British Naval Policy since World War II*. Annapolis, Md.: Naval Institute Press, 1987.
Gurkan, Ihsan. *NATO, Turkey, and the Southern Flank: A Mideastern Perspective*. New York: National Strategy Information Center, 1980.
Gwyer, J.M.A., and J.R.M. Butler. *Grand Strategy*. Vol. 3, *June 1941–August 1942*. London: Her Majesty's Stationery Office, 1964.
Hackmann, Willem. *Seek and Strike: Sonar, Antisubmarine Warfare, and the Royal Navy, 1914–1954*. London: Her Majesty's Stationery Office, 1984.
Halle, Louis J. *The Cold War as History*. Rev. ed. New York: Harper & Row, 1991.
Hallion, Richard P. *The Naval Air War in Korea*. New York: Zebra Books, 1986.
Hamilton, Nigel. *Monty*. Vol. 3, *The Field Marshal, 1944–1976*. London: Sceptre, 1986.
Hampshire, A. C. *The Royal Navy since 1945*. London: Kimber, 1975.
Hanks, Robert J. *American Sea Power and Global Strategy* Washington, D.C.: Pergamon-Brassey's, 1985.
Hansen, Chuck. "Nuclear Neptunes: Early Days of Composite Squadrons 5 and 6." *Journal of the American Aviation Historical Society* (1979): 262–68.
———. *U.S. Nuclear Weapons: The Secret History*. New York: Orion Books, 1988.
Harrison, Stanley L. "Defense of the Atlantic Community." *U.S. Naval Institute Proceedings* 95 (1969): 44–49.
Hastings, Max. *The Korean War*. New York: Simon & Schuster, 1987.
Hattendorf, John, and Richard Jordan, eds. *Maritime Strategy and the Balance of Power*. New York: St. Martin's Press, 1989.
Henderson, Nicholas. *The Birth of NATO*. London: Weidenfeld & Nicholson, 1982.
Henrikson, Alan K. "The Creation of the North Atlantic Alliance, 1948–1952." *Naval War College Review* (1980): 4–39.
Herrick, Robert. *Soviet Naval Strategy: Fifty Years of Theory and Practice*. Annapolis, Md.: Naval Institute Press, 1968.

Higham, Robin, and Jacob W. Kipp, eds. *Soviet Aviation and Air Power*. London: Brassey's, 1977.
Hill, J. R. *Antisubmarine Warfare*. London: Ian Allen, 1984.
Hogg, Ian, and J. B. King, eds. *German and Allied Secret Weapons of World War II*. London: Chartwell Books, 1976.
Holloway, David. "Entering the Nuclear Arms Race: The Soviet Decision to Build the Atomic Bomb, 1939–1945." *Social Studies of Science* 11 (1981): 159–97.
Hone, Thomas C. *Power and Change: The Administrative History of the Office of the Chief of Naval Operations, 1946–1986*. Washington, D.C.: Naval Historical Center, 1989.
Horne, Alastair. *A Savage War of Peace: Algeria, 1954–1962*. London: Penguin Press, 1977.
Howard, Joseph. "The Navy and National Security." *U.S. Naval Institute Proceedings* 77 (1951): 748–53.
———. *Our Modern Navy*. Princeton: Van Nostrand, 1961.
Howard, Michael. "Civil-Military Relations in Great Britain and the United States, 1945–1958." *Political Science Quarterly* (1960): 35–46.
———. *Grand Strategy*. Vol. 4, *August 1942–September 1943*. London: Her Majesty's Stationery Office, 1972.
Howe, George F. *The Mediterranean Theater of Operations: Northwest Africa Seizing the Initiative in the West*. Washington, D.C.: Department of the Army, 1957.
Hubbard, K., and S. Simmons. *Operation Grapple: Testing Britain's First H-Bomb*. London: Ian Allen, 1985.
Huston, James A. *One for All: NATO Strategy and Logistics through the Formative Period, 1949–1969*. Newark: University of Delaware Press, 1984.
Hyland, William G. *The Cold War: Fifty Years of Conflict*. New York: Random House, 1991.
Ismay, Lord. *NATO: The First Five Years, 1949–1954*. Utrecht: Bosch, 1954.
Jackson, Robert. *Avro Vulcan*. Wellingborough, Northamptonshire: Partik Stevens, 1987.
———. *Canberra: The Operational Record*. Washington, D.C.: Smithsonian Institution Press, 1989.
———. *Strike Force: The USAF in Britain since 1948*. London: Robson Books, 1986.
Jackson, William. *Britain's Defence Dilemma: An Insider's View*. London: Batsford, 1990.
Jampoler, Andrew. "A Central Role for Naval Forces? . . . To Support the Land Battle." *Naval War College Review* (1984): 4–12.
Jane's Fighting Ships, 1949–1950. London: Jane's, 1950.
Jane's Fighting Ships, 1954–1955. London: Jane's, 1955.
Jane's Fighting Ships, 1958–1959. London: Jane's, 1959.
Jockel, Joseph T. *No Boundaries Upstairs: Canada, the United States, and the Origins of North American Air Defence, 1945–1958*. Vancouver: University of British Columbia Press, 1987.
Jordan, John. *Soviet Submarines, 1945 to the Present*. London: Arms & Armour Press, 1989.

Jordan, Robert S., ed. *Generals in International Politics: NATO's Supreme Commander, Europe.* Lexington: University of Kentucky Press, 1987.
Kahan, Jerome H. *Security in the Nuclear Age: Developing U.S. Strategic Arms Policy.* Washington, D.C.: Brookings Institution, 1975.
Kaplan, Lawrence, and Robert Clawson, eds. *NATO after Thirty Years.* Wilmington, Del.: Scholarly Resources, 1981.
Kaplan, Lawrence, et al., eds. *NATO and the Mediterranean.* Wilmington, Del.: Scholarly Resources, 1985.
Kassell, Bernard M. "1,000 Submarines—Fact or Fiction." U.S. Naval Institute *Proceedings* 77 (1951): 266–75.
Kasulka, Duane. *U.S. Aircraft Carrier Air Units.* Vol. 1, *1946–1956.* Carrollton, Tex.: Squadron/Signal Press, 1985.
Kealy, J.D.F., and E. C. Russell. *A History of Canadian Naval Aviation, 1918–1962.* Ottawa: Crown Printers, 1967.
Kennedy, Paul M. *The Realities behind Diplomacy.* London: Fontana, 1981.
———. *The Rise and Fall of British Naval Mastery.* New York: Macmillan, 1983.
Kidd, Isaac. "NATO's Double Dependence on the Atlantic." *NATO Review* (1978): 3–8.
Knaack, Marcelle Size. *Encyclopedia of U.S. Air Force Aircraft and Missile Systems.* Vol. 1, *Post–World War II Fighters, 1945–1973.* Washington, D.C.: U.S. Government Printing Office, 1986.
———. *Encyclopedia of U.S. Air Force Aircraft and Missile Systems.* Vol. 2, *Post–World War II Bombers, 1945–1973.* Washington, D.C.: U.S. Government Printing Office, 1988.
Knorr, Klaus, ed. *NATO and American Security.* Princeton: Princeton University Press, 1959.
Krulak, Victor H. *Organization for National Security: A Study.* Washington, D.C.: U.S. Strategic Institute, 1983.
Laqueur, Walter. *Europe since Hitler: The Rebirth of Europe.* Rev. ed. London: Pelican Books, 1982.
Lewis, D. D. "The NATO ASW Situation." U.S. Naval Institute *Proceedings* 85 (1959): 55–63.
Lewis, Nigel. *Channel Firing: The Tragedy of Exercise Tiger.* London: Penguin, 1990.
Lockheed P2V Neptune. Surrey: Profile Publications 1989.
Loth, Wilfried. *The Division of the World, 1941–1955.* London: Routledge, 1988.
Lusar, Rudolf. "The Red Fleet Is Being Built Up." U.S. Naval Institute *Proceedings* 80 (1954): 56–66.
Mackay, R.S.G. *Lancaster in Action.* Carrollton, Tex.: Squadron/Signal Press, 1982.
Maier, Charles S., ed. *The Cold War in Europe: Era of a Divided Continent.* New York: Marcus Wiener, 1991.
Marshall, S.L.A., et al. *The Simon and Shuster Encyclopedia of World War II.* New York: Simon & Shuster, 1978.
Mason, R. A. *War in the Third Dimension.* Washington, D.C.: Pergamon-Brassey's, 1987.
Matloff, Maurice. *The War Department: Strategic Planning for Coalition Warfare, 1943–1944.* Washington, D.C.: Office of the Chief of Military History, 1959.

Matloff, Maurice, and Edwin M. Snell. *The War Department: Strategic Planning for Coalition Warfare, 1941–1942.* Washington, D.C.: Office of the Chief of Military History, 1953.

McGwire, Michael, ed. *Soviet Naval Developments: Context and Capability.* Halifax, N.S.: Dalhousie University, 1973.

Menaul, Stewart. *The Geostrategic Importance of the Iberian Peninsula.* London: Institute for the Study of Conflict, 1981.

Milberry, Larry. *Sixty Years: The RCAF and CF Air Command, 1924–1984.* Toronto: CANAV Books, 1984.

Miller, David, and Chris Miller. *Modern Naval Combat.* New York: Crescent Books, 1986.

Miller, David, and John Jordan. *Modern Submarine Warfare.* New York: Crescent Books, 1987.

Millis, Walter, ed. *The Forrestal Diaries.* New York: Viking, 1951.

Milner, Marc. "The Dawn of Modern Antisubmarine Warfare: Allied Responses to the U-Boats, 1944–1945." *RUSI Journal* (1989): 61–68.

———. *North Atlantic Run: The Royal Canadian Navy and the Battle for the Convoys.* Toronto: University of Toronto Press, 1985.

Molony, C.J.C., et al. *The Mediterranean and the Middle East.* Vol. 5. London: Her Majesty's Stationery Office, 1973.

Monsarrat, John. *Angel on the Yardarm: The Beginnings of Fleet Radar Defense and the Kamikaze Threat.* Newport, R.I.: Naval War College Press, 1985.

Morison, Samuel Eliot. *History of United States Naval Operations in World War II.* Vol. 1, *The Battle of the Atlantic, September 1939–May 1943.* Boston: Little, Brown, 1947.

———. *History of United States Naval Operations in World War II.* Vol. 2, *Operations in North African Waters, October 1942–June 1943.* Boston: Little, Brown, 1947.

———. *History of United States Naval Operations in World War II.* Vol. 9, *Sicily-Salerno-Anzio, January 1943–June 1944.* Boston: Little, Brown, 1954.

———. *History of United States Naval Operations in World War II.* Vol. 10, *The Atlantic Battle Won, May 1943–May 1945.* Boston: Little, Brown, 1956.

———. *History of United States Naval Operations in World War II.* Vol. 11, *The Invasion of France and Germany, 1944–1945.* Boston: Little, Brown, 1957.

———. *The Two-Ocean War.* Boston: Little, Brown, 1963.

Morton, Louis. *The War in the Pacific: Strategy and Command, the First Two Years.* Washington, D.C.: Department of the Army, 1962.

Moss, D. M. "The Impact of Technology on the Relationship between Sea and Air Power." *Naval Review* 73 (1985): 4–12.

Mountbatten, Louis. "Allied Naval and Air Commands in the Mediterranean." *RUSI Journal* (1955): 171–86.

Muir, Malcolm. "A Stillborn System: The Submarine-Launched Cruise Missile in the U.S. Navy, 1945–1964." Unpublished paper.

Mulley, F. W. *The Politics of Western Defense.* New York: Praeger, 1962.

Murphy, Paul J., ed. *The Soviet Air Forces.* London: McFarland and Co., 1984.

Neustadt, Richard. *Alliance Politics.* New York: CUNY Press, 1970.

Newhouse, John. *War and Peace in the Nuclear Age.* New York: Knopf, 1988.

Nowarra, Heinz J., ed. *Russian Civil and Military Aircraft, 1884–1969.* London: Fountain Press, 1971.
Palmer, Joseph M. "The Channel Command: Sea Highway to Europe." U.S. Naval Institute *Proceedings* 102 (1976): 178–89.
Palmer, Michael A. *Origins of the Maritime Strategy: American Naval Strategy in the First Postwar Decade.* Washington, D.C.: Naval Historical Center, 1988.
———. "The U.S. Navy and the Mediterranean, 1946–1948." Unpublished paper, 1991.
Paolucci, Dominic A. "The Development of Navy Strategic Offensive and Defensive Systems." U.S. Naval Institute *Proceedings* 96 (1970): 206–23.
Park, William. *Defending the West: A History of NATO.* Boulder, Colo.: Westview, 1986.
Pearson, Lester B. *Mike: The Memoirs of the Rt. Hon. Lester B. Pearson.* Toronto: University of Toronto Press, 1972.
Peebles, Curtis. *Guardians: Strategic Reconnaissance Satellites.* Novato, Calif.: Presidio, 1987.
Playfair, I.S.O., et al. *The Mediterranean and the Middle East.* Vol. 4. London: Her Majesty's Stationery Office, 1966.
Pocock, Rowland F. *German Guided Missiles of the Second World War.* New York: ARCO, 1967.
Pogue, Forrest C. *The Supreme Command.* Washington, D.C.: Department of the Army, 1954.
Polmar, Norman. *Soviet Naval Power: Challenge for the 1970s.* New York: National Strategy Information Center, 1972.
———. *Strategic Weapons: An Introduction.* New York: Crane, Russak, 1975.
Polmar, Norman, and Siegfried Breyer. *Guide to the Soviet Navy.* Annapolis, Md.: Naval Institute Press, 1977.
Poole, Walter S. *History of the Joint Chiefs of Staff.* Vol. 4, *The Joint Chiefs of Staff and National Policy, 1950–1952.* Washington, D.C.: Historical Division of the JCS, 1980.
Prados, John. *The Soviet Estimate: U.S. Intelligence Analysis and Russian Military Strength.* Garden City, N.Y.: Doubleday, 1982.
Price, Alfred. *Aircraft versus Submarines: The Evolution of the Antisubmarine Aircraft, 1912–1972.* London: William Kimber, 1972.
Ranelagh, John. *The Agency: The Rise and Decline of the CIA.* London: Cambridge Publications, 1987.
Ranft, Bryan, and Geoffrey Till. *The Sea in Soviet Strategy.* Annapolis, Md.: Naval Institute Press, 1988.
Ranken, M. "Have We Got It Right?—Reflections on NATO's Strategy." *Naval Review* 79 (1986): 322–29.
Reardon, Steven L. *History of the Office of the Secretary of Defense.* Vol. 1, *The Formative Years, 1947–1950.* Washington, D.C.: U.S. Government Printing Office, 1984.
Reinhardt, George. "Sea Power's Role in Atomic Warfare." U.S. Naval Institute *Proceedings* 79 (1953): 1279–87.
Richards, Denis, and Hilary St.-George Saunders. *The Royal Air Force, 1939–1945.* Vol. 2, *The Fight Avails.* London: Her Majesty's Stationery Office, 1954.

Richelson, Jeffrey. *American Espionage and the Soviet Target*. New York: Quill, 1987.
Ries, John C. *The Management of Defense: Organization and Control of the U.S. Armed Services*. Baltimore: Johns Hopkins University Press, 1964.
Riste, Olaf. *Western Security: The Formative Years of European and Atlantic Defense, 1947–1953*. New York: Columbia University Press, 1985.
Rodger, N.A.M. *The Admiralty*. Lavenham: Dalton, 1979.
Rosecrance, R. N. *Defense of the Realm: British Strategy in the Nuclear Epoch*. New York: Columbia University Press, 1968.
Rosenberg, David Alan. "American Postwar Air Doctrine and Organization: The Navy Experience." *Air Power and Warfare: Proceedings of the Eighth Military History Symposium*. Colorado Springs, Colo.: Office of Air Force History, 1978.
———. "The Origins of Overkill." *International Security* (1983): 3–71.
———. "U.S. Nuclear Stockpile, 1945–1950." *Bulletin of the Atomic Scientists* (1982): 25–31.
Roskill, Stephen. *Churchill and the Admirals*. London: Collins, 1977.
———. *The War at Sea, 1939–1945*. Vol. 2, *The Period of Balance*. London: Her Majesty's Stationery Office, 1956.
———. *The War at Sea, 1939–1945*. Vol. 3, *The Offensive, Part 1*. London: Her Majesty's Stationery Office, 1960.
———. *The War at Sea, 1939–1945*. Vol. 4, *The Offensive, Part 2*. London: Her Majesty's Stationery Office, 1961.
Ross, Steven T. *American War Plans, 1945–1950*. New York: Garland, 1988.
Ryan, Paul B. *First Line of Defense: The U.S. Navy since 1945*. Stanford, Calif.: Stanford University Press, 1981.
Sanders, David. *Losing an Empire, Finding a Role: British Foreign Policy since 1945*. London: Macmillan, 1990.
Scarborough, William E. "The North American AJ Savage: Establishing the Heavy Attack Mission." *The Hook* (1989): 28–43.
———. "The North American AJ Savage: Launching the Heavy Attack Mission." *The Hook* (1989): 16–37.
Schnabel, James F. *History of the Joint Chiefs of Staff*. Vol. 1, *The Joint Chiefs of Staff and National Policy, 1945–1947*. Wilmington, Del.: Michael Glazier, 1979.
Schnabel, James F., and Robert J. Watson. *History of the Joint Chiefs of Staff*. Vol. 3, parts 1 & 2, *The Joint Chiefs of Staff and National Policy: The Korean War*. Wilmington, Del.: Michael Glazier, 1979.
Schratz, Paul R. "The Admirals' Revolt." U.S. Naval Institute *Proceedings* 112 (1986): 64–71.
———. *The Evolution of the U.S. Military Establishment since World War II*. Washington, D.C.: George C. Marshall Research Foundation, 1979.
Schurcliff, W. A. *The Technical Report of Operation Crossroads*. Washington, D.C.: Defense Atomic Support Agency, 1946.
Scrivner, Charles. *TBM/TBF Avenger in Action*. Carrollton, Tex.: Squadron/Signal Press, 1987.
Seymour, William. *British Special Forces*. London: Sidgewick & Jackson, 1985.

Sherry, Mike. *Preparing for the Next War: American Plans for Postwar Defense, 1941–1945.* New Haven: Yale University Press, 1977.
Sherwin, Nicholas, ed. *NATO's Anxious Birth: The Prophetic Vision of the 1940s.* New York: St. Martin's Press, 1985.
Shuckburgh, Evelyn. "Why NATO Is Necessary." *Military Review* (1961): 23–35.
Siegfried, Doug. "Carrier-Based Airborne ASW." *The Hook* (1989): 56–75.
Sked, Alan, and Chris Cook. *Postwar Britain: A Political History.* London: Pelican Books, 1984.
Slim, William J. *Defeat into Victory.* London: Papermac, 1956.
Snyder, W. P. *The Politics of British Defence Policy, 1945–1962.* London: Benn, 1964.
Sokol, A. E. "Sea Power in the Next War." U.S. Naval Institute *Proceedings* 78 (1952): 519–31.
Sokolsky, Joel J. "Seapower in the Nuclear Age: NATO as a Maritime Alliance." Ph.D. diss., Harvard University, 1984.
Stacey, C. P. *Arms, Men, and Governments: The War Policies of Canada, 1939–1945.* Ottawa: Queens Printers, 1970.
Stambler, Irwin. *The Battle for Inner Space: Undersea Warfare and Weapons.* New York: St. Martin's Press, 1962.
Sullivan, Jim. *P2V Neptune in Action.* Carrollton, Tex.: Squadron/Signal Press, 1985.
———. *Skyraider in Action.* Carrollton, Tex.: Squadron/Signal Press, 1983.
———. *The S2F Tracker in Action.* Carrollton, Tex.: Squadron/Signal Press, 1990.
Swartz, Peter M. "Contemporary U.S. Naval Strategy: A Bibliography." U.S. Naval Institute *Proceedings* 112 (1986): 41–47.
Terraine, John. *Business in Great Waters: The U-Boat Wars, 1916–1945.* London: Mandarin, 1990.
Thomason, Tommy H. "Carrier-Based ASW." *The Hook* (1985): 16–32.
Thursfield, H. G., ed. *Brassey's Annual: The Armed Forces Yearbook, 1947.* New York: Macmillan, 1947.
———. *Brassey's Annual: The Armed Forces Yearbook, 1948.* New York: Macmillan, 1948.
———. *Brassey's Annual: The Armed Forces Yearbook, 1949.* New York: Macmillan, 1949.
———. *Brassey's Annual: The Armed Forces Yearbook, 1950.* New York: Macmillan, 1950.
———. *Brassey's Annual: The Armed Forces Yearbook, 1951.* New York: Macmillan, 1952.
———. *Brassey's Annual: The Armed Forces Yearbook, 1952.* New York: Macmillan, 1952.
———. *Brassey's Annual: The Armed Forces Yearbook, 1953.* New York: Macmillan, 1953.
———. *Brassey's Annual: The Armed Forces Yearbook, 1954.* New York: Macmillan, 1954.
———. *Brassey's Annual: The Armed Forces Yearbook, 1955.* New York: Macmillan, 1955.

———. *Brassey's Annual: The Armed Forces Yearbook, 1956*. New York: Macmillan, 1956.
———. *Brassey's Annual: The Armed Forces Yearbook, 1957*. New York: Macmillan, 1957.
———. *Brassey's Annual: The Armed Forces Yearbook, 1958*. New York: Macmillan, 1958.
Till, Geoffrey. *Maritime Strategy and the Nuclear Age*. 2d ed. London: Macmillan, 1984.
———. *Modern Sea Power: An Introduction*. Washington, D.C.: Pergamon-Brassey's, 1987.
Trachtenberg, Marc. *The Development of American Strategic Thought, 1946–1969*. Vol. 1, *Basic Documents from the Eisenhower and Kennedy Periods, Including the Basic National Security Policy Papers, 1953–1959*. New York: Garland, 1988.
———. *The Development of American Strategic Thought, 1946–1969*. Vol. 2, *Writings on Strategy, 1945–1951*. New York: Garland, 1988.
———. *The Development of American Strategic Thought, 1946–1969*. Vol. 3, *Writings on Strategy, 1952–1960*. New York: Garland, 1988.
———. *History and Strategy*. Princeton: Princeton University Press, 1991.
Veremis, Thanos, and Yannis Valinakis. *U.S. Bases in the Mediterranean: The Cases of Greece and Spain*. Athens: Hellenic Foundation for Defense and Foreign Policy, 1989.
Watson, Mark S. *Chief of Staff: Prewar Plans and Preparations*. Washington, D.C.: Army Historical Division, 1950.
Watson, Robert J. *History of the Joint Chiefs of Staff*. Vol. 5, *The Joint Chiefs of Staff and National Policy, 1953–1954*. Washington, D.C.: Historical Division of the JCS, 1986.
Werrell, Kenneth. *The Evolution of the Cruise Missile*. Maxwell AFB, Ala.: Air University Press, 1985.
West, F. J. *Naval Forces and Western Security*. Washington, D.C.: Pergamon-Brassey's, 1987.
Wettern, Desmond. *The Decline of British Seapower*. London: Jane's, 1982.
Wilkinson, Nicholas. "Inside NATO." *Naval Review* 74 (1986): 13–17.
Williams, Ray. *Royal Navy Aircraft since 1945*. Annapolis, Md.: Naval Institute Press, 1989.
Wolfe, Thomas W. *Soviet Power and Europe: The Evolution of a Political-Military Posture, 1945–1964*. Santa Monica, Calif.: RAND Corp., 1968.
Wright, Jerauld. "The North Atlantic Treaty Organization." U.S. Naval Institute *Proceedings* 77 (1951): 1253–65.
Y'Blood, William T. *Hunter-Killer: U.S. Escort Carriers in the Battle of the Atlantic*. Annapolis, Md.: Naval Institute Press, 1983.
Yenne, Bill. *SAC: A Primer of Modern Strategic Air Power*. Novato, Calif.: Presidio, 1985.
Yergin, Daniel. *Shattered Peace: The Origins of the Cold War*. 2d ed. London: Penguin, 1990.
York, Herbert F. *The Advisors: Oppenheimer, Teller, and the Superbomb*. Stanford, Calif.: Stanford University Press, 1976.

Young, John W. *The Foreign Policy of Churchill's Peacetime Adminstration, 1951–1955*. Leicester: Leicester University Press, 1988.
Ziegler, Charles. "Waiting for JOE-1: Decisions Leading to the Detection of Russia's First Atomic Bomb Test." *Social Studies of Science* 18 (1988): 197–229.
Ziegler, Philip. *Mountbatten*. New York: Harper & Row, 1985.

Index

AASSB. *See* Allied Antisubmarine Survey Board
ABC-1 talks, 8–9, 31
ABC-22 talks, 31, 54
ABC relationship, 47, 54–55, 78
ACCHAN (NATO Allied Command, Channel). *See* CinCCHAN
ACE (NATO Allied Command, Europe). *See* SACEUR
Acheson, Dean, 135, 186
ACLANT (NATO Allied Command, Atlantic). *See* SACLANT
aircraft
    AD-4B Skyraider, 159
    AJ-1 and AJ-2 Savage, 91, 158–59, 161
    B-29, 85, 89
    B-36, 89
    B-50, 89
    F2H3 Banshee, 158–59, 161
    fighters, 89
    FJ Fury, 158–59
    IL-28, 89
    Lincoln strategic bombers, 90
    for maritime patrol, 113, 125, 151, 153, 154, 157, 167, 190
    P2V3C Neptune, 91, 158–59
    Scimitar, 158
    TU-4, 88, 98, 139–40
    V-bombers, 198
aircraft carriers, 91, 110, 130, 140, 156, 159, 161, 162
    and command problems, 160, 175, 192–93, 198, 199

airspace coordination problems
    in the Mediterranean, 19–22
    in Newfoundland, 33–35
    between SACLANT and AFNORTH, 147, 159–60, 163–64
Algeria, 179–80
Allied Antisubmarine Survey Board (AASSB), 46
Altican, Admiral, 194
Andrewes, Vice Adm. Sir William, 150
Anglo-American-Canadian Atlantic Convoy Conference, 40
antisubmarine warfare
    and attack-at-source doctrine, 64, 134, 157, 161, 162, 167
    and barrier operations, 198
    and differences between U.S. and Royal Navy policies, 33, 42, 157
Arcadia conference, 10
Area Combined Headquarters system, 26–29, 35, 142–43, 147, 150
Atlantic Approaches Pact of Mutual Assistance, 67
atomic weapons. *See* nuclear weapons
attack at source, 64, 134, 157, 161, 162, 167. *See also* antisubmarine warfare
Attlee, Clement, 123, 127, 132
Azores, 95, 116

barrier operations, 198
base area and main support area concepts and Plan Broiler/Doublequick, 60–65

269

base area and main support area concepts *(continued)*
  and Plan Crosspiece/Galloper, 88–91, 93
  and Plan Masthead/Binnacle, 140–41
Berlin crisis, 47, 56, 69, 79, 84
Bermuda, 28
Bevin, Ernest, 75
Bidwell, Adm. R.E.S., 151
Binnacle, Plan, 139–40, 141, 174
Black Plan, 29–30
Blandy, Adm. W.H.P., 93, 99
Brind, Admiral, 110, 164, 190
British Chiefs of Staff Committee, 8, 9, 76, 127, 154, 167
  and IBERLANT problem, 166
  and Mediterranean command problem, 176, 180, 181–82, 192
British Joint Staff Mission, Washington (BJSM), 10, 82, 118, 127, 174
Broiler, Plan, 56–64, 67–69, 79, 84, 88–89, 171
Brussels Pact, 48, 66–69, 75
Bullmoose, Plan, 67, 72, 74, 81, 84, 88–89, 92, 95, 101, 171
Burke, Adm. Arleigh, 199

Canada–U.S. Basic Defense and Basic Security plans, 97
Canadian Chiefs of Staff Committee, 30, 54, 97, 135, 151
Canadian Joint Staff Mission, Washington, 10
Canadian–U.S. Regional Planning Group, 80, 83, 97–98, 106, 151
CANUSA proposal, 54
Carney, Adm. Robert, 108, 123, 132, 172, 174, 175, 190, 191, 194
  and Edelsten, 173–74
  and Eisenhower, 175–76
  and Mountbatten, 191
CCS. *See* Combined Chiefs of Staff
CHANCOM. *See* CinCCHAN
Chief of the Imperial General Staff, 8, 12
CHOP lines
  during World War II, 38–42, 51
  in postwar period, 66, 95, 114–16, 118
Churchill, Winston S., 7, 10, 123, 127, 130, 132, 182
  and summit with Truman, 134–35, 186
  views of, regarding American control of the Atlantic, 133
CinCAFMED, 170–71, 194, 197. *See also* SACEUR
  disbanding of, 201
  final organization of, 195–96
  and regional planning groups, 171
  and strategic concepts, 171
CinCAFSOUTH, 171–72, 176, 181, 190, 191, 194. *See also* SACEUR
CinCAIREASTLANT. *See* SACLANT
CinCCHAN, 107, 139, 142–49
  British concept for, 143–44
  and the Channel Committee, 145
  Dutch proposal for, 145
  final organization of, 148–49
  relationship of, to SACEUR and SACLANT, 146–48
CinCCONAD, 152, 198
CinCLANT, 37, 42, 73, 80, 116, 120. *See also* SACLANT; WESTLANT
CinCLANTFLEET, 16, 152, 160, 172
CinCME, and World War II, 14
CinCMED, 22–23, 172–73, 186, 191
CinCNELM, 52, 72, 172, 190
CinCWA, 26, 29, 35, 40, 129
Combined Canadian–British–U.S. Working Group on Antisubmarine Doctrine, 89
Combined Chiefs of Staff (CCS), 8, 9, 47, 51, 64, 69–71, 77, 80–81, 102–3, 125, 171, 190
Commanding Officer, Atlantic Coast (COAC), 29, 32, 40–42, 150
command organizations, in postwar period, 71–72, 76
command systems
  joint committee system (U.K.), 12, 32, 53–54
  unified command system (U.S.), 12–13, 25, 33, 51, 54, 186, 188
communication systems, and Mediterranean command problem, 173–74
COMNAVFE. *See* Korean War
COMNAVNAW controversy, 16–17
  effects of, on postwar planning, 47, 52, 66, 93
COMSUBEASTLANT, 201. *See also* SACLANT
Creasy, Adm. Sir George, 150, 156, 161, 174

Index

Crosspiece, Plan, 88–93, 98, 100–101, 103, 112, 115, 139–40, 141, 171
Cunningham, Adm. Sir Andrew, 15, 19–20
Cyprus, 90

Defense Plan 1-50, 98
Denfield, Adm. Louis
    and 1949 Atlantic command proposal, 93
    and objections to Plan Broiler, 62–64
Desert Air Force, 22
destroyers-for-bases deal, 32
Dixon, Sir Pierson, 132
Doublequick, Plan, 57–65, 67–68, 84, 88–89, 171
Doublestar, Plan, 67–71, 74–75, 79, 81, 84, 88, 92, 95, 101, 171
Douglas-Pennent, Admiral, 127
    and "Gentleman's Agreement," 18–19, 126, 154
DuBose, Vice Admiral, 152
Dunkirk talks, 56, 67

Eastern Mediterranan Command proposal, 183–84
EASTLANT, 125, 127, 128, 129, 130, 134, 153, 154, 161, 164, 177, 199. *See also* SACLANT
Eden, Anthony, 7
Edlesten, Admiral, 173–74, 191
Eisenhower, Dwight D., 108, 110, 123, 133, 137, 174, 182
    becomes SACEUR, 107, 109
    and concept of NATO operations, 108, 140
    opinion of, regarding SACEUR command organization, 109
    and World War II, 14, 17
Emergency Defence Plan 1-52, 162, 167

Fechteler, Adm. William, 122, 123, 130, 132–33, 136, 154, 174, 190–94
    and appointment to SACLANT, 121
    and Churchill-Truman summit, 134–35
    and "Gentleman's Agreement," 118–19, 126, 154
    and Korean War model for STRIKE-

FLEETLANT, 162–63
Ferrari, Admiral, 192
Fife, Adm. James, 194
Flag Officer, Atlantic Coast (FOAC), 151, 198
Flag Officer, Western Europe (FOWE)
    in NATO, 107–8, 111–12, 142
    in WUDO, 70
Fleetwood, Plan. *See* Doublestar
flexible response, 198
force comparisons, between Western allies and Soviet Union, 49–50, 58–59, 88–89, 139–40
Forces Maritimes D'Airienne, 147
Forces Maritimes De Rhin, 112
Foulkes, Gen. Charles, and organizational concept for NATO, 77–78
Fraser, Adm. Lord Bruce, 99–100, 124, 129
    and CinCCHAN, 143
    and problems with Sherman, 131
French Navy, 112, 116, 190
    and the IBERLANT problem, 164–65
    and Mediterranean command problem, 179–80, 190

Galloper, Plan, 88–93, 98, 100–101, 103, 112, 115, 139–40, 141, 171
"Gentleman's Agreement," 118–19, 126, 154
Gibraltar, 17, 28, 91, 113, 118, 126, 164, 194
Girosi, Admiral, 194
Global Strategy Paper (U.K.), 158
Grant, Admiral, 118
Greece, 180, 182, 183, 186, 191, 195
Group Able, 162–64

Halfmoon, Plan. *See* Doublestar
Hewitt, Adm. H. K., 16, 19
higher direction of war
    in NATO, 83, 103, 121, 123, 140, 153, 183
    in postwar period, 47–48, 67–70, 76–77, 84, 99–100, 101, 109
    in World War II, 5–12
Horton, Adm. Sir Max, 35
hunter-killer groups. *See* antisubmarine warfare
Husky, Operation, 17, 19, 20

IBERLANT, 120, 132, 179, 201. *See also* SACLANT
  British arguments against, 126
  French objections to, 164
Iceland, 88, 95, 116
Ingersoll, Adm. Ralph, 16, 35, 42
Ismay, Sir Hastings, 8, 75, 133
Italian Navy, 194–95

Jaujard, Admiral, 111
Johnson, Louis, 121
Joint Chiefs of Staff (JCS)
  and Mediterranean command problem, 181–82, 184, 187–88
  and postwar period, 51–52, 79, 97, 121, 127, 176, 177
  and World War II, 8, 13, 21
joint committee system, 12, 32, 53–54. *See also* unified command system
Joint Planning Staff (JPS) (U.K.), 72
  and Atlantic command idea of 1951, 124–25
  and coalition warfare in 1950, 100
  and Dunkirk talks, 56
  and Mediterranean command problem, 186–87
  and Plan Broiler/Doublequick, 64, 66
  and Plan Crosspiece, 92
  and Plan Doublestar/Speedway, 72
  and Plan Offtackle, 87
  and regional planning groups, 76, 78, 81
Joint Strategic Planning Committee (JSPC) (U.S.), 51
  and Mediterranean command problem, 183–84, 186–87
  and Plan Broiler, 56, 62, 79
  and Plan Doublestar, 72
  and regional planning groups, 80–81, 100, 101
Joint Strategic Survey Committee (JSSC) (U.S.), 183–84
Joubert, Air Chief Marshal Philip, 44–45
Joy, Adm. C. Turner, 200
Juin, Marachel, 111

Karachi option (Plan Broiler), 62–64, 68
King, Adm. Ernest, 8, 35, 42, 47
King, William Lyon Mackenzie, 10
Korean War, 87, 100, 103, 121, 132, 137
  naval command organization for, 200–201

Lambrecht, Capt. W. O., 164
Lappas, Admiral, 194
Lisbon meeting of North Atlantic Council, 189–90

Mainbrace, Exercise, 153–56, 161
  and Carrier Striking Force, 156–57
Marshall, Gen. George C., 13, 21
Masthead, Plan, 139–40, 141, 174
MC 14 strategic concept, 88, 139
MC 14/1 strategic concept, 139, 140
MCC. *See* Military Cooperation Committee
McCormick, Adm. Lynde, 98, 148, 150, 151, 152–53, 154, 161, 167
  approval of, as SACLANT, 136
  and inspection trip of SACLANT area, 136
  and problems with U.S. Navy over NATO, 166
McGrigor, Adm. Sir Rhoderick, 133, 154, 161, 190
  and McCormick-McGrigor status quo, 167
  and McGrigor proposal, 128–29
McMahon Act, 51, 73, 159, 161, 166–67, 172, 186. *See also* nuclear weapons
Mediterranean Allied Air Forces (World War II), 22–23
Medium Term Defence Plan (MTDP), 95–96, 99, 103, 140
Middle East Command (MEC), 182
Middle East Command Organization (MECO), 188–89
Middle East Steering Group, 185–86
Military Cooperation Committee (MCC), 54–55, 80
mine countermeasures, 142, 146–47, 151, 152, 174
Montgomery, Field Marshal Sir Bernard Law, 110
Morrison, Herbert, 127
Mountbatten, Adm. Louis, Earl of, 191
  and relations with Carney, 191–92
Murray, Rear Adm. L. W., 42

NATO (North Atlantic Treaty Organization). *See also individual commands and regional planning groups;* SACEUR; SACLANT

Index

area of, 95
and DC 24/2 and 24/3 recommendations, 120, 132–33, 136
and interim arrangements for the Channel, 144–45
and MC 14 strategic concept, 88, 139
and MC 14/1 strategic concept, 139, 140
and Medium Term Defence Plan, 95–96, 99, 140
North Atlantic Council of, 83, 103, 121, 123, 140, 153, 183
North Atlantic Defence Committee of, 83, 95, 101, 104
North Atlantic Defence Council of, 119–20, 126
North Atlantic Military Committee of, 83, 95, 104–6, 132–33, 183, 185
and North Atlantic Treaty, 79, 82
organization of, in February 1952, 136
origins of, 75, 76–77
and regional planning groups, 77–78, 80–81, 83, 95–97, 99–101, 104
relationship of, to Middle East, 170–95
Standing Group of, 83, 93, 97, 99, 101–2, 121, 122, 125, 127, 129, 130, 140, 153, 176, 185, 188–92
Strategic Reserve Group of, 77
Working Group of, 75
naval control of shipping (NCS)
in World War II, 28, 37–38
after 1945, 73, 128, 151, 152, 164, 192
"New Look" (U.S.), 158
Noble, Adm. Sir Percey, 35
Nomy, Admiral, 150, 190, 192
NORAD, 199
Norstad, Gen. Lauris, 111
North Atlantic Ocean Regional Planning Group, 80, 83, 98–99, 101, 112–14, 121, 136, 150, 151, 153
and Defense Plan 1-50, 98
and Short Term Defence Plan, 98–99
Northern Europe Regional Planning Group, 96, 101, 105
nuclear tests
by Soviet Union, 85–86
by U.K., 167
by U.S., 166, 197
nuclear weapons
and attack at source, 157, 158, 159
in CinCLANTFLEET's strike plan, 159, 161
command and control of, 159, 161, 167
delivery aircraft for. *See* aircraft
Mk III, 140
Mk IV, 158
Mk VII, 160
Mk VIII, 160
and McMahon Act prohibition against foreign command, 51, 73, 159, 161, 166–67, 172, 186
and SACEUR's Special Air Staff, 159–60, 162–64
Soviet arsenal of, 50, 85–86, 98, 140, 198–99
and STRIKEFLEETLANT, 157, 161, 167
tactical vs. strategic, 161, 162
targeting of, 62, 68

Offtackle, Plan, 87
Ogdensburg summit, 29
ON 113 controversy, 39–40, 47
Operations. *See specific names*
Overlord/Neptune, Operation, 23–25

Paukenschlag, Operation, 37, 125
Pearson, Lester B., 135
Permanent Joint Board on Defense (PJBD), 29, 53–55, 77, 97
Pincher study, 48–51, 64
Plans. *See specific names*
Power, Adm. Sir Arthur, 147
Premar I, 145, 147
Premar II, 142, 147

Quemoy-Matsu crisis, 199

regional planning groups (RPGs). *See* Canadian–U.S. Regional Planning Group; NATO; North Atlantic Ocean Regional Planning Group; Northern Europe Regional Planning Group; Southern Europe/Western Mediterranean Regional Planning Group; Western European Regional Planning Group
Rhine River, 69, 89, 112
Rio Pact, 67

Roosevelt, Franklin D., 8, 10
Royal Air Force
  Bomber Command, 159, 162–63, 167, 198
  Coastal Command, and World War II, 17, 24, 26, 45
  Desert Air Force, 22
  HQ Middle East, 18, 171
  Middle East Air Command, 19
Royal Canadian Air Force
  after 1945, 151
  in World War II, 31–32, 40
Royal Canadian Navy
  Canadian Northwest Atlantic Command (CinCCNA), 41–42, 150
  Commanding Officer, Atlantic Coast (COAC), 29, 32, 40–42, 150
  Commodore Commanding, Newfoundland, 32, 34
  Flag Officer, Atlantic Coast (FOAC), 151, 198
  Joint Service Committee, Atlantic Coast (JSCAC), 29, 33, 40, 42, 150
  Joint Services Subcommittee, Newfoundland (JSSC), 29, 42, 150
  in World War II, 29, 31–32
Royal Navy
  CinC America and West Indies Station (CinCAW&I), 28–29
  CinC Home Fleet, 28, 119
  CinC Levant, 14
  CinCME, 14
  CinCMED, 14, 17–18
  CinC Western Approaches (CinCWA), 26, 29, 35, 40, 129
  Force H, 18
  Rhine River Flotilla, 112

SACAO, 113–14, 116, 118–19
  British proposal for, 117
  and CinCHAN, 143
SACEM proposal, 182–83
SACEUR (NATO Supreme Allied Commander, Europe), 87, 104–6, 121, 122, 157, 172, 181
  AFCENT, 111
  AFMED, 6, 124, 170, 194, 195–96, 201
  AFNORTH, 96, 110, 129, 130, 146, 161, 164, 167, 190
  AFNORTHWEST, 201
  AFSOUTH, 111, 171–72, 175, 176, 190, 191, 194
  Allied Land Forces, Southeastern Europe, 191
  British proposal for, 107–8
  Eisenhower is selected as, 107, 109
  Eisenhower's concepts of command and strategy for, 108
  Flag Officer, Western Europe, 111–12, 142
  Naval Striking and Support Forces, 201
  nuclear strike coordination with SACLANT, 161–62
  problems of adding Greece and Turkey to, 181–85
  and rivalry with Carney, 194
  SHAPE, 104, 110, 127, 193
  STRIKEFORSOUTH, 193, 194, 195
  terms of reference for, 106–7
  working concept for, 106
SACLANT (NATO Supreme Allied Commander, Atlantic), 6, 75, 87, 104–5, 112, 121, 122, 124, 126–27, 130, 135, 172, 181
  African Atlantic Sub-area, 115–18
  British proposal for, 117
  Canadian Atlantic Sub-area, 117, 151–52
  is changed from SACAO to SACLANT, 121
  CinCAIREASTLANT, 153
  COMSUBEASTLANT, 153, 201
  EASTLANT, 125, 127, 128, 129, 130, 134, 153, 154, 161, 164, 177, 199
  and Emergency Defence Plan 1-52, 162, 167
  final organization of, 167–68
  Iberian Atlantic Sub-area (IBERLANT), 120, 126–27, 132, 153, 154, 164, 168
  organization and boundaries of, in 1952, 155–56
  relationship of, to CinCHAN, 146–47
  and SACAO proposal, 113–14, 116, 118–19
  STANAVFORLANT, 201
  STRIKEFLEETLANT, 18, 155, 161, 164–66, 167, 176, 177, 192, 193, 199
  SUBNA and SUBLANT, 74–75
  terms of reference for, 122–23
  WESTLANT, 120, 151, 153, 154, 166

Index

SACME and CinCANFME proposals, 176–79, 185
SACMED (World War II), 21, 107, 171
St. Laurent, Louis, 75
Sala, Admiral, 194
Scapa Flow, 28
SCAT proposal, 45, 73
SEAC (Southeast Asia Command), 13
SHAEF, 6, 21, 23, 67, 84, 112
SHAPE, 104, 110, 127, 193
Sherman, Adm. Forrest, 51, 96, 98, 109–10, 118–19, 121, 124, 127, 178
   death of, 154
   and discussions with Carney over command, 123–24, 176
   and problems with Fraser, 131
Short Term Defence Plan, 98–99
Simpson, Adm. George, 154
Slessor, Air Vice Marshal, 124, 132–33, 174, 178–79, 190
Slim, Field Marshal Sir William, 124, 131, 133, 174, 190
SLOCs (sea lines of communication)
   in the Atlantic, 16, 26, 54, 89, 91–92, 98, 115–16, 128–29, 154
   in the Mediterranean, 57–59, 64, 69, 87, 91, 116, 167, 170–71, 174, 175–76, 180, 187, 195
Smuts, Field Marshal Jan, and the Atlantic command idea, 45
SOSUS, 198
Southern Europe/Western Mediterranean Regional Planning Group, 83, 105, 171
Soviet Union, 47
   naval forces of, 50, 58–60, 64, 88–89, 91–92, 139–40, 153, 198–99
   nuclear weapons of, 50, 85–86, 98, 140, 198–99
   threat to Europe posed by, 48–50, 57–59, 64, 69, 86–88, 140
Spain, and NATO war plans, 57, 69, 89, 92, 140
Special Air Staff, 163–64
Special Boat Service, 112
Speedway, Plan, 72, 74, 81, 84, 88, 92, 95, 101, 171
STANAVFORLANT, 201
Stark, Adm. Harold, 35
Stevens, Air Marshal, 147
Strategic Air Command. *See* U.S. Air Force
Strategic Reserve Group, 77. *See also*

Foulkes, Gen. Charles
STRIKEFLEETLANT, 18, 155, 161, 164–66, 167, 176, 177, 192, 193, 199. *See also* SACLANT
STRIKEFORSOUTH, 193, 194, 195. *See also* SACEUR
submarine threat, Soviet, 59–60, 64, 88–89, 91–92
Suez Canal, 89–90, 189, 195
Suez crisis, 199

Torch, Operation, 16–17, 19–20
Trojan, Plan, 87
Truman, Harry S., 75, 133
   and summit with Churchill, 133, 134–35, 186
Turkey, 180, 182, 183, 185, 186, 191, 195
type XXI submarine, 89, 139

Unified Command Plan, 51, 118
unified command system, 12–13, 25, 33, 51, 54, 186, 188. *See also* joint committee system
U.S. Air Force
   49th Air Division, 163
   375th Very Long Range Air Weather Reconnaissance Squadron, 85
   Special Air Staff, 162, 163
   Strategic Air Command, 52, 64, 140, 163, 167
U.S. Army Air Force, 38, 43–44, 118
   9th Air Force, 19
U.S. joint commands, in the postwar period, 51, 118, 152, 161, 198
U.S. Navy. *See also* aircraft carriers; nuclear weapons
   2nd Fleet, 160, 161. *See also* SACLANT; STRIKEFLEETLANT
   6th Fleet, 52, 72, 91, 109–10, 172, 174, 175–76, 179, 186, 190, 191, 193. *See also* SACEUR; STRIKEFORSOUTH
   8th Fleet, 19, 23
   10th Fleet, 42–44
   Caribbean SEAFRON, 36
   CinCLANT, 37, 42, 73, 80, 116, 120
   CinCLANTFLEET, 16, 152, 160, 172
   CinCNELM, 52, 72, 172, 190
   CinCUS, 35
   COMINCH, 16, 35, 37

U.S. Navy *(continued)*
   COMNAVEUR, 24
   COMNAVMED, 52
   COMNAVNAW, 16, 52, 66, 93
   Eastern SEAFRON, 32, 36–38, 42, 115, 151–52
   Gulf SEAFRON, 36, 38
   Hemisphere Defense Plan No. 4 (WPL 51), 31, 33
   Panama SEAFRON, 36
   Task Force 24, 32–35, 40, 42
   Task Force 34, 16
   Rhine River Patrol, 112

Vandenberg, Gen. Hoyt, 162

Western European Regional Planning Group, 83, 96, 101, 105, 146
Western Union Chiefs of Staff Committee, 65, 67–71, 76, 78, 80, 84, 109, 142
Western Union Defense Organization (WUDO), 47–48, 67–70, 76–77, 84, 99–100, 101, 109
   and evacuation plans, 70
   and Flag Officer, Western Europe, 70, 108–9
WESTLANT, 120, 151, 153, 154, 166. *See also* SACLANT
World War II, 5-46. *See also individual operations*
   combined bombing offensive of, 10, 12
   and COMNAVNAW controversy, 16–17
   effects of, on postwar planning, 47, 52, 66, 93
   and higher direction of war, 5–12
   ON 113 controversy during, 39–40, 47
   and strategic zones, 11
World War II command arrangements
   in Asia, 13
   in the Atlantic, 25–46
   in Europe, 23–25
   in the Mediterranean, 14–23
   in the Pacific, 13
WPL 51. *See* U.S. Navy Hemisphere Defense Plan No. 4
Wright, Adm. Jerauld, 161, 190, 191, 199

About the Author

Sean M. Maloney is a Canadian military historian specializing in the Cold War. He is the author of *War Without Battles: Canada's NATO Brigade in Germany, 1951–1993.*

The **Naval Institute Press** is the book-publishing arm of the U.S. Naval Institute, a private, nonprofit society for sea service professionals and others who share an interest in naval and maritime affairs. Established in 1873 at the U.S. Naval Academy in Annapolis, Maryland, where its offices remain, today the Naval Institute has more than 100,000 members worldwide.

Members of the Naval Institute receive the influential monthly magazine *Proceedings* and discounts on fine nautical prints and on ship and aircraft photos. They also have access to the transcripts of the Institute's Oral History Program and get discounted admission to any of the Institute-sponsored seminars offered around the country.

The Naval Institute also publishes *Naval History* magazine. This colorful bimonthly is filled with entertaining and thought-provoking articles, first-person reminiscences, and dramatic art and photography. Members receive a discount on *Naval History* subscriptions.

The Naval Institute's book-publishing program, begun in 1898 with basic guides to naval practices, has broadened its scope in recent years to include books of more general interest. Now the Naval Institute Press publishes more than seventy titles each year, ranging from how-to books on boating and navigation to battle histories, biographies, ship and aircraft guides, and novels. Institute members receive discounts on the Press's nearly 400 books in print.

For a free catalog describing Naval Institute Press books currently available, and for further information about subscribing to *Naval History* magazine or about joining the U.S. Naval Institute, please write to:

> Membership & Communications Department
> U.S. Naval Institute
> 118 Maryland Avenue
> Annapolis, Maryland 21402-5035

> Or call, toll-free, (800) 233-USNI.